Multimedia Journalism

Multimedia Journalism: A Practical Guide, second edition builds on the first edition's expert guidance on working across multiple media platforms, and continues to explore getting started, building proficiency and professional standards in multimedia journalism.

The second edition features new chapters including:

- getting started with social media
- live reporting
- building proficiency with WordPress
- building apps for smartphones and tablets
- building a personal brand and developing a specialism
- creating a glossy magazine for tablet, phone and web.

The new edition also includes an extensive range of new and updated materials essential for all aspects of multimedia journalism today. New areas explored include editing video and slideshows for mobile and tablet devices, the advanced use of mobile devices for reporting, location-specific content creation and delivery, the use of video and audio slideshows, and live blogging. Other updates include more material on photojournalism as a storytelling technique, using and transferring digital images and sound, the use of Google Analytics, and practical guides to storytelling through infographics, timelines, interactive graphics and maps.

The book fully engages with multimedia journalism in relation to a range of social media and web publishing platforms, including WordPress, Blogger, Tumblr, Twitter, Facebook, Google+, YouTube, Instagram, Pinterest, SoundCloud, audioBoom and iTunes.

The book is also supported by fully updated online masterclasses at www.multimedia-journalism.co.uk.

Andy Bull has been a journalist for over 30 years, working in senior positions on *The Times*, AOL, *The Independent*, *Conde Nast* and *The Mail on Sunday*, among others. He is also the author of *Brand Journalism* (Routledge, 2013).

Multimedia Journalism

A Practical Guide

Second Edition

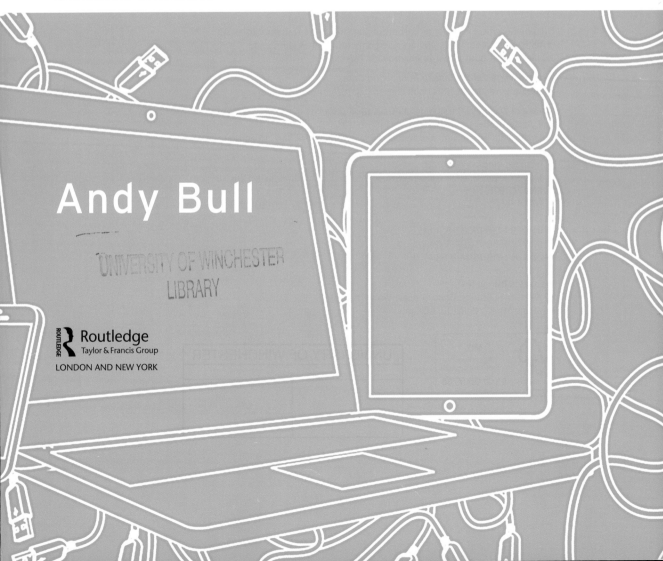

Andy Bull

Routledge
Taylor & Francis Group

LONDON AND NEW YORK

This edition published 2016
by Routledge
2 Park Square, Milton Park, Abingdon, Oxon OX14 4RN

Simultaneously published in the USA and Canada
by Routledge
711 Third Avenue, New York, NY 10017

Routledge is an imprint of the Taylor & Francis Group, an informa business

First published 2010 by Routledge

Trademark notice: Product or corporate names may be trademarks
or registered trademarks, and are used only for identification and
explanation without intent to infringe.

British Library Cataloguing in Publication Data
A catalogue record for this book is available from the British Library

Library of Congress Cataloging in Publication Data
Bull, Andy, 1956-
    Multimedia journalism: a practical guide / Andy Bull. – Second edition.
        pages cm
    Includes index.
    1. Journalism. 2. Online journalism. 3. Interactive multimedia. I. Title.
    PN4775.B76 2015
    070.4–dc23   2015010714

ISBN: 978-1-138-79283-8 (hbk)
ISBN: 978-1-138-79284-5 (pbk)
ISBN: 978-1-315-76174-9 (ebk)

Typeset in Interstate
by Keystroke, Station Road,Codsall, Wolverhampton
Printed by Bell & Bain Ltd, Glasgow

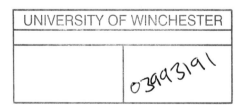

For Elena, for everything

Contents

Multimedia Journalism: A Practical Guide, second edition remains a truly hybrid project, interlinking the textbook materials with essential resources on the companion website, which is accessible at www.multimedia-journalism.co.uk.

Through the book you will be directed to further online activities, exercises, quizzes, videos, and links, all expanding on the areas explored in the book.

The companion website is arranged in sections matching the parts, chapters and numbered chapter section in the book. Whenever you see numbered sections in the book like this you can match these to the same numbered section on the website.

On the companion website you will find:

- Interactive quizzes, allowing you to test your knowledge and the skills covered in the book
- A broad range of embedded videos and audio guides, illustrating and informing the concepts explored in more depth
- Annotated links to further web materials offering more expert guidance and training
- More in-depth discussion of working with specific social media platforms including Twitter, Google+, Facebook and YouTube, and on key skills like making infographics and smart phone apps
- Masterclasses, designed to cover new developments in multimedia journalism practice and to provide any essential updates to material covered in the book.

Visit the site at www.multimedia-journalism.co.uk.

Guided Tour

Multimedia Journalism: A Practical Guide, second edition isn't just the book in your hands – it's a website too, featuring tons of audio, visual and textual material. At **www.multimedia-journalism.co.uk**, you'll find fully cross-referenced material that links with and builds on the book material, keeps it current, and is updated regularly.

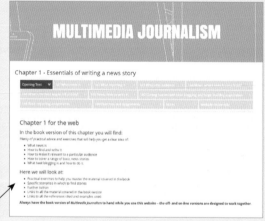

At the start of each chapter in the book, and online, you'll see a summary of what's in each version.

Boxes throughout the book chapter will direct you to related material online.

Each chapter is split into sections that are numbered and coded so you can go directly to the relevant area of the website, or book, and back again.

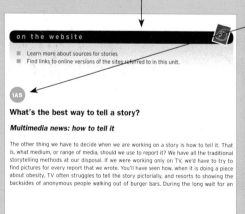

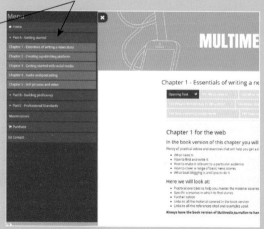

In the textbook, blue boxes highlight real story examples.

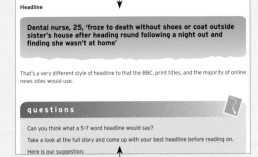

Take online multiple-choice quizzes to test your knowledge.

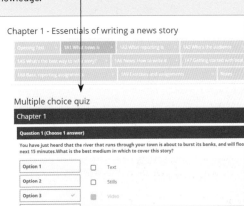

Question boxes prompt you to think about what you've read before you move on.

At the end of each chapter in the book you'll find exercises and projects

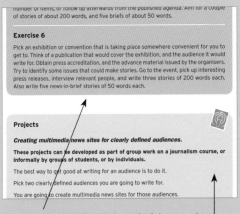

Exercises related directly to material covered in the chapter.

Projects are wider, longer-term enterprises that you will be able to develop as you work your way through the book and website.

Look out for regular masterclasses from the author and experts in the particular field covered; a range of topics in both video and audio form. Check the masterclasses tab on the site to see what's coming up.

You'll find loads of video and audio throughout. It's a truly multimedia project!

Acknowledgements

Dental nurse, 25, who froze to death in the snow outside her sister's house after night out made 27 calls in failed bid to contact friends before dying by Rosie Taylor, *Mail Online*, 20/6/2013. Reproduced courtesy of the *Daily Mail* and Solo Syndication.

Lily Allen shows off boobs and nipple pasties as she performs in sheer top at charity gig by Zoe Shenton, *The Mirror*, April 2nd 2014. Reproduced courtesy of *The Mirror* and Mirrorpix.

Food phobia woman who lived on nothing but CHIPS hypnotised into eating first proper meal for 15 years by Richard Wheatstone, *The Mirror* 15 April 2014. Reproduced courtesy of *The Mirror* and Mirrorpix.

Paul McKenna: Look into my eyes by Polly Vernon, *The Observer*, 12 December 2004. Copyright Guardian News & Media Ltd 2004.

Plebgate: Geldof in defence of Mitchell by Sean O'Neill (*The Times*, 18 November 2014). Reproduced courtesy of *The Times* and News Syndication.

'Banker blames 'interference' as wife who killed disabled children is spared jail by David Brown' (*The Times*, 18 November 2014). Reproduced courtesy of *The Times* and News Syndication.

A revolution in Romanian city sightseeing (*The Times*, Lee Karen Stow, 4 December 2004). Reproduced courtesy of *The Times* and News Syndication.

Robert Crampton quote (ROY)

St Pancras (*The Sunday Times*, 29 May 2005). Reproduced courtesy of *The Sunday Times* and News Syndication.

Scarlett Johansson: The sexpot superhero's great power is invisibility (*The Sunday Times*, 24 August 2014). Reproduced courtesy of *The Times* and News Syndication.

Review of *Small Wars Permitting: Dispatches from Foreign Lands by Christina Lamb*, Patrick French (*The Sunday Times*, 20 January 2008). Reproduced courtesy of *The Sunday Times* and News Syndication.

Stock images used courtesy of Getty Images.

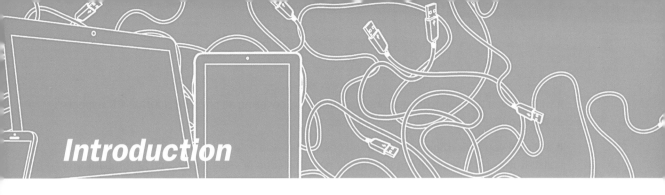

Introduction

Equipping you for the fourth revolution in journalism

Yet again, journalism is undergoing radical change.

James Harding, the BBC's director of news and current affairs, speaks[1] of a fourth revolution in journalism.

First there was print, and then came the first three revolutions:

- Radio
- Television
- Online.

Each caused radical upheaval in their turn.

The fourth revolution, which is taking place right now, is being caused by mobile technology.

Harding, who is responsible for shaping the BBC's vision for news coverage, told staff: "In the age of the smartphone, we have entered the age of smart news, of handheld, news of what, for want of a better term, I will simply call interactive news - news that is portable and personalised; news that is fully internet-enabled and responsive; news that is available to everyone, everywhere, right now; news in which everyone has a hand on the microphone, i.e. not just broadcast, transmitted or distributed, but shared, exchanged, checked, investigated and explained as much by the audience as the author; news that can plug you in to what's happening anywhere in the world, but equally root you into where you live and work; news that puts the world, with all this implies, in the palm of your hand."

The Multimedia Journalism (MMJ) project is designed to equip student journalists - and, indeed, working journalists - with the skills they need to join this revolution.

With its textbook in paper and ebook form, its companion website, its mobile and social media presences, MMJ teaches how to do journalism across all media and on all platforms.

It will take you through from day one to graduation, covering all practical, journalistic aspects of your course.

It will give you everything you need to know to develop as a fully rounded multimedia journalist. It will start by assuming absolutely no knowledge or experience, and accompany you through to full competence: the level of competence required to graduate from a practical undergraduate or postgraduate journalism course.

It will take you through the practice of reporting - of storytelling - in text, audio, still and moving images, mobile platforms and on social media.

MMJ takes as its starting point the way news, information and entertainment is consumed today.

How do you consume your news?

Chances are, you use a mix - something along the lines of the following:

- News alerts on Twitter
- Status updates on Facebook or other social networks
- News headlines from a range of titles you like
- An app - either free or (possibly) paid for - on your mobile phone or tablet computer
- A free print product (if you live in a city) that you pick up before or after your morning commute
- TV news.

You may, just possibly, also buy a newspaper.

What about your other information and entertainment needs?

You might buy one or more glossy magazines that fall into the categories of general consumer or specialist consumer titles. That's particularly likely if you are into fashion, movies, or gaming. Or you may read them on a tablet.

Your interests and hobbies may also be served by a range of other apps, headline alerts or email newsletters. So if you follow a particular sports league or team, for example, you are likely to be signed up for news from them, and this news will often be produced not by independent journalists but by journalists employed by the club or league itself.

A lot of what you read or watch will come to you - those in your social circle will share or like a video on YouTube, say, or a news story that has been shared by someone you know on Facebook, or linked to on Twitter.

You might listen to a radio station, or download podcasts of news or other information to listen to on your smartphone, iPod or tablet while you are on the way to work, at the gym or on a run.

So that's a pretty complex media landscape, and because we have so much choice about where we get our news, information and entertainment, everyone's pattern of media consumption is likely to be unique to them.

How you learn to deliver news and information in the age of the fourth revolution

So if you want to be a journalist, how do you find a way to make a living in this complex landscape?

The answer is to acquire all the skills it takes to produce that news and information, across a wide range of media. To become, in short, a multimedia journalist. Someone who can use all the modern tools that are available to us as gatherers and disseminators of news and information – to be equally at home writing for print or online, doing an audio or video report, taking still images, crunching data to reveal the stories hidden within it, and using a wide range of social media to find, research and publish stories.

That's what the MMJ project sets out to help you do.

And, because this is a revolution, MMJ can't stand still. So, while the textbook will remain a guide to the unchanging principles of good practice, in whatever medium you operate, the online versions will be constantly updated to take in new technologies – new software, hardware and ways of doing journalism.

Note

1 www.bbc.co.uk/mediacentre/speeches/2014/james-harding-bbc-staff

How to use this book in conjunction with the online version

You'll notice that each chapter of the book is divided into short modules, beginning with 1A1, which stands for Chapter 1, in Section A, Module 1, and moving up through 1A2, 1A3 and so on.

Each of these modules has a twin on the website. The two versions are designed to work together so, when you are using the book, it's often a good idea to have the equivalent module open on your computer or tablet.

Here's how the book and online versions are intended to work together.

Modules in the book

Cover the unchanging principles of good practice in the area under discussion such as:

- What news is
- What reporting is
- How to find stories.

and so on.

Modules online

Offer supplementary information to that contained in the book including:

- Further, step-by-step tuition in the concepts outlined in the book for those who need more information
- Links to material referred to in the book, including examples and case studies
- Embeds of videos referred to in the book – including examples and further tuition
- Essential updates to the tuition in the book – so if anything changes post publication, you'll get new examples, case studies or tuition online.

A note on the software referred to in the text

Throughout this tuition I have sought to use free, or inexpensive, software and applications to demonstrate the journalistic principles and practices covered.

In this way, I hope to avoid excluding any reader who does not have access to, for example, InDesign, FinalCutPro or any other industry-standard tools. But for readers who do have access to them, through their universities or employers, all that is taught here can be applied to their use.

Getting started

Introduction: What multimedia journalism is

This part of *Multimedia Journalism* is called Getting Started, and that's what we are going to do - straight away. We won't spend a lot of time theorising about things. Instead, you'll jump straight in.

This is what we'll be covering in part A of *Multimedia Journalism*:

Aims of this section

To give you core journalism skills and show you how to:

- Write a good basic news report
- Build a simple WordPress multimedia website and beat blog
- Use social media as an integral part of your news gathering and reporting
- Take good news pictures and create a stills picture story
- Film, edit and publish a video story
- Record, edit and publish audio reports and podcasts.

chapter one

Essentials of writing a news story

In the book version of this chapter we will cover:

- What news is
- What reporting is
- How to identify and serve a particular audience
- Where to find news
- How to write and structure a text-based news report
- Multimedia reporting - the effective use of text, still pictures, video and audio
- Why you need a journalistic specialism
- How to write a specialist or beat blog
- How to tackle a range of basic reporting assignments.

At the end of the chapter are a range of assignments and projects to enable you to practise what you have learned.

In the online version of this chapter you will find:

- Interactive quizzes to test your understanding of the principles of news gathering and writing
- A wide range of videos illustrating the material covered here
- A wealth of links to further information
- Any essential updates to the tuition contained in the print and ebook editions
- Footnotes to the book version chapter.

Always have the companion website to this book open at www.multimedia-journalism.
co.uk. That way you can easily click on the links to the stories discussed here.

1A1

What news is

Teenager dies after confronting attacker

A BOY of 16 died in his brother's arms yesterday after confronting a youth who was
threatening staff in a baker's shop in south London.[1]

That's news. It is clearly a tragic story, and very worrying. Here are some of the reasons we
see it as news:

1   **It's new** - it has just happened, and we are learning about it for the first time.

2   **It's factual** - in that 25-word sentence, there are numerous facts.

questions

Can you work out what they are?

List them before reading on.

Here are the facts covered:

- A boy
- aged 16
- died
- in his brother's arms
- yesterday
- after a confrontation
- with a youth
- threatening staff
- in a baker's shop
- in south London.

3   **It's about people –** that short first paragraph – known as an intro – drops us into a compelling human drama. We can picture the scene, and empathise with the characters in it.

4   **It's relevant to readers; it affects them –** in the immediate area this story will have had a great effect on people, but this was also a big national story. It affected most readers not because they were directly caught up in it but because it was shocking, and they felt great sympathy for the victim and his family. It also affected them because it probably made them feel a bit less safe – either for themselves or for their family.

5   **It's dramatic and out of the ordinary –** the amount written about an event can depend on how dramatic and out of the ordinary it is. In some inner city areas, a murder warrants only a couple of pars (paragraphs) on a local news website, or in a local paper. In a quiet rural area, it would probably be the lead – the main story on the website's home page, and the paper's front page. The difference in coverage reflects the extent to which such an event is relatively common or uncommon.

This story was given great prominence because it involved a law-abiding young man who was completely blameless, and who was attacked for no reason.

6   **It involves conflict –** a fatal attack involves a very high level of conflict.

So that gives us six things that tell us what news is.

Take a look at the next story. Is it news?

IRA and UDA 'held secret talks'

Secret talks between the UDA and the Provisional and Official IRA 30 years ago have been revealed in confidential Cabinet papers. They have been made available under the 30 year rule.[2]

This story can hardly be called new - it happened over 30 years ago. So how can it be defined as news under our item 1 above?

It's news because we have only just learned about it. So let's refine that first item and say:

News is new to our readers

So it doesn't matter if an event happened a long time ago, or if some people know about it. As long as our readers don't, then it is news to them.

Here's another story

Ireland's police watchdog has launched a criminal investigation into allegations that the Garda Siochána is secretly reading journalists' phone records.[3]

How many elements in our definition of news does it cover? Can you think of something else about it that means we should add another element to our definition of news?

Make your list, and decide what further element we may need to add to our definition, before reading on.

Here are the elements in our news definition that this story covers:

> This story is **new to the reader**, it's **factual**, it's **about people**. Its **relevance to the reader** is that this overt reading of phone records may have compromised the work of journalists. It might not be dramatic but it does disclose **events that are – or should be – out of the ordinary**. It doesn't involve dramatic conflict, but what it reveals is likely to concern many who read it – particularly journalists. We often need to protect the identity of our contacts. Our phone records may help reveal who has given us sensitive information.

But is there something else about this story that means we should add a new element to our definition of news?

Think about the senior officials who ordered this snooping to take place. Would they rather this story had not been written, and that this practice had remained secret? I think we can assume that they would. And that gives us another element often found in news stories:

News is something someone, somewhere, doesn't want you to report

As is becoming apparent, not all stories fit every element in our definition of news. We will have to be a little flexible over this.

Here's a fourth story

Is it news? Does it fit none, some or all of the elements in our definition of news?

> **Our recent home page featured a request to help find George the cat.**
>
> George had gone missing from his home in Upper Bush. He was spotted in the area of Charles Drive and James Road Thursday evening and Friday morning.
>
> Following a leaflet drop by his owner, in the area, a resident of Ladywood Road reported that they had taken George in after finding him in their back garden.
>
> George's owner is very grateful for the help of all those involved in George's safe return.[4]

This might not seem like the most exciting news (it appeared in the Cuxton Parish Council newsletter) and it's not written in a way that makes the most of the story, but it is new, it is factual and it is about people. And a cat.

It's not dramatic or out of the ordinary and it doesn't involve conflict.

But does it *affect* people? And is it *relevant* to readers? Yes. It affects not just George's owner, but those who received leaflets about his disappearance, and the lady who found him. And, indirectly, it will affect cat owners who live in the area and can sympathise with the owner's anxiety, and relief that the pet was found.

A lot of stories aren't of earth-shattering importance, but that doesn't mean there isn't an audience for them. For example:

Lily Allen and a lot of Lily's side/underboob took to the stage at London's Royal Albert Hall on Tuesday night. . .

The brunette *Hard Out Here* singer was dressed in a daring sheer sleeveless William Vintage creation, which barely covered her cleavage. . . Before she took to the stage she told her followers she had to be sewn into the top, which we think seems like a lot of hassle for something that hardly covers anything. A lot like those nude Nicki Minaj-esque nude pasties she decided to wear, too.[5]

The story above had a picture with it. Indeed, the picture *was* the story. Sometimes text is not the best way to tell a story, but more of that later.

Audience is key to news

Perhaps the most important thing to grasp about news is that we can't see it in the abstract. We have to look at it in relation to a particular audience. Readers of *The Guardian* would not be interested in Lily Allen's boobs - or, at least, they probably wouldn't admit to being interested. But tabloid gossip columns and online celebrity news sites carried the story prominently.

The *Sunday Times* or the *News of the World* would not be interested in George the cat's adventure, but many of those who read the appeal to find him in the parish newsletter would be interested in the happy ending to the story.

A good question for a journalist to ask themselves is: do our readers, viewers or listeners care about this story?

Get used to asking yourself that. Before long an editor will ask it of you, when you are telling them what a fantastic tale you have uncovered. If you say, "Yes, they will," you'll need to be able to justify that claim.

One further thing to remember as we define news. News is only news the first time we hear it. Once we've heard about a story, it's old hat. So:

News is perishable

questions

So what is news? Define news in 50 words, covering the eight key points outlined above. Don't read on until you have written your definition.

Your answer should include the following key points:

News:

- is new to our readers
- factual
- about people
- relevant to our readers, viewers and listeners - it affects them
- is often dramatic and out of the ordinary
- it often involves conflict

- can be something that someone doesn't want us to report
- is perishable.

Here's one way of turning those points into a crisp definition:

> News is factual information that is new to its audience. It must be relevant to, and affect, that audience. It is about people. It often involves conflict, is dramatic and out of the ordinary. It can be something someone doesn't want reported. It gets stale very quickly.

PS News is a good story well told

This is not so much an element in our definition, but a pointer to how we approach finding and writing news stories.

Journalists often call their news reports 'stories'. Why do you think they do that?

It is because news reports share many characteristics in common with good fictional stories that appear in novels, or make up the plots of films.

Good fictional stories involve colourful characters, dramatic events, conflicts, unexpected happenings and – sometimes – tragic or very lucky occurrences.

Fictional stories also have a clear beginning, middle and end.

If we are to turn factual events into a good news story we need to use the techniques of fiction to help us do that.

One of the first things reporters realise is that everyday events – real life stories – are very messy. There is no real clear beginning, middle or end.

Whether key characters are acting well or badly can be hard to determine.

So, while we try very hard not to distort events, we have to present them in the form of a coherent story. The best way to do that is to identify the two sides in a situation, and give their points of view – their interpretation of the story and how it has unfolded. That way, the reader can decide which version of events they choose to believe.

Here is an example. A football manager is sacked because his team performs badly and gets relegated. He tells reporters that the team's poor performance is the fault of the team's captain, who did not train hard enough and has lost interest in winning games.

The team captain says that this is a lie, and that the manager didn't care whether the team was relegated, because he had already agreed to manage another team.

We may not be able to tell whether either of these stories are true. They are both versions of events. When we write our story, we can include both sides of the story. And that takes us on to the other half of the phrase news reporting – the reporting part.

on the website

Find a further, detailed discussion of what news is.

1A2

What reporting is

Reporting is about finding the answers to questions. To function as news reporters we need to take an event and ask the right questions in order to find out about it. Once we have done that we are ready to file our report. And whether our report is filed in text form, or uses audio, or video, we still need to answer the same essential questions, so that our audience understands what has happened.

There are six essential questions we must answer for our report to be complete. They are:

- Who?
- What?
- When?
- Where?
- Why?
- How?

By the way, sometimes "How?" can be further defined by saying "How much?", or "How many?". Numbers are very useful in intros and headlines – they are specific, unlike words such as "massive" or "tiny" and enable the reader to assess how important they think the story is.

questions

Look back, and apply the Who?, What?, When?, Where?, Why? and How? test to the very first story we looked at. Don't read on until you have done that.

Here is how five of the six key questions are answered:

> A BOY of 16 **[that's the who]** died **[that's the what]** in his brother's arms yesterday **[that's the when]** after confronting a youth who was threatening staff **[that's the why]** in a baker's shop in south London.**[that's the where]**[1]

The only question that hasn't been answered is: **How?**. In fact the boy was stabbed to death. So, in the next sentence, our news report would need to answer that question.

The other vital thing we will have to do is say who is telling us all this. That's called **attribution**, and is essential in any news story. We are *reporting*, so we must say who is giving us this information.

When we write a news story we often find we split our presentation of essential information as follows. First, we say

- Who did what/had what done to them?

Which means we answer two of our six questions.

Then we fill in the answers to our other four questions

- When, where, why and how did they do it/have it done to them?

These six questions are the essential ones we all use, in our everyday lives, in order to find out about things. Our readers will be asking the same set of questions as they begin to read any news report that we write. It's our job to answer their questions as clearly, quickly and interestingly as we can. And we need to answer them in the right order.

Here is some information that forms the basis of a news story

- Who? Hundreds of people
- What? Missing from a Philippine ferry that capsized
- When? On Saturday
- Where? On its way from Manila to the island of Cebu
- Why? There was a typhoon
- How? [The answer to that question is often very closely caught up with the Why?, and in this case there is nothing to add under this heading].

Have a go at taking the information listed above, and write a sentence that turns it into a report of the incident.

Don't be self-conscious, and don't worry about formal writing. If you get stuck, just tell yourself the story, then write it down, using the same words as you would use to speak the tale. Do it in about 20 words.

Don't read what's below until you have done that.

Here's our intro:

> Hundreds of people are missing after a Philippines ferry capsized during a typhoon while sailing from Manila to the island of Cebu.

We could end our first sentence after the word typhoon, and begin a second sentence about the route. We could then say more about the destination. Cebu is a popular holiday destination, and we could mention that.

Here's another string of bits of information. Have a go at turning them into a story.

- Who? 250,000 council workers
- What? Have voted to take industrial action
- When? This summer
- Where? In England and Wales
- Why? Inflation is affecting their standard of living and they want a 6 per cent pay rise
- How? Banning overtime and working to rule

And don't forget:

- Attribution: the union Unison has announced this action.

Write two or three sentences. Don't read on until you have written your version

> Council workers have voted in favour of industrial action in a dispute over pay, the union Unison has announced.

A quarter of a million union members in England and Wales will take part in an overtime ban and work to rule this summer. They are demanding a 6 per cent pay rise.

There you go, now you are a reporter. I don't mean to suggest that being a really good reporter is easy. I just want to demonstrate that there is no mystery about being a journalist. It takes a lot of practise to get really good at it, but the principles behind what we do are very simple.

It's all about answering key questions, and making sure we say where the information comes from.

What we have just done is called news reporting. We took some news, and we wrote a report about it.

on the website

Find a further, detailed discussion on how to be a good reporter.

1A3

News: who's the audience?

News doesn't exist in the abstract. It must be directed at – and relevant to – a particular audience. If it isn't of interest to your chosen audience, it's not worth reporting. So let's think about audience in some detail.

Your audience might be international, national, regional, local or hyper local (which is jargon for very local indeed).

It might be a very general audience – people with all sorts of backgrounds and interests, or it might be very clearly defined.

Your international audience might be a specialist one. It might be made up of investors, or those involved in reinsurance or risk management. It could be pianists. Your national audience could be made up of planning officers or those involved in the retail food business.

You need to know about your audience in order to write news that will be relevant to its members. Remember, if it isn't relevant to them, it isn't news to them.

If the following story appeared in *Golf World*, it wouldn't be news. But it didn't. It was in a magazine for journalists.

> Freelance journalist Sylvia Morris was named journalist of the year last night at the headlinemoney.co.uk awards for personal finance journalists.[6]

Can you think of another audience for that story?

What about the people Sylvia Morris writes about, and the industry she covers?

questions

Come up with three audiences for the following piece of information. If you haven't heard of Christopher Lloyd, Google him.

Photo: Jonathan Buckley

> The late Christopher Lloyd's house and garden, Great Dixter in East Sussex, has been allocated more than £4 million from the Heritage Lottery Fund to help safeguard its future.[7]

Make your list before you read on.

Among the audiences for this information are:

- **Keen gardeners** - so the story is of interest to the readers of gardening magazines and websites.
- **People who visit gardens** - so the story is of interest to those who provide news and information to them.
- **People who live near Great Dixter** - so the story is of interest to local newspapers and websites.

As well as these specialist, clearly defined audiences, there might be a general audience for this story. Great Dixter is often featured in colour supplements, so a magazine editor might decide this is a good peg (a peg is an event to hang a story on) for running a Great Dixter feature now.

So you know what news is. And you know how important it is to know who your audience is.

Very often, news stories published for a general audience can be the source of new, much more detailed and targeted stories, for specialist audiences. If I give you some general news stories and tell you what your specialist audience is, you will be able to come up with some stories directed at those audiences.

Here are the general news stories:

New rules for consumer protection

A new law aimed at protecting consumers against rogue traders has come into force in the UK.

For the first time in UK law there will be a duty on all businesses not to trade unfairly.

The law aims to tackle everything from aggressive sales tactics by rogue builders to bogus closing-down sales.

Fortune-tellers, astrologers and mediums are among those affected by the rules, which require them to say their services are for "entertainment only".[8]

Here are some audiences. What stories would you pursue for each of them, from this information?

- Consumers in general
- The boss of a building company
- Trading standards officers.

Don't read on until you have your ideas written down.

The stories you could pursue for them:

- **Consumers in general**
  You could tell them how they will be protected by this new legislation – and against what dodgy practices – and give them details of what to do if someone tries to con them

- **The boss of a building company**
  You could tell him what 'aggressive sales tactics' he must not indulge in

- **Trading standards officers**
  You could tell them in detail what practices they must look out for and the action they should take if they discover them.

Here is another piece of information:

'Care flawed' in many bypass ops

The care given to many patients having heart bypass surgery may be flawed, according to an expert report.

The study suggested that as many as one in five of the 20,000 patients a year undergoing the operation do not get the best possible care.[9]

Here are your audiences:

- Hospital managers
- Patients facing heart bypass surgery.

questions

What stories could you pursue for them?

Don't read on until you have your story ideas.

- **Hospital managers**
  How to ensure your surgical and nursing teams give the best possible care
- **Patients facing heart bypass surgery**
  What level of care you can expect, how to recognise when you don't get it, and what to do about it.

on the website

Find an interactive quiz on matching a story with an audience.

1A4

News: Where does it come from?

So how do you find news? Most stories start from an initial germ of an idea, and need following up. A press release, for example, should be the start of a reporter's quest for a story, not the end.

We take the initial piece of information and we add to it. We find out more, we look for updates, more interesting angles, we talk to those involved, we go along to an event, get pictures, video, audio where appropriate.

Let's look at some stories and see where they came from

Here are three stories from the front page of the BBC News website on one particular day.

1 Here's a story about a murder

Youth 'brutally' killed in park

A murder inquiry has been launched after the battered body of a teenager was found in a park in West Yorkshire.

Detectives said the youth, aged 17 or 18, was found in Crow Nest Park in Dewsbury at 1930 BST on Sunday.[10]

W<small>HERE THE STORY CAME FROM</small>

As the second par makes clear, the police are the source of this story. On the West Yorkshire Police website there was a press release that alerted the media to the story.

Here's what that press release said. It contains a number of additions to an initial release, organised in order of publication, with the latest at the top:

Dewsbury suspicious death update

At about 7.30 last night police were contacted by the ambulance service who had been called to Crow Nest Park at Dewsbury, where the body of a 16 yr old youth was found.

The 16 yr old appears to have been subject to a serious assault. We are still investigating the cause of death.

Police are keen to identify the young man, who is Asian and smartly dressed in white tracksuit bottoms, a white "Bench" top and black trainers.

We know there were a number of groups of young people in the park throughout yesterday and we need them to come forward as a matter of urgency.

We also want to hear from anyone who has information about what might have happened, or who knows the identity of the young man. Anyone with information is asked to ring the Incident Room on 01924 431000.

0925am update – we now believe we know the identity of the young man, though at this stage we are not in a position to release that. We hope to be able to do so later today

Det Supt Chris Thompson, speaking at a media briefing at 11am today said:

> Last night at 7.30pm a young man aged about 17 was found in a walled garden inside Crow Nest park. The cause of death has not yet been established but he had

been subjected to a sustained and vicious beating. A post mortem will be carried out later this morning.

We would like to appeal for anyone who was in the park between 2pm and 8pm yesterday to come forward and help us build a clearer picture of events.

We know the park was very busy yesterday with a lot of groups of young people around during the day.

We have not yet established a motive for the attack."

On the force website is a page where all its news and public announcements are issued:

www.westyorkshire.police.uk/news

Press releases have their own page off that: **www.westyorkshire.police. uk/news/releases**. News is also available via Facebook, Twitter, an RSS feed and on a mobile phone app. (We'll look at RSS feeds in Chapter 3)

Not all those sources are targeted specifically at those in the media. Some are focused much more at the general public.

Here are the links to each of them:

www.facebook.com/westyorkshirepolice

https://twitter.com/WestYorksPolice

www.westyorkshire.police.uk/news/rss-feeds

www.westyorkshire.police.uk/wypuploads/mobile/#home

questions

Take a look at each of the means by which, if you were a reporter covering crime in West Yorkshire, you could get breaking news from this source. Decide which would be the most useful for you, and in what circumstances.

Don't read on until you have decided.

The Facebook page is focused very much on the general public. It regularly carries appeals for information about crimes, and pictures of wanted people. Like the page and you get updates on your wall. Those appeals are still news, but the Facebook page does not give the same detail as that available in the press releases.

The Twitter feed is very similar in content to the Facebook page, so while it can be a good way to get alerts, it has the same shortcomings.

The RSS feeds are more specialised. RSS stands for Really Simple Syndication. To subscribe to an RSS feed you click on the RSS logo and add it to your reader. You can learn about readers in Chapter 3, or get some suggested ones at this link: **http://lifehacker. com/google-reader-is-shutting-down-here-are-the-best-alter-5990456**

West Yorkshire Police actually has a wide range of RSS feeds, as you'll see here: **www. westyorkshire.police.uk/news/rss-feeds**. There are feeds for appeals, campaigns and missing persons, in addition to several news release ones. News releases are the only information feeds targeted at journalists, and you can choose from force-wide ones or those for a particular area.

The mobile app feed has both force-wide and divisional news, along with all the other information contained in the Twitter and Facebook accounts.

You'll probably find different news sources most useful depending where you are and what device you have with you. At your desk, the website press releases page may be best. On the move, the mobile app may be most convenient.

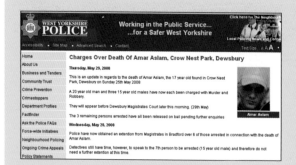

Whichever channel you use, you want to be sure to get alerts when new stories are posted. We'll look at how you set up such alerts in Chapter 3.

The West Yorkshire force has a very systematic way of updating their releases, which makes it easy to follow the latest developments in any case. Here is a grab of the page quoted from above, with some further updates on it.

Once you have subscribed to the appropriate RSS feed, all the releases that are added to it come automatically to your reader and are on your desktop whenever you want to look at them.

If you were covering crime in West Yorkshire, that feed would be an invaluable source of news stories.

2 Here's a story about space exploration

Historic pictures sent from Mars

A NASA spacecraft has sent back the first historic pictures of an unexplored region of Mars.[12]

WHERE THE STORY CAME FROM

NASA issued a press release on its website.

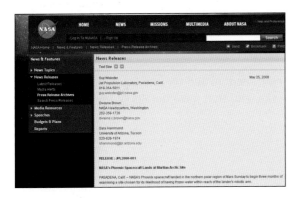

It began like this:

NASA's Phoenix Spacecraft Lands at Martian Arctic Site

05.25.08 - NASA's Phoenix spacecraft landed in the northern polar region of Mars Sunday to begin three months of examining a site chosen for its likelihood of having frozen water within reach of the lander's robotic arm.[13]

3 Here's a story about an eccentric event

Cheese racers in steep challenge

Dozens of competitors have been hurling themselves down a steep hill in the annual bank holiday cheese-rolling event in Gloucestershire.[14]

WHERE IT CAME FROM

The organisers of the event have publicised it, and invited the media along. There was a link from the story to the organisers' web site, and that gave details of how to get media accreditation.[15]

Common news sources

Here are some common sources of stories. Which are relevant to any given online publication, newspaper, magazine, radio or TV channel will depend on its audience.

- Social media
- Court cases
- Local and national government
- The stock market and company reports
- The emergency services – police, fire and rescue, ambulance and coastguard

- Product launches
- Press releases from a wide range of organisations
- News wire services
- Anniversaries
- News from your own publication, your readers and from your contacts
- News from other media outlets
- Campaigns, opinion polls, surveys.

On- and off-diary stories

News stories fall into two types: ones that can be predicted, that we have notice of; and those that we cannot predict.

Stories we have notice of are called on-diary stories.

Stories that cannot be on the diary because they cannot be predicted are, you guessed it, off diary.

Some examples

Here are some examples of stories gained from some of the sources on our list. Our list is not an exhaustive one, by the way. You might like to think about additional sources to add to it.

Social media

Many celebrities choose to break news themselves, on their Twitter and/or Facebook accounts, via their own blogs or official websites.

Many organisations choose to do the same.

This is one of the effects of the ability social media, and the web in general, gives any individual or organisation to become their own publisher.

Because of this, it is vital that you follow the online accounts of individuals and organisations in the fields you cover. If you report on football, for example, there will be a wide range of players, managers and others you need to follow.

When it comes to general news events, eye-witnesses are often the first to report, via their mobile phones.

Many major stories have broken on social media in recent years.

Major ones have included the downing of a passenger jet into the Hudson River in New York. Eye-witness Janis Krums posted the first picture on Twitter here: **http://twitpic.com/135xa**

It is one of the longest-trending (which means: consistently popular) pictures on the service.

His accompanying tweet said: "There's a plane in the Hudson. I'm on the ferry going to pick up the people. Crazy."

on the website

Find links to a range of other stories that broke on social media.

Court cases

A US court is to hear the opening statements in the trial of a UK man accused of killing his family.[16]

Local government

The people of a Mid Wales town have won their battle to keep their local library open.

Ceredigion council's cabinet had decided to close Tregaron library as part of its aim to save £9.6m this financial year... but the local authority has now agreed to keep the library open three-days-a-week.[17]

National government

The UK government has issued an explicit warning to British businesses over the risks of involvement in Israeli settlements in the West Bank, including potential damage to a company's reputation.[18]

theguardian

News | Sport | Comment | Culture | Business | Money | Life & style

News World news Israel

UK government issues warning over doing business with Israeli settlements

For the first time, UK government issues guidelines on the risks of trading with Israeli settlements

Harriet Sherwood in Jerusalem
The Guardian, Monday 9 December 2013 18.28 GMT

A Palestinian labourer at a construction site in the Jewish settlement of Maale Adumim in the West Bank. Photograph: Baz Ratner/REUTERS

The stock market and company reports

Phone makers Samsung and HTC have reported discouraging first-quarter results, with Samsung recording its second year-on-year decline in operating profit and Taiwan's HTC suffering its third loss in three quarters.[19]

The emergency services – police, fire and rescue, ambulance and coastguard

Nineteen firefighters have died in Arizona after being caught in one of the deadliest wildfires in the US for decades, which destroyed scores of homes and forced the evacuation of two small towns north-west of Phoenix.[20]

Product launches

These are often important for B2B (business to business) publications where the readers need to know about the latest products and services coming on to the market, and also for consumer publications. Often they are newsworthy to both sectors. Here's an example:

> Sales of electric cars could move out of the slow lane with the arrival of an electric version of the world's best-selling car.
>
> The Ford Focus Electric, which goes on sale in the UK on Thursday, runs entirely on battery power for up to 100 miles between charges.[21]

The information above is from a Ford press release that formed the basis of stories in a wide range of publications, from *The Guardian* to B2B publications dealing with the motor industry, specialist car magazines aimed at motorists considering buying an electric car, and a Facebook page called Energy Share, which deals with alternative energy issues.

The release also contained the information that the car has a top speed of 85mph, and costs £28,500. Most reports on the story added the fact that this price meant that, even after a government grant, it would cost twice as much as the cheapest petrol-powered Focus.

Press releases and press conferences

These can come from a very wide range of organisations. From the police alerting the public, via us, of a dangerous individual on the loose, to a company launching a new product.

> Today, the Supervisory Board of HUGO BOSS AG has resolved on the appointment of Claus-Dietrich Lahrs as member of the Managing Board and CEO of HUGO BOSS AG.[22]
>
> Morton Plant Hospital has been recognized as a 100 Top hospital in a national study. . . the Thomson 100 Top Hospitals: Cardiovascular Benchmarks for Success, formerly the Solucient 100 Top Hospitals study.[23]

The release adds that this is one of only two hospitals in the United States to have received recognition in the Top 100 for heart care for nine consecutive years.

You will have noticed that the press releases above - one from the Hugo Boss clothing company, the other from an American hospital, are not well written. It will take some work for a journalist to establish what the story is - if any - and for which audience it will count as news. That's where we come in. Journalists are good at spotting information that is of interest to the audiences they serve - even when those providing the information haven't a clue how to present it.

News wire services

There are international, national, regional and local agencies. Some supply general news, some specialise in, for example, financial news or sport.

Media outlets will usually subscribe to a feed of news from such services but, depending on the service and how often it is used, might buy items individually.

INTERNATIONAL

> Reuters: Britain's economy looks to have grown at its fastest quarterly rate since early 2010 during the first three months of this year, a leading economic research body estimated on Tuesday.[24]

NATIONAL

> Press Association: The Archbishop of York's charity skydive should go ahead, the Red Devils parachute display team said.[25]

LOCAL

> Solent News and Photo Agency: People could soon be donning revolutionary mittens to keep them cool rather than ward off chilly weather. Scientists are developing gloves and boots which people will be able to put on in hot weather to stop them overheating.[26]

Anniversaries

Anniversaries are very popular pegs for stories. Sometimes they can be an excuse for lazy journalism. An audience isn't always interested in something just because it happened 10, 20 or 25 years ago. For example:

> The 25th anniversary of the visit by the Space Shuttle Enterprise to Stansted Airport has been marked.[27]

But at other times there is good reason to return to a story one year on:

> The family of hostage Peter Moore have made an emotional appeal for his release on the anniversary of his abduction.[28]

News from your own publication, your readers, and from your contacts

Monitoring your own website, newspaper, magazine, TV channel or radio station is vital. Not only because you must be familiar with what you are publishing, but because your own publication can be a great source of new stories to follow up.

Responses from readers to news items - via comments on your stories on your website, posted on social media, in blog posts, emails and letters - can include new information that pushes a story forward, and gives something new to write about.

Also, readers may raise subjects that you were unaware of.

Tips from a reporter's contacts are another important source of news. Contacts are people who know you well enough, or trust you enough, to give you stories in preference to other reporters. They may do so because they want the story to appear in your publication, because they know you will treat the story fairly, or that you will keep their name out of it if they have requested anonymity. The great advantage of tips is that they often put you ahead of your rivals.

Leaks from individuals or organisations may also put you ahead of the game. Leaks are unofficial, unattributable announcements, or the surreptitious release of documents. A person or organisation may leak to you because they know you, trust your publication, or want to manage the release of a story that they believe you will treat sympathetically.

Campaigns, opinion polls, surveys

News organisations often decide that a particular issue has great resonance for their readers, viewers or listeners, and decide to take a stand on it. They usually have a goal in mind - persuading major retailers to stop issuing plastic bags, for example.

Asking for opinions is very easy to do online. Getting readers to vote on a topic is easy for us to organise, and for them to participate in.

At a more organised level, media outlets often commission a survey from a recognised polling organisation. This means that the poll will have been scientifically designed and that results will carry some weight. Below is one from *The Guardian*/ICM, which asked about housing concerns and found:

> Affordability - and, most particularly homebuyers' struggle to get a foot on the property ladder - emerges as by far the biggest issue in housing in a new *Guardian*/ICM poll.[29]

A survey can be less formal. We can do what is called a ring-round - or an email round - in which we ask respondents their views on one or more key questions. Such a survey might be less scientific than a poll, but it enables us to get a range of particular individuals engaging on a topic.

We can also go out and do a vox-pop. The name comes from the Latin, *vox populi* or voice of the people. We can take still pictures of the people who talk to us, or video / audio record them and create a package of their responses.

News from other media outlets

Journalists are great recyclers. A great deal of what we do is inspired, to be polite, or nicked, to be honest, from another publication of some kind. TV and radio often feed off newspapers. Newspapers often feed off broadcasters. All the traditional media feed off the web, and web journalists feed off the comments and input of readers, bloggers, Tweeters, Facebookers, and those who post their comments on stories, and about issues, that are in the news.

At its best, this process is a positive one. We take the germ of an idea from something that has been published elsewhere, and adapt and update it for our audience and for the particular medium we are working in.

Recycling is increasingly common today because there are no deadlines, no restriction on how often we can update a story. Or at least, there are no restrictions imposed by printing deadlines and distribution schedules. We don't have to wait for a video or audio report to be edited. If there is no time for that, we go live to air or web. If we work on a weekly newspaper and there is no print edition for four days, no problem. We probably publish first to social media, particularly Twitter, as a story is just breaking, and then with more, as we get it, on the web. If we work on a monthly magazine, where it is impossible to cover news effectively, again no problem. We establish a news website with daily updates, publish an email bulletin, offer an RSS feed, SMS or Twitter subscription.

on the website

- Learn more about sources for stories
- Find links to online versions of the sites referred to in this unit.

1A5

What's the best way to tell a story?

Multimedia news: how to tell it

The other thing we have to decide when we are working on a story is how to tell it. That is, what medium, or range of media, should we use to report it? We have all the traditional storytelling methods at our disposal. If we were working only on TV, we'd have to try to find pictures for every report that we wrote. You'll have seen how, when it is doing a piece about obesity, TV often struggles to tell the story pictorially, and resorts to showing the backsides of anonymous people walking out of burger bars. During the long wait for an

election result, TV has to use endless shots of people hanging about in halls, and elaborate 3-D graphics.

With multimedia journalism we choose the medium that best fits the story we are telling. If there aren't any good pictures to be had, then we don't have to use video or stills. If a story does not lend itself to a pictorial treatment, then we can use text to tell it.

Each medium – text, video, stills and audio – has its strengths and weaknesses.

- Broadly, **text is good for explanation and analysis**. If you need to give readers a lot of detail, that can best be done through the medium of text
- Unedited **live audio gives great immediacy**, and presents no time lag at all. It's great for eye-witness accounts, where dramatic events are unfolding. Recorded audio, built into what is known as a package containing good actuality can also bring a story to life
- We can **use live moving images to show events as they unfold, and to capture the immediacy of dramatic situations**
- We can **use still pictures to capture events after they have happened,** and allow the viewer to savour them
- We can **use data visualisations, also called graphics, to simplify the presentation of statistics and complex figures.**

And that's by no means all that we can do with multimedia journalism.

- We can **use interaction to create a dialogue with the reader**, to make them a part of our storytelling, and to develop our stories through them.

With the web, social media and multimedia, we are free to use none, some or all of the full range of storytelling techniques – in addition to the key one of text – to tell a story to best advantage.

questions

Let's think about the three stories in the last unit. They were the Dewsbury murder, the Mars landing and the cheese-rolling event. Take another look at them. What is the best medium to tell them in?

Jot down your thoughts before you read on.

1 The Dewsbury murder story

Little is known at present other than what the police have released. A straightforward text story is a good basis. You could also go to the scene, and conduct audio or video interviews. Residents might well want to discuss the situation and make their feelings clear. They may have things to say about the level of violence they experience in their community. They might also want to express their views via comments on the story you publish. So interaction on the web would be an effective way of adding to your coverage.

2 The Mars landing story

Text can be used to tell the story in detail, to give a clear summary of what has happened and some background to it. But text can't do full justice to it, so there must be some other elements.

The BBC website coverage also included an embedded video of the first pictures sent back from the craft.

There was also an embedded video to capture the drama of the moments just before and after landing, and to record the delight of the NASA team at mission control.

There was a still-picture slide show to combine the photos that the craft sent back to earth, and the NASA crew's celebrations.

3 Cheese-rolling

This is an annual, diary event so you have plenty of time to plan your coverage. On the day, you really have to go to this event to cover it properly, and it is best told in pictures. A video combining footage of cheeses being hurled downhill, interviews with those who do it, and the spectators, would work well.

You could do something in advance, too. The organisers' website talked about the cheeses, made by the only Double Gloucester manufacturer using traditional methods. An interview with her might be fun. Doesn't she mind her skilfully made cheeses being hurled down hills? You could even use this as an angle for a piece about the Double Gloucester dying out, or a broader piece on the English cheese industry.

The three stories we have just been looking at all have strong visual possibilities. But that's not true of every story.

Take this one for example:

EALING'S council tax will rise by 1.9 per cent this year, less than the rate of inflation.[30]

Council Tax stories require a good deal of detail and explanation. Readers want to know how much the increase will affect them. There will be complex explanation of how the council arrived at the figure it has set. There will be information on how much it is going to spend on a range of key services.

If you are going to explain such a story in detail, then text is your best option. But for presenting the story at a glance, data visualisations - also called graphics - really come into their own. A list of figures is hard to absorb and make sense of; a graphic can show readers instantly what the figures mean. That's not to say you can't augment your facts-and-figures text and graphics-based coverage with pictures, video, audio and text interviews with council tax payers.

Multimedia storytelling – what works best for each type of story

Here, in more detail, is a run-through of the main media and an outline of the benefits of each.

Text

Text gives depth. It is good for context, background and analysis. It connects with our audience's intellect - with their desire to comprehend.

When you really want to understand something, text is best. Text is also good for providing links to other material related to a story - both current and archive material. It's great for displaying searchable databases of information. So, for example, the reader can go to a database of university courses and find the one they are interested in, and how it is rated.

Text is also good for interaction. If we want readers to vote, or comment, or join a debate, then text is quick and simple.

Text is good as an anchor for a story that contains other elements. You can give the facts, outline the nature of the story, and offer stills, video or audio as additional elements.

Text is fast and cheap to produce. You can knock out a fair number of news stories in the time it takes you to film and edit one video package.

But text is not always good when we want to draw a reader in to a story - to empathise with the victims of a natural disaster or a terrible crime, for example.

Video

Video is great when we want to enable our audience to see and hear an event, or people, or a mix of the two, directly. Video puts the audience at the scene.

Video is good when we have action and drama to capture and convey. It connects with the audience's emotions. In text we can *tell* them about a famine, for example. With video, we can *show* them the suffering of individuals.

If the story warrants it, we can go live to an event and broadcast video from it straight to our website and/or social media. Apart from the fact that we have to be at the scene, this is quick and easy reporting.

Where video becomes very time-consuming is if we have to create a well-crafted video package, involving a range of interviews. For such a package, we have to go to places, arrange interviews, edit footage into a coherent package and publish it. For this reason, many web publishers are reluctant to use video in anything other than a live broadcast situation.

CCTV footage can be a good source of a video story. Greater Manchester Police (GMP) released dramatic cctv footage taken in a prison van which was attacked by armed men, who released prisoners from it. They put it on YouTube.

GMP presented that video as part of its press release on the incident. You can see that video on the MMJ website, or by following this link: **http://youtu.be/Le87BeehXjc**

The *Mail Online* used the video as part of an extensive story with text and many stills – even adding 30 seconds of commercials at the front of the video when they embedded it on their site. That's on our website too.

Stills photography

Good stills photography captures a moment. It is incredibly valuable in sport, when things happen fast, and even an action replay can't capture the real drama of a shot at goal, a momentary lapse, or a split-second decision.

Of course, not all stills photography is that vital. Often a still is used to show what a person looks like – a classic head and shoulders mug shot.

It can also be used to bring home something that words can't convey with full effectiveness. If a much-loved park has been vandalised, if racist graffiti has been sprayed on graves, or if a horrible crash has occurred, stills are very useful in effectively conveying what has happened.

With a still (and this is why they are called that) we get a split-second frozen in time. Great stills can be incredibly memorable. You can probably picture some stills that have been imprinted on your brain.

Stills are also very popular with readers. They buy them, so giving us a source of revenue. Traditionally-edited local papers often have a policy of publishing as many people's pictures as they can, partly because it sells papers, but also because those people might buy a print of the picture that is published.

Stills can tell a story in themselves, and hence stand alone from text.

They are much cheaper and quicker to produce than video.

Audio

Audio has the immediacy of video without the disadvantage that the audience member has to give it their full attention.

Audio gives a quick impression of a speaker – their accent, age, personality.

An audio interview can be woven with narration to give context and comment on what is being said.

It is very portable – audio podcasts are very convenient ways of obtaining news or information when the audience is on the move and doing other things.

We must choose the right medium for the story we are covering

Before the advent of multimedia, if a journalist came from a print background they would tend to favour text. If they came from a TV background they would tend to favour video, and if they came from radio, then audio was their chosen way of telling stories.

In multimedia journalism, we have no favourites – we choose the right medium for the story we are working on. We use the best format every time.

questions

Is video and audio used to the same extent on all news websites? Before you read on, compare use of video on the BBC (**bbc.co.uk**) with that on *The Guardian* (**www.the-guardian.com/uk**). Do you notice any difference?

Generally, you will find that an online publisher with roots in broadcasting will use a great deal more video than a publisher coming from a print background will. The broadcaster has the resources and expertise to produce a considerable amount of video as a by-product of what they screen on their TV channels. Print publishers often team up with a broadcaster: for example, *The* (London) *Times* uses Sky News videos on the *Times*'s web, mobile and tablet platforms.

Combining storytelling techniques

With multimedia reporting we don't just have to pick one way of telling a story.

We can combine two or more elements in order to present each aspect of a story most effectively.

We can use text as our main means of storytelling, and add in a video or sound clip to give better coverage to one element in a story. We can twin a text report with a stills slide show.

We can use video as our main medium but give a URL that will take viewers to, for example, a report that the video is based on.

We can combine audio and stills to make an audio slideshow.

This combination of sound and still images is very effective. It can combine powerful, evocative stills images with, for example, the comments of the subject of those images on what is taking place.

Stills of a footballer receiving a career-ending tackle can be combined with his commentary on what happened, how it felt, what he thought at the time, and how he looks back on the incident. Video of the tackle would be over in a second and would not have the impact of good stills.

This combination - often called an audio slideshow - expands on the traditional picture story, and adds to the traditional radio package. It is a true child of multimedia journalism and the web.

Tailoring one story for print, web, video and audio

Often, we will have to create versions of a story we are working on in a range of media - a text report, a video, and an audio version. For speed we don't want to make our audio and video versions too different. Indeed, if the audio track of our video will stand alone that's great. On the BBC, one report usually serves both TV and radio.

We can take any given story and decide how best to tell it in each of the media at our disposal.

We can create a video package, an audio package, a text report that links to them both and has an opportunity for the reader to get involved - by voting, commenting, chatting, linking or any number of other interactions.

Where are they reading you?

The other vital aspect of multimedia journalism is our knowledge of where our audience is consuming our news, and which medium of storytelling best fits those situations.

For example, if we are giving traffic information to the residents of a particular town – or drivers on a certain stretch of motorway – then they need us most when they are out and about. Maybe we can give commuters on public transport updates via Twitter, a mobile app, or a website that is optimised for mobile phones. With drivers it's harder. Radio is probably the best outlet for them, if our publisher has one.

Many media companies offer packages of their content in different forms. So Sky News is available on TV, or on a mobile platform optimised for both phones and tablets. Subscribers to *The* (London) *Times* and *Sunday Times* can choose from packages that give them a combination of print product, mobile app or tablet versions of the content.

Subscribers can choose the medium that best suits them at different times of the day or week.

On a Sunday, our audience may be sitting in their armchairs, or relaxing in the garden, and could be most happy with a print publication. On a weekday, they may prefer a mobile app. While travelling, they might just want Twitter updates.

on the website

- ■ Take our interactive quiz to see how well you have grasped the principles of multimedia storytelling
- ■ Find links to all the story sources discussed here, plus see the videos referred to.

1A6

News: how to write it

We are concentrating on text in this chapter, but in the multimedia world text is not just static words on a page. Text also covers links to other information; opportunities for readers to take part in polls; to share our material via social media such as Twitter and Facebook; to recommend it to others via services such as StumbleUpon, Reddit, Digg and Upworthy; and to add their comments to our stories.

Text is the bedrock of multimedia journalism - the glue that binds the video, audio and stills together.

We are concentrating on text for electronic publication. That's very similar to text for print, but with a few refinements that make our words as effective as possible online and in multimedia packages.

We are teaching you to write for online - for websites, tablet editions and mobile apps - because that is where news first appears. We don't have time to write it twice, so it makes sense to write in a way that optimises our stories for online, but which works for print too.

How to begin a story

Two key questions that help us focus on how we begin an online news story are: What's the intro? Or: what's the headline?

If we get the beginning right, we have cracked the hardest thing about writing news. We have started in the right place, and can move on from there, following the correct course.

Get it wrong and you'll have no clear idea of how to structure your information from then on.

If you think back to unit 1A2 in this chapter, what we wrote there were a couple of intros - one about a ferry disaster, the other about a council workers' strike. If we wanted to write more, we have begun at the right place, by answering the key question: what is new, or what has happened?

If you are writing breaking news, you might well only know a very little. But you can publish that straight away - maybe in the form of a tweet. You could also publish a headline, and an intro, on your website.

By the way, there is another, online-native, form of storytelling for breaking news stories that needs constant updating. It's called live blogging, but because it is very different from the structured news writing we are looking at here, we'll save an exploration of it for Chapter 6.

As you learn more you can build your story from the headline and intro you have already written.

Once, stories would have to be written in full before they could be published. That's no longer the case. Now we can publish what we know, then build on it with new versions of the story as we learn more. But what stays true - now as in the past - is the way news is structured.

So let's learn how to structure a news story right away.

Headlines and intros, or heads and sells, or heads and blurbs

There are various terms being used to describe the headlines and first paragraphs on text reports. Whatever they are called – here's what they need to be. . .

If we think back to our definitions of news, a key one was that something should be new – or, at least, new to our audience. This is key to our intro-writing. We want information that is new, that says what is the latest, that tells the reader what has just happened, is happening or will happen.

The two styles of online news writing: BBC and *Mail Online*

Two distinct ways of doing that are developing, and two contrasting styles of online news writing have emerged.

One is typified by the BBC's news website.

The other has been developed by the *Mail Online*, the digital version of the (London) *Daily Mail*, a midmarket tabloid newspaper.

Many other websites – perhaps a majority – use what I'm calling the BBC's style, and it is much closer to the traditional way of writing for print. But plenty of online news brands use a similar style to the *Mail Online*. I'm using these two as examples because they are among the most successful news sites in the world: the BBC has 64m unique users a month, the *Mail Online* 190m per month, according to the Audit Bureau of Circulations.

We'll look at both BBC and *Mail Online*, and demonstrate how to write stories for each.

But what is true of both of them is that the key thing we must do first is to tell readers what's new.

The BBC's style of online news writing

This style of online news writing sets a premium on using as few words as possible. So we don't have much room to say what's new.

Often, heads are restricted to five, six or seven words, and sells/intros to about 20 words. Some content management systems – the set-ups that we feed our content into in order to publish it online – are very unforgiving. If we go a character over on the head, or a word over on the sell, it just cuts the extra off. So we get heads that end in mid air, and sells that are missing a vital final element.

Let's look at some BBC-style heads and sells and how they work. By the way, you'll see the present tense used.

Alcohol squad to target 10 towns

A specialist squad is to help advise English towns with the most drink-related hospital admissions.

Deadline for school 'rescue plan'

The government warns the poorest-performing secondary schools to improve or face "formal intervention".

West End is 'celebrity obsessed'

Theatre director Sir Jonathan Miller accuses West End producers of having "an obsession with celebrity".

How do we decide what to say in a head/headline, and what to say in a sell/intro?

Think first about what's new. Then see if you can include some of the how or why it happened.

If we think of an intro as the summary of a story, then the headline is a summary of the intro. But we don't want to make them too similar, or it will feel like we are repeating ourselves. So we use the technique of giving more detail in our intro/sell than we could in our head.

So, in the first example, 'alcohol squad' becomes 'specialist squad' and '10 towns' becomes 'English towns', then the intro goes on to explain why the ten have been targeted.

Take a look at the second two examples and analyse how the head and intro work together. Look also at how many of our 'who what when where why and how' are being answered in them.

Let's come up with some heads and sells of our own

Here are four stories. Come up with a head of between five and seven words, and a sell of between 18 and 22 words, for each of them.

If you get stuck, ask yourself this: if there was one thing I could say, what would it be? That one thing is likely to be the most important, and will form the basis for what you write. Think of the intro and sell as the conclusion of the story or – if events are still unfolding – the very latest thing that has happened.

1   Coordinated attacks on trains have brought chaos to the city of Mumbai, which is India's financial centre, and rescuers fear that the number of casualties will increase. Heavy monsoon rains are hampering the rescue effort.

Indian television news channels showed images of the wounded lying on train tracks and being carried on sheets through stations.

"People began jumping off our running train when a bomb went off and filled the carriage with smoke and fire," said a commuter with serious injuries to his left arm and shoulder.

More than 100 people have been killed and around 300 others injured after seven explosions tore through commuter trains during the evening rush hour in Bombay.

2   For the 13 weeks to July 1 like-for-like sales at Marks and Spencer rose 8.2pc compared to the same period last year. Like-for-like sales of general merchandise jumped 10.5pc while food gained 5.8pc. A spokesperson said the company was gaining market share across all areas of its business, save children's wear.

The company is creating 4,000 new shopfloor jobs in its stores as a result of this sharp increase in quarterly sales.

The spokesperson said the company operated a "lean machine" but needed the extra staff to cope with the unexpected surge in volumes at its stores.

3   James Fairbright, 23, an accounts administrator earning £16,000 a year, exploited his position at a building firm to transfer money to his bank account then into his Ladbrokes Internet account

The online gambling addict stole more than £1 million from his employers to pay for betting sprees, forcing the company to go into liquidation and lay off staff, a court heard yesterday.

He spent up to £7,000 a day, placing bets on sports of every kind, including horse racing and football matches, and on internet poker and other online casino games.

4   The body of 21-year-old horsewoman Hazel Finnegan was yesterday found by a passing motorist who saw her horse staggering in the road until it collapsed and died. Police believe the animal may have been taken ill and thrown Miss Fletcher, an experienced rider, before dying from a possible heart attack.

Police, who were investigating the death in which the horsewoman found on a country road with her mount lying dead beside her, are looking at the possibility that it might have fallen and crushed her, before getting to its feet again.

Don't read on until you have written your heads and sells.

Here are our suggestions:

1   **100 dead in Mumbai terror attacks**

Over 100 commuters were killed and 300 injured when terrorists detonated bombs on evening rush hour trains in India's financial capital.

2   **4,000 new jobs at M&S**

An 8 per cent increase in sales figures at Marks and Spencer has led to the creation of 4,000 shop floor jobs.

3   Online gambling addict steals £1m from firm

A £16,000-a-year accounts administrator forced his employers into liquidation by stealing to fund his £7,000-a-day gambling addiction.

4   Rider killed by dying horse

An experienced young rider may have died after her horse suffered a heart attack and fell on her, police believe.

Where to go from there: how to structure the rest of a BBC-style news story

Getting the intro right is the most important thing to do when writing a news story. After that comes writing a good second par. Between them, those first two paragraphs set things up well. If you get them right, you will find that writing the rest of the news story is relatively easy.

There is a simple structure that governs the writing of a news story. It's like a multi-purpose ground plan on which we can construct any news report.

Perhaps you haven't realised this yet, but you already know what the first two instructions are on the ground plan.

Below is a graphic that shows you what I mean. The structure we use for writing a news story – the ground plan – is called:

The inverted triangle

The top of the triangle is the start of the story. The inverted triangle is at its widest up there at the start because you need the most important things at the top.

You are starting your story at the widest point: at the point of greatest interest for the reader.

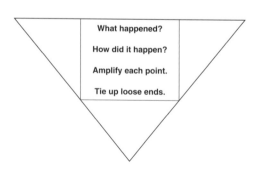

What happened?

How did it happen?

Amplify each point.

Tie up loose ends.

From there, the triangle gets narrower, to denote that the information in the triangle - in the story - is placed in descending order of importance, finally tailing off to bits and pieces which are less important than everything else that has gone before them.

You'll notice that What happened? comes right at the top, just as it has when we have been writing intros.

Next comes the How or Why it happened? - just as it has when we have been writing second pars.

If we get our first two or three pars right, we will have touched upon everything that is of importance in the story - even if we have only done so very briefly.

When we go on to write more of the story, our task is to take each of those important points that have been briefly introduced and to explain them. We go back over the points we have made and tell the reader more about it.

Finally comes the instruction to tie up loose ends. This means we can finish the story off with less important material.

There are two virtues in writing a story that follows the inverted triangle structure. One is that the reader can stop reading when they have satisfied their interest in the story, without worrying that something important may be buried further down the story and that they might miss it unless they read to the end.

The second is most relevant when we are writing for print. If we are writing for print there will be a finite number of words assigned for each story. The decision on story length comes only when the page is laid out, not when you are asked to write your story. When it comes to cutting the story to fit a slot given to it on a page, the person sub-editing (or subbing) the story can cut it pretty much from the bottom so that it fits. They can do this quickly. If they had to cut bits throughout the story that would take longer.

Traditionally, in print publications, dedicated sub-editors took reporter's copy, corrected it, cut it and put it on the page. Today, on newspapers, there are often very few subs, and reporters often have to sub their own copy. On magazines, where layout and design is often of great importance, traditional subbing is still more common.

The acronym **WHAT** might help you remember this structure:

- **W**hat happened? (Or what's new?)
- **H**ow or why did it happen?
- **A**mplify each of the points made in the above
- **T**ie up loose ends.

There is another way of helping you ensure you have written your news story correctly.

Remember our check-list of six questions that must be answered in every news story. We can begin to answer all of them high up in a news story - certainly within the first three or at most four pars. They are:

- Who? What? When?
- Where? Why? How? (and/or How much? How many?)

It is not always possible to answer all these questions in a news report. Sometimes information is not available. For example, if people are killed the police may not release their identities immediately.

The golden rule we must follow when we can't give the answer to an obvious question is to say so. Then the reader is not left wondering why certain information is not contained in the story. So, in the case of deaths, you often see a sentence such as: "A police spokesperson said the names of the dead would not be released until their families had been informed."

Below is an example of a complete news story, written in BBC-style.

The head and the first two pars are these:

6.4 million vehicles recalled by Toyota

Toyota is to recall 6.4 million vehicles globally, including 35,000 in the UK, due to five safety issues.

Around 3.5 million of the recalls are over problems with airbags.

The head and the intro say what is new.

The second paragraph says why this has happened. Let's also apply the Who What When Where Why How test to the first three paragraphs of this story.

> Who? Toyota
> What? Recalling 6.4m vehicles
> When? Now (implied: if it's now we don't need to say so, if it's some other time we do)
> Where? Globally, including in the UK
> Why? Five separate issues including airbag problems
> How? How, as in how could the issues affect car safety, is not addressed here. We'll need to learn about the how very soon.

We have begun to answer five of our six questions.

If a story is well written, the first two paragraphs are a self contained mini-story that could be run without any further words, if space were tight.

Those two paragraphs introduce the important elements in the story: each key point.

After that, a news story is written by going back over the points - the answers - that have been given and amplifying on them. That is why the third main section of a news story is covered in the diagram with 'amplify each point'.

With this story, the who, what, when and where are straightforward and have already been dealt with in the opening pars. The main question that gives room for further reporting is the why: why is this recall necessary, why have Toyota cars developed this range of faults?

There is also the how question to address: how dangerous are these faults, and how could they affect car safety?

Let's see how the Toyota car recall story goes on to amplify these points.

I have explained in bold type where each point in the first two pars is amplified. I have also pointed out where two other characteristics of a web-based text story – side headings and bulleted lists – have been used.

The fault in driver's side airbags means a cable attached to them may be damaged when the steering wheel is turned. As a result, the airbag may not be deployed in a crash. **[addressing the how point, which had not been answered in the first two pars, as in how could the airbag problem affect car safety?]**

Other issues include a problem with engine starter motors that poses a fire risk, and issues with steering columns, windscreen wipers and the rails on which seats run. **[amplifying both the why of why the recall and the how of how dangerous]**

The carmaker said it has had no reports of crashes, injuries or deaths caused by these problems. **[an obvious question is, why have these recalls occurred – have people been injured in the cars? If the recall had been due to a series of deaths, that fact would be important enough to put in the headline and first par]**

It had, however, received two reports of fires in connection with the engine starter problem.

Toyota said that **[here comes some attribution, and a quote to support the assertions made earlier in the story]** "due to inefficiencies in the design of the starter motor relays, metallic particles might accumulate on the contacts within the relay". **[further amplifying the why]**

The company said that particles could come off the relays and enter the relay's circuitry. In what it described as the worst case, "this could lead to the starter relays catching fire". **[further amplifying the how, as in how dangerous]**

Around 20,000 vehicles across six Toyota models, plus the Subaru Trezia, are being recalled for the replacement of both engine starter motors and relays.

Other recalls include: **[Next comes one of the characteristics of writing for online: the use of bullet points to break up dense information into easily digested chunks]**

- 2.32 million vehicles over seat rail problems
- 760,000 vehicles because of a potential defect with the steering column bracket
- 160,000 vehicles to replace windscreen wiper motors.

[Next we see another characteristic of online writing: the side heading, designed to break up a long run of text and give an indication to the reader of what they will be told next]

Toyota's reputation at risk

[Now we are in the tying up loose ends section. We get background and context, with information on previous recalls]

This recall, affecting 27 models, is the fifth Toyota has issued in a few months.

In February, 1.9 million of its Prius hybrid cars were recalled because of a software fault that might cause the vehicle to slow down suddenly.

Late last year, Toyota issued recalls affecting more than 2.2 million vehicles.

In total, the company has called back over 25 million vehicles in two-and-a-half years.

This is far higher than the numbers recalled in 2009 and 2010 - considered to be the worst years in terms of reputation damage.

Toyota's sales suffered following those recalls, which were due to accelerator pedals getting trapped under floor mats.

The recalls triggered a criminal investigation against the carmaker in the USA.

Earlier this year, Toyota made a $1.2bn (£720m) settlement after a four-year inquiry by US regulators into its reporting of safety issues.

The firm is not the only carmaker to suffer major recalls. General Motors is currently recalling millions of vehicles.

Making text scannable

Why do we use side headings and bulleted lists, and write in such short sentences and paragraphs?

We write like this for one very good reason. Online, people don't read very much. They certainly don't take in every word and wade through long blocks of text. Instead, they scan. They look at a headline, and a sell, and decide on the information contained in them whether this story is worth reading.

They won't even read a full sentence if it doesn't look interesting. Instead, they judge the relevance or otherwise of a piece of text to their interests or concerns on the strength of the first few words. We must make our text work for scanners - it must be scannable.

So, the first few words in our head or sell have to hook the reader.

If we have hooked them, we have done well, but we can't relax. They treat each new par in the same way - looking at the first few words to decide whether it is worth reading. That means we must keep our pars short - because if the reader doesn't like the look of the first piece of information presented, they won't move on to the second.

Therefore, we try to keep to just **one piece of info per paragraph**.

We also break up our text with **side headings**. These are clear, descriptive phrases that tell the scanner what the next few paragraphs in an article will give them.

If, within a piece of text, we have to convey dense, complex pieces of information we try to cut them up into **bullet points**. Turning a big chunk of text containing several different elements into a bulleted list makes dense information easy to absorb.

There are a couple of very important characteristics of writing for the web that we haven't yet covered. They are:

Hypertext links

These are links that, when clicked upon, take us to another web page. Hyperlinks might take us to a page containing another current story on our website, an archived story of ours, or to a page on someone else's site - either current or archived. There will be much more on this in Chapter 2, where we will create web sites, and in Chapter 8, where we will look in more depth at writing news and other types of online story.

Thinking in screens

In this style of online news writing we can think of each web screen as being like a page in a book. We don't want to cram too much onto it. If we do, the reader will have to do a good deal of scrolling to see everything we have put there. Instead, if we have a long and complex story with various aspects to it, we can split the material over several screens. Doing that effectively is often called **thinking in screens**. Again, there will be more on this in Chapter 2.

However, in the *Mail Online* style of news writing, a very different approach is taken - as we shall see later.

A couple of other things to mention before we move on

Quoting

Quotes are very important in a story. They are evidence that you have obtained the material you are reporting from reliable sources that are prepared to be named in a story. They also give a clear account of a person's views.

You don't have to quote everybody in a news story. Quotes are there for when someone has said something important, and when their words give a strong sense of their views.

Otherwise, it is quicker to use what is called reported speech. That is, when we summarise what someone has said. When we do that we do not use quote marks, but put their comments into our own words.

When quoting, you should say who is speaking before the quote, not after it. Otherwise, the reader does not know who is speaking until the end. For example: "The world will end," says the man wearing the sandwich board, is less of a story than "The world will end," says the US President. Say who said it first, and the reader immediately knows the value of the statement.

So that's one style of writing news for multiple platforms.

Now let's look at another, which has grown up in contrast to the first, and which is directed solely at online.

The *Mail Online* style of writing news online

The *Daily Mail* is a midmarket print newspaper published in London. You might think the *Mail Online* (**www.dailymail.co.uk/**) would not be too different from its print stable-mate. In fact it is.

It uses a way of writing and structuring a story that is very different from that employed in print, and from the BBC-style of writing for online which many outlets use.

For want of a better word, The *Mail Online*'s style is far more tabloid.

Let's take a look at how *Mail Online* stories are written, and why.

The 10 to 20 word headline, combined with bullet points, and an intro

Where the BBC uses five, six or seven words in a headline, the *Mail Online* regularly uses between 10 and 20 - sometimes even more.

Here's an example:[31]

Headline

Dental nurse, 25, 'froze to death without shoes or coat outside sister's house after heading round following a night out and finding she wasn't at home'

That's a very different style of headline to that the BBC, print titles, and the majority of online news sites would use.

Bullet points

The *Mail Online* follows its headlines with a long run of bullet points, which give most of the key details of the story. Here they are for this one:

- Bernadette Lucy Lee discovered by a dog walker in Deal, Kent, on Sunday
- It was just hours after 25-year-old dental nurse was seen at local nightclub
- 'Beautiful person' was in garden of the property next to her sister's home
- Lee was due to stay with a friend but went to sister Jodie's home instead
- However her sister had lost her front door key and also stayed with a friend
- A Facebook tribute page set up in her memory described her as 'truly loved'
- Father: 'I loved her so much, she was a very popular girl – I'm devastated'.

For a lot of readers, that might well be all the information they need. And it's presented in the bullet points style that, as we've seen above, is great for scanners.

There is another reason for using this style, which we'll look at in a second.

First three pars

Following all this, the *Mail Online* still runs a conventional intro and following two paragraphs. Here they are in our example:

A young dental nurse found dead outside her sister's house is believed to have frozen to death in the snow.

Bernadette Lee should have been staying with a friend after a night out, but went to her older sister Jodie's instead.

Finding the house empty, it appears that she either slipped and banged her head, or that she fell asleep and succumbed to the freezing temperatures, which dropped below minus 2C.

questions

Why do you think the *Mail Online* does this? Decide before reading on.

A proportion of readers will no doubt stop reading after the bullet points. If their level of interest in the story is fairly low, it probably tells them all they need to satisfy that interest.

However, those with a higher level of interest will want to know more. And this is, after all, a pretty compelling human interest story, published during a period of extremely bad weather, of a young woman tragically losing her life because, it seems, of a series of trivial mishaps.

Those readers, having got the gist by scanning the headline and bullet points, are now ready to get all that information fleshed out with the full detail.

The inverted triangle

The *Mail Online* gives that detail by now following the inverted triangle structure, and amplifying each point, before going on to tie up loose ends.

It does this over several hundred words, and often goes into other areas that give general background to the story. In this example, there is boxed-out material on hypothermia.

Multimedia content

Another characteristic of *Mail Online* storytelling is the way it displays multimedia content in a story.

While BBC-style reporting often includes a video and a picture gallery of ten or so still images, those images are presented in just one place in a story.

In this example there are 14 pictures. Each of them appears alongside the text story, but click on any one of them and you are into a gallery of all 14.

The Mail regularly trawls social media, such as Facebook pages, to gather images.

So the Mail policy is, while presenting a traditional inverted triangle story at the core of its news stories, to top and tail it. To top it with a great deal of search-engine and scanner-friendly summarised information, and to tail it with as much detail, background and illustrations as it can possibly find.

Why does the *Mail Online* use this style of storytelling?

Ruud Hein of Search Engine People[32] compares the *Mail Online* with the *New York Times* website - a site that uses the traditional BBC-style writing style.

He says that, while both sites have about the same number of stories on their home page - around 100 - the *Mail* uses far more words to sell them to search engines, and consequently out-performs sites such as the NYT on Google.

He says: "To sell its copy, to get its clicks, the *Daily Mail* uses 7,900 words; almost 80 words per story. The *New York Times* uses a sparse 1,900: no more than 19 words per story."

The reason the *Mail Online* does this has to do with the way search engines such as Google rank news stories in their search results. We'll look at this in more detail later but, essentially, Google sees the words in headlines, intros and in other display text as being important, so it uses them when deciding how to rank a given page in search results.

With the NYT/BBC-style, it is considering the five to seven words in the headline and the 20-odd words in the intro when it decides how to rank a story.

When it comes to the *Mail Online* style, Google takes into account the 10-20 words in the headline and the 60-80 in the bullet points, plus the intro and other display text.

So there are many more opportunities for the *Mail Online* style of headline to rank well on Google. Some search engine optimisation specialists see this as the reason the *Mail Online* is among the most popular news sites in the world.

Style guides

The English language gives us a great deal of choice in the way we write. Simple things such as how we present dates, for example: is it 1 July, 1st July, July 1 or July 1st? It could be any of them. When we have choice such as this, we need what is called a Style Guide to tell us what the preference of our publication is.

A style guide will tell us whether we spell a word specialise or specialize. It will tell us whether we use initial capitals for Prime Minister and other titles.

If you don't have a style guide to follow, you need to get one. One simple solution is to use *The Guardian* style guide, which is online, and free. Here's a direct link:

www.theguardian.com/guardian-observer-style-guide-a

You can also find it by typing 'style guide' into the site's search engine.

This is a very valuable guide, because it is highly readable and gives a good deal of information about words which, in *The Guardian*'s view, should not be used, styles of writing it approves and disapproves of, and explanations of a wide range of points of grammar and English usage.

on the website

- Find the BBC's own video guide to writing news for the corporation
- See how the Toyota story looked online
- See how the *Mail*'s snow death story looked online
- Find out more about the theory and practice of writing for the web.

Getting started with beat blogging, and begin building a specialism

Let's start with a question: What's wrong with blogs?

Too often, they are self-indulgent, trivial, highly personal, introspective diaries. Many such blogs read like poor-quality first-person pieces in newspapers or magazines.

That's not the sort of thing we want to produce as professional journalists.

Some online news titles call themselves blogs, often because they started as simple blogs, but have actually become extensive websites employing a number of journalists. Examples include Tech blogs such as Mashable and TechCrunch, or personal finance blogs including MoneySavingExpert.

What I want to look at here is a third form of blog: what is known as the beat blog. We are referring here to beat as in a journalistic beat or specialism, so we are talking about a blog in which a journalist focuses on their area of expertise.

We are going to look in detail at why a modern, multimedia journalist needs a specialism in Chapter 14 but, briefly, it's because the days of the generalist are pretty much over. That's because there is a far greater value placed on specialist information, and so - to make yourself marketable as a journalist - you need to be an expert in a given field.

That field could be anything from politics, health or the environment to film, music or computer gaming.

Let's take the BBC journalist Robert Peston as an example. Robert is the BBC's economics editor. He says he writes five or six blog posts a day, as well as broadcasting on major BBC news programmes.

Here's Robert Peston on the value and power of beat blogs like his:

> "For me, the blog is at the core of everything I do, it is the bedrock of my output. The discipline of doing it shapes my thoughts. It disseminates to a wider world the stories and themes that I think matter."[33]

He says that his blog gives him unlimited space to publish the kind of detail on an important story that he can't get into a three-minute, two-way Q and A piece conducted with a presenter on Radio 4's *Today* programme, or a two-minutes-forty-seconds package on the Ten O'Clock News.

It connects him to the audience, he says, in a very important way. The comments left by readers contain useful insights - and they help him understand what really matters to people.

Most important of all, he goes on, the blog allows Peston and the BBC to own a big story and create a community of interested people around it. Sharing information - some of it hugely important, some of it less so - with a big and interested audience delivers that ownership and creates that committed community.

So that's the sort of blog we are talking about - not just a reflective first-person column, not a big media organisation that chooses to describe itself as a blog. Peston's is a beat blog, one on which he can really show the detail of what he knows, interact with an interested community of readers, and learn what that community most wants to know.

He also says something which goes directly to the heart of why we need to see ourselves as multimedia journalists. He says that it is increasingly clear that much of the audience doesn't care whether they receive their information via the blog, some other Internet channel, the TV, newspapers or radio.

He reports that a BBC audience survey of where British people get their information about the economy revealed that 84 per cent still turn to television first, but 53 per cent used the Internet, as opposed to 52 per cent who go to a newspaper, and 37 per cent radio. For young people in the ABC1 category, 61 per cent turned first to the Internet - although even for this group TV was out in front with 74 per cent.

Peston says that convergence has already happened for TV, radio and newspapers. As a consequence, all journalists working on these previously distinct areas now do video, audio and the written word.

And, he adds, we compete with all sorts of other titles across all media and all over the world. Because he is indifferent as to how he communicates a story, whether in text, audio or video, he sees his competition as not just other broadcasters, but also media brands with a background in print. And, because the Internet internationalises the availability of what journalists produce, he also sees himself competing with news brands such as the *Wall Street Journal*, CNN, the *New York Times* and the *Washington Post*. All, he says, are his direct rivals.

When your competition is so widespread, and so easily accessible to anyone interested in your topic, you really have to be good at what you do - to be a specialist.

The blog also lets Peston reveal the detailed work that goes into discovering stories: ploughing through company accounts or Bank of England data.

His blog gives him an outlet for when he spots a trend or something hidden away in statistics that he thinks carries major implications. He says it gives him a way of taking the reader through the argument and coming up with informed conclusions.

What Robert Peston's approach tells us about beat blogs

Beat blogs are:

- Places where journalists can go into depth about stories within their area of expertise
- Demonstrate their grasp of their subject
- Show they are authoritative and can be trusted
- Connect with audiences and
- Find out what matters to those audiences.

The concept of layered reporting, and how beat blogging fits into it

The beat blog is one element of what former editor of *The Guardian*, Alan Rusbridger calls layered reporting.[34] He says: "you can layer reporting - with the most specialist material in the blog (linked to yet more specialist source material on the web - and the most general material in newsprint. It's called through-editing".

He characterises it like this:

- The paper carries a short story on a controversial topic that will be of limited interest to general readers, but of great interest to a particular specialist audience
- The reporter explains the significance of this story in their beat blog
- The blog will link to any documents that enable the reader to go to the source of the story and find as much detail as they need
- Readers debate the story on the blog.

So, once again, the beat blog is the place where the journalist demonstrates the depth of their expertise.

on the website

Find more about layered reporting, with examples of how it works.

How a beat blog differs from a straightforward news story

In beat blog posts, a journalist is not just reporting the news. Posts are often a mix of opinion and informed analysis, so they don't have to follow the same rules we have for straight news reporting, where any opinions must be attributed to one of the people who appear in the report.

on the website

- Find an analysis of a Peston blog post
- Discuss what it teaches us about writing a beat blog
- Read more about layered reporting
- Find a wealth of links to blogs of all kinds
- Read a post on how blogging changes what journalists do
- Read 50 blogs by journalists.

1A8

Basic reporting assignments

Let's look at some specific story-finding and writing assignments that will give you a good introduction to general reporting.

In order to keep these assignments fresh and relevant, you will find them at the online version of this module, where they can be updated as necessary.

on the website

Find examples and guidance on how to get stories, including from

- Emergency service press calls
- Press releases
- A council committee meeting
- A conference, exhibition or convention.

1A9

Exercises and projects

The exercises relate directly to material covered in this chapter.

The projects are wider, longer-term enterprises that you will be able to develop as you work your way through this book.

Exercise 1

Monitor a breaking news source for a day.

You could use the BBC website, or an agency such as Reuters. Look for stories that are breaking, and see how they develop during the day.

If you are part of a group, divide the day into blocks, or shifts. Take an hour or two each to monitor the news. If you can, cover several sources – two or more agencies, or two or more news outlets – and keep a log of what story breaks, when, and how it develops. See who is first with this news and how fast rivals catch up with it.

Exercise 2

Take a story that is high in today's news agenda and see how it has been handled in various media. If you can, pick a story that has local, national and specialist-audience interest. Look at how it is handled for a local audience, a national one and a specialist one.

Exercise 3

Take a range of press releases that relate to a particular audience and follow them up.

Exercise 4

Go to the website of your local police force. Take a day's news releases – or a week if you prefer. Select the most promising stories and follow them up.

Exercise 5

Take your local council and check the agendas of forthcoming committee and council meetings. Although anything a committee decides must be ratified by the full council, they almost always do, so it is the committees where the stories unfold and you get the detail you need. Select one or more committee meetings that look interesting from the agendas, look at any reports and try to identify some interesting stories.

You might be able to pursue the stories before the committee meeting, particularly if there is a clearly controversial matter that will be debated. You can talk to the protagonists and write a story before the meeting. Go to the meeting and write reports on a number of items, or follow up afterwards from the published agenda. Aim for a couple of stories of about 200 words, and five briefs of about 50 words.

Exercise 6

Pick an exhibition or convention that is taking place somewhere convenient for you to get to. Think of a publication that would cover the exhibition, and the audience it would write for. Obtain press accreditation, and the advance material issued by the organisers. Try to identify some issues that could make stories. Go to the event, pick up interesting press releases, interview relevant people, and write three stories of 200 words each. Also write five news-in-brief stories of 50 words each.

Projects

Creating multimedia news sites for clearly defined audiences.

These projects can be developed as part of group work on a journalism course, or informally by groups of students, or by individuals.

The best way to get good at writing for an audience is to do it.

Pick two clearly defined audiences you are going to write for.

You are going to create multimedia news sites for those audiences.

These sites will develop into substantial demonstration of your all-round abilities as a multimedia journalist.

They will give you a focus for many of the exercises, and all of the practical guidance, that you will find in this book and on the accompanying website.

Your newspapers and magazines do not have to have a print edition, but if you are able to produce one, that would be good. Primarily what you will be working towards is two web-based publications that use the full range of multimedia storytelling skills. So far we have only looked at news writing, and text reporting. As you work your way through this book you will learn about other writing - features, interviews and so on - and also about storytelling through audio, stills photography, video and data visualisations. As you move along you will be able to practise these skills on your projects.

Here are some areas in which you might consider creating projects.

A LOCAL WEBSITE

To get used to writing for people in an area, define a place you are going to cover. It might be a university campus, a college, a housing estate, a tower block or a postal code area. You could cover a village or a town, but that's a broad canvas, and will be too challenging unless you are tackling this project as part of a group.

A PROFESSION, A TRADE OR AN INDUSTRY

Magazines, newspapers and websites that cover a trade, profession or an industry are called business to business or B2B titles. Learn to write for such a group and you will be demonstrating a second highly marketable skill.

You should probably keep your magazine's subject matter within clearly identified limits - both by subject and geography. So, for example, you might choose to run a magazine for stall-holders at Camden Market in London, or for traders in a particular city centre or major shopping mall.

Tackling a national magazine can add too many logistical challenges - getting reporters out to remote places to conduct interviews, take pictures and film reports, for example.

If you are planning a B2B title, you need to focus on helping your reader do their job or run their business better, and to understand their industry more clearly. Through informing them, you are helping them make sound business decisions and to make - or save - money. Typical B2B magazines include *Management Today*, which is for those in management roles, and *GP*, which is for family doctors (general practitioners).

A SPORT, HOBBY OR PASTIME

These magazines are called specialist consumer titles. They are for a group of people that can easily be defined through their interest in a particular activity. You could, for example, run a magazine for footballers in a particular amateur league, for those involved in amateur dramatics, or who go to live gigs in a particular area. Go for something you know and/or have an interest in.

A GENERAL INTEREST MAGAZINE

In contrast to specialist consumer titles, we have general consumer titles. The difference is in the range of content they cover. *Vogue* is general interest, *Your Cat* is specialist interest. If you plan a general interest magazine, beware of giving yourself too wide a brief. It can be hard to focus on your audience if you are covering too much.

How to choose your projects

In order to demonstrate your ability to write for different audiences, and in different types of publication, we suggest that you choose contrasting projects.

If one is local then you will demonstrate your ability to work on a local newspaper. There are around 1,300 of those in the UK.

If the other is B2B you will demonstrate your understanding of that market. And it is a key one for newly qualified journalists. Of the 9,000 magazines in the UK, around 7,500 are B2B. It is much more likely you'll get your first job on a B2B than on a consumer title.

To firm up your ideas do these things for each of your projects.

- Choose a name for the publication
- Write a short descriptive line that supplements your title
- Come up with a 50 word 'mission statement' that says what the purpose of your publication is, who its audience is and how it will be of value to them
- Write a description of a typical member of your audience. Think about their interests and concerns
- Come up with some content ideas. Think about news areas that you will cover, and other content and services that will be of interest and value to your reader.

Now I want you to create some news stories for each of your website projects

You will need these news stories to work on in the next chapter, where we will build your websites and create your beat blogs.

For each of your websites, write five news stories. They should be of at least 200 words, and can be up to 400.

You can write them in either of the two main styles of online newswriting that we have discussed in this chapter, and which I have characterised as BBC and *Mail Online*. Whichever style you choose be sure to follow the characteristics of that style carefully in terms of the number of words in heads and sells, use of bullet points and other structural and stylistic details.

Come up with a subject on which you would like to build a beat blog

Make it a subject you have a keen interest in, about which you are knowledgeable and which offers plenty of scope for reporting and comment.

You could choose a subject you'd like to specialise in as a journalist. That might be a heavyweight topic such as health, environment or politics. It could be a lighter one. For example, if you go to a lot of live gigs, follow football closely, or are very interested in cinema, you have the basis for a beat blog in one of these areas.

You might have a very esoteric hobby or interest. When it comes to beat blogging, having a keen interest in a narrow area can help give focus to what you write. Maybe you want to blog about just one band, or one actor or director.

Gather some ideas for a couple of initial posts. Do some research into the subject you are covering. Identify good sources of information and other interesting blogs. See what multimedia elements you might be able to link to, or cut and paste into your site. Perhaps there are relevant videos on YouTube or elsewhere? For now, just get some ideas together so that, when we look at blog platforms in the next chapter, you have some content to put into it.

Notes

You will also find details of the source material referenced above on the web version of this chapter.

1 The *Sunday Times*, 11 May 2008
2 bbc.co.uk 24 January 2005
3 *The Guardian,* 26 March 2014
4 Cuxton Parish Council newsletter, 20 April 2008
5 *The Mirror*'s 3am column, 2 April 2014
6 Press Gazette, 9 May 2008
7 *The Garden*, May 2008
8 bbc.co.uk 26 May 2008
9 bbc.co.uk 4 June 2008
10 bbc.co.uk 26 May 2008
11 westyorkshire.police.uk 26 May 2008
12 bbc.co.uk 26 May 2008
13 nasa.gov 25 May 2008
14 bbc.co.uk 26 May 2008
15 cheese-rolling.co.uk May 2008
16 bbc.co.uk 6 June 2008
17 bbc.co.uk 8 April 2014
     www.bbc.co.uk/news/uk-wales-26922218

18 guardian.co.uk 9 December 2013
    www.theguardian.com/world/2013/dec/09/uk-government-warns-over-business-israeli-settlements

19 guardian.co.uk 8 April 2014
    www.theguardian.com/technology/2014/apr/08/samsung-and-htc-record-disappointing-first-quarter-results-as-smartphones-slow

20 guardian.co.uk 1 July 2013

21 guardian.co.uk 5 September 2013

22 Hugo Boss, 1 August 2008

23 Thomson 100 Top Hospitals, 2010

24 Reuters, 8 April 2014

25 PA, 6 July 2008

26 Solent News and Photo Agency, August 2008

27 bbc.co.uk 5 June 2008

28 bbc.co.uk 2 June 2008

29 guardian.co.uk 12 February 2014

30 *Ealing Times*, January, 2007

31 dailymail.co.uk 21 January 2013
    www.dailymail.co.uk/news/article-2265735/Bernadette-Lucy-Lee-Woman-25-dead-collapsing-snow-walk-home-winter-coat.html

32 www.searchenginepeople.com/blog/daily-mail-top-site.html

33 bbc.co.uk 29 August 2009
    www.bbc.co.uk/blogs/legacy/thereporters/robertpeston/2009/08/what_future_for_media_and_jour.html

34 guardian.co.uk 25 January 2010
    www.theguardian.com/media/2010/jan/25/cudlipp-lecture-alan-rusbridger

chapter two

Creating a publishing platform

In the book version of this chapter we will cover:

- How to choose a URL
- Finding your way around the WordPress dashboard
- What a home or welcome page is and what it should contain
- How to create a logical structure for a website
- What WordPress themes are and how to choose one
- How to make a website easy to navigate
- How to make content easy to read
- Adding pages and posts to your WordPress site
- What WordPress widgets are and how to use them
- How to integrate multimedia content
- Measuring the success of a website
- Beat blogging on WordPress, Tumblr and Blogger.

At the end of the chapter are a range of exercises and projects to enable you to practise what you have learned.

In the online version of this chapter you will find:

- All the links you need to follow the tuition in this chapter
- A wide range of videos illustrating the material covered here
- A wealth of links to further information
- Any essential updates to the tuition contained in the print and ebook editions.

2A1

Creating a website

Have the companion website to this book open at www.multimedia-journalism.co.uk. That way you can easily click on the links to the stories discussed here.

At the end of the last chapter we got working on some journalistic projects - two websites and a beat blog.

Now we are going to create the publishing platforms for these projects. I am going to use WordPress to build a website and beat blog, and also look at two alternative beat blogging platforms: Tumblr and Blogger.

If you have access to other publishing platforms as part of your journalism course, all well and good. You may be able to build a site hosted on your university's own servers. In that case you can gloss over the specifics of how to use the particular platforms I have chosen.

But what I will be saying about content - and organising and presenting that content - is relevant to you whatever publishing platform you are using. You can't say this too often - with multimedia journalism, content is king. It's the quality of the journalism that matters, and the only way to judge the platforms we use is how effectively they allow us to deliver that journalism to our community of interested and engaged readers.

Please note

From time to time platforms such as WordPress get an update. So while the description of how the site looks, and how to work with it, are current at the time of publishing, they may change over time. That's where the companion website to this print and ebook edition comes in. If things change, we'll update our tuition on the website.

Introduction to Wordpress.com as a publishing platform

Go to **www.wordpress.com** and click the **Get Started** button.

Just to avoid confusion, you need to know there are two versions of Wordpress - **Wordpress. com** and **Wordpress.org**

Wordpress.com is the simple version that you can get to work on without any preliminaries, which is why we are using it in this Getting Started chapter.

Wordpress.com is simple because your site is hosted by WordPress itself. So you don't have to worry about downloading it to your computer, unzipping and hosting it, or finding a hosting provider as you do with Wordpress.org.

But .com has its drawbacks - your ability to change the look and feel of the site you create is limited, while with .org you can customise the look and feel of your site to a far greater extent.

In this Getting Started guide we'll look only at Wordpress.com, and take the most straightforward approach to getting a WordPress site up and running.

We'll delay looking at using Wordpress.org until Chapter 8: Building proficiency with WordPress.

But don't worry about what you create on Wordpress.com being wasted if you decide to upgrade to Wordpress.org - you can transfer your site from one to the other.

How to choose a URL

During sign-up, WordPress invites you to choose a name for your website. They call them blogs, but I like to keep a clear distinction between websites and blogs.

The thing about WordPress is that it began life as a blogging platform, but grew.

A blogging platform, at its simplest, adds in your latest post at the top of the page and pushes older posts down. A website allows you to create a framework to hold your content, and you decide the hierarchy and where each item sits in it. Things don't get shoved down the ranking just because something newer but not necessarily as newsworthy has come along. Today, WordPress lets you create a simple blog or a structured website - we are going to do the latter.

As you sign-up, WordPress also asks you to choose a URL.

The website name you choose will form the key part of your URL. URL stands for uniform resource locator, and it's your site's domain name or web address. You need to think about two things when choosing a URL:

- What's the perfect URL for the site I am creating?
- Is it available?

questions

Have a think about what your site should ideally be called before you read on. What makes your idea a good one? What do you think the criteria are for choosing a website name and URL?

The perfect URL will be one that very clearly describes what your site is about. Many people will come to your site through Google and other search engines, and to get the right traffic you need a URL that accurately describes your topic.

The URL should be the same as your site's title - the name you put at the top of your home page. That will reinforce to Google's bots what the subject matter of your site is, and help flag you up as an authoritative resource for information on your given topic.

However, many URLs with the most popular suffixes - .com, .net and country identifiers such as: .co.uk, .es, .it etc. - are taken. You might find the URL you want with one of the newer suffixes. There are many very specific ones, for example: .coffee, .guitars and .retirement, which could be perfect if you are creating a B2B or specialist consumer site in one of these categories. There are also individual city suffixes, which could be good for a local news site.

But you must avoid confusion with existing sites: **ilovecoffee.coffee** will be confusing if **ilovecoffee.com** already exists - and you may be accused of trying to pass your site off as the already-established one.

You can check within WordPress for the domain you want as you are setting up your website. A drop-down shows you the main URL suffixes and what they cost to rent per year.

I'm creating a hyperlocal website called 'London W5', designed to serve the people who live in that postcode.

But just before you settle on a name, there is one more vital check you must make.

Is your chosen name available on Twitter, Facebook, YouTube and the rest?

You want consistency of naming on all your presences, so before fixing on a URL, you need to check that this name is available on social media too.

You can find out what names are available across the top 20 social media platforms here: **www.usernamecheck.com/**

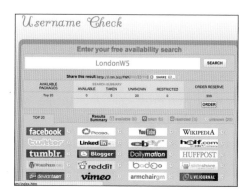

That search shows me 'LondonW5' is available on Twitter, Facebook, YouTube and a wide range of other social platforms.

So what's your domain going to be?

If you are not ready to choose a URL yet, don't worry. First, you can build your WordPress site under a temporary URL, with the free suffix they offer, and switch to a permanent URL later, when you've decided.

You can also click the option to keep your site private for now. You don't need to show it to the world until you are ready.

Choosing a WordPress theme

Once you have signed up for a WordPress.com account you are taken through to the dashboard, which is the private area where you create your site, add pages and posts and fill them with content: text, video, stills and more.

This WordPress video gives a great introduction: **http://youtu.be/WUJ-OfpbgOs**

(It's embedded in the online version of module 2A2).

The dashboard is where you can set your design, or what WordPress calls your theme. We are going to do that first, before posting any of our content to it.

So go down the list of items on the dashboard's left hand navigation bar and hover over **Appearance**. From the sub-menu that appears, click the top item, **Themes**.

By default, WordPress gives you a theme. The default is updated each year, and the current one will load automatically when you create your site. There are loads of other themes, some good for a professional journalism site, others not so good.

Some are free, some you have to pay for. You can click to get details of a particular theme, to see a demo of it and to apply it to your website. As it only takes another click to change your chosen theme you can experiment as much as you like.

If your focus will be on text, a simple theme such as 'Truly Minimal' might suit.

Then there is 'Responsive', which pitches itself as a theme that will work well on mobiles and tablets as well as the web - that's a key point to consider as we look more at how to tailor our content for the full range of devices.

For this demonstration I am using a theme called 2014. It has a magazine feel and also adjusts for web, tablet and mobile viewing. But you can use any theme you like for now because, whatever theme you use, the way WordPress functions does not change.

The theme you choose sets the design of your site.

At this stage, while your site is private, it doesn't really matter which you choose. Once we get some content into it you can see how it shapes up, and, by browsing through the available themes again, see how that content looks in a wide range of themes.

Once you activate a theme you get options for customising it, changing colours, backgrounds, header images and so on.

For now, we'll leave that and look at adding content to your site.

on the website

Find further guidance in choosing a WordPress.com theme.

Adding content to your WordPress site

We'll use the copy that you wrote as part of the projects at the end of Chapter 1 to get some news onto your site.

WordPress offers two ways to add content: **Posts** and **Pages**. You'll see those two tags are also in the left hand nav where we found Appearance.

By default your home page is set up to take blog-style posts.

But you can change the front/home page to a static one if you wish, and have your blog posts appear on another page.

We are going to make that change, because the blog-style page will be useful for other things – maybe our beat blog, or perhaps for when we cover a fast-moving story on a live blog (we'll look at doing that in Chapter 6).

To prepare for making that change, click on **Page** and create a page called **News.**

Cut and paste into it the five heads and sells from the copy you wrote as part of your projects. Define each headline in turn and click the **B** icon above the post area to turn it bold.

Under **Page attributes** on the right, make sure the option 'no parent' is selected, and publish the page. That means this is the top level of your navigation or hierarchy. We'll look at page hierarchy in a moment.

Take a look at the page you have created as readers will see it by clicking the **View page** option at the top of the screen.

Now create five more pages, and put one of your stories in each, with the text in the main posting area, the headline in the title field. In the **Page attributes** area, choose the **News** page you created first as the parent to these child pages. Then go to the **Order** box and choose the order they will appear in by giving the story a number from 0 to 4. WordPress orders stories with the lowest number first.

Now you need to link each of your heads and intros on your news index page to the individual story pages. Do that by opening the **News** page and highlighting the headline on the first story. Then click the link icon at the top of the posting area (it looks like the link in a chain) and choose the **Link to existing content** option at the bottom of the dialogue box that opens. You can also link to the intro itself if you like, or add the word *More. . .* at the end of the post and make that a link as well. What you are creating are called hypertext links or sometimes hotlinks. Do this on each of your stories.

Most news sites used to add a 'more. . .' link at the end of the sell, today many don't, believing that readers are sufficiently aware of linking conventions to know that the headline will link them to the full story. You could add an icon such as '>>>' and make that a link. Later, when we add pictures, we can make them link to full stories too.

Always remember to click to **Update** the page once you have finished working on it.

Now click to view the page, and it should look something like this:

Check that all the links you have added go through to the right pages.

Now go back to the dashboard navigation and to **Settings > Reading**, where you'll see this:

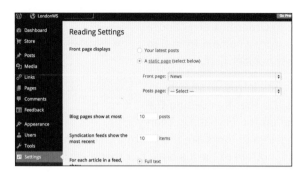

on the website

Find further guidance on adding content to your WordPress site.

How to make 'News' your home page

Click to activate **A static page** and then, in the drop down menu beneath it, select the **News** page you just created.

So now you have a home page called News, which is the welcome screen/landing page for your site, and you have five stories linked from it.

So we have begun to create a logical structure - a hierarchy - for our website.

Creating a home page, and a logical structure for your website

Let's just review what we have done in creating these pages, and linking them as we have.

First, we have created a home page. The home page is the one that users see when they go to your site - either by typing your URL into a browser or by clicking on a link to you. It has to impress them, and should be used to promote all the best content from deeper into the site.

Then we have created a second layer of content.

Think of a website as being a bit like a family tree. The home page is at the top of the tree and is at the head of the family. It's the parent page. We can create subsidiary screens to this one, and they are like children to that parent page. For now, our **News** page is at the top of our family tree and doubles as the home page/landing page for the site.

The reader goes to the parent page first - that's the point from which they start reading our stories. When they decide to read more than just the head and sell, they click the hyperlinked headline or >>> icon and are taken to the child page. On the child page they get the whole story.

Here's what I mean:

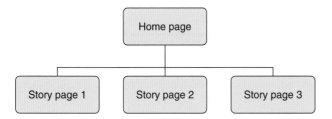

If you take a look at any news website, you'll see that structure followed.

In fact, there are more than two layers - levels of navigation to use the technical term - to anything but the very simplest of websites.

Most news websites have a general home page with top news stories and other important items, and subsidiary pages at the second level of navigation for key areas of content: news, sport, features and so on.

Each new level we create takes its place on a new line. So a typical site might have four or five levels of navigation - or generations in its family tree.

We'll look at adding to that hierarchy, and posting more complex content, later in this chapter. For now, let's get the site looking more professional.

on the website

Find more about hierarchies and how to make them easy for the user to navigate.

2A4

Working on the design and appearance of your website

The site looks pretty minimal at the moment, so let's do some work on the design. You might also run through some different themes, now you have content to show in them, just to see how they look.

I'm going to work with '2014', about which WordPress says: "In 2014, our default theme lets you create a responsive magazine website with a sleek, modern design. Feature your favourite homepage content in either a grid or a slider. Use the three widget areas to customize your website, and change your content's layout with a full-width page template and a contributor page to show off your authors. Creating a magazine website with WordPress has never been easier."

There is more about the theme and how you can customise it here:

http://codex.wordpress.org/Twenty_Fourteen

'2014' is a responsive theme, which means that it can tell whether a visitor is looking at it on a computer, a tablet or a mobile, and will adjust how content is presented accordingly. As you are building, you'll see these icons:

Click on them and you see how your content looks in each format.

Here's my content in tablet format:

Here it is in mobile phone format:

Adding a header image

The '2014' theme allows you to add an image to the top of your site. With my site, a landmark from the area I'm covering would be appropriate.

To do that go to **Appearance>Header**, where you are told: "Images should be at least 1260 pixels wide. Suggested width is 1260 pixels. Suggested height is 240 pixels."

That's a long, shallow image, but when you click to upload a picture from your computer or choose it from your media library, the crop you will need is superimposed on the image.

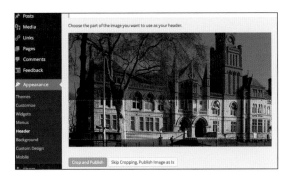

You can override this by choosing to publish the image as it is, but you'll change the look of the site if you do.

You can also take an image and run it through Photoshop Express, editing for special effects and adding text.

Here's how the image appears on my site:

Adding images to stories

You can add pictures using the grey **Add media** icon just above your page's tool bar. You can also insert video, a poll or a custom form, but we'll deal with those later.

Have some pictures on your computer and select the one you want for the story you are adding to the website. It will be added where the cursor is in your story.

Crossrail have released a picture of how they propose the new Ealing Broadway station will look, so I add it, choosing to place it as a medium-size image. I write a caption, and copy that into the alt text field, which is there for those who have images turned off or are visually impaired.

Here's the image as I edit the story:

Here's the image as the reader sees it:

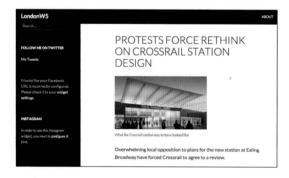

How to make a website easy to navigate

Our website will be easy to navigate if the structure is clear and logical, and if we provide links that mirror the paths readers would like to take to get from one piece of information to the next. There must always be a link back to the Home page from wherever the reader is in the site. We'll also add other links back to key places in the site as we build it.

The stories we have worked on so far are simple, one-page units of information. With more complex subjects we might want to create some additional supplementary screens that lead off from this page. We'll tackle this next.

Thinking in screens – creating a content area within your website

Let's say we have a more complex story to tell. It's going to be far too long to include all the information we have on one screen. Instead, we need to split it across several screens.

To do that effectively we need to think about how the material will break logically. Also, if it is fairly detailed, we need to make sure we introduce it effectively, so that the scanner can see what is on offer and – we hope – make the effort to go through it.

This approach to organising web content is known as 'thinking in screens'.

You see that done on big news stories, where there are several major aspects to the story that need to be dealt with separately. Here's an example from the *Guardian* where there is a head and sell on the main news story, a live blog beneath it, followed by two links to other related reports:

I'm going to take one of the big news stories I have - about a multimillion pound investment which has secured the future of Ealing Studios, and create a content area called News Focus: Ealing Studios.

I want to look at various aspects of the studios - their days as the home of Ealing Comedy movies in the 1940s and 1950s, a look at the big stars who have worked there and what the future holds.

That's a lot of aspects to a big local story, and I'll give a logical structure to my content by creating a page for each of those key elements. I'll make those child pages to a parent which I'll call News Focus: Ealing Studios.

That page will not have a parent and will cover the subject in general - focusing on the latest news. A scanner might just read this and go no further, and still get an idea of the scope of the material, but those with a deeper level of interest in the story can click down to get more.

I'll also write a news story that will appear in my news digest, and which also links to the News Focus page.

Here's the navigation, showing how the child pages are revealed when you hover over the News Focus parent page.

Here's my main News Focus page, which uses bullet points as hypertext links to those child pages. I used the option of adding images as thumbnails, and setting them left and right respectively, to begin to add some interest to the layout of my stories.

How to make content easy to read

We do that by making our story scannable. We follow the principles of copy organisation and presentation that we worked through in Chapter 1. With the simple stories we have worked on so far, all that is needed really are some side heads to break the text up into logical blocks of information, and give the scanner an idea of what they will find if they read on from any of the side heads. When you come to the exercises and projects at the end of this chapter, you'll have to use your judgement and decide what devices are appropriate for each piece of copy you produce.

What we must avoid are grey slabs of text that the scanner will fail to engage with.

Some examples of website structure

On some news websites, the head and sell are repeated verbatim on the full story page. On others, the head and sell on the index page differ in some ways to those on the story page. Sometimes by a little, sometimes by quite a lot.

Here are some examples of different practice.

questions

Can you work out why some heads and sells on story pages differ from those on the index page? Are any of the approaches more effective than the others? Is there a right and a wrong way to make heads and sells on index and story pages work effectively?

First, **The Times**

The Times very often keeps the same wording for heads and sells. On the occasions when it chooses to change a heading on the story page, it still rarely alters the intro.

Here are a couple of examples of occasions when it has altered headlines.

> **Plebgate: Geldof in defence of Mitchell**
>
> Bob Geldof rode to the aid of his "unlikely friend" Andrew Mitchell today in the plebgate libel trial.

Becomes:

> **Geldof support for 'unlikely friend' Mitchell revealed at plebgate trial**
>
> Bob Geldof rode to the aid of his "unlikely friend" Andrew Mitchell today in the plebgate libel trial.

In another example on the same day:

> **Mother who killed disabled children spared jail**

Becomes:

> **Banker blames 'interference' as wife who killed disabled children is spared jail**

A banker whose wife was spared jail today after killing their three disabled children said he wanted to ensure that no other family endured the "unbearable pressure" of interference from doctors and social workers.[1]

The *Mirror*

Food phobia woman who lived on nothing but CHIPS hypnotised into eating first proper meal for 15 years

Fries fanatic Hanna Little, 20, developed a severe eating disorder at the age of five and became terrified of all other foods

Becomes:

Food phobia woman who lived on nothing but CHIPS hypnotised into eating first proper meal for 15 years

A woman who lived on a diet of chips since the age of five has finally eaten a proper meal after being HYPNOTISED to overcome her fear of other foods.[2]

The BBC

Ex-Met boss heads 'Islam plot' probe

An ex-counter-terrorism chief will oversee an inquiry into an alleged Islamist takeover plot – an appointment described as "desperately unfortunate".

Becomes:

Trojan Horse probe headed by ex-Met chief Clarke

The former national head of counter terrorism is to lead an inquiry into 25 Birmingham schools. . .[3]

This sell goes on to say that this is over allegations of a hard-line Islamist takeover plot.

What has been changed and why

The Times's Geldof headline is extended on the story page, to bring in the additional detail that Mitchell is an 'unlikely friend' of Geldof's. It's likely this element was left out of the headline on the story index page solely because of lack of space, as it's a key reason we are interested in the story.

In the story of the mother who killed her children, there was in fact no intro on the index page, just a picture of the husband with two of the children. The story page headline is like a second headline, which does not repeat the key news that the mother has been spared jail. This has the effect of moving the story swiftly on and adding a second line to the sell.

The habitual repetition of intros on both index and story pages shows *The Times* is not concerned that giving readers the same intro twice will put them off.

The *Mirror*'s sell on the index page is like a strap line – a subsidiary heading – rather than a traditional tabloid intro. When we come to the story page, the strap-style text is replaced by a traditional intro.

On the BBC site, the longer headline on the story page amplifies what we learn from the head on the index page. The sell on the story page amplifies what we learn in the sell on the index page.

What we effectively get when we add this material together are a main head plus a strap line or subsidiary head, and two sells that are really the first and second pars of the story.

So what do you think of these different approaches? To my mind, there is no fixed right and wrong way to do this, and the range of approaches shows that sites are experimenting with how to write most effectively for the web.

Using widgets on WordPress

Widgets are little bits of code that add extra features to your website.

If you go to your dashboard and click through **Appearance>Widgets** you'll see what widgets are currently applied to your site, and a range of others you can use.

To activate them you simply click and drag them to the areas labelled **Primary sidebar**, **Content sidebar** or **Widget footer area**. **Primary sidebar** appears on the left of your webpage, **Content** to the right, and **Footer** at the bottom.

There are already a number of widgets in your content and primary sidebars:

If there are any you don't want, just drag and drop them into the main widget area on your dashboard.

Scroll down the list of available widgets and you'll see several that are very useful.

Widgets such as your Twitter feed, a Facebook 'Like' box, and a link to Instagram connect your activities on social media to the content you publish on your website.

We are going to look in detail at how to use social media as a journalist in Chapter 3, and you can decide then what social media platforms you want to use professionally.

How do you decide where to put such widgets? With this theme I have two main areas to choose from - the primary and content sidebars. The footer is of less use because it's at the bottom of the page.

I could put, say, my social media widgets on the left, where they appear against the black vertical band of the site's wide border.

Widgets placed on the right appear against the white area that your story appears in, so look as if they are related to that text. I could use widgets here that relate to the content on the website, such as Top Clicks and Top Posts and Pages.

Choosing a publishing platform for your beat blog

So far we've only used pages on our WordPress site. We also have a blog-style page, and if the subject of your beat blog is the same as the site you are building, that's a perfectly sensible thing to do. If, with my London W5 site, I was an expert in local history and wanted to beat blog about this aspect of local interest, that might be a good fit. Or if I had a deep interest in and knowledge of the local council, a beat blog might also be a good fit with my local news website.

How to create a beat blog on your WordPress site

Create a page - I'm calling mine 'The History Man', and save it with no parent. Then go to **Settings>Reading** and, in the drop down beside **Posts page** choose the page you have designated for your beat blog content.

Now, each time you create a post (as opposed to a page) that post will drop in to the top of your beat blog page.

However, I have other plans for the blogging page on my WordPress site. In Chapter 6 we are going to use it to create a Live Blog area. So I'd rather publish my blog on another platform. There are plenty to choose from. Here are a couple you might like to consider.

Beat blogging on Tumblr

Most people on Tumblr (**tumblr.com**) use it less for long-form posts, and more for sharing interesting snippets that they find. It's often seen as something of a cross between blogging and Twitter.

That's not to say you can't beat blog on it. The reason I suggest it as an option is because of the audience you get on it. If you were to beat blog about music, movies, gaming or some other aspect of popular culture, then our content could be a good fit with the interests of the community you'll find there.

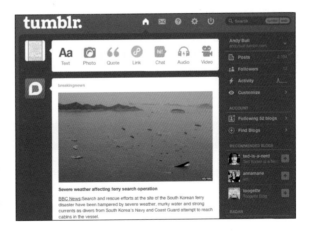

Most of the 70m-plus visitors to the site have blogs (or tumblelogs) of their own, so you are likely to find many experts in your field to interact with.

It's very simple to blog on. Open an account and you get blogging right away - posting is like writing an email. You can go on to customise your blog if you wish.

There is a search facility so you can find other bloggers in your field and follow them. There are thousands under headings such as film, fashion, food and drink, and Tumblr highlights some popular and recommended ones in each category.

on the website

Find video guides to using Tumblr.

Beat blogging on Blogger

Blogger (**blogger.com**) is part of Google, and as such is closely integrated with Google+ (which we'll look at in Chapter 3) and Google Search, meaning that it's second-to-none as the place to beat blog if you want your work to feature prominently in search returns.

There's a lot to be said about Google's key role in disseminating our journalism, but I'll have to save it for Chapter 3.

Like WordPress.com, Blogger has grown into a website creation and hosting platform, but sites built on it using the available tools don't look as professional, in my opinion, as those built on WordPress.

You can read about its features here:

www.blogger.com/features

on the website

- Find a detailed video guide to Blogger
- Find all the resources linked to and referenced here
- Get essential updates on all the tuition contained here.

2A8

Exercises and Projects

Exercise 1

Take a website that interests you and analyse its content and structure. Look at the policy on the use of heads and sells. How long are they? Look at how they link to individual news pages. Does wording differ between index page and story page? If it does, can you see why? See if you can draw a structure diagram – in family tree form – for the site. Is it logically organised? How are links back from individual items handled?

Exercise 2

Pick a busy beat blog that you like and follow it closely for a week. How often does the blogger post? How long are the posts? What is their content made up of? How reliant is the blogger on links to other blogs? Do they use pictures and video? If so, what do these add to the blog? How many links do they include in each blog?

Exercise 3

Look for some areas on websites where a number of screens have been grouped together to cover a particular story. Look at how this has been done. Has an initial screen been written that summarises the subject, and contains links to other screens that cover aspects of the story in more detail? How many external links are there?

Projects

We are going to create some more content for your websites and beat blog.

Over the next week

1   Write five news stories of between 300 and 400 words for each of your websites, following the guidance in Chapter 1 on how to write and structure text for the web. Publish those stories online, giving them heads and sells and using side headings and bulleted lists as appropriate.

2   Post to your beat blog at least daily for a week. Find others who blog in the same field and follow them. See how your blog compares with others.

Notes

1   times.co.uk 18 November 2014
2   www.mirror.co.uk 15 April 2014
3   bbc.co.uk 14 April 2014

chapter three

Getting started with social media

In the book version of this chapter we will cover:

- The importance of social media to modern journalism
- How to establish professional presences for yourself and/or the media entity you work for
- Using essential social platforms: Twitter, Facebook, YouTube, Google+
- The importance of RSS feeds
- Using social media dashboards to manage your use of social media.

At the end of the chapter are a range of exercises and projects to enable you to practise what you have learned.

In the online version of this chapter you will find:

- Detailed tuition in the use of Twitter, Facebook, YouTube and Google+
- Examples of best practice by media organisations in the use of social media
- Tuition in using RSS feeds to gather and publish news
- Step-by-step guides to using social media dashboards in managing your social media accounts.

Have the companion website to this book open at www.multimedia-journalism.co.uk. That way you can easily click on the links to the stories discussed here.

3A1

Social media guidelines for journalists

Most organisations now have social media guidelines, which outline how their journalists should conduct themselves on social media. Any sensible publisher will make adherence to its social media policy a part of all employment contracts.

Such concerns inform the tuition that follows. If you'd like to consider this aspect of social media engagement, the BBC's strategy offers a good example.

on the website

Find links to social media guidelines from the BBC, Reuters and the *Guardian*, plus further consideration of this topic.

3A2

Why should journalists use social media?

That's a good question. And it's often followed by: what do we get out of it?

Well, we can actually get a lot out of social media, but it's important that we also think about what we are prepared to put into it.

The old saying - you get out what you put in - applies demonstrably to social media. As with any relationship, a relationship via social media grows through sharing, and developing trust.

Social media has had a huge impact on the way people find and consume news. Here's a quote:

"If the news is that important, it will find me."

A student in a focus group is meant to have said that, although it may be apocryphal. In any case, it's a quote that gets to the heart of how the web is developing, and also of how we - journalists and publishers - must adapt if we are to thrive in the age of social media.

What the student said turns the traditional relationship between journalists and the audience on its head.

We used to rely on people coming to us for their information – to our print publications, radio and TV stations, and our websites. Now we can't be nearly so sure that they will.

Today, people are much more likely to learn about news, and other information that interests them, from their social circle and via social media.

The friends and contacts they have, on whatever social networks they use, will be alerting them to news, information and entertainment by sharing video clips about it, links to it and talking about it.

So, to reach people, we need to get our content on the social networks that they use. Today, it's much more likely that audiences – particularly new and young ones – will find us on social media sites. So we need to be on them to have a hope of making that first, tentative connection.

Here's another saying: fish where the fish are.

If the fish, our potential audience, are on Facebook – and over 1bn people are – or on Twitter or elsewhere, we need to put our content before them in such a way that they engage with it, and want to connect with us.

We hope, then, to build on that first connection, and forge ever-stronger links with individuals.

So, to recap, one reason we use social media is:

■ Because that's where our audiences, and potential audiences, are.

But there is a second, equally important reason:

■ Because it's a great place to find stories.

As we saw in Chapter 1, many stories now break on Twitter, and other social media. It's often evident when you read a story that a smart journalist has found it on Twitter, Facebook or other social platform.

For example, this tweet from former cricketer Shane Warne was the spark for this story in the *Guardian*

www.theguardian.com/sport/2014/may/29/shane-warne-selfies-killed-autograph

Find more stories that began on social media.

The online media pyramid

There are various visuals used by publishers, PRs, marketers and others to demonstrate the way they hope to build relationships with their readers/clients/audiences through social and other online media.

The graphics are often represented as triangles, or pyramids, with the first connection being made at the wide, base level, with a series of levels of deeper engagement rising above it.

Here's one that takes elements commonly found in many such pyramids.

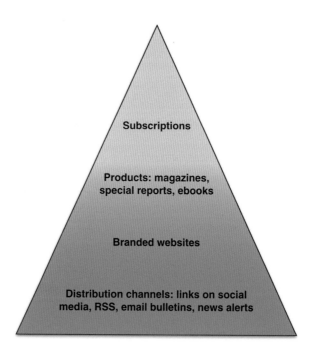

It has at its base distribution channels, which include links on social media, RSS feeds and email bulletins.

If readers find content on those distribution channels useful or interesting, they will click on the links, and be taken to the next stage up in the online media pyramid: branded websites.

That's where a publisher's titles have their main online presences. Delivering new audiences to those branded websites is one goal of social media posts.

We'll look at the others as we go through this chapter.

Above Branded websites come levels including products – that might mean buying a tablet computer or print edition of a title.

Above that comes Subscriptions, where readers are paying us a lump sum to receive our news, information and/or entertainment for several months or a year at a time.

If you can get a person who first engaged with you on social media to that level you've essentially cemented them as a paying customer, and regular consumer of your journalism.

That's not to say your engagement with them via social media is no longer important. It is. Many of us find it easiest to get our news initially from social media, so it's hugely important to continue to use it.

Which social media platforms should you use?

I'd say Twitter for sure. It has established itself as the ultimate breaking news service. YouTube is also hugely important – it's the second biggest search engine globally, after Google.

With Facebook, opinion is divided. Some publishers find it a great place to engage with audiences, others find they get relatively little engagement on it.

If you are starting from scratch, you'll have to see what level of engagement your journalism gets on Facebook.

Google+ also divides opinion. At times during its development, Google appeared committed to using Google+ as a way to present authoritative content to audiences, and did a good deal to aid journalists to confirm themselves as authoritative sources, but the policy has not been consistent. Nevertheless, Google+ requires serious consideration.

There is also a range of more specialist platforms, but we'll look at them in later chapters.

Please note: Because social platforms regularly undergo radical overhauls, detailed advice on how to use them can quickly become outdated. For that reason, we will concentrate in the book on a summarised, essential look at the strengths and uses of each platform, and save detailed, step-by-step tuition in their use for the website, where it can be updated as necessary.

on the website

Find more on why journalists use social media.

3A3

Twitter

The following tuition assumes a working knowledge of Twitter. If you are unfamiliar with the platform, you'll find a step-by-step guide to setting up an account and using Twitter professionally on the website.

I rate Twitter as the best social platform for journalism. That's because it is simple (you're limited to 140 characters in a post), direct, and most easily used as a breaking news platform.

When important stuff is happening, that's where people go. Whether it's a national disaster, a riot, a revolution or a war, Twitter usually leads the way in breaking news.

The one huge caveat is that not all sources on Twitter and other social media are reliable.

There are fundamental issues of balance, attribution and verification.

There is also the vital issue of how you conduct yourself on Twitter, and other social networks.

on the website

Find a step-by-step guide to setting up an account and using Twitter professionally.

Your presence on Twitter must be professional

Do you already have a personal account on Twitter? If you do, you need to consider whether to turn that into a professional one, or to start a new, separate professional presence.

To some extent, having a personal account where you can chat with friends as you would if you were face-to-face with them, and an entirely separate professional account, makes sense. On the professional account, you only say things that you'd be happy to see under your byline in an online or print publication or express in a broadcast. You keep your personal opinions and general chat for your personal account. But there are still dangers.

My own view is that it's safest to have as your guiding principle that you will never say anything on social media that could damage your reputation as a journalist, or embarrass the organisations that you work for, whether or not the account you are tweeting from identifies you as a journalist.

When you sign up with Twitter you should also add the Twitter app on to your smartphone, because you need to get news alerts, and to publish your own breaking stories when you are on the move.

Think of Twitter as a contacts book

Find the people who are most relevant to the journalism that you do – or plan to do – and follow them (which is like putting them in your contacts book). Some of them will quickly follow you back.

on the website

Learn how to find people on Twitter.

The benefits of using Twitter

Twitter gives you a presence

If members/potential members of your audience – your community – can't find you in the places they go to communicate, then you can't be a part of the conversation.

Twitter lets you listen and learn

It links you in with the community you seek to serve and be a part of. You can connect with the movers and shakers and absorb their knowledge and expertise, and find out what the average punter is most interested in.

Twitter drives traffic to your website or blog

Use it as a breaking news service for your latest stories. Tweets that include a shortened link will drive traffic to your website or blog. That's known as internal linking.

on the website

Find out how to write a great tweet, and use shortened links, on the MMJ website.

Other types of tweet that you should use

We've mentioned internal links, but there are others. You should vary things, and engage with the community, by also tweeting:

External links

To good material not created by you, or that's from colleagues on your publication - material that your industry/interest group will find valuable.

Replies @

These are replies to people whose tweets you find interesting, useful, annoying – even plain wrong. A reply@ is when you include the name of a Twitter account-holder in your tweet, placing the @ symbol before that name, without a space: @useraccount.

Such replies@ do two things:

- They send a personal response to the individual you has communicated with you. Those replies are filed in the @Mentions column of the account-holder
- This reply is also public, and seen by all who follow you and the person you have communicated with. So they know you are engaged in a conversation.

Retweets of tweets that you have found valuable, interesting, amusing

Retweeting spreads information throughout your community, reaching some who may not be following the original tweeter, or who may have missed that particular tweet.

Use #hashtags in your tweets

If you put the # symbol before a key word in a tweet, without leaving a space, it makes that tweet easily findable by someone searching Twitter for that subject. While @ links you to a person, # links your tweet to a story or topic.

Big events get hashtags associated with them. TV shows that want to be discussed put their hashtags on screen during the broadcast - eg #bbcqt for the BBC's *Question Time* show. Organisers of events such as conferences publicise the hashtag they'd like those discussing it to use.

If those engaged in a conversation on a particular topic all use the same hashtag, that can bring together the threads of a conversation, linking tweets from many different sources. A search for say #bbcqt brings up all the tweets using that tag, so the live conversation of viewers flows before you, making it easy to contribute.

Major breaking news stories quickly gain a hashtag.

Add your Twitter feed to your WordPress site

You need to make it easy for your content to be shared, and for people to follow you on Twitter.

Website-building platforms such as WordPress make it easy to integrate your work with Twitter - and other social platforms - in a couple of ways.

For one thing, many themes automatically place a 'tweet this' button on each story you write, making your content easily shareable. With those themes that don't do this automatically (and 2014 is one of them) we can easily add this feature.

For a second, you can add a widget to your site which contains your latest tweets.

on the website

Find out how to add your Twitter feed to your WordPress site, and a **tweet this** button to each of your stories.

Use Twitter as a story-finding and researching tool

Bring Twitter into the processes of discovering, researching and reporting stories.

Finding stories on Twitter

Many famous people use Twitter to break news about themselves. Many organisations do the same.

To find those stories you need to be following the right individuals and organisations. But how do you follow hundreds of people without being overwhelmed, and risk missing the newsworthy needles in the giant tweet haystack? The answer is to organise Twitter and your social media accounts so that they are easy to follow.

Set up lists of people you follow on Twitter

If you create lists that focus on categories of people you need to follow, you have a quick way of keeping up to speed with these key individuals. You can create a list for each category of contact you have. For a local reporter that might include a list of local politicians, community leaders, influencers and manic tweeters. Another list might focus on emergency services, and include official news feeds plus key police officers, fire fighters and others who are big tweeters.

You'll also need to follow local news sources and reporters so you can see when your rivals have got a story you ought to know about.

A showbiz reporter could create lists of various categories of celeb and showbiz news outlets.

on the website

Find out how to create lists.

Clicking on a list brings up the tweets of its members, so if you have – say – a politics list, then when a big political story is breaking you should be able to go to this list to see the key figures in the story tweeting about it.

If a story or subject has a hashtag then you can search that hashtag and follow the news that way.

Check on those lists regularly, and go to the relevant one when you get the first whiff of a breaking story.

Find Twitter's advice on lists.

Researching stories on Twitter

Twitter can be invaluable for spotting ideas, researching, finding case studies and interviewees.

You'll find eyewitnesses tweeting about an event, posting photographs and video clips, and those involved in or affected by a story commenting on it. And you'll see requests from journalists who want to talk to someone about a particular story.

The Twitter search tool we used to find people can also be used in our story-finding and reporting.

Twitter search is here: **https://twitter.com/#!/search-home**

Reporting on Twitter

At its heart, Twitter is a breaking news service. That's why journalists immediately recognised its potential. If you are on a breaking news story, one of the easiest ways to report it is to do so, blow-by-blow, via tweets. We'll look in detail on doing that in Chapter 6, on live blogging.

Find Twitter's advice on making your tweets more popular, and see examples of how journalists have used the platform effectively.

Twitter is a conversation

Some people, and some media outlets, just use Twitter to broadcast links to their news and other content, and often publish several tweets at once. That's hardly conducive to a conversation.

It's the old, top-down, 'here is the news' approach to journalism that social media allows us to vastly improve upon.

That may be all they feel they have the resources to do, but it is not using social media to anything like its true potential.

getting started

To get the benefit of Twitter you should follow people, listen to them and respond. In short, you should be part of a conversation.

Making Twitter use manageable

Some journalists still dismiss Twitter and other social media, saying "I haven't got time for it." Well, duh. Actually, you haven't got time not to use it.

You don't have to let it swamp you, or get in the way of your news gathering, writing and reporting.

Make Twitter a key part of your working day.

Make tweeting a by-product of your work as a journalist.

If you are looking for ideas, for case studies or interviewees, researching a story, tweet about it.

Ask for help, suggestions or advice.

Rather than setting aside time to tweet, tweet as you work – if you are set to work on a piece of breaking news, tweet it and add that there'll be more later.

If you are interviewing someone, tweet about it in advance. Ask what your community would like you to ask that person. Maybe tweet a picture of your subject when they arrive for the interview.

After the interview, tell your community how it went; let them know when and where you'll be running the full thing.

At a press conference or other live event, tweet as appropriate – and possible – during it.

Such tweets should take no more than a few seconds of your time, and make your journalism a collaborative process with your social-media community.

Tweets are just a by-product of your note-taking. Indeed, you'll sometimes find you can use your tweets *as* your notes when you come to write up your piece.

Using a social media dashboard such as TweetDeck or Hootsuite makes it easier to organise and follow tweets, plus feeds from other social networks. We'll cover that later in the chapter.

3A4

Getting started with Google+

on the website

Find a full guide to Google media tools.

Twitter and Facebook have entered the language. We talk about tweeting something, or liking something on Facebook. But we don't talk much about Google plus-ing something.

Google+ has not taken off as a social network in the way that Twitter and Facebook have, but it is still highly powerful. The reason for that is Google's wider power, as the foremost search engine in the world, and the owner of the biggest video site – YouTube – plus all of the other Google-owned platforms that Google+ is designed to pull together.

The power of this network of services means that when you post on Twitter (and Facebook) you really need to post on Google+ too.

Google+ is also a vital tool when you are building your personal brand, but we'll save discussion of that until Chapter 13.

How Google+ is structured

Where Twitter is simple, Google+ is complicated. It's a collection of different social products including:

- **Stream** (a newsfeed),
- **Hangouts** (a video chat service),
- **Circles** (a friend management service).

There are also communities, a personal photo album and games.

One key difference over Twitter is that you can create pages on Google+. Pages are sort of semi-detached entities, related to what you might call your personal page, but designed to stand independent from it.

So while your Google+ profile page can be used for you as a journalist, you can also create a page to support a news website, newspaper, a blog, a TV show or any other media entity. And that page can bear the name of the media entity.

So the *Guardian*, along with most other news brands, has a *Guardian* Google+ page on which it publishes links to news stories and other elements such as communities it has built in order to engage with groups of its readers.

Another thing that keeps Twitter distinct from other social networks is that tweets are limited to 140 characters. On Google+, and also Facebook, there is no such restriction. So while posts still often contain a link that takes the reader through to the branded website of the media entity, the post will usually contain a headline, a paragraph of text, a picture and often a video.

Which means that when you are using Google+ as a promotional tool for your website, you have a lot more opportunity to sell your story than you do on Twitter. But as each new iteration takes Twitter away from its spartan roots, it may not be long before it drops its character-count.

One role Google sees Google+ performing is to: "visually and socially improve the way people consume news."

By that they mean: "Google+ allows journalists and media organisations to gather, report and analyse the news in innovative ways, while developing online communities and driving discovery among new audiences. Google+ unifies your presence across Google products where your content is discovered, including Search, YouTube, Google News, and others."

So let's set up a professional Google+ account you can use to find, research, and publish news.

How to use Google+ for journalism

As with all social media platforms, you need to engage with them if they are to work for you. So while you can exploit them by finding contacts, stories, story sources and case studies, you should also share generously by offering your information and insights on, say, a breaking story, and commenting positively on the status updates of other journalists.

Signing up with Google+

Google is designed so that one account gives access to all its many services. The key is to have a Gmail account. Once you have that, you can set up Google+. The sign up involves adding all your other Google presences and is the feature that makes Google so useful in building your personal brand. I'm going to save that aspect of things for Chapter 10, but if it suits you better, by all means go there now and set up your full profile.

Also, be sure to add the Google+ app to your smartphone.

on the website

Find full, step-by-step guides to setting up your Google+ account, and using the various elements within it.

Build up your following/followers count and use Circles

On Twitter you have one big group of followers (although you can organise them into lists, as we discussed earlier). On Google+ you can divide those you choose to follow, and your followers, into a series of Circles. You can then choose, when you post an update, whether to send it public, and hence open to be read by all, or to direct it at one or more Circles – restricted audiences who, if we have set up our Circles correctly, will find the post of particular interest.

You can also send your status updates public, making them visible to all.

on the website

Find a guide to setting up, using and sharing Circles.

The idea behind Circles is that we as individuals - and journalists - have a range of groups of contacts, colleagues, friends etc. By assigning each individual to a relevant circle, we can ensure we only send appropriate content to them.

People can be in more than one circle. So you might have an umbrella circle - all journalism contacts, plus separate Circles for each of the beats you cover, maybe one for press officers, one for PRs, whatever suits the way you work.

Join and start conversations

When you see a status update that is interesting, useful, insightful or whatever, add a comment of your own. In that way status updates can develop into a dialogue, or a debate, about a piece of breaking news, an issue or an area of discussion that is of interest to your community.

Join communities or start your own

Communities are a big step up from Circles. On the communities page - **https://plus.google. com/u/0/wm/4/communities** - you can search out topics relevant to your journalism and, if there isn't one for a particular area of interest, you can create one.

This is a great tool for, say, starting a campaign or building a pressure or support group. A local journalist might join or start a community around a campaign to save a local hospital threatened with closure, around a controversial planning proposal, or any other hot issue.

You can search for existing communities at the communities page. Type in an issue relevant to your journalism beat and see what comes up. All sorts of communities have been created - from local residents' groups to victims of a particular crime, from support groups around a particular medical condition to fans of a band, movie, actor or comedian.

Such communities give you access to a ready source of experts, specialists, obsessives and case studies.

on the website

You'll find a video on communities.

Post status updates regularly

Post whenever you have a story to promote. But what does a perfect post contain? And what can you post right now?

The perfect status update on Google+

Whereas Twitter is great for a crisp, breaking news headline, Google+ status updates offer more opportunity to present a richer mix of content: headline, picture, intro, link and video can all be posted together, giving a more extensive 'sell' on a story.

You can also incorporate a hashtag, as with Twitter.

on the website

Find a detailed guide on how to post.

Hangouts

Hangouts are video chat rooms where you can link with up to ten people you are connected with on Google+. Journalists can use hangouts for video conference calls, as a more personal way of interviewing someone we can't chat to in person, or as a way to bring two or more people together for a debate.

Broadcasting hangouts live to air

You can also broadcast your hangout via YouTube, meaning Google+ gives you an easy way to broadcast live video about a breaking story. We'll look at this in Chapter 6.

on the website

Find a video on using Hangouts, and another on broadcasting live via YouTube.

3A5

Getting started with Facebook

on the website

Find guides to setting up Facebook.

Many journalists are suspicious of Facebook as a publishing platform. They get Twitter, but with Facebook they're not so sure. It's just too social for them, too much about friends sharing stuff that's very personal to a small circle.

But if that's where a sizeable proportion of our audience is, then we can't afford to ignore it. And if they prefer to find news alongside much that is personal or trivial, we can either go along with them in that, or decide that Facebook is not the right platform for our news.

If Facebookers choose to follow us or the news brands we work for, they will see our content alongside all the other personal stuff from friends, material from brands and whatever else makes up their news feeds.

In fact, Facebook users are creating what we can think of as **personalised news stands** of the material they are interested in. They may not know that's what they are doing, but they are. So they may have news from the *Guardian* or another news brand, content from a number of magazines they like, from the sports teams they support, the fashion labels they wear and content from their own personal social circle presented to them in the one place.

The result is a hybrid of personal communications from friends, and material from people and organisations that an individual likes, enjoys, values, and wants to follow.

Facebook users are very social. They interact, comment and share. In short, they are the sort of people who may create a vibrant community around your content.

So Facebook can be a very significant place for journalists to work in - but it doesn't work for all journalists or all news outlets.

Keep your Facebook presence professional

You probably already have a Facebook account.

If so, you'll no doubt want to retain it as the place you chat to friends and family. If Facebook had a facility along the lines of Google+ Circles, this would not be a problem, but at the time of writing they don't.

Facebook is aware of this shortcoming and, as it wants to encourage journalists to use the platform, it has come up with a solution, which we'll look at in a minute.

If you *don't* have a Facebook profile already, and you are happy for your Facebook account to be an official, journalistic one on which you will never post anything that would conflict with your role as a journalist - drunken partying springs to mind - then you can start from scratch and set up a new account.

on the website

If you want to follow that route, you'll find a guide on the MMJ website.

The basic geography of Facebook

Facebook is complex and confusing. Even those who have used it for years are often hard-pressed to explain to a newbie how all the elements of the account they give you are supposed to work together. So let's summarise things.

Facebook consists of:

- Home page and news feed (what you see when you check in)
- Timeline/profile/wall (what you see if you click on your name at top right on the Facebook screen).

The distinction is that **the News Feed is about those you follow** - your friends, brands, journalists, news organisations and other individuals and entities that you follow - while **the Timeline is about you**.

on the website

If you'd like a run-through on the basics of how Facebook is arranged, you'll find one on the MMJ website.

Using Facebook as a journalist

Facebook has set up a Journalists on Facebook community which has a great deal of useful guidance on how we can use the platform to best advantage. You'll find it at **www.facebook.com/journalists**.

on the website

Find a full, up-to-the-minute guide on using Facebook for journalism, including how to create a page.

There are two options or those who already have a Facebook account: **create a page** or **enable 'follow' on your profile**.

Both let you update readers and sources on the stories you are covering.

Whichever beat you cover, Facebook says, having a professional journalistic presence gives you the opportunity to share public photos, links and analysis about the latest news with your readers and viewers.

Creating a Page, says Facebook, is a great way to share your updates with your community on the platform.

However, if you feel more comfortable using your current profile, you just turn on Follow. That enables readers to see your public updates without adding you as a friend.

So what's the difference between the two options? Facebook says: "Pages offer features like Insights, targeted posting, promoted posts, multiple admin support and more.

"Follow, however, enables you to maintain your personal and professional connections from one profile, giving you the option to toggle the audience you want to communicate with: friends or public."

on the website

■ See how to set up Follow on your personal profile
■ Find a guide to setting profile and cover pictures for your account.

Integrate your Twitter and Facebook accounts

To integrate these two platforms, and to make it easier to use them in tandem, you should:

- Link your Twitter account to Facebook
- Add the Facebook mobile app to your smartphone and link to your account, so you can post on the move
- Add the Facebook Like box to your WordPress stories
- Link your WordPress website with your Facebook account.

on the website

Find guides on the above steps.

Posting to Facebook

One of the prime things you'll want to do, as with Twitter and Google+, is to post headlines, intros and other tasters from content you have created back on your website. As with Google+, you can post several media together and are not restricted to 140 characters of text.

Breaking news works well

Facebook says: "In a recent analysis of posts from journalists and news organizations on Facebook, posts that included 'breaking' or 'breaking news' in a posting received an increase 57% in engagement."

Here's an example of how the *Guardian* posts to Facebook, with a comment on the post above a picture, the headline and intro of the story and a link to read more at the *Guardian*'s own branded website:

That post also got a good deal of feedback, and the comments thread beneath the post shows that *Guardian* readers are sharing, liking and discussing the story:

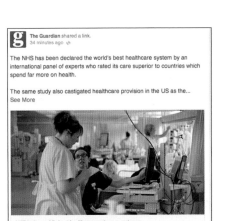

Eyewitness reports that include powerful pictures work well

You should keep readers updated as the story develops. If you have linked your Twitter account to Facebook you can double up by having Twitter posts automatically republished on Facebook.

Share behind-the-scenes photos and videos

Facebook says: "people are fascinated by the journalistic process."

Share your expertise

Your followers want to hear your personal voice and, more importantly, your expert analysis on the story you're sharing.

You can also share content you didn't originate; content that will interest the Facebook community you are a part of.

But, as we want to use social media including Facebook as that first point of contact with an audience that will find value in what we do – remember that bottom level of the social engagement pyramid we discussed above – we also want to link our weightier content posts back to our main website or blog.

Researching stories and finding eyewitnesses or case studies

Facebook offers this advice to journalists using the platform: "Your followers are a powerful network of sources that help you gather information and content for stories you're reporting. When you're trying to find individual sources, casting a wide net to your followers can be a good start to find people to interview.

"Facebook can also be a great way to source commentary from your readers about a news event. Whatever the content you're looking to source from your community, make the prompt clear and simple."

Be social. . .

Facebook says: "Interact with your readers: Ask questions, solicit feedback, and crowdsource content on your page's wall."

. . .and personal

Whenever possible, write in the first person.

You should also click to 'Like' items that others put in their news streams, and comment when you have something to say.

Best practices when posting your own content on Facebook

All the advice we have heard so far in relation to other social platforms applies equally to Facebook.

on the website

Find Facebook's own data-supported guide to using the site for journalism.

3A6

Getting started with YouTube

on the website

Find detailed tuition and demonstration videos on setting up and using a YouTube account.

Why use YouTube for your journalism?

We don't necessarily think of YouTube as being in the same category as Twitter, Facebook and Google+. Is it even social media?

Let's check it against Wikipedia's definition of social media:[1] "The term Social Media refers to the use of web-based and mobile technologies to turn communication into an interactive dialogue".

So, it's more how we use media that makes it social, rather than some narrow definition of its characteristics. If we let our video be shared, and commented on, it's social.

Let's also remind ourselves of one of the goals of using social media that I outlined above. It was to publicise our journalism, and to connect with an audience that will value it. We hope that community will further disseminate our content - whether it be in text, video, audio, or stills-photography format - and introduce others in their social circle to it.

So if we create video - and, as multimedia journalists, we almost certainly do - we can make it social by broadcasting it via YouTube.

As ever, we will decide which social platforms are worth us practising our journalism on by the response we get.

Many publications find YouTube a convenient place to host their video. As with a website, video needs to be hosted if it is to be published on the web. We'll look at the question of hosting in detail in Chapter 5 and also explore how to upload your own videos to YouTube and other hosting platforms.

What if you don't create video?

Even if you don't create video, but do include video from others in some of your reporting, it's still worth being on the platform.

You can create what is called a **YouTube Channel** on which you can aggregate the videos from others that you've used. That might work brilliantly for a really big story, where you'd like to gather - curate - all the video shot by others about it in one place.

So, YouTube is very valuable, and very useful, but - as with Twitter and Facebook - it wasn't originally designed for use by journalists and publishers. It's designed for people to browse around. Viral videos are the big hits: things you stumble across. It isn't good at organising videos coherently. But it can be, with some tweaks. Here's what you do.

Creating and customising your YouTube account

Sign up, create an account, and make the username either your own name or the title of your website, newspaper, TV show etc, as is appropriate. Also sign up to YouTube on your smartphone. If you are creating a publication, it is important to grab the YouTube username soon after you buy your URL.

If you do, you'll get a URL from YouTube that mirrors that of your main site, and makes you easy to find. So the *Guardian*, for example, has: **www.youtube.com/user/TheGuardian**

You can choose to share what you do on YouTube - everything from uploading a video to liking or commenting on one - with Facebook, Twitter, Google+ and other platforms. This helps pull all your activity on social media together. It means that when you do something on one social platform, that activity gets reported on all the others. So even if someone doesn't follow you on YouTube, but does follow you on Twitter or Facebook, they still get to know you have posted a video.

on the website

You'll find a comprehensive range of links to YouTube tuition on the MMJ website, covering all aspects of setting up and customising your account.

Develop your YouTube presence

YouTube places tabs on your user page for **Videos**, **Playlists** and **Channels**.

Under **Videos**, everything you have ever uploaded is lumped together. It's searchable by various criteria, but it's still pretty hard to navigate.

Playlists are a bit like chapters in a book - you can create them for sub-topics of your coverage or even for major stories. So, when I looked, the *Guardian* had a playlist called 'Modern Day Slavery' with eight videos, another called 'The Oscars', again with eight videos, and a third for a major UK floods story with 19 videos.

Channels are like whole books: useful for establishing really major areas of your coverage.

on the website

Get further guidance on how to use playlists and channels.

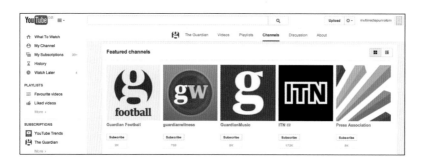

So the *Guardian* has these among others: Football, Guardian Witness (a citizen journalist area) and two for major agencies whose video the *Guardian* uses: ITN and the Press Association. Any channel you subscribe to will also appear in this area.

Channels have sub-categories called sections within them. As YouTube says: "Channel sections are a great way to organise and promote content you create and content created by others that you wish to curate and highlight on your channel home tab."[2]

You can have a maximum of ten sections on your channel home tab.

"A channel is the page which is viewable by the general public and contains a user's profile information, videos, favourites."

on the website

You'll find a comprehensive guides to creating and customising your channel, including:

- adding artwork
- setting a trailer video
- linking your YouTube account to your WordPress site and other social media accounts.

How to embed YouTube videos in your WordPress or other website

Embedding in WordPress is much simpler than with most other websites. You just copy and paste the video's URL. You'll find it in your web browser's address bar, or by clicking the share button beneath any video you are watching. Paste it into your story at the point you want it to appear.

Save the change and click to view the page, and the video will be in place.

I've done that with one of the stories on the WordPress site I created in Chapter 2. Here it is embedded:

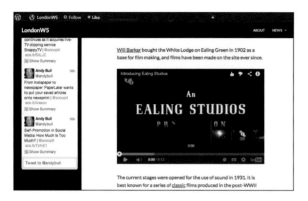

With most other sites, embedding is more complicated. It involves clicking on the embed button beneath a video you are watching, and then copying and pasting the html code presented there into the page on the website.

To do that, you have to be in the text version of the page, where the html code is presented rather than the visual or wysiwyg (what you see is what you get) version. You may also have to customise the html code before grabbing it from YouTube so that the video is the right dimensions for your page.

on the website

Find out how to use YouTube as a promotional tool for your main website, and how to become part of the YouTube Community.

Finding stories on YouTube

YouTube is massive, globally the second biggest search engine, and if you want to get your video on Google search results, you have to have a YouTube account.

The Pew Research Center published a report which detailed how what they term citizen witnesses are using the site to reach millions of people. CNN reported:[3] "A prime example was the tsunami that hit Japan. In the week following the earthquake that caused the deadly wave, the 20 most-watched news videos on YouTube received 96 million views, according to the report."

Mostly, that footage came from users who were in the middle of the disaster that killed more than 18,000, rather than professionals.

Citizens, the report notes, are creating their own videos about news and posting them online. They also share news videos produced by professional journalists. News organisations take advantage of citizen content and incorporate it within their journalism.

Pew found that consumers of news are embracing the interplay between what they watch and share. This is creating "a new kind of television news."

In effect, Pew describes an emerging partnership of sorts between traditional media outlets and citizen journalists. While many of the tsunami videos were user-generated, they received most of their views after being shared by professional outlets on the site, the report said.

The key to finding relevant stories – or video to illustrate stories you are writing – on YouTube is to use the available search facilities. In addition to the general search facility there are a couple of other video-finding devices on the site. Let's look first at how to use the general search facility.

Searching on YouTube

The key to finding what you need is to filter your search. You can filter by city or country, and use keywords to narrow things down.

You'll find advanced search tips here:

> **https://support.google.com/youtube/answer/111997**

Kevin Allocca, YouTube Trends manager, said that, when news is breaking "search is still the most efficient way for quickly finding clips on a certain topic".[4]

on the website

Get more tuition on finding video via YouTube, and seeking permission to use it.

3A7

Getting started with RSS feeds

In Chapter 1 we looked briefly at RSS feeds as sources of news: for gathering information. We can also use them for distributing it: by setting up our own RSS feeds.

WordPress and many other website and blogging platforms make that easy for us. There are two RSS feeds on the site I created in Chapter 2: one for posts, and one for comments. If a visitor clicks on either of those links they get an interface asking how they want to access those feeds. If, like me, they have a social media dashboard set up, they can add my feeds to that dashboard. I use Hootsuite, and so can add any useful feeds I find to it. We'll cover dashboards in the next module.

questions

Why do you think RSS feeds might be useful? Don't read on until you have given this some thought.

RSS feeds help us greatly in our role as consumers of information.

Feeds bring us breaking news, press releases and other material instantly, from all the sources we need to monitor.

Feeds save us having to remember to go to dozens of individual web addresses to check what's new.

Publishers often set up RSS feeds for closely defined categories of information:

- Breaking news
- Latest headlines in various news sub-categories
- Job adverts, and so on.

The *Mail Online* offers a huge array of RSS feeds here:

www.dailymail.co.uk/home/rssMenu.html

You can choose to follow news or sport headlines, a full range of sub-categories of news, individual columnists, even select from a wide range of RSS feeds for individual celebrities. Here are some of them:

They would be a great resource for a showbiz reporter.

The *Mail* also gives a selection of RSS readers which you can choose to have them delivered on.

| Main RSS Feeds | Headlines | Football | Columnists | Money | TV & Showbiz | Health Directory |

Click on the RSS icon or on your favourite RSS reader to bookmark the feed(s) you wish to keep up to date with

Amy Winehouse	RSS	Google	MY YAHOO!	Bloglines
Britney Spears	RSS	Google	MY YAHOO!	Bloglines
Charlotte Church	RSS	Google	MY YAHOO!	Bloglines
Cheryl Cole	RSS	Google	MY YAHOO!	Bloglines
Coleen McLoughlin	RSS	Google	MY YAHOO!	Bloglines
Daniel Radcliffe	RSS	Google	MY YAHOO!	Bloglines
David Beckham	RSS	Google	MY YAHOO!	Bloglines
David Tennant	RSS	Google	MY YAHOO!	Bloglines
Elton John	RSS	Google	MY YAHOO!	Bloglines
Eva Longoria	RSS	Google	MY YAHOO!	Bloglines
Geri Halliwell	RSS	Google	MY YAHOO!	Bloglines
Gordon Ramsay	RSS	Google	MY YAHOO!	Bloglines
Hugh Grant	RSS	Google	MY YAHOO!	Bloglines
Jude Law	RSS	Google	MY YAHOO!	Bloglines
Justin Timberlake	RSS	Google	MY YAHOO!	Bloglines
Kate Moss	RSS	Google	MY YAHOO!	Bloglines
Katie Holmes	RSS	Google	MY YAHOO!	Bloglines
Keira Knightley	RSS	Google	MY YAHOO!	Bloglines
Kimberley Walsh	RSS	Google	MY YAHOO!	Bloglines

Some specialist websites, such as journalism.co.uk, also offer feeds of relevant press releases for the subjects they cover.

We can further distribute our own published news and information by making it available as an RSS feed or feeds. So RSS feeds also benefit journalists and publishers by letting us syndicate content automatically.

Set up the feed and it automatically pumps new information published on your website or blog down the pipe to the consumer.

on the website

Find guidance on how to choose a feed reader.

What feeds should you subscribe to?

That depends on what you need to know to do your journalism:

- What's your specialism?
- What beat do you cover?
- What are the areas of news that interest you the most?

You may have several beats or areas of interest.

In which case, you'll want to scoop up the best RSS sources for each of them, and organise those feeds into groupings on your reader, so they are in one place and you can zip through them in turn, picking up what you need in each subject area.

Begin with any sources that you already use. Then search for new sources relevant to your journalism. If your beat is a geographic area, look for RSS feeds from all the organisations that are important to doing journalism in that place.

Getting started with social media dashboards

The great challenge to any journalist using social media and RSS is to keep on top of two things:

- Monitoring all the sources they are using
- Publishing their own news to all the platforms they have a presence on.

Social media dashboards let you manage several social media accounts from one place. So you can bring your Twitter, Facebook, Google+, YouTube and WordPress accounts together.

Dashboards are typically arranged as a series of columns, with each account you are monitoring allocated a column.

I will demonstrate this using Hootsuite (**www.hootsuite.com**).

You can sign up for Hootsuite using your Twitter account.

on the website

- Find tuition in setting up and using a Hootsuite account
- Find alternatives to Hootsuite.

Hootsuite organises the accounts it follows for you into a series of columns. You can further segment your Twitter and Facebook account into several columns, featuring (for Twitter) your home feed, mentions of you, sent tweets and so on. You can also add RSS feeds and WordPress accounts.

So that's the monitoring sorted. Also, you can post to these social presences from the dashboard, so your publishing is also taken care of in one place. Hootsuite's Apps facility (**http://appdirectory.hootsuite.com/**) lets you add more platforms, some for free, some at a monthly fee. You can link your Blogger blog and Instagram, for example.

You can schedule tweets, status updates and other postings across your social accounts over a period of days. There is also a built-in link shortener. So you can stack up posts that relate to predictable content and have them roll out automatically. For breaking news, obviously, you have to take over and handle things in real time.

The free version imposes restrictions on the amount of use you can make of Hootsuite, but paid-for plans remove these constraints. Terms are adjusted periodically, so you'll need to check the latest position at the site.

Hootsuite also offers browser extensions for Chrome and Firefox, enabling you to post without even opening Hootsuite.

Scheduling social media posts with Buffer

Buffer (**www.bufferapp.com**) is a simpler alternative to Hootsuite and other dashboards.

Buffer's free version lets you stack up ten pending tweets/Facebook status updates (more if you pay). You can also post to Google+ pages and to LinkedIn.

Posts are spread out through the day, and Buffer's analytics tell you how many are clicked, retweeted or shared, and the total reach achieved.

Exercises and projects

Exercise 1

Look at the BBC's guide to social media usage, linked to from the MMJ website, and consider whether you abide by it. Is it a good policy? What would you change?

Exercise 2

Go through one day's newspapers or news websites and see how many stories rely, at least in part, on other social media for their existence.

Exercise 3

Research what have been the biggest stories to break via social media and write an assessment of how the main platform used has been instrumental in that story's dissemination.

Projects

1   Establish professional presences on the social media platforms covered in this chapter, following the guidance given.

2   Build a resource of RSS feeds you follow.

3   Sign up for Hootsuite or another social media dashboard and use it to monitor sources and publish to your social media platforms.

Notes

1   http://en.wikipedia.org/wiki/Social_media
2   https://support.google.com/youtube/answer/3027787?hl=en-GB
3   http://edition.cnn.com/2012/07/16/tech/web/youtube-news-pew/
4   http://ijnet.org/stories/6-tips-journalists-seeking-news-youtube

chapter four

Audio and podcasting

In the book version of this chapter we will cover:

- How to create audio news reports and podcasts
- Using your smartphone to record and publish audio
- More specialised audio recording equipment and formats
- Recording audio reports and podcasts
- Editing audio reports and podcasts
- Publishing your edited audio.

At the end of the chapter are a range of exercises and projects to enable you to practise what you have learned.

In the online version of this chapter you will find:

- An interactive quiz to test your understanding of audio recording and editing
- A wide range of examples of audio reports
- Links to video tutorials illustrating the material covered here
- Links to further information.

Have the companion website to this book open at www.multimedia-journalism.co.uk. That way you can easily click on the links to the stories discussed here.

4A1

How audio can be used

Many reporters record their interviews. Recording them for broadcast can be a simple by-product of the reporting process. After all, the recorder is on anyway. You may only be able to use a couple of quotes in your text story, but perhaps there is more from the speaker that could be of interest to readers – particularly those with a deep level of interest in the story.

Likewise with a feature interview. You may well have had an hour with the subject. In a typical 1,000 to 1,500 word feature for a print publication or online text-based piece, you probably only have the equivalent of five to ten minutes of what the subject said. For readers with a keen interest in the person, or the subject, the chance to listen to another five or ten minutes – or even more – can be very attractive.

Audio clips to enhance a text-based story

So, at its simplest, your audio report might be just a very basic edited – or even unedited – addition to your text report.

But there is more we can do. Perhaps you have some sound that powerfully illustrates the story you have written. Just as footage from a CCTV camera might offer a powerful visual addition to the story (as we'll see in the next chapter) a dramatic sound clip might add a powerful audio element.

Here's an example, in which the headline tells all: **'We've Been Abducted': Kidnapped Teens' Emergency Call to Police Released**

on the website

Find links to this and other examples.

www.algemeiner.com/2014/07/01/weve-been-abducted-kidnapped-teens-cellphone-call-to-police-released-audio/

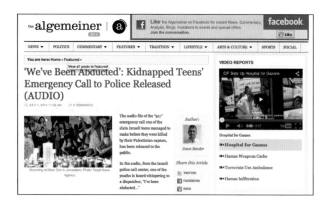

The news of three Israeli teens' abduction and later murder by Palestinian captors was a dramatic and tragic one. The release of the audio of the call they managed to make to the police is a powerful part of the story, bringing the drama of their plight into even sharper focus, particularly as we know they were killed shortly after making it.

Such audio is often released in similar cases, and when you are covering a crime or other dramatic story involving the emergency services, it is worth asking if they have any audio they can make available.

Here are a couple of other examples, also linked to on the MMJ website:

> An eye-witness's call to the police about an Australian politician's dangerous driving. **www. abc.net.au/news/2014-04-30/police-release-audio-of-emergency-call-about-troy- buswell27s-n/5422192**

> A passenger on a plane that crashed at San Francisco airport telling emergency services that they have critically injured passengers with them and no ambulances. **www.theguard- ian.com/world/video/2013/jul/11/asiana-airlines-plane-crash-san-francisco-audio**

But audio isn't only of value in dramatic stories. Here's a contrasting example of the use of sound from the Bristol Post. **www.bristolpost.co.uk/ AUDIO-People-8217-s-History-Arnos-Vale- Cemetery/story-21740876-detail/story. html**

This much less dramatic text story about a local cemetery has audio clips of interviews embedded at points within it. The text covers the news of an audio history project about the cemetery, and the clips demonstrate what has been learned from those interviewed.

Using audio clips as part of a video, or stills slide show

Here are a couple of examples from the MSNBC news channel. They use audio as an element in a video report. The first is another emergency call. Here's the text story:

www.msnbc.msn.com/id/12208992/

Here's the video report which contains the audio (sorry, you'll have to put up with an advert before you can watch it).

www.msnbc.msn.com/id/21134540/vp/12204821#12204821

Here's another MSNBC story: **www.msnbc.msn.com/id/17023604/** which is about some audio that has come to light that records an airport worker making a call to the Federal Aviation Administration (FAA). It is significant because his call, enquiring about a plane on which John F Kennedy Jr was aboard, was made four hours before a search and rescue operation was launched. Kennedy died in the crash.

Again, the audio has been used not as a self-contained element in a story, but has been built into a video report.

Here's the video report containing the audio:

www.msnbc.msn.com/id/21134540/vp/17023736#17023736

Adding audio to a slide show of stills is very popular. It's less time consuming than filming and editing video, and is also a great way to bring life to a series of images that would not work too well on their own.

Here's an example from the BBC, of a slide show of archive images used in conjunction with interviews and music to mark the 100th anniversary of the Chelsea Flower Show: **www.bbc. co.uk/news/uk-england-london-22512074**

Perhaps you have video and audio available for a particular story, but they are not directly related. The *Middlesbrough Gazette* (www.gazettelive.co.uk) had audio of the confession of a woman who helped her husband fake his own disappearance in order to claim on his life insurance policy. They also had video of her arriving at the police station. They brought the two elements together like this: **http://youtu.be/9mwUhAAAZAO**

on the website

Watch the audio and video package.

questions

What do you think of this package? Could better video or stills have been used with this audio? Don't read on until you have decided.

They could also have used still images instead of this video, perhaps telling the story of the arrest, or the criminals' lives, more fully.

It's always possible to use an important audio clip as the basis for a video report, as we'll see in the next chapter, but you don't have to do that. You can also use a piece of crucial audio in an audio package. It's that approach we are concentrating on in this chapter. We'll look at audio slide shows in Chapter 11.

The audio package

You will be familiar with the concept of an audio news package if you listen to radio news or features - particularly if you tune in to local radio. Where a reporter has had time to cover a story in some detail, they will record a number of elements and pull them together into a well-crafted report of two or three minutes. Typically, such a report - known as a package - will have an introduction from the reporter, some interviews and some sound that identifies the place in which the recording took place. Such sounds are a crucial element in an audio report and their effective use is vitally important to its success.

Such reports paint pictures with sound - the sounds are there to give the listener an instant understanding of location. Sounds often start a report. If the sound is of a cow mooing and a man saying "come on girl" they expect to discover the report is taking place on a farm.

The voice of the reporter might come in next explaining where they are, who they are with and what the story is about. If the reporter has said they are with farmer John Mackenzie and we then hear another voice, we will have a clear understanding that this is Mr Mackenzie speaking.

Here are a couple of examples of traditional audio packages

This one is from BBC Radio and is called Metal Guru. Here's the link:

www.bbc.co.uk/stoke/content/articles/2007/10/13/road_roller_feature.shtml

questions

Before you read on, have a listen. Analyse the elements in the report and its structure. Don't read on until you've done that.

It has an introduction, which sets the piece up. It's about a man who kept active in his retirement by making something (we aren't yet told what). The intro ends on the words "It all started when he bought himself a lathe. . ."

The next sound we hear is the actuality of the lathe being turned on. Without the word lathe in the intro we wouldn't know what the sound was. The interviewee talks over the sound and we can imagine him in his workshop. This background sound was actually recorded separately from the interview as what is known as wild track – more about that later. The interviewer's questions have been edited out so we get a very natural, uninterrupted chat from the subject. At points the wild track changes, from the lathe turning to a file being used, for example.

We learn he is actually making a quarter scale model of a steam engine. We have had to listen for a little while to get that information, but the device works because we are intrigued to discover what exactly it is that this man has taken years creating.

The USA's National Public Radio regularly features audio packages.

This story about how climate change threatens migratory birds contains a good deal of wild track featuring bird cries and the sounds of waves on the shore, interspersed with audio interviews and voice-over from the reporter. Here's the link (it's easier to access online): **www.npr.org/player/v2/mediaPlayer.html?action=1&t=1&islist=false&id=319092192&m =335986180&live=1**

on the website

Listen to more audio packages:

- Find a link to current BBC Radio 4 Today programme packages
- Find more NPR audio packages by searching their archive.

Podcasts – and RSS feeds

Then there is the podcast. But what is a podcast, and does it differ from a bog-standard bit of audio or an audio package? In a word, yes. But not necessarily in terms of content.

Because, while a podcast might contain all the elements of an audio package, and be as slickly produced, it is different in one key way: how it is distributed.

Podcasts are not just available on a website or blog. They are also available independently of your main publishing platform. BBC Radio 4's Today programme has a Best of Today podcast that you can subscribe to by clicking a link on their website:

http://news.bbc.co.uk/today/hi/default.stm

Here are some examples of different styles of podcast

An unscripted chat podcast

Let's listen to a podcast to be found on the website of *The Word* magazine

It is a very relaxed, unscripted chat about music. Every Monday afternoon David Hepworth and Mark Ellen gather with a couple of contributors in a spare room at his office to record the Word podcast, a highly informal 40-minute chat session.

This is how its creator, David Hepworth, described it in the *Guardian*:

> We happen to have among the team a disproportionate number of people with extensive broadcasting experience. Or just experience of talking.

Hepworth says that the podcast medium leaves these experts free to do something that they can't do anywhere else: chat about their favourite topics for an audience prepared to go along with the informal style in which they ramble around a range of subjects.

> "It's an inch away from a complete shambles," he says, but "it's also one of the most liberating things I've ever done."

on the website

Find a link to it. Have a listen.

questions

What do you think of it? Does it work for you? Don't read on until you have decided.

Clearly, such a podcast is not like a mainstream radio show. It won't work for many people. Listeners really have to be on the right wavelength to appreciate it. But notice that David Hepworth says it is liberating. Podcasts can be a lot of fun. They free you from the constraints of formal, objective reporting. You can sound off, have a laugh, rave about your pet love or rant about your pet hate. Listeners know podcasts are different from our formal work – they are us with our feet up. A podcast of you and some friends chatting like this would work for listeners who are on your wavelength – just as long as you have something to say!

A radio package-style podcast

Here is an example of a podcast that uses the format of a radio show, with a presenter introducing a short package put together by a reporter.

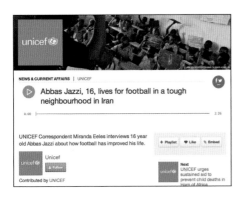

The headline on the text link to it reads:

Abbas Jazzi, 16, lives for football in a tough neighbourhood in Iran

on the website

You'll find the link to it on the MMJ website, or you can type in this URL: **https://audioboom. com/boos/1520361-abbas-jazzi-16-lives-for-football-in-a-tough-neighbourhood-in-iran**

Unicef is the United Nations' Children's Fund. The podcasts on what it calls Unicef Radio are designed to illustrate the work that the organisation does, to bring it to life and to show individuals who have been helped.

questions

What are this podcast's strengths and weaknesses? Don't read on until you have decided.

It could be a lot more interesting than it is. Click on the link and you get not one but two introductions to the item - the first from some sort of presenter, the second from the journalist. It is some time before you get to the boy and the football. And where's the passion? The report could have started with the sound of him playing football, perhaps the scuff of a football on the ground, the pants, grunts and scuffling feet of the players, followed by them yelling in joy at a goal. Opening with such audio would have put the listener in a place and with a person. Once the scene is established, the reporter could then come in. You don't need the presenter at all because the text link does their job quite adequately.

The polished, radio show-style podcast

The *Guardian* runs a range of highly professional podcasts. The link here is to an episode of one called Music Weekly.

Find the link, or you can type in the following URL:

www.theguardian.com/music/audio/2014/may/01/music-weekly-manic-street-preachers

questions

What do you think of it? Don't read on until you have decided.

This podcast is pretty much up to the quality of a radio show, give or take a bit of the sort of informality we heard on the Mark Ellen audio. It is entertaining and informative, and might be just the thing to load on to your phone, iPod or tablet and listen to on the way to work or while out running.

Such a podcast is very resource-intensive. It has a presenter, the footage must be edited, guests must be coordinated. Such programming takes time and resources.

on the website

Find additional examples of podcasts.

Why you should podcast

You should be creating regular podcasts as part of your development as a multimedia journalist. Be disciplined. Whether your podcast is on a website – and several people may be contributing to it – or on your blog and done by you alone, publish regularly. That way listeners know when to expect more from you and – if you get good at it – will look out for your new posts.

If you are blogging about music, for example, you can do a weekly gig guide podcast. If you blog about movies, your podcast could be a review of the week's releases. If you get one or two other people together you can turn your podcast into a lively discussion along the lines of a radio feature or short programme. Sports podcasters can offer a weekly preview of the big game, and a post-match analysis.

If you are specialising in a fast-moving area of journalism – politics, financial markets or any of the beats that a newspaper or B2B magazine journalist has to follow – you might do a daily podcast.

4A2

Recording and publishing audio using just your smartphone

So that's a taster of what can be done, here's how to get started.

An iPhone or Android smartphone is a powerful multimedia journalism device, and you can record and publish simple audio straight from it.

You can record on the phone's voice memo app, and that process is covered in the BBC video linked to from here.

on the website

Watch a video with beginners' tips on audio for smartphones from the BBC.

www.youtube.com/watch?v=q8ngvpZwxDg&list=PLom7Q2FZ5qMNr3au-k4tg-5kG6j_roUzY&feature=share&index=1

I prefer to use an app such as audioBoom (**http://audioboom.com**), because it also provides a publishing platform. If you simply want to record quick clips and get them to air, audioBoom is all you need. The clips you publish with audioBoom can also be embedded in text stories, enabling you to do a lot of what we've discussed so far. Another alternative is SoundCloud (**https://soundcloud.com**).

There are also apps such as Vericorder 1st Video which let you edit audio, audio slideshows and video to a professional standard within your phone, and to publish a polished package. We'll look at such software in Chapter 5.

If audio doesn't play a central role in the journalism you do, then the smartphone option will be fine for you. But if audio is going to be a key part of your journalism, if you want to create polished packages, then you need to delve deeper into the subject.

It's up to you, but to facilitate both levels of learning we'll cover both options in this chapter.

The simplest way to record and publish audio

Sign up for audioBoom (**http://audioboom.com**) on a computer, and then add the app to your smartphone or tablet, linking it to the account you created on your computer.

Note: the free version limits you to ten minutes recording time per piece. Paid options offer 30 minutes or more.

on the website

Watch an introductory video from audioBoom.

Here's a run-down on what audioBoom lets you do

If you are at a desk computer, you can record and published audio from there. If out and about, you can record and review your audio in the phone app. When you are happy with it, you can add a title, picture and location. You can share your podcasts via links, set up automatic posting to social platforms, and embed individual podcasts in your blog or website.

You can also embed a player that presents all your podcasts in one place.

You can use the RSS feed audioBoom gives you to embed your podcasts in a dedicated place on your WordPress website or elsewhere.

If you have an iTunes account, you can add audio podcasts to an iTunes channel.

Using audioBoom to record and publish audio

Because the processes for doing this are likely to change over time, you'll find full tuition in using audioBoom on the MMJ website.

on the website

Find step-by step guides in

- Recording your audio
- Publishing your audio automatically on social media, website and Blogger blog

- Publishing your audio as part of a text story
- Adding audio to your Wordpress site
- Adding an audioBoom player to your Blogger or other non-WordPress website
- Getting your podcasts onto iTunes
- Perfecting your podcasting.

4A3

The professional approach to audio journalism

The simple approach is all well and good, but let's look now at developing a deeper understanding of how to use audio.

If you plan to regularly record audio to a professional standard, you may decide to buy a dedicated recorder. While modern phones can produce good audio, and let you publish directly from the device, professional audio journalists usually use a good digital recorder in addition. Recorders come in all shapes, sizes and costs.

on the website

Find up-to-the-minute buyers' guides.

Audio recording equipment and formats

Know more about audio formats

If you are thinking of using a dedicated audio device, you need to know a bit about digital file formats right at the outset. Audio that is available on a website will have been compressed so that it downloads faster.

If you have an MP3 player it is called that because the files on it have been compressed in the MP3 format. Other compressed formats include:

- WMA, used in Windows Media
- Real, used by the Real Audio brand
- MPEG-4, used in the QuickTime brand
- MPEG-4 AAC, used by iTunes.

Then there are uncompressed formats which are not found on websites:

- WAV, which is pronounced wave
- AIFF, which is Apple's standard format.

We are going to stick with the MP3 format because it is so universal – almost any computer can play an MP3 file, and so can programs such as iTunes, Real Player and Windows Media Player. But try to play a file in one of these formats on one of the others and you will have a problem.

Here are the essentials you need to take into account when choosing – at whatever price you pay.

Is it easy to use?

One-touch recording is best.

How much recording time does it have?

Recorders with 20 or 30 hours may seem excessive, but if you only have an hour or two it is surprising how quickly the memory fills up. If the machine has a slot for a memory card you are restricted only by the capacity of the card, and how many of them you have.

What digital file format does it use, and is that format compatible with your computer?

MP3 is best, because you can edit it on any system. If the recorder uses Windows Media and you work on a Mac, you'll need a file converter to switch it to MP3 or another format that is compatible with Mac software.

Does it have a USB port?

It needs one, so that you can easily plug it in to your computer and transfer files from it.

Does it have mic and headphone input points?

It must have both. You need an external mic to focus on the sound you want – such as a person talking – and screen out general background noise.

You need headphones to listen in to your recording and make sure the quality is good. Particularly before an interview, checking that sound levels are neither too high nor too low is very important.

Some people like to keep headphones on while they record, others don't. When recording in a noisy place, headphones help you make sure your subject can be heard and, if recording on the street and a motorbike shoots past, you know whether your speaker was drowned out or not.

An external mic will vastly improve the quality of your recording, and good sound is the key to a good audio report. Without it the listener is not going to bother.

You can either get a standard mic with a cord that attaches it to the recorder, or a wireless or lavalier mic. A standard mic is useful if you are interviewing more than one person, as you can direct it to a given speaker, and also towards yourself when you want to ask a question.

It's also good for getting natural sound – actuality – to add a flavour of where your interview is taking place and what is going on.

A wireless mic is useful if you want to record one person and it is hard to keep close to them at all times. For example, if you mic up a runner in a race, or someone moving through a crowd and describing what they are seeing.

Wireless mics come in two parts. There is a battery pack and a small mic that you clip to your subject's clothes so that their voice can be heard clearly. This transmits to a second, base unit that receives the sound. You attach this to your recorder.

Adding a mic to your phone

You can also add a microphone to your phone, using the earphone jack. You can either buy a mic designed for the phone or, by plugging in a short adapter cable, attach any standard external mic to the phone.

on the website

Find video on using an external directional mic to record professional-quality audio on your phone.

Good sound is vital

You can't create good audio reports if the sound quality of your recordings is poor. So, while you can use low quality audio to practise interviewing, editing and uploading to your editing software, you really need decent equipment to create good reports that you can be proud of.

Recording audio reports and podcasts

When you are worrying about getting someone to talk to you at all, thinking of also getting them on audio might seem too much to take on. In fact, recording audio when you go about your everyday reporting work becomes second nature once you have done it a few times.

Of course, not all reports need audio. A standard news story in which you have a couple of pars of quotes from each of three people probably doesn't benefit from it, but it can add to many other everyday stories. Take a vox pop, for example. If you record the people who answer your questions, their comments can be edited into a lively audio track. If they say funny things, the humour will come across much better in audio. If an interview is very emotional, the emotion will be fully felt in a sound report.

Record somewhere quiet

When you are conducting your interviews, you need to be keenly aware of sounds that will become distracting when broadcast. For example, a ticking clock might not bother you in normal circumstances, but if it comes out on your recording it can become intrusive. A whirring fan is another distraction. Turn such appliances off, or move your subject somewhere else.

The importance of natural sound

Natural sounds give a sense of place. Having your interviewer speaking, or you describing a scene, is one thing. But good natural sound effects will give the listener a much stronger sense of being in the place.

You might be tempted to simply record your interview close to the source of natural sound.

questions

So, for example, if you are interviewing a man who went over a waterfall in a barrel, why not interview him with the sound of rushing water behind him?

Think about that before you read on.

You could do that, but the danger is that you won't have a good balance between his voice and the sound of the water. The background - natural - sound may be too loud for the speaker to be heard properly. You've probably heard interviews conducted by busy roads. Even if they are meant to illustrate how horribly noisy the traffic is, your listener does have to be able to hear what is said.

If you record your interview somewhere quiet, and the natural sounds separately, you can run both audio tracks simultaneously when you come to edit, and adjust the balance so background does not drown out foreground.

You might not want much natural sound at all, but it is always worth getting a few minutes of it. Audio obtained in this way is known as wild track. Perhaps you just want some natural sound to open your audio. If you are on a farm, the sound of cows mooing at the start of an audio report immediately tells the listener where you are.

Record natural sound - wild track - in uninterrupted 20-second segments. Record a minute or two for a short report. That ensures you have enough wild track to drop into your report.

How to conduct your interview

There are three approaches to conducting an audio interview.

The first is to do your initial interviewing without recording it. Once you have a clear idea of the story you can switch to record mode and conduct a formal, structured interview. This approach can be advantageous if you only want a short piece of audio from an interview. You avoid recording a lot of material you can't use.

The potential drawback is that spontaneity is lost. Your interviewee either doesn't give as good an answer the second time or refuses to repeat something they now realise they were unwise to say.

The second approach is to begin recording straight away. If you do this you need to have a clear structure to your questioning worked out. You can't interrupt and say "sorry, when did this happen" or "can you spell that". If you are used to interviewing for print or text reporting it can be hard to get out of the habit of butting in, or of simply murmuring agreement or other responses to what you are being told.

And you really want to ask your questions pretty much in the order you expect to run the answers you get, or you will have a big editing job on your hands.

The best approach is a sort of halfway house. With this, you ask a few preliminary questions to get the basics, but don't put your key questions. Then you start recording and put the key questions.

How to phrase your questions

There are what is known as closed questions, and open questions.

Here's an example of a closed question: "Do you think the litter in the park is a disgrace?"

Here is an open version of the same question: "How would you describe the state of the park?"

questions

Which is best? Don't read on until you have decided.

The open question is best. The closed question risks a one word, yes or no answer.

If you are conducting a vox pop, make sure you ask everyone the same question. If you do you can easily edit the question out of all but the first interview and run the answers on. If you need to ask a second question, ask it of everybody and you can then splice these answers together to form the second part of the interview.

For example:

First question: "What do you think about the state of the park?"
A string of answers follows.
Second question: "What do you think the council should do about it?"
A second string of answers follows.

What order should you ask your questions in?

If the interview is non-controversial, asking questions in the order you expect to broadcast the answers is the best approach. However, if you are interviewing a reluctant interviewee, or have some difficult questions to ask, it is often best to keep those difficult questions back until towards the end of the interview.

The reasoning here is that we want to get as much on tape as we can. If there is a danger that certain questions will provoke the interviewee into terminating the interview, then we ask the most innocuous questions first, gradually building up to the trickiest ones.

That's when we are recording. If the interview is going out live then we should get straight to the point and ask the key question first, however awkward it is.

How to plan your interview

Know what you want to get out of it. Know what your goal is. Have a focus. Have clear open questions. Get straight to the point. If you have a list of questions you need to ask be careful not to stick religiously to them. You must listen to the answers and respond, pick them up on things. Don't ignore unexpected but interesting things that are thrown up in the answers you get. Follow them up. Make the interview a conversation.

And remember that you only want two or three minutes at most. That's very little time, and only allows you to ask a handful of questions. You have much less time to conduct the interview than you would have for a text-based piece, and you will publish far fewer words from your interviewee.

Before you begin

Tell your subject how long the interview will take. If you want them to begin their answer by telling you their name or other details, make that clear. Get levels from them. A good recording level oscillates between half and two thirds up the range. Check that your recording equipment is working by recording them telling you, for example, what they had for breakfast, and playing that back through your headphones to confirm all is well.

As you interview, keep eye contact, nod to encourage, don't speak.

When you are finished, check you have a useable recording. If you don't you'll have to apologise humbly and ask to go again.

Creating a podcast

There are only a few main elements to audio – a vox pop, an interview, a discussion and a voice piece or audio diary. Any of those elements can occur in any piece of audio. Podcasts can also include one or more of them.

Podcasters often concentrate on voice pieces or audio diaries. Many podcasts are just the subject talking, others are chat sessions.

Podcasts are often less formal than more traditionally journalistic audio. The challenge for us as podcasting journalists is to bring high journalistic standards to our podcasts in terms of accuracy, fairness, telling a good story while retaining that informal web-friendly, personal style.

More ambitious podcasts with high journalistic standards may well be very personal in that the podcaster will place themselves in the item, and take a personal slant on whatever issue they want to cover. But they can also include the elements we find in general audio reports – an interview or discussion, and maybe a vox pop too.

The package will be cleanly put together, with a strong narrative drive, good logical links between the items and a clear beginning, middle and end.

The podcast's immediacy can be boosted - like any audio report - with appropriate sound effects. So recording wild track is just as important for a podcast as for other audio.

Editing and publishing audio reports and podcasts

You need software to do that. You can do it in iMovies or Windows Moviemaker. Alternatively you can use dedicated software. The industry leader is probably Adobe Audition.

For this chapter, we are going to use a free service called Audacity.

You can download it here:

http://audacity.sourceforge.net/download/windows

Note: To ensure our tuition is up-to-date, we'll keep the step-by-step guide to editing and publishing with Audacity on the MMJ website.

on the website

Find full tuition in using Audacity.

Now that you have completed this part of the chapter. . .

on the website

Take the interactive quiz to find out how much you have remembered.

4A6

Exercises and projects

Exercise 1

Record your voice. You can do it straight to Audacity on your computer if you have a plug-in mic, just to give yourself something to work with. Perhaps read out several stories from a news website. Record two minutes then edit it down to one minute. Use this as an exercise to get used to Audacity, and to see how you sound

Exercise 2

Monitor the audio on websites of two publications from any two of the following categories: a local newspaper, a B2B magazine, a general consumer magazine and a national newspaper

What format does it follow? How well is it produced? Are there ways you think it could be improved?

Exercise 3

Monitor the audio and podcasts on the website of a broadcaster such as the BBC. Choose the website of a local radio station, and of a network programme that you enjoy or which is relevant to your websites and podcasts.

Again, consider these questions: What format does it follow? How well is it produced? Are there ways you think it could be improved?

In addition, compare the quality of this audio with that you have found on the sites you are covering for exercise 2. Is the quality better from the broadcaster? If it is, identify why.

What can we learn from broadcast journalists about the art of audio reporting and podcasting?

Projects

1 Set up audioBoom as described in the online version of this chapter, then experiment with recording and publishing audio. Find a story where you can interview a series of people, or where there will be plenty of updates you can broadcast, and post regular audio updates to social media and your website.

2 Choose a current news story that is relevant to your website or blog and go out and conduct a vox pop. Record an introduction to the piece in which you tell the listener what you are trying to find out. Ask six people one clear, concise and open question. Follow up as necessary with additional questions. If necessary record a closing voice piece. Record some wild track. Edit the package to no more than two minutes, using Audacity or another audio editing programme.

Write a news story that introduces the vox pop for your WordPress site, add a link from it to the audio you have created and publish.

3 Conduct an interview of no more than four minutes' duration with a person involved in a current news story that is relevant to your website. Record any additional material you need - such as an introduction, conclusion or any necessary links between points in your subject's answers.

Edit it down to no more than two minutes and publish on your website.

4 Record a four-minute package. It should include these elements:

- An intro from you
- A vox pop
- An interview.

Record some wild track and any other elements to complete the package, such as introductions or links from you and possibly a concluding statement.

5 Come up with the subject for a podcast that would fit in to your website or beat blog. Have a clear idea of your subject matter. Try to get colleagues, friends or other enthusiasts for your chosen subject to take part. See yourself as the anchor or chairperson for the discussion that takes place. Record a new episode of the podcast each week. Publish each edition via a feed and place it on your website or blog.

chapter five

Still pictures and video

In the book version of this chapter we will cover:

Stills

- ▪ Shooting still pictures with smartphones and digital cameras
- ▪ Cropping and editing stills within your phone and on web-based editing software
- ▪ Captioning
- ▪ Telling stories through still picture galleries and slide shows
- ▪ Publishing pictures to social media and on websites and blogs.

Video

- ▪ Shooting video on smartphones and with video cameras
- ▪ How to film a wide range of video reports
- ▪ Telling a story through moving pictures
- ▪ Writing to pictures
- ▪ Presentation skills
- ▪ Editing video to create effective packages
- ▪ Publishing video on social media, websites and blogs.

At the end of the chapter are a range of assignments and projects to enable you to practise what you have learned.

In the online version of this chapter you will find:

Stills

- An interactive quiz to test your understanding of the principles of picture taking and editing
- A wide range of videos illustrating the material covered here
- Links to further information.

Video

- An interactive quiz to test your understanding of the principles of video journalism
- Updates on latest best practice
- A wide range of videos illustrating the material covered here
- Links to further information.

At the end of the chapter are a range of assignments and projects to enable you to practise what you have learned.

Have the companion website to this book open at www.multimedia-journalism.co.uk. That way you can easily click on the links to the stories discussed here.

Stills photography

Smartphones have made photographers of us all. And, thanks to their autofocus and auto-flash facilities, pretty good ones at that.

Our phones don't really let us take bad pictures. All we have to do is get the subject in the frame. After that, the camera takes over. And if there are any problems with the image we take, there are a range of apps such as Photoshop Express that will enable us to correct just about anything.

With modern phones fitted with cameras of 8 megapixels or more, opinion is divided as to whether even many professional photographers still need a separate digital camera.

Much stills photography is either routine – which anyone can do – or opportunistic. That means, if you are in the right place at the right time and you happen to have a smartphone with you, you can grab pictures that have news (and commercial) value.

However, we must acknowledge that there will always be some photography that needs a really well-trained and talented professional photographer. Action sports photography for example, where you have a split second to capture an image. We aren't going to cover that area in this book/website. But the routine and the opportunistic leave us loads of scope, and cover the majority of news photography for print and online.

Not every story needs a picture, and not all pictures can be taken by the general reporter. So how do we decide whether a picture is needed, and whether we need a photographic specialist to take it?

With multimedia journalism, one key determinant of the need for pictures is whether a story can be told better, or more easily or clearly, with the addition of one or more pictures. We also need to bear in mind that, online, a story of any length can look very dull without a picture. Many websites, plus smartphone and tablet apps, use templates that require a picture to be added to the story – often above the text. This can mean that an awful lot of stock, generic pictures are used which don't have any direct relevance to the particular story. Such pictures will usually come from a database; a reporter won't be expected to take them.

Mug shots – straightforward head-and-shoulders portraits of the people involved in a story – can also be very useful. If we feature a particular individual regularly on our website or in our newspaper or magazine, we will probably have pictures of them on file. But it is a very good idea to get into the habit of taking straightforward pictures of people when we interview them.

In this chapter we are going to look at taking straightforward pictures – the sort that anyone, with a bit of guidance, can take with a smartphone or digital camera – and also at telling stories through a sequence of still images. We'll also cover publishing these pictures to social media, your websites and blogs.

5A2

The simple approach to stills photography

So let's look first at the simple approach to stills photography with a smartphone, before going on to look in more depth at photography as a key skill of the multimedia journalist.

Taking pictures on your smartphone

Get into the habit of taking smartphone pictures whenever you are on a job. If you arrive at a dramatic scene such as a crash, tweeting a picture as soon as you arrive is the quickest way to get your coverage underway. Regular photo updates will boost interest in your story.

Get close to your subject and keep the image simple. Detail and strong, clear objects work well, cluttered images are confusing and don't grab the viewer. (More on taking pictures below)

Don't use the digital zoom; it's not a real zoom, and merely crops the image and blows it up, reducing quality.

Turn the phone sideways, so you are taking landscape rather than upright photos – or take both a landscape and upright of each subject. You'll find landscapes much more useful.

On many phones, tapping on the screen adjusts the area the camera will focus on, so you can ensure the key element in your shot is pin sharp.

Most phones allow you to take a sequence of photos: hold the button down and instead of one single image you get a burst of shots. That can be great for fast-moving events – such as the final seconds of a neck-and-neck race.

on the website

Watch a BBC video on stills photography with a smartphone.

Hardware and software to enhance your phone

You can add external lenses, supporting frames and tripods to your phone or tablet.

on the website

■ Find links to comprehensive guides to devices that let you take better pictures on your smartphone or tablet
■ Find links to the apps discussed below.

Editing smartphone pictures

There are several apps that enable you to edit your pictures within your smartphone. Here are some of the best and what they can do.

Photoshop Express

Adobe's Photoshop Express enables you to correct the exposure, remove red eye, remove blemishes, crop and – if you wish – add a filter to the image. You can take photos within it or add previously-taken shots from your camera roll.

Camera+

Camera+ lets you improve clarity, add effects such as backlighting, remove blemishes, and crop, add filters and frames.

Instagram

Instagram lets you crop and enhance photos using filters, but you'll need to do any necessary corrective work in Photoshop Express or another app first.

on the website

Find advice on using Instagram for journalism.

Autostitch

Your phone may well have a panorama setting enabling you to take a long shot – ideal for a landscape or big group photo. If it doesn't, apps such as Autostitch let you take a series of overlapping images and have the app knit them together for you.

It's worth experimenting with these apps, perhaps with a range of images taken previously on jobs, to see which you prefer, and decide whether some are more appropriate than others depending on what needs doing to your image.

Publishing smartphone pictures on social media platforms

Add a picture to your tweets whenever reporting live. Likewise with Facebook or Google+ posts.

If photography is important to the journalism you do, open an account at Instagram in the name you use on your website or blog. Instagram is the place for those who appreciate good photography, so it's a great place to present yours.

You can also publish your Instagram photos on your other social networks.

Pinterest

Pinterest (**Pinterest.com**) gives users a kind of digital notice board or scrapbook onto which they can pin images of things they like. Users create boards on given topics and others can like them and repin items onto boards of their own.

It's a very visual medium, and much of the subject matter pinned falls into consumerism in the broadest sense. If your journalism concerns any kind of product – clothing, home design, items for the home, cars or any other consumer item, then Pinterest could be a place for you to do your photo-journalism.

If it is of use, be sure to add the **Pin It** button to your posts on your WordPress site – we covered how to add such links in Chapter 2.

on the website

Find out more about Pinterest and other social platforms for photo-journalism.

5A3

A more professional approach to photography, using smartphones and digital cameras

So that's the simple approach to photography and it may be that, for your journalism, it's all you need. However if, or example, you are a travel journalist, then more may well be required of you.

So let's look at the more professional approach to digital photography. We'll need to cover some of the technical aspects of the subject, including pixels. Pixel is short for picture element. A pixel is a single rectangular point in a larger graphic image composed of many such points.

Computer monitors can display pictures because the screen is divided into millions of pixels arranged in rows and columns.

Take a look at the technical specification of any digital camera or smartphone lens and you will see it has a pixel rating expressed in megapixels.

Megapixels

A megapixel is a million pixels. Each pixel is one element of data, one tiny pinpoint of information about the scene you have captured. Add all those dots together and you have the digital version of the scene you photographed.

The power of a digital camera is measured through its megapixel rating. Modern mobile phones have a camera of 8 megapixels or more.

To give you an idea of how a megapixel rating converts into the size and quality of the picture you can take, let's look at what a, 3.2 megapixel camera, a 6 megapixel and a 9 megapixel can do.

A 3.2 megapixel camera can take a picture that is 2,048 pixels by 1,536 pixels. Multiply the second figure by the first and you get 3,145,728 pixels. As with the cc rating on cars, the makers round the figure up to 3.2 for marketing purposes.

A 3.2 megapixel camera can take a high-quality image that measures about 180mm by 130mm. Which is about the size of a standard snapshot, and would be enough for a standard size picture for a newsprint publication, but not for anything larger than, say, four columns wide. It follows that a 6 megapixel camera can take an image almost twice as big, and a 9 megapixel nearly three times as large.

Digital cameras store the images they contain on a memory card - a reusable storage device.

You can lower the number of pixels that are contained in the image you take, but that will lower the quality of the photograph.

Does that matter?

That all depends on the medium you will publish it in. Because the other measure of a photograph is its resolution. Resolution is the number of pixels in an image of any given size.

Resolution

Most computer monitors display images at 72 pixels per square inch - 72ppi. They do that to speed up download times, so your reader is not left waiting for images to load in a page.

Newspapers are usually printed in 200ppi, and glossy magazines at 300ppi.

This means that, while you don't need a high-quality image for a website, you need a reasonably good one for general print and a high-quality one for a glossy magazine.

If you've ever taken an image from a website and printed it out - as part of a document perhaps - you find that the dots that make up the picture are visible. So it follows that you can't use an image taken for the web in a print publication unless you are prepared to put up with poor quality reproduction.

Conversely, if you have a high-quality image and are going to use it on a website, you need to compress it - reduce the number of pixels it contains. We can do that easily with any piece of digital picture-editing equipment.

One final piece of acronym soup for you to get your head around relates to the various formats digital images can be in. We aren't going to go into too much detail about that now, but here is a quick run-through.

The three most common are TIF, JPG and GIF.

TIFs, JPGs and GIFs

These are different ways to encode an image. Each format is good for some uses, and not so good for others. Web pages must have pictures encoded as either JPG, GIF or another format called PNG because browsers can only show these three. On websites, JPG (pronounced jpeg but actually standing for Joint Photography Editors' Group) is best for photographs because it produces the smallest file sizes, and small files mean fast downloads. It does, however, cause some loss of image quality. GIF (Graphic Interchange Format) is used most commonly for graphic images - diagrams, tables and charts. Artwork, to use another name for it.

TIF is most often used away from the web when high-quality images are needed.

For now, we are going to use jpegs. Your camera will use jpegs, although it might also offer TIF and yet another format, called RAW. We won't worry about them for now.

getting started

5A4

Shooting pictures

Many mobile phones have sophisticated cameras in them, and may well be good enough to take pictures for the web and print. However, they will probably only have a fixed lens, unless you add an external one, which means that you won't be able to get up close to your subject without putting the camera pretty much in their face. Such a camera will be good enough to learn the basics of photography in this chapter, but a more sophisticated camera would be better for later sections.

In this chapter we are going to use the automatic settings on your camera – where the camera decides, for example, whether flash is needed or not, and sorts out focus. In later chapters we will look at turning those settings off and being more creative with our photography.

Get into the habit of taking lots of pictures as you go about your reporting duties. If you are at an event where many people are taking part, and a number of activities are happening, then you have a good opportunity to shoot a sequence of pictures that will tell the story of the event through still images.

So a carnival, protest march, battle of the bands, talent show, exhibition or convention will give you the opportunity to capture the event photographically.

Always check that you have a good image – even if you are only taking a head-and-shoulders. Look for things to improve in the image that you have shot and put any problems right in your next shot.

Here are some basics you need to think about while you are shooting.

Light

There are three types of photographic lighting:

- Natural - or available, or ambient - light
- Flash as the main light source
- A mix of ambient light and flash.

Shooting in bright sunlight poses problems. If you have the sun on your subjects' faces it can cast deep, ugly shadows. If you have bright sun behind your subjects, they can be thrown into compete shadow. Be careful to avoid placing your subject between you and a brightly lit window. If your early shots throw up such problems, try to move your subjects into less harsh light.

Wherever possible, use available light. Flash can cause red eye which will need fixing in your photo editing software, and can bring shiny spots to people's faces.

If you don't have enough light, see if you can move your subject somewhere brighter.

A clear indication of not having enough light comes when your camera flash comes on automatically.

Get in close

Fill the frame with your subject. Remember that, particularly if your picture is going on to a website, the image is going to be small. A straightforward mug shot (showing head-and-shoulders only) will probably only be something like 25mm wide and 35mm tall. Your subject's face should be near the top of the photo, not in the middle. If you leave a lot of space around your subject when you shoot, you'll have to crop it out when you come to edit.

Keep your pictures simple

Particularly with the web, your image must not be cluttered up with lots of small items. If it is, they will be very hard to make out on screen. So go for detail. If you are photographing a display of prize-winning flowers, you'd do best to concentrate on one bunch of flowers, or even one bloom. If you want the winner and the bloom in one shot, get them to hold the flower up to their face, so you can crop in tight.

If you have to photograph a shop or a factory, go for a detail - the sign, perhaps with the face of any central person in your story alongside it.

And remember, whenever photographing a thing - a place or an object - to try to get a person into the shot. A picture to accompany a restaurant review that shows an empty restaurant

makes a very dull picture. If you are on a B2B magazine there is no getting away from the need for lots of product shots, but try to use people whenever you can.

Learn the Rule of Thirds

If we are to produce professional photographs we need to plan their composition carefully. Photographers follow what they call the Rule of Thirds. To understand it, picture your photo divided with two lines horizontally, and another two vertically. This gives a grid of nine parts to the picture. For compositions to look professional, the key elements in the photograph should correspond to one of four intersections of those horizontal and vertical lines. That means we don't put the main subject of our picture bang in the middle, we offset it to one side. Cameras often superimpose such a grid over the viewfinder as an aid to composition as you shoot.

on the website

Find illustrations of this and the other points we are covering here.

Shoot vertical and horizontal versions of each image

Give yourself some flexibility. If you have upright and landscape versions of all your pictures, then you won't end up with a photograph that doesn't fit the space you have for it.

Shoot action

Posed pictures often look dull and stilted. Instead, try to photograph people while they are doing something, so the picture looks more natural. If you are photographing a footballer, have them keeping the ball in the air. If you photograph a teacher, have them sitting by a pupil helping them with something.

Be careful about the background

That means avoiding having something odd or distracting behind your subject. Will that lamp post look like it is growing out of their head? Will that shrub make them look like they have a massive afro? Is there a pile of rubbish behind them?

on the website

Find further tuition in taking good photographs.

 5A5

Editing pictures

There is plenty of choice when it comes to photo editing software. The more sophisticated and expensive include Adobe, which you will probably have access to if you are on a journalism course. Then there are the free systems you get as part of your PC or Mac. There are also free systems available online such as Adobe Photoshop Express.

Whatever system you use, there are some fundamentals to remember.

Edit a copy of each photo, not the original.

Crop the pictures

Decide if there is any wasted space, or if the composition can be improved. Maybe you need to zoom in on one key element, or crop in on one person, and leave another out.

If your photograph is for the web, compress the image

Compressing means reducing the number of pixels to an appropriate size for the web.

Many content management systems (CMS) automatically compress photos, and blogging software resizes them automatically as well.

If you are working on a PC, Windows Photo Manager lets you edit and compress an image. On a Mac, iPhotos does the same.

on the website

Find guides to photo editing and compression on PCs and Macs.

How to size pictures for your WordPress site

When you upload a picture to WordPress you are given three options on size: thumbnail, medium or full-size. Whatever the size of the original image, WordPress won't let the picture you publish be wider than the width of your page or post.

Publishing the picture on WordPress

Open the story file you want to add an image to, click on **Add media**. Locate the image and it will be uploaded into the file you have open at the point where you last had the cursor. Once it is there you can move it around by using the cut and paste commands. The text commands enable you to position the picture with text running to its left, its right, or you can avoid what is known as a wrap of text and your words will begin beneath the image.

Telling stories through picture galleries and slide shows

Very often, in a print publication, the restriction on space means we use just one or two pictures to illustrate a story. We have no such restriction online. Indeed, if a story warrants it, we can include a dozen pictures or more. We don't have to have all those pictures present on our story screen either. Instead, we can arrange them in one of two related ways.

Picture galleries and slide shows

A picture gallery is a sequence of pictures. Often we have a separate, dedicated template for galleries, and - depending on what our content management system lets us do - it can either be included as an element of the main story screen, or linked to from that screen.

One form of picture gallery template presents one picture in a large format, and the rest in a series of thumbnails. If the viewer flicks on one of the thumbnails, it appears in the main picture window, replacing the image that was there before. The viewer can click on any image they are interested in to see it enlarged.

A slide show differs from a picture gallery in that it is automated. The images follow each other automatically, in a sequence, once the viewer has clicked on either the link to the slide show, or on the opening image.

Using a sequence of pictures has two main uses. One is that it enables us to tell a story as it unfolded - the progress of a fire or a flood for example.

Also, it gives us the opportunity to play to one of the web's great strengths: we can satisfy a (perhaps small) audience that has a deep level of interest in a particular story.

Captioning

Good captions are important. Not quite as important as good headlines, but they still deserve some effort. A caption is another way of 'selling' a story to a reader. Readers often look at pictures as they scan the opening of a story, and an interesting picture can be one of the key triggers to reading that story. A caption can help as well, if it tells the scanner something that appeals to them.

Too often, captions really don't say anything very much. But a caption on a mug shot can say more than the name of the person pictured. If the person is a murder victim, and even if we only have very little space for our caption, saying: **Murdered: John Smith** or **Victim: John Smith** is better than giving just their name because the reader now knows their context within the story. Incidentally, we could switch the captions around so the person's name comes first. And if the words 'murdered' and 'victim' are already in our head and sell, we can go for another keyword. Perhaps the murder victim was strangled. In which case **John Smith: strangled**.

Creating a picture gallery and slide show on WordPress

An image gallery will display a set of small images attached to a particular post or page. Readers can click on any image to launch a full-size carousel that allows them to scroll through the entire gallery one image at a time. With the slideshow option, images will automatically move from one to the next after a few seconds.

To create one, open a new page, name it and click to add images. Select **Create a gallery** and drag your images into the upload area. Then click **Create gallery**. Now caption your images.

Here's my gallery, half built:

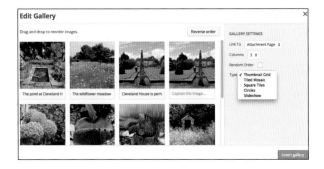

You can choose to have various presentations, including a thumbnail gallery or an automatic slide show. Once you are done, click on **Insert into page**.

I chose the slideshow option, so when readers come to my page they get the images presented before them in a sequence.

Here's how it looks on my site:

5A7

Stills exercises and projects

Exercise 1

Study the pictures in a newspaper and a glossy magazine. Look at how they are composed and cropped. Do the pictures always add to the story?

Exercise 2

Look at how pictures are used on a number of news websites. How often are they stock pictures that have no direct connection with the story they illustrate?

Exercise 3

Look at a range of picture galleries and slide shows on websites. How are they introduced in the text? How are they captioned?

Projects

1   Take your camera along when you interview someone. Take pictures of them, rang-
    ing from simple mug shots to full-length portraits and pictures of them in action
    – doing their job, their hobby or in any other appropriate context. Pick pictures that
    would work for a glossy magazine, a newspaper and for a website. Edit, crop and
    resize them as appropriate. Publish the interview on your website.

2   Attend an event appropriate to the subject matter of your website. Take pictures,
    as appropriate, of individuals, places and events to illustrate this story effectively.
    Edit, crop and resize your pictures as appropriate. Publish these illustrated stories
    on your website.

3   Create a picture gallery or slide show. Attend a major event that is of interest to the
    audience of one of your websites. Cover the event pictorially so that you have sev-
    eral dozen pictures to choose from. Make sure you have the information you need
    to write comprehensive captions. Edit this total down to about 15 or so. Organise
    the pictures so that they tell the story of the event. They don't have to appear
    chronologically; place them in order of interest and importance – using your news
    judgement to guide you. Give the gallery a title, and write some opening text that
    introduces the story. Write captions and, if you choose to, give headings to each
    picture. Publish this gallery on your website.

Video

In the book version of this chapter we will cover:

- The hardware and software needed to create video reports
- How to film a wide range of video reports
- Telling a story through moving pictures
- Writing to pictures
- Presentation skills
- Editing video to create effective packages
- Publishing video on a website and blog
- Streaming live video reports to your blog and website.

At the end of the chapter are a range of assignments and projects to enable you to practise what you have learned.

In the online version of this chapter you will find:

- Updates on latest best practice
- A wide range of videos illustrating the material covered here
- A wealth of links to further information.

Introduction to video

Online video reports come in many forms, from the very simple to the highly ambitious. The simplest could be a live stream from a mobile phone, or a clip from a CCTV camera.

Then there are more advanced packages - a combination of clips of people, places and events that tell a story primarily through moving images. The reporter will have shaped this package, and may well have added a voice-over to tie it together. They may do a piece-to-camera as part of the report.

The most complex is a full online news bulletin presented by a newsreader who introduces a series of individual video reports. Some of those reports may be fairly complex packages, others may be simple video clips over which they talk.

We are going to look at the full range of what is done, and learn to create such video reports. First, to whet your appetite, here are some examples of the various types of video that we can produce.

Have the companion website to this book open at www.multimedia-journalism.co.uk. That way you can easily click on the links to the videos and other resources discussed here.

Smartphone journalism has undeniably revolutionised reporting. With it, any reporter can broadcast live in multimedia.

questions

There's one big problem with producing the more sophisticated types of video. Can you think what that problem might be? Don't read on until you have considered.

The problem is this: sophisticated video packages take a long time to plan, record and edit. Because of this, many formerly print-based media organisations have stopped producing them. Some with a print background form a partnership with a broadcaster and get their video that way. The link between *The* (London) *Times*'s online offerings and Sky News is one example.

However, publishers with a background in consumer magazines - such as the Haymarket group - use sophisticated video packages on the websites of many of their titles, often in the form of product reviews.

This means that the level of skill in video reporting you will need will vary, depending on what branch of journalism you work in.

Many multimedia journalists will only routinely produce either live video or short clips that require a minimum of editing. Others will find video is an essential reporting tool.

Whatever form it takes, video is hugely popular with audiences. While viewing figures for mobile video rise, those for terrestrial and satellite/cable TV, and readership of print publications, are in decline.

on the website

- See a one-hour debate about the impact smartphones have had on the changing face of news
- Find other resources that identify the impact video has had on the media.

Examples of video use in journalism

Live-streaming of video

The most straightforward video is live footage, streamed straight from your camera phone to a website or blog. Many news organisations supply their reporters with a mobile phone or tablet containing an app that allows live video reporting. The BBC has its own Portable Newsgathering (PNG) app, which lets the reporter send video straight to the newsroom.

on the website

Watch the BBC's introduction to video reporting on a smartphone.

Others use a third-party app such as Vericorder 1st Video, which we'll look at later in this chapter.

There are also micro-video services, such as Twitter's Vine, that let you shoot between 6 and 15 seconds of video. We'll look at Vine in Chapter 6.

One way you can see live news being broadcast from mobile phones, is to go to www.bam-buser.com. Sign up for an account (we'll be using it later) and click the discover tab. There you'll see whatever is being broadcast right now.

on the website

There are other apps that offer the same facility and you'll find details of some of them on the MMJ website.

A video clip, and text-plus reporting

The simplest edited video report is really just a video element to a text report. This is often called a text-plus report.

Here is an example:

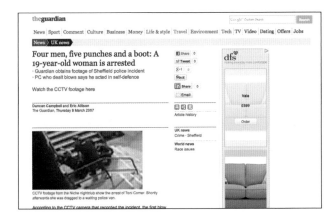

on the website

Find this and all other examples.

The video is crucial to this report, as it shows the arrest of a young woman involving a number of police officers and a high level of violence. It adds greatly to the text report that accompanies it, which goes into detail on the claims and counter claims about what the video is said to show.

A key opportunity for the reader to see the evidence and draw their own conclusions from it would be lost without the video.

There are other ways of handling such material. It could be used as one element in a video package.

questions

What elements do you think you'd need to make a short but comprehensive video package built around this CCTV footage? Take a look at the report for ideas. Don't read on until you've decided.

For one thing you would want to talk to the victim, Toni Comer. We learn from the text report that she doesn't remember the incident, and that she is an epileptic. She admits that she had been drinking that night, and became aggressive. Some thorough questioning would be appropriate.

PC Mulhall has issued a statement, and it would be good to get him – or his lawyer – reading it on camera. We want to see him if at all possible so, failing his agreement to appear on camera, footage of him arriving or leaving court during the case would be useful.

Ruggie Johnson, coordinator of The Monitoring Group North, which obtained the footage, should probably be interviewed.

We could get the police force spokeswoman reading its statement to camera, and something from the Police Complaints Commission. But these last two are not going to add much visually, and could be covered in the reporter's voice-over.

By the way, what do you think of the headline on this report? How does it fit with the guidance on using key words that we discussed in Chapter 1? Don't read on until you have reached your conclusions.

This headline is a problem. It contains none of the keywords readers are likely to use to find the story. Consequently, although the *Guardian* had the video exclusively, it did not get to the top of Google. Instead, bloggers who covered the story and linked to the *Guardian* report trumped them because they did use keywords such as police, assault, woman, and beaten.

This is the simplest form of multimedia journalism. If you know that the format you are expected to follow is text-plus – that is, your text report will appear as a screen on the website, with a link to a video or audio clip – then you don't necessarily need to film the whole of the interview. Instead, once you have gathered the material you need for your text report, you can set up your camera and ask the key questions that you know will get you the sound bites you need for the video. That's a much more efficient way of getting material for a video or audio clip.

The simplest example is where you have obtained a piece of footage – it might be from a CCTV camera of a brawl between rival groups of football fans, it could come from the emergency services and show a fire, a rescue, a horrific crash or a high-speed chase between a speeding motorist and a police car shot from a helicopter.

This piece of self-contained video might be allowed to stand on its own, with your text report filling in the details of the incident and containing quotes from those involved.

A slightly more advanced version of such a story would add a voice-over to the clip, which could be, for example, a police officer talking us through the incident.

The audio might be a voice-over from us, giving a similar description, or it might be a mini audio package, including clips from one or more of those involved, linked by our commentary.

A video news package

A package has a mix of elements within it – one or more interviews, a piece-to-camera segment or two from the reporter, and appropriate video and stills photography of people, locations and events.

Here's an example from Gazette Live on Teesside; watch it on the website.

Drugs network jailed on Teesside

Video feature packages

Sophisticated video packages are used widely in consumer journalism. The Haymarket title Stuff.tv, for example, runs regular, professionally produced, product reports. Here's an example:

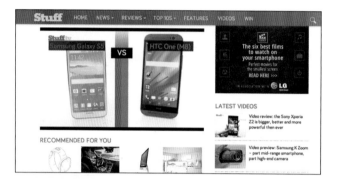

Watch it on the website.

What Car? another Haymarket title, creates car road test videos that are of broadcast media quality.

This example is on the website.

Video news bulletins

Online news bulletins can follow the format of TV news, with a studio presenter, or news-reader, who reads from a script that introduces each item. Generally you'll find five or six items in a two or three minute bulletin. Some of the items have accompanying video. Often, the studio newsreader's script is the only soundtrack on some of them while, for others, there is an audio track.

When video first became available to print publications as a tool for their online versions, they jumped at it, often producing daily news bulletins that aped TV ones. Now many have dropped them, finding they were too resource heavy.

on the website

Find examples of how print-legacy news organisations adopted and then dropped video news bulletins.

In the main, TV-style online news bulletins now come from media organisations with a back-ground in broadcasting.

Examples include Al Jazeera

www.aljazeera.com/video/

The BBC streams its News channel's bulletins online

www.bbc.co.uk/news/video_and_audio/video/

Other broadcasters, such as the UK's ITV News, prefer to offer a menu of individual video reports that the viewer can select from. ITN calls its offering On Demand News:

www.ondemandnews.com/Home/TopStories#

on the website

Find all these examples.

5A9

Recording and publishing video using your smartphone

Reporting live via video

You can broadcast live to the web or your blog from your mobile phone or desktop computer. You sign up to a service such as Bambuser (**bambuser.com**), UStream (**www.ustream.tv/**) or Livestream (**http://new.livestream.com/**). YouTube also offers a live event broadcast facility called YouTube Capture.

Bambuser and other live-streaming apps generally give you four things:

- An app on your phone or tablet to do the filming
- A channel at their website on which your material appears
- Links to your social media platforms
- Code to embed a player so you can show your video on your own website or blog.

The live broadcasts you make are also recorded and stored on the service, so that you can link to each of them after the live event, if you wish, and keep them available to your readers.

You aren't going to get great quality video like this, but imagine you find yourself caught up in a newsworthy event, or are sent to cover a fire or other incident. You can stream live footage of the event straight to the web. You could conduct interviews and provide your own, unscripted voice-over commentary to the pictures you are streaming.

This technology can be very useful in a press conference. While other reporters plonk their audio machines on the desk in front of the speaker, you can attach your camera phone to a discreet mini tripod and set up a live video feed of the conference to your site.

We'll look in much more depth at live reporting in Chapter 6.

Note: Because live video apps are developing rapidly, we'll keep step-by-step tuition in using them for the MMJ website. There you'll find a detailed guide to using what I consider the best one currently available.

on the website

You'll find a comparative review of live-streaming services, and guides to their use, on the MMJ website.

We'll cover:

- Installing the app
- Publishing live video to your channel page and to social media
- Adding a video player to Blogger or WordPress
- Publishing video as part of a text story.

Whatever video application you use to report live, that video will also be recorded, so you can use it later to edit into a package if necessary.

5A10

The professional approach to video journalism

If you have access to a video camera, great, if not, don't worry for now. Your smartphone will do. You don't need any fancy editing software for now either.

We are going to edit using an inexpensive smartphone app called Vericorder 1st Video, plus the free software that comes with your computer – Windows MovieMaker on a PC or iMovies on a Mac.

We are going to publish via YouTube, from which your video can be shared via other social media, and also embedded in your WordPress website, on blogger and elsewhere.

If you already have some technical proficiency in video filming, editing and publishing, you could follow the more sophisticated equipment and technical specs you will find in Chapter 12.

However, what we are really concentrating on here is the content of our videos. So if your editorial experience does not match your technical know-how, you should follow the tuition and exercises at this level. Don't make the mistake of thinking video is all about technical expertise. As ever in MMJ, content is king.

Types of camera and basic operating techniques

If you are on a journalism course you no doubt have video cameras you can use. If not, here is some guidance on what to look for when you buy. Because models are frequently updated, we'll stick to the general things to watch for here.

There are two broad types of video camera - 1CCD and 3CCD. CCD stands for charge coupled device. The difference is 1CCD has one computer chip and 3CCD has three. Why does it matter? Because cameras use these chips to process colour, and 3 CCD cameras produce higher quality video, but are more expensive.

1CCD is fine for shooting video for the web, but if you need TV quality, 3CCD is necessary.

Your camera may record onto tape, a mini disc or a card. It doesn't matter which, all will give you an hour or so of video recording capacity and, when the recording device is full, you just pop another one in.

What is harder to get enough of is battery power. Many cameras have less than an hour of juice in them. That's no good if you are out and about shooting a range of stories - or even stuck at a major fire or accident with no socket to plug in to. So you need spare batteries. Buy the largest capacity batteries you can. Many manufacturers offer a three-hour battery. You need two or three of them to be really sure you will never get caught short.

Using a tripod, a microphone and additional lenses

Try shooting a video without a tripod and you'll get very jerky results. For a steady picture, a steady camera is essential. Sometimes you can improvise, propping or resting the camera on something solid. But a tripod is pretty important. Cameras usually have a thread in their underside, and tripods have a bolt you screw into it.

You can buy tripods for smartphones and tablets, and clamps that attach the device to a conventional tripod.

You can also buy additional macro (for close-ups), fish-eye and wide-angle lenses for smartphones and tablets.

However good your video pictures, they are worthless if the audio track is poor. The microphone in your video camera, smartphone or tablet is ok for getting general sound. But it can't distinguish between the sound you want – from the person speaking, say – and the general background noise. A hand-held mic – or a directional, 'shotgun' mic that clips to the top of the camera – enables you to select and capture the sound that you want, and push the rest into the background. (See also what we said about mics in Chapter 4.)

Headphones help you get that all-important audio right. With them, you can hear how things sound and judge whether your levels are ok. Without, it's harder. Your camera, phone or tablet will have a headphone jack, all you need is a basic headset to plug into it.

So, you have the gear, now to do some filming.

Setting up the camera

Most cameras have controls that handle focus and exposure automatically. Professional video camera people will tell you to turn them off and learn to use the manual controls because they give you much greater control over the pictures you get. But then, if you were Sebastian Vettel or Lewis Hamilton, you might well turn off the traction control on a road-going Ferrari. Do that as an average driver and you'll be off the road in an instant.

Here's why they suggest it. Auto focus is great, but it can be fooled. If you are filming action and something moves across the screen between you and it, the camera auto focus will try to readjust to this new object, and lose focus on the subject you are interested in. If you lock your focus, that won't happen. But at this stage, with so much to think about, that's going to cause confusion, so we'll wait until we know more about filming before we take the pros' advice.

Many cameras also have automatic exposure controls – they make sure you have the right amount of light in most situations. Again, you can switch them off. This can be helpful where there is a very low level of light. But it's much easier, as we start out, to avoid filming in such circumstances if you possibly can. Another option is to use artificial lighting. Again, that's too complicated for now.

Framing a shot

Remember the guidance on following the Rule of Thirds we covered in our discussion of stills photography above? Well, it also applies to shooting video. Look back to page 154 to refresh your memory, or go to the MMJ website version of module 5A10 for the rule demonstrated with video in mind.

You don't want your subject bang in the middle of the shot. When filming a person, you want their eyes roughly aligned with the top horizontal line. That should leave enough 'head room' above them so it doesn't look like they are banging their head on the ceiling, but not so much air above them that they appear to be sinking.

This person is too high in this frame

She's just right in this one

In this frame she is sinking horribly

And if you are interviewing someone as part of a report, you don't want them looking straight at the camera and positioned in the centre of the screen. You want one of your vertical thirds lines running down through their face. And you want them looking into the shot.

Set your camera up just to one side of you, so that when the interviewer talks, they look across the camera at you. This gives a clear sense of a conversation taking place and which the viewer is observing. It also gives what is known as lead space - two thirds of the screen is in front of the speaker. If you were panning to follow someone walking, or a car travelling, you'd follow the same rule.

Shoot your subject at roughly their eye level

Shoot the subject from above and they look as if they are sinking down a hole. Shoot them from below and they may loom over you menacingly. If your tripod is too short, you'll need to improvise to get your camera at the right level.

Get in tight

You want your subject to appear prominently in your shot. For that you need to use what is known as a Medium Close Up (MCU). This is the most commonly used shot on web video.

This is a medium close-up (MCU)

You don't want a tiny head filling just a tenth of the frame. If you film like that, when your video is screened on the 4in sq screen of most websites, the person talking will have virtually disappeared. Your subject needs to be the biggest thing in the screen. An artist standing alongside a sculpture that dwarfs her is not going to be the focus of the picture. OK for an establishing shot but, if we want to see the artist speaking, we'll need a MCU of them. Your subject should dominate the screen, but there should be some background visible around their talking head.

So, for each shot, get that right. It may mean moving the camera closer to the subject (if you are using a mobile phone) or using the zoom facility on a video camera to frame the shot correctly.

Avoid distracting backgrounds

Activity behind your subject can be distracting for the viewer. They might watch the drunk trying to pick up a coin and stop listening to your interviewee. Likewise, you don't want an overflowing rubbish bin to mess up your shot, or to have a tree growing out of your interviewee's head. Adjust things to avoid such distractions.

Avoid distracting backgrounds

Once you have your shot framed. . .

Turn on – and wait

With each shot, set your camera recording for five to ten seconds before you begin the action. That gives you some empty tape to edit out and a clear start to things. Turn on and immediately ask a question and you can get a messy start to things, and you leave yourself no footage to edit out. Also, if you are interviewing someone, you may want to add a voice-over later introducing the person you are talking to, or creating some other audio link from whatever your previous scene was. Having five to ten seconds of them sitting doing nothing can be very useful. The viewer gets to see them and hear who they are before they start speaking.

When you have finished recording a video clip, again keep the camera running for 5-10 seconds before you switch it off. That gives you spare footage you can talk over or simply use to effect a transition to your next clip.

Oh, and don't forget. . .

Keep quiet as you film. Avoid the temptation to mutter agreement with what your interviewee is saying, or to add your own comments. You can do that in a text interview. With a video, everything you say - even your throat clearing - is picked up, and can ruin your footage.

The basic shots we use

Panning and zooming

Panning is when the camera moves across a scene.

Zooming can be either in or out. Zooming in is when the camera moves from a general view and progressively focuses in on one element of the original scene. Zooming out is the opposite.

Many people will say zooming should be banned. Too much camera movement can be confusing for the viewer, and zooming makes them seasick. Instead of zooming in, it is generally much better to frame your first shot, shoot it, and then stop filming and frame your second, close-up shot, hence avoiding the need to zoom.

However, hard and fast rules are really not something the multimedia journalist needs to adhere to. We can zoom if we have a good reason. The reason, as with everything we do, must be editorial. Does a zoom help our story-telling?

A zoom shot might be useful editorially if, for example, we are covering a case of vandalism to a town centre. We might start with a general shot of the damage, and then zoom in on a CCTV camera that caught what happened. A logical next shot here might be footage from that camera. Our voice-over would make it clear why we had chosen to use this sequence of images.

Panning shots are less controversial. If, for example, we want to demonstrate that a hurricane has ripped the roofs off a whole street of houses, and we can get a good vantage point, we might want a panning shot – starting at one end of the street and panning along it, demonstrating the geographic extent of the damage.

When we decide to film such a shot we can be thinking of the voice-over we might put with it. For example: "Five houses in Tooley Street had their roofs torn off. The worst damaged was Nancy Jones's at No 3."

The next logical shot would be of Nancy Jones, talking about what has happened.

Panning shots should not be overused. A sequence of still shots is often preferable.

Establishing shots and detail shots

These are also known as long shots and close-ups. You need to ensure you have enough video for your report, and that you have sufficient variety in terms of shots and the things filmed, to make a visually interesting report. The pictures you shoot need to be logically related in sequences.

An establishing shot, long shot or general view gives a broad picture of the scene. We use them sparingly because, on the small screens of online video, detail is lost, and the shot can be boring if held for too long, or if long shots are repeated too often.

If you are covering a road accident in which a bus has ploughed into a shop front, you might start with a general view of the scene – a wide shot that gives you the bus and the shop.

Editorially, that gives you the opportunity in your voice-over to give the essential details of the accident. You might do this segment of your report to camera, if you are able to stand with this scene behind you. You might look back to it and, if you have the luxury of someone else to operate your camera for you, they could then zoom in past you onto the scene of wreckage.

Then you should shoot lots of detail.

A close-up – or detail shot – of the crumpled front of the bus, the shattered windscreen, a headlamp hanging out of its housing, would give you a good variety of shots. With the shop you might take a picture of what is left of the front, then focus on the point of impact between bus and building, then the shop display that has been sent sprawling.

These shots could be used in sequence, or broken up with interviews – an eyewitness, perhaps, the fire and rescue officer at the scene, the shopkeeper.

Your report will probably be not much longer than two minutes, but you should shoot a good deal more than that. A ratio of five to one between what is shot and what makes it to the final edit is a reasonable guide for news reports. So aim for 10 minutes of footage for each two minute report. Don't do much more, or your editing will be too slow.

Lead space

This is the amount of space between the person in your shot and the edge of the frame that they are facing. As with stills photography, we don't want our subjects looking out of the frame. They should be looking in. If our subject is walking, they should be walking into the frame, with about two thirds of the frame kept in front of them – as lead space.

Reverse shots

A reverse shot is where you edit into an interview some footage of the interviewer. You will need to film these after your interview – unless you have the luxury of two cameras set up. You can just use them as reaction shots – a picture of you as interviewer nodding, or smiling

- or you could ask some of your questions to camera, so there is the option to cut to you at one or more points during the interview.

Reverse shots are useful when you need to cover an edit. If you have two pieces of an interview that you want to bring together, simply butting the shots up against each other can leave a messy join. To avoid such awkwardness, the option to cut to a reverse can be useful. To do that effectively you need to know about crossing the line. . .

Crossing the line

When you are filming two people talking - in a classic interview situation, say, you need to be careful of the angles from which you shoot them. If you shoot one person over the left shoulder of the interviewer, and then film some shots from the interviewee's perspective of the interviewer asking questions, you should shoot it over the interviewee's right shoulder. That way, when you cut between the two shots, you see each speaker from the other's perspective. You keep your angles of shooting within 180 degrees of each other - a straight line, in other words. Go beyond the 180 degrees and you are crossing the line, and you get a strange effect. If it helps, think of a straight line drawn between the noses of the interviewer and interviewee. If you film each of them individually, keep to the same side of that straight line.

Cutaways

You may have noticed some other devices being used - a shot of the interviewee's clasped hands, a shot of a photo of the person they are talking about or any number of other devices. The generic name for these shots is cutaways.

At a press conference a general view of the assembled reporters scribbling in their notebooks is sometimes used, or a MCU of a cameraperson filming.

Those sometimes rather contrived shots are useful when you need to edit. Gather them, by all means, but avoid including them in your reports if you can.

Pieces to camera

This is when you talk directly to the camera. In a very simple filming situation - for example where you are standing outside a court relating the verdict of the jury - the entire clip may be of you speaking. In more complex video reports, one or more shots of you talking to camera can be useful as part of the visual mix.

Sometimes you will find yourself at the scene of an incident but the pictures you have are very limited - maybe non-existent. So you set up your camera as close as you can to the incident, ideally with relevant activity shown in the background, and refer to it. In your report you need to fill in the description and detail that you can't show in pictures.

If, say, you are at the scene of a motorway pile up, you can add some drama to your description of the incident. "Rescuers describe a really shocking scene just 100 metres behind me," for example.

Or, if you are outside a company AGM in which a chief executive is being harangued by shareholders, you need to give some of the drama of the angry scenes you can't show.

Even if you are going live to air you need a rough script, if it is simply the points you want to cover in order in your notebook, plus one or two key quotes you must get right. That's particularly important if you are outside a court and quoting from what a witness has just said inside.

You should warm up your voice (see Going Live below). You need to be relaxed, and use your hands to add expression to what you are saying. Stand or sit as straight as possible.

Take care with the location you choose. It shouldn't be so noisy that the viewer can't hear you, or finds the extraneous sound distracting. Make sure the light is good - don't stand in the shadows, or have brilliant sunlight behind you.

A good balance of shots to aim for

A good balance between the various styles of shot would be around 25 per cent establishing, wide angle or general shots, 25 per cent close-ups, and 50 per cent MCU shots. Most shots will be five or six seconds in duration, except for the most important ones in which you have an interviewee delivering key sound bites. They can be longer. Detail shots might last for just two seconds, but make sure the viewer has time to take in what you are showing.

Plan

It might be tempting to pitch straight in to an interview. If at all possible - don't. Take time to prepare, or the footage you film will be messy and hard to edit.

The questions to ask

When you interview for print, you have a great deal of leeway in how you frame your questions, and the order you ask them in. You can use questions to gain basic information that you have no intention of using in direct quotes.

With video you need to be more disciplined. Ask your information-hunting questions before you start the camera rolling. Don't waste video and battery power on fundamentals. When you come to film you need to ask fully rounded questions. You can't interrupt to gain clarification, and you can't hunt for quotes. You need fully rounded answers. Your initial questions, before you film, will give you a good basic briefing about the story and your interviewee, which means you can effectively and efficiently direct the interview.

Ideally, you want to be able to cut out all your questions and let their answers flow from one to another.

Shoot to edit

Another piece of jargon to learn: shoot to edit. That means, when you are on a story, think of how you are going to tell it in pictures. Shoot the pictures that you need to tell the story, just as in reporting for a text story you will be gathering the quotes, facts and information you need to make your story hold together on the page. This story has to hold together on screen. You don't want any gaps, you need to be able to set the scene for the viewer, take them into the story, explore it, give all the relevant angles, get comments from all sides.

Remember you are not just *telling* stories on video, you are *showing* them. The pictures are your illustrations.

Think about how your shots fit together before you take them.

Shoot a wide, medium and tight shot of each thing that happens, each element of your story.

Consider how you want to place yourself, as the reporter, in the story. Perhaps you just want to do a short piece-to-camera to stand at the top of the report. Maybe you also want to tail it with a final comment to camera. Maybe you want to appear at some point in the story. You could use one, some, all or none of the above.

Sequencing

The key to good shooting is known as sequencing. You need to think of sequences of pictures that tell the story, and that lead effectively from one to another. Good sequencing enables us to tell a story quickly. So, for example, if you want to tell the story of a disabled person's difficult journey to work in their wheelchair you would follow that journey. At each point along it you need to get a range of shots that show what problems they face in detail. So, at the bus stop, we have a shot of them waiting for the bus. It would be ideal to cut from that to a shot from inside the bus – although this requires some planning and extra time – as it pulls up alongside them and the doors open. You might then shoot from the person's perspective, at a low angle, showing the challenge of getting up onto the vehicle.

The sequence of getting the chair onto the bus can then be followed, with a mix of shots showing the whole scene, close-ups of faces, perhaps of a hand reaching out to help. When these shots are cut together into a fast-moving sequence we get a very clear and fluid piece of video.

Getting material on video gives you the essentials for all sorts of reports. Your video can be edited into packages of different lengths.

The sound can be used for audio reports, either as stand-alone stories, for podcasts or in a blog post. You could also use it as the soundtrack on a slide show of still images.

■ Test your knowledge with an interactive quiz on the shots we use
■ Watch a comprehensive introduction to video equipment and shooting
■ Get the best, fully up-to-date advice on choosing a camera and other equipment
■ See the full range of video shots we use demonstrated.

5A11

Writing for video

In writing for video, your words must be designed to be spoken, not read. No doubt you will want to write your script down, but don't be fooled into using words and phrases in a script that look great on the page, but which jar when read out.

The real test of your video script is how it sounds when read out loud. Your tone of voice matters very much here. Imagine you are telling your story to a friend in a coffee shop. That should help you remove formalities and wordiness. You need to be direct and informal.

What you say must be crystal clear or the viewer will miss it and, unlike text where the reader can easily run over the last sentence again if it didn't make sense the first time, video viewers are unlikely to go back for a second attempt at understanding you. So, restrict your sentences to 20 words on average, and focus on one thought per sentence.

Keep things concrete. Don't say: "The current crisis in the financial sector has leached in to the mortgage market with the cost of a home loan increasing by .5 of a per cent from tomorrow."

Say: "Householders face a rise of £50 a month in their mortgage payments."

One other key difference is that, if your video package is to be part of a bulletin, the newsreader will need some words – a cue – to introduce it. This cue is often very similar to an intro on a hard news story in print. It is normal practice for the reporter to write this cue, so that they can then make sure they don't repeat the cue at the start of their video report. It doesn't always work out like that, but that's the idea.

The cue often robs you of your hard news line, and means you may have to take a more feature-style approach to the start of your script for the video.

For example, here's a cue for a murder story:

Cue:

"Police seeking the killer of prostitutes Annette Dowling and Kerry Harker fear their murderer has struck again."

"The body of a young woman was discovered this morning by a man walking his dogs in woods at Sefton Hall in Warwickshire. Andrew Knight reports."

Script for video:

"It was shortly after dawn that Adrian Jenkins's two Alsatians drew him to what he at first thought was a pile of rags. It was only when he touched the bundle that he realised he had come across the body of a young woman. . ."

When you are reporting using video, start with the pictures. The big pitfall for reporters who are more comfortable with text can be that they write their text story – which is incredibly wordy by video standards, and then try to fit pictures to it. That's putting the cart before the horse. You'll find you simply don't have the footage to cover your words and that, even if you did, your video would be far too long. You won't get more than 150–180 words per minute of video, which means that even on a two minute story you don't have much more than 300–350 words to play with. So your 20-second voice-over has to be delivered in 60 words or so.

Another key difference between a video report and a text news story is the ending. In text our ending is the least important part of our news story. With video our final line should have impact. We need to end with a punch.

Never forget you are telling your story through pictures. When you get back to edit, first put your pictures in sequence. Some, perhaps all, of those clips will have voice to go with them. The interviews you conducted drive the report forward. Usually you will want some voice-over, but your job as a video reporter is to introduce the report and end it – top and tail it to use some more jargon – and then to interject to move the story on and to provide essential links between the elements you have drawn together and the various people you have interviewed.

That's not to say that words aren't important. There will be things you have to say to make your report complete, and for viewers to follow it, and sometimes you will be fitting pictures to cover those key points.

Your words should add to the pictures – not simply describe what the viewer can see. If you are showing a scene of a burning boat, there is no point saying the boat went up in flames. Give additional information, such as how long it took to put the fire out, how many rescuers fought it, or what the damage is estimated to have cost.

And your tone of voice is crucial. The conversational style we spoke of as an ideal for text reporting in Chapter 1 is even more important here. When you record your voice-over, imagine you are telling your friends the story.

5A12

Presenting skills

Learn to speak well

You may have a good script, but reading it badly can ruin your video. A monosyllabic mumble does not enhance even strong pictures. So take a tip from professional performers and warm your voice up before you tackle recording your narration. Stretch your facial muscles by opening your mouth as wide as you can and moving your jaw from left to right. Then do some humming or singing. Go through the vocal range from high to low and back again. Sing a couple of verses of any song you know.

You want your delivery to be conversational, but with a few enhancements. Stresses on important words will help.

Go through your script and decide on the words you need to emphasise to keep what you read interesting, and easy to understand. You need to find the essential words in your script – the ones that, when emphasised, give the gist of the story and make meaning crystal clear.

They are often known as the **operative words**.

- ◼ Raise or lower the volume of your voice when speaking the operative words
- ◼ Alter your pitch on these words, going either up or down the scale a notch
- ◼ Alter your rhythm, pausing either before or after the operative word
- ◼ Change speed. Keep your speed up as you move through less important information, but slow down when you get to the key bit that needs emphasis
- ◼ But don't become stagey.

5A13

Editing your video

We are going to get on and edit our pictures now, using:

- ◼ Vericorder 1st Video or Voddio in your iPhone, iPod or iPad, and
- ◼ iMovies or MovieMaker, the free software that, respectively, comes with your Mac or PC.

Note: Because these software packages develop fast, we'll offer just an overview of them here, and keep the full, step-by-step tuition for the MMJ website.

Editing on your mobile phone using Vericorder 1st Video or Voddio

Some apps let you do basic editing – trimming a clip, and switching the order in which clips appear, for example. Others, such as Vericorder 1st Video, let you do a complete edit on your phone or tablet. Vericorder also has Voddio which adds on the facility to upload video and audio directly into a publisher's content management system. That makes it a commercially available version of something like the BBC's PNG app which we looked at earlier.

The functionality of 1st Video and Voddio is very similar, so what we look at in relation to 1st Video also goes for Voddio.

I like it because the style of editing – using your fingers on the phone or tablet screen just as you do with many other apps, makes for a very instinctive way of using the software. You tap, slide, pinch and stretch with your fingertips.

Vericorder calls 1st Video: "an audio and video editing studio in the palm of your hand".

It's an iPhone/iPod/iPad-specific editor of professional quality – and you can use its paid-for (but inexpensive) app, to record, edit and publish not just video, but also audio and audio slide shows. At the time of writing it was not available for Android, but Vericorder is working on that, and we'll update on the MMJ website when they launch that version.

With these Vericorder packages you can:

- Film within the app or upload clips from your camera roll or elsewhere
- Rough-edit individual video clips
- Add them to a timeline, fine-edit and reorder them
- Add two additional audio tracks, allowing for voice-over and wild track
- Create smooth transitions between clips
- Adjust audio levels and introduce professional fades
- Publish to YouTube.

Get the quick-start guide

If you buy the app it's worth registering it and getting Vericorder to send you their Quick Start guide. You'll get a 22-page document which – bearing in mind this is a quick guide and by no means a comprehensive manual – gives you some idea of the time it'll take to become as familiar with 1st Video as you may be with whatever system you use for office-based video editing.

on the website

Find a comprehensive video-based guide to filming, editing and publishing with Vericorder's apps.

Editing video with Movie Maker and iMovies

on the website

Find comprehensive guides to both Movie Maker and iMovies.

5A14

Publishing online

So now you have your finished video report, ready to be published online. The video file you have edited is too large to put on the web. It has to be compressed first. At this stage, you don't need to worry about how that happens, because Blogger or YouTube, Facebook or any of the many other platforms that allow you to publish video, do it automatically.

As a general rule, they reduce the file size to 1MB per minute or less.

Your video needs to be hosted. Many media organisations host their video themselves, but many others use the biggest video website: YouTube. Once uploaded to YouTube, you can make your video available on your YouTube branded channel, via your social media accounts and embed it into your websites and blogs.

Uploading to YouTube

Click the upload button on your YouTube account, navigate to the relevant video and hit upload. YouTube hosts the video and gives you a link, and the code to enable you to embed it anywhere you like. Many publishing organisations use YouTube to do this, particularly if they are keen to have readers take videos that they like and embed them in other sites.

By no means all publishers embrace this viral element of the web, but many others see the vast potential in getting their name known for good video. They let anyone who likes it take it because the payback is that they become much better known and expect the videos copied to drive traffic back to them.

on the website

■ Find a video guide to uploading to YouTube, and guidance on writing a good headline, description and tags
■ See an alternative to YouTube: Vimeo, and what it can offer.

5A15

Exercises and projects

The exercises relate directly to material covered in this chapter.

The projects relate to the longer-term enterprises that you are recommended to develop as you work your way through this book.

Exercise 1

Watch online video reports. How well has the reporter tackled the essentials we have covered in this chapter?

Assess the framing of shots, the length and sequencing of shots. The variety of video material. How well is the story told? Does the voice-over work well? If the reporter does a piece-to-camera, how effectively has it been handled?

Exercise 2

Watch TV news. Analyse the make-up of their video packages. Are they more sophisticated than those you see online? If so, in what ways? Are there things you can learn from them that could be applied to your web video reports?

Exercise 3

Practise your interviewing. If you can get a friendly official, activist, press officer or other person to take part in a training session, practise on them. Tell them what you want to interview them about, and go through the recommended process. Carry out an initial interview to get the essential facts clear in your mind, then do a taped interview. Analyse your tapes to see how you have done.

Exercise 4

Take a number of reports from newspapers – up- and down-market – and read them out loud. How close are they to good video scripts? Rewrite them so that they work well when spoken.

still pictures and video

185

Exercise 5

Listen to a number of video news bulletins. Look at how the news readers present their script. How natural do they sound? What mistakes do they make? Now take a close look at a couple of TV news readers. Is their delivery different? Is it possible to identify things that they do better?

Exercise 6

Identify some news organisations that have channels on YouTube, and subscribe to them. Look at the videos they post.

Projects

These projects relate to the website and blog you are recommended to be working on as you go through this book. The stories you choose to cover must be tailored to the interests and concerns of the audiences you are catering for.

These projects can be developed as part of group work on a journalism course, or informally by groups of students, or by individuals.

1   Select a fast-moving story and do a series of live video broadcasts from your mobile device to your website or blog. It could be a major event such as a marathon, or a conference. Later, build the clips into a coherent text-plus news story along the lines of those discussed in this chapter.

2   Create two or more video packages for your website. Find a story, contact the individuals you need to help you tell it, set up interviews and go through the process from preparation and filming to editing and posting online. Get colleagues, tutors or friends to watch and critique them. Learn from your mistakes and try again. Do such reports regularly until your feedback tells you they are professional.

3   Attend an event – a sports game, a performance or anything else that you find newsworthy. Do a two-minute piece-to-camera. Get colleagues, tutors or friends to watch and critique it. Learn from your mistakes and try again. Do such reports regularly until your feedback tells you they are professional.

part B

Building proficiency

This section of *Multimedia Journalism* is about building on all you learned in Part A. We'll take you to the next stage across the media.

Aims of this section

Here you will develop the ability to:

- Live blog using the full range of media and social networks
- Curate stories and topics
- Conduct highly effective research
- Develop your interviewing skills
- Build proficiency with WordPress
- Improve your social and community journalism
- Create email bulletins and RSS feeds
- Use a DSLR camera to take high-quality stills
- Record, edit and publish audio-visual packages
- Produce video that approaches broadcast quality
- Produce video that puts you and the reader at the heart of the story
- Find stories within data and create visualisations that tell those stories effectively
- Build a personal brand, develop a specialism or become an entrepreneurial journalist.

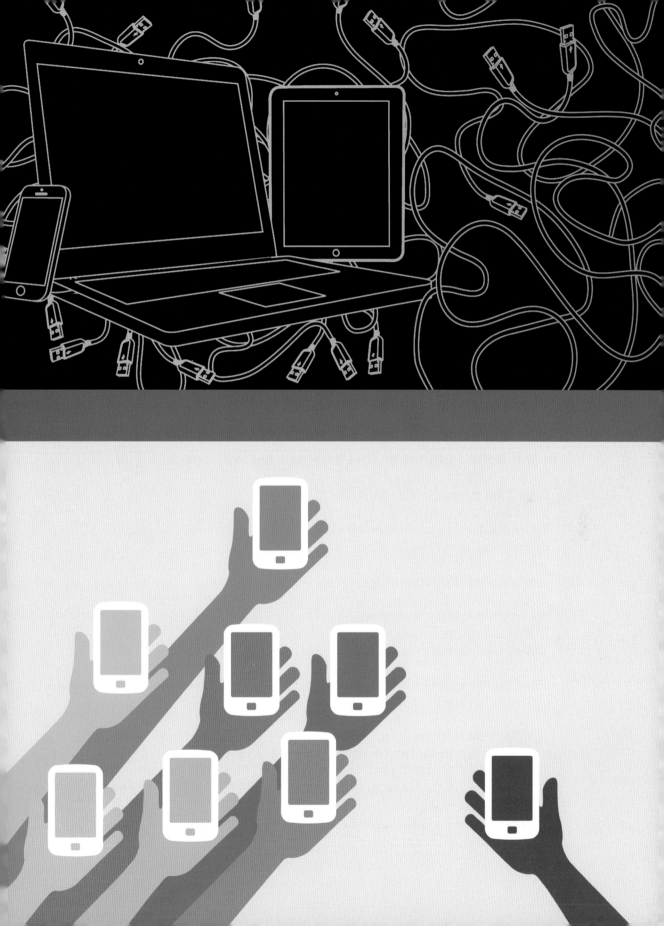

chapter six

Live blogging and curation

In the book version of this chapter we will cover:

- What live blogging is and how to do it
- The advantages and disadvantages of live blogging
- Live blogging as a reporting, editing and curatorial enterprise
- The sort of stories that lend themselves well to live blogging
- The different styles of live blog that are emerging
- How the BBC, the *Guardian*, and others do it
- Apps and software that will enable you to create a multimedia live blog
- Platforms on which to live blog
- The issues of balance, attribution and verification
- What curation is and how to do it.

At the end of the chapter are a range of assignments and projects to enable you to practise what you have learned.

In the online version of this chapter you will find:

- Step-by-step guides in how to use WordPress, CoveritLive, Storify and Spotify as live blogging platforms
- Links to all the resources covered in the book version
- A wealth of additional material.

Have the companion website to this book open at www.multimedia-journalism.co.uk. That way you can easily click on the links to the stories discussed here.

6B1

Introduction to live blogging

We looked at reporting live at various points in MMJ Part A, and saw how we could use mobile phones and tablets to report live using text, stills, audio and video on our websites, and on social media platforms.

We are going to build on that by looking at live blogging, which is a technique of live reporting whereby journalists cover a fast-moving and often very messy and confused event with a very regularly updated stream of latest snippets of information.

While live blogging certainly encompasses live reporting on the ground - filing text, stills and perhaps audio and video, where possible, from the location of a developing story - there are other aspects to it.

It can also be an editing or curatorial task. The content in a live blog may be drawn from a range of sources beyond the reporting ranks of a given publisher or broadcaster. It may be pulled together from eye-witnesses, or from other professional reporting sources.

Often the two come together - and you get one or more reporters out in the field, and one or more editors or curators putting a live blog together from their output, and that of others.

These live bloggers will be sifting a wide range of potentially curatable content from official sources, other media outlets, eye-witnesses and those using social media - Twitter, Facebook and the rest - to add their coverage and comment on a story.

Advantages of live blogging

questions

What do you think they might be? Don't read on until you have decided.

Here are some advantages of live blogging:

■ Live blogging is a useful way of telling stories characterised by incremental developments and multiple layers

- On fast-moving stories, reporters can post significant developments more quickly than through editing and re-editing a news article
- Live blogs allow us to link out to other coverage, include comments from Twitter and Facebook, display pictures, video, audio.

Disadvantages of live blogging

questions

What do you think they might be? Don't read on until you have decided.

Here are some of the disadvantages of live blogging:

- Muddle: with no inverted triangle to structure our reporting, a live blog can be hard to follow
- It can be hard to evaluate sources, corroborate their information
- On stories without a defined timescale, such as the Arab-Israeli conflict, live blogs can get long and confusing
- Live blogs sometimes merely provide readers with raw material rather than telling them a story
- Journalists tend to get swept up in the rush of events
- Journalists don't have time to think about what's happening and make connections, or write news analysis.

on the website

Read more about live blogging as transformational journalism.

6B2

Examples of live blogging

Live blogs are best on a major event. I've chosen the 100th anniversary of the outbreak of the First World War to show some contrasting examples of the format. War centenary commemorations will continue through to 2018, a century after the conflict ended, so you can look out for other examples.

As you run through these examples, think about the disadvantages of the live blog format which we listed earlier, and see how well the particular news organisation has overcome them.

The BBC

Broadcasters have an advantage when it comes to live blogging because they have access to plenty of live video. Media organisations with a background in print tend to struggle to get enough multimedia.

Formats change rapidly in this area but, at the time of writing, the BBC was tackling live events with three main themes:

- Key points
- Key video
- Live coverage.

Here are grabs from the three screens used on a live blog on the anniversary of the outbreak of the First World War:

Key points

The key points area brings context to the live blog, and helps balance the stream of latest – but sometimes trivial – events.

Key video

Another opportunity to bring context. Some videos were about events on the day, others were about events during the war, and provided a rich resource for those who wanted to understand what the conflict was all about.

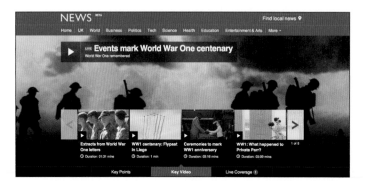

Live coverage

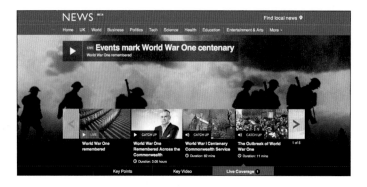

This live blog ran on a day of celebrations throughout Europe and beyond. With its enormous resources, the BBC was able to draw in a huge amount of eye-witness reporting, meaning that its live blog was updated every minute or two.

Updates were mainly in text format, but stills were frequent, and regular 'get involved' requests brought in many items from the public, including reminiscences and archive material.

Items are short, rarely longer than tweet-length.

The Guardian

Guardian live blogs differ from the BBC's in some key ways.

The *Guardian*'s live blogs have a bullet-point of context at the top, but there is no 'key video' area. Readers can choose whether to read the blog in chronological order, or reverse posts so the latest comes first.

The live blog is bylined with the main contributor, and his Twitter handle is given.

Posts are much longer than the BBC's – often giving context and running to 100-200 words or more. The live blogger is very much the voice of the blog, and often curates content from *Guardian* journalists and others. He quotes at length from articles by journalists on rival papers and press agencies, and links to them. Tweets, images and other social media posts are pulled in from both the famous and plain eye-witnesses around the world.

Posts come every five or ten minutes rather than every minute or two.

There are also summaries at key points, giving further context.

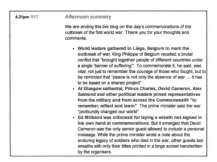

ABC Australia

The Australian broadcaster ABC is an example of a live blogging style halfway between those of the BBC and the *Guardian*.

It concentrates on one flow of material, as the *Guardian* does, but uses video in that time line, has films by correspondents giving context, and drops in news reports from reporters about contemporary aspects of the story:

In a side bar it offers items including: video of the First World War explained, a timeline, and little-known facts about the conflict.

on the website

Find more examples of live blogs in contrasting styles.

6B3

How to plan your live blog

Just because you'll be reporting live doesn't mean you can't plan your coverage. Most of the major events that make good topics for live blogging are flagged up in advance. Approach a live blog like any other coverage of a major story.

For example, if there is a major demonstration and violence is possible (the illustration here is from the *Guardian*'s live blog of a TUC [Trades Union Congress] anti-cuts demo in London, you can do a lot of research into the event - the people taking part, the locations they will use - so that you are as prepared as possible for what will happen.

Planning is particularly relevant if you are live blogging a conference or other event with a substantial itinerary.

So you need to research:

- Itinerary
- Participants
- Location
- Likely developments
- Background
- Is there a hashtag?

Not all events worthy of a live blog are predictable - nor can you always get to the location of the story.

If you are covering events far away - an earthquake, a war or other major story - you need to do a lot to familiarise yourself as much as possible with what you are covering.

And the social web offers us great opportunities for researching, and for identifying significant individuals and organisations that can provide us with vital information for our reporting.

Whether the event you are live blogging is on-diary (hence predictable) or off-diary (non-predictable), you need to find sources: official and unofficial, participants and eye-witnesses.

Pick a hashtag

If it's a well-organised event those behind it will pick and advertise the hashtag well before it. Nevertheless, most big events end up with more than one hashtag. The UK Treasury tends to use this format at Budget time: #budget15, but a large number of tweeters use #budget2015. You should use the one that a search on Twitter shows is the more popular, but don't be afraid to change it if usage shifts.

If there is no hashtag, create one of your own, and promote it.

Find sources

Everything we discussed in Chapter 1 applies here. You need to receive information from official sources, to work out who is participating, and who is covering the event, and lock on to whatever social media they will be using during it.

Official sources

It may be organisers, governments, charities, aid organisations. Identify and follow whatever publishing processes they are using.

Participants

You need to find out where they will be publishing their comments, analysis, eye-witness reports or whatever content is appropriate to the event you are covering.

Some will have websites, some blogs, others (particularly those who fall into the category of eye-witness, or simply individuals caught up in the flow of events), will be using social media. That means you need to search for them on Twitter, Facebook and any other relevant social network. They may be using live streaming video services such as Bambuser or UStream.

Those covering the event

It's very common in live blogging for journalists from one organisation to draw material from rivals in to their live blog. It's possible, even in the dog-eat-dog world of journalism, for you to co-operate with other reporters to create complementary material that you share.

Here are some ideas for beginning to identify those who will become your valuable sources.

Blastfollow

Blastfollow (**http://brianmcarey.com/blastfollow/**), an application created by Brian M. Carey, enables you to follow everyone using a particular hashtag with one click. Carey says: "This application will allow you to search for Twitter users based on a keyword. It will then return the number of users who have tweeted that keyword recently. You will have the option to follow all of those users en masse, which is a really efficient way to follow people who share your interests on Twitter."

Read more about it here: **http://brianmcarey.com/about-blastfollow/**

Let's take a look at the 26 March event discussed above. With #26march (the official TUC march hashtag) 343 followers were identified. You'd need to find other appropriate hashtags, including that for one of the more radical participants in the event, UKuncut. #ukuncut throws up 318 people using the hashtag. You'd also need to tap into those policing and stewarding the event, and any potential breakaway or disruptive elements.

Use Twitter lists

Once you have identified reliable sources, you can add them to private Twitter lists. Scanning the tweets from that list, using, for example, Hootsuite as we did in Chapter 3, will enable you to curate eyewitness accounts.

There is a limit to what you can do in advance, but it will make live coverage much easier if you can identify useful tweeters in advance and make sure you are following them.

on the website

Find further guidance on planning your live blog.

6B4

Reporting live on the ground

You might not be able to get reporters on the ground. We'll cover that scenario in the next module. For now, let's look at when you can do the reporting yourself.

We'll be using the apps we have covered in Part A of *Multimedia Journalism* for live reporting using, text, video etc. If you need to refresh your memory of what they are and how to use them, refer back to the relevant section.

Text

The hardest thing to file from a smartphone is text. It's actually much quicker to take stills, shoot brief video clips or audio soundbites.

Even if you are using a tablet computer, or have a keypad attached to your phone, you'll probably want to keep your text pretty much at tweet length. That's great for quick updates on a fast-moving story, poor for context, depth and analysis. That's why if you can twin your on-the-spot reporting with a live blogger at a desk, things will work so much better.

And if the big picture is being collated by others, that leaves you free to bring individuality and personality to the bits of live coverage you add. Check out a live blog from the publishers/broadcasters we looked at earlier and you'll see plenty of updates that focus on an individual or a small detail of the event. You are an eye-witness, so it's what your eye sees that will bring colour to your live blog.

If you were reporting in this situation for the BBC, you could well be using their Portable Newsgathering (PNG) app that delivers your multimedia content straight to the newsroom, where editors or producers would process it. If the media organisation has such a system, or if you are able to use the Voddio app we discussed in Chapter 5, you can do the same.

Stills

Good stills need good subject matter. If you are live blogging a conference, those opportunities may be few and far between, but at least pictures of speakers and other key participants give those following your coverage something more than just text.

If you are covering a demo, and if things turn violent, stills become really important. The pictures you shoot on your GPS-enabled device will be geotagged and time-stamped, so you have a record of exactly where and when they were taken. That helps establish you as a reliable source. If, for example, there is debate about whether a group of protesters or the police became violent first, your images are part of the evidence as to where the truth lies.

Audio

audioBoom or UStream are among the apps that offer the easiest ways to broadcast snippets of audio from an event – unless you have access to a news-gathering app. One difference is that with audioBoom you record and then post, but can add a picture and caption, and your content will be presented to listeners as a neat package, complete with your location on a map. Some apps, including UStream, let you broadcast live audio.

You really need an external mic, so you can improve quality, and avoid the wind noise that bedevils recordings made on the internal mic on your phone. Refer back to Chapter 4 for more on this.

Video

If things are moving fast, then you'll need to grab short, say 30-second, clips of dramatic action and stream it live, or as near to live as you can. Bambuser and UStream both let you do that. Refer back to Chapter 5 for all the detail.

For really short, sharp video clips, you could use Vine (**https://vine.co/**), Twitter's 6-second video clip publisher, or another micro-video app.

If you have the time to fully edit video on your device, you can use Vericorder 1st Video. If there's only time to partially edit – trim clips and change their order, for example – you can choose from a range of free apps, including YouTube Capture, or the paid-for app version of iMovies.

But you can only consider editing video if there is time.

One of the problems with live streaming video from an event is that your ability to broadcast live is only as good as the signal on your phone. And if you lose your connection your video is delayed. But one video app has a solution to that.

Why Bambuser may be best for reporting live

Bambuser scales the quality of its broadcast to the strength of the connection. As reported here:[1] On fast connections it pushes out high-quality video, but on weaker connections it drops the number of frames it sends per second, but maintains continuous broadcasting.

It can spot key frames, ones which are substantially different to those before it, and judges them to be important, as they probably indicate the start of a new shot. Key frames get broadcast in preference to others.

When you have finished your live broadcast, the app will replenish the frames it stripped out of the first broadcast so that a full-quality video will be available for replay after the event.

Interaction is built in

People watching your live broadcast can comment on what they're seeing through the embedded Bambuser video viewer, and you can respond. If you are interviewing, they could send questions they'd like you to ask.

Curating other content while on location

If you are live reporting from a fast-moving event, you are unlikely to have time to break off from your own reporting to bring in material from others.

At a conference or another, more structured reporting occasion, you may be able to, but I've kept all curatorial ideas to the next module, on live blogging from your desk, as that is the place, and the role, where curation is much easier. But, if you have the time, then a lot of what is contained there will be relevant to you when out and about.

on the website

Find links to all the apps discussed here, plus additional resources.

6B5

Live blogging from your desk

If you are in the live blogging role away from events, then your skills as a curator will be vital to the success of your live blog.

You may be in the position of being able to blend material from your own reporting resource on the ground and other news sources – both professional and citizen or eye-witness.

If you've done your preparation, then you should have some good sources to refer to right at the start of your live blog. With the right Twitter lists and other social monitoring devices in place, you are well set up. Those lists are probably best viewed in one of the social media dashboard tools such as Hootsuite or Tweetdeck (covered in Chapter 3). With those, the lists you have created on Twitter, and, if relevant, Facebook and other social platforms, can be brought together so you can easily monitor and compare the streams of information you are receiving.

Monitor that dashboard to keep an eye on incoming tweets, and set up columns for official and other hashtags and searches that are relevant to the live story.

Live search: for when you can't plan ahead

If you need to live blog immediately about unforeseen events, you need to carry out some effective and targeted searches to make up for the fact that you don't have any existing sources lists to draw on.

That goes for when you need to find eye-witnesses to something unforeseen that has just happened. Using the Twitter live search facility at **http://search.twitter.com/** lets you see what's being said on a given topic right now, and you can set up your dashboard to identify sources on Facebook and elsewhere. See also the module on advanced search techniques in Chapter 16.

Live blog publishing platforms

For your live blog to have coherence, you need a place where people can follow it. The BBC, *Guardian* and so on have dedicated areas, usually with some sort of 'Live' label on them.

If you are lucky enough to have access to a CMS with suitable live blogging functionality already built into it, that's great. If you don't, we'll look at how to set up live blogging on your WordPress website, and also at some dedicated live blogging platforms that you can embed into your site.

How to broadcast live to your website

We'll introduce two options here, in the book version of MMJ, and keep detailed, step-by-step tuition on how to use the software described for the online version of this module. That way, any updates or changes to the way things are done can be instantly added to the text.

Two easy ways to broadcast live to your website or blog are:

- To activate the live blog facility on your WordPress site
- To use a platform such as CoverItLive, which enables you to embed a player wherever you like, and have the multimedia elements of your live blog appear in it.

You can send material to your WordPress live blog via the app on phone or tablet, or via email.

CoverItLive is a free live blogging platform that you can embed into any blog or website simply by copying and pasting a bit of code they give you. You can also publish to it from the CoverItLive smartphone app. It is a perfect platform for a live blogger to curate content from a range of sources, including reporters in the field.

It can take stills, audio and video as well as text, and it has an inbuilt comment facility so you can interact with readers.

on the website

- Find detailed tuition in broadcasting a live blog to your WordPress site
- Get full guidance in using the CoverItLive live blogging platform
- See further live blogging platforms.

6B7

Issues of balance, attribution and verification

When we live blog we are exposed to all kinds of dangers. With the pressure to publish fast, we may be tempted to put our concerns about balance, attribution and verification aside.

We can't afford to do that. Each is just as vital when live blogging as it is when conducting any other form of journalism. It's not always possible to verify when live blogging, but if we can't verify we must clarify. We need to say who is saying something has happened or will happen.

If we are getting unconfirmed reports about events, we need to make that clear.

There are those who see live blogging as the enemy of professional journalistic standards. Live bloggers need to be aware of the pitfalls, and to do all they can to guard against them. Because if your live blog is any less than professional, it's pretty much worthless.

on the website

The NYT's live blogger, Robert Mackey, talks about how he approaches issues of verification.

Robert Hernandez, Web Journalism professor at USC Annenberg, blogged in the *Online Journalism Review*[2] about a dramatic situation in which he used social media to find eye-witnesses. The post also reveals how social media can help you verify the facts in a story.

He talked about the occasion when a gunman entered the Discovery Channel's headquarters, taking several people hostage.

Immediately, he writes, the real-time web began to throw up first-hand witnesses.

Hernandez was in his office, elsewhere in the country, when the news broke.

He tweeted these two tips:

He writes: "Searching Twitter, I was able to find people sending updates from the Discovery Channel's zip code (Here are some highlights that I found). Using FourSquare, I was able to find someone who had "checked in" to the building before the incident.

"Possible witnesses, potential sources."

The power of the real-time Web was in full swing, he writes, but the dangers of the web were also becoming evident. Some were posting incorrect information, albeit with the best of intentions.

One false post was of a picture of someone the poster believed to be the gunman.

Look at these next two tweets. The first says the gunman has been identified. The second is from the person pictured, saying they are not the gunman.

Robert Hernandez makes the point that, in the real-time web, speed is highly valued. However, that is outweighed by the need for publishing responsibly, with credible information. Journalists must become known for getting it right first, not for getting it first but wrong.

This, he says, is where being a professional matters. He included in his blog post the photo that @techsavvymama retweeted, along with an explanation from a former Discovery Channel employee as to why the person in the photo is probably not the gunman.

@yankeetrini
@ezstreet if that was the gunman he would have needed a badge to get in the building that pic is of the side botanical gardens
Wed Sep 1 11:39:33 2010 via twidroid in reply to ezstreet

As you live blog, and are monitoring sources, you will sometimes come across material that you know to be false. In the spirit of keeping things factual and balanced you should refute it. To be portentous about it, live blogging is about writing the first draft of history. Sure, that first draft will need to be amended as events become clearer, but we should do what we can to help get things right from the outset.

The best way of doing that is to keep things factual. Keep opinion out of your reporting, and label any comment as such.

6B8

Curation

Curation is a new word for doing something that old-school journalists might call copy tasting.

On a traditional national newspaper, or a broadcaster's newsdesk you'll find a copytaster who sifts through the incoming reports from news agencies – Thomson Reuters, AP, PA, Agence France Presse and the rest – rejecting some, selecting others and pushing the most promising ones towards reporters, or the relevant specialists, for their assessment and follow-up.

So some of those wire stories are developed, expanded and taken to a new level. Other, less promising ones, are printed straight, with or without reference to the source.

In the new world of journalism, the sources for stories have multiplied, and become available to all.

Eyewitnesses, industry experts and citizen journalists all have the ability to publish their material direct to the public if they wish. There is a far greater wealth of information being disseminated, on a wide range of open publishing platforms.

If we are talking about eyewitness accounts, Twitter probably comes first to mind. There's also a lot of material filed to Facebook, video to YouTube and other platforms.

If there is a really big story – such as wars and revolutions in a range of Middle Eastern countries or the Japanese earthquake, tsumani and nuclear meltdown of 2011 – then the resources of profession journalists and broadcasters/publishers are completely inadequate to the task of reporting the situation in full.

It's down to eyewitnesses – or citizen journalists – to provide the vast majority of first-person material for the many reports that will be crafted about these events.

OK, there will be a few hard-news honchos striding in their flack jackets or anti-radiation suits through a scene of conflict or devastation, but what they can tell us is often actually pretty superficial.

Given that many big events can't be covered adequately by professional journalists, what do we need to do? We need to look to social media, and the vast amount of eyewitness material and informed comment they hold.

The problem with all this eyewitness stuff is that it is unverified, sometimes unreliable, sometimes inaccurate. What it lacks is the eye of a professional journalist, who can sift, evaluate and seek to corroborate the material that is presented.

That's the process an old-school copy taster sets in train. And it's the same process we embark upon when we try to take these raw sources of information, compare them, and seek patterns in information that reveal a truth.

That process describes what curatorial journalism is. But it doesn't just relate to really big stories.

Because everyone with a smartphone has the capacity to file multimedia reports, many people can contribute to the raw source-material for a story.

Curatorial journalism is about bringing an objective journalistic eye to all that raw data, sifting it, and presenting the best of it to a wider audience.

And it doesn't just apply to fast-unfolding events of world-wide significance.

In another journalistic field, that of comment and analysis on an industry, there will be many commentators, some who describe themselves as journalists, others who are key members of that industry, some with less elevated roles but still with potentially illuminating insights.

Curating an industry, an issue, a hobby or pastime is also a valuable and rewarding journalistic enterprise.

So the old-school skill of copy tasting can be reinvented in the modern world as one in which many news sources – both official and unofficial, eyewitness, citizen journalist and/or experts – can be scanned, appraised and either added to the report or rejected.

Potentially, anyone could do this, so what will make our curations worth reading?

It comes down to a fundamental journalistic skill – the ability to present information in the most dramatic and engaging way. Have we curated, selected and packaged source-material in such a way that people want to read it? If so, we have created successful journalism. If not, we've failed.

We may at times be unsure of the reliability of our sources, but we can at least identify what those sources are. That way, the reader can decide whether to trust them.

There are a range of platforms that promise the opportunity to curate successfully. Which platform is most appropriate for you depends in part on the sort of curation you want to practice, and how much work you want to put in.

How does curation differ from live blogging?

If live blogging is the first draft of history, curation is the second. While live blogs are essentially immediate and disorganised, curation aims to make more sense of things: to put things in context. I suppose it's really an extension of live blogging. Some curation is pretty close to live blogging, some is a substantial step forward from it.

on the website

Want to know more about the reasons for curating? Read a great Mashable article on why curation is important to the future of journalism.

Decide what you want to curate

There are all sorts of curation you can practise. So you need to decide what you want to curate:

- One big story
- An ongoing issue
- An industry
- A pastime
- A sport.

We have looked at live blogging one big story. Curating one big story would involve following it over a longer period than just a day or week.

You need a coherent area for your curation. If the content you gather doesn't hold together, your curation won't be valuable for others who are interested in a particular story, issue, industry, pastime or sport.

You also need to think about what you are going to curate for another reason: because some platforms are designed for single story curation, others for long-term coverage. Storify, for example, is good for gathering and publishing quickly on a particular story. Scoop.it is set up to facilitate very regular curation of an issue, industry or other content topic. More on which platform to use in a moment.

Do you want to work alone or in a group?

Solo curation has the advantage of coherence, but it may suffer in that your view is partisan and partial. That might or might not be a problem. Editing is not a democratic process. A strong, focused editor can create a great, coherent publication, and a great solo curator can do the same.

But group curation can work well if a subject is huge, fast-moving and complex. Wikipedia is a great example of this.

How much work do you want to do?

You also need to decide how much work you want to do on your curation.

Because there is a sliding scale of involvement from you. Here are the broad levels of involvement you could choose:

Automatic curation platforms

The easiest way to curate is to do nothing. There are various platforms that collect and publish content from, for example, your Twitter feed – followers and followed – and publish it as a daily digest of the most popular items. Paper.li does that, for example. Here's mine:

On such platforms, curation is a by-product of your social engagement. Just by having a (hopefully good) range of people you follow and who follow you, by being involved in a good conversation online, you are curating well.

If you follow a range of Paper.li accounts you'll see that some work better than others. If an individual or organisation has a thin range of contacts on Twitter, the content of their Paper.li will be equally poor and thin. If they have a good range of contacts, it'll be rich and vibrant. And if their range of followers and followed represents key people in an industry, or around a particular topic or range of topics, their Paper.li will be a really valuable curated information source.

Curating a story with Storify

Storify (**www.storify.com**) is good for curating a particular story. As the platform develops it is being made easier, also, for live blogging, and you could certainly use it for that. But we'll look at it here in relation to curation.

Note: we'll keep detailed tuition in using Storify for the MMJ website.

You pick your sources, post them, design the page. You can curate as many or as few stories as you like, and pick any subject at any point, depending on what is in the news and what interests you.

Storify allows users to aggregate Twitter messages, Facebook updates, online video and more into an aggregated chronology that contains links to the source material. This makes collecting and displaying web content in a timeline format incredibly easy. It can be used for a mix of live blogging and curation. You can embed your story wherever you like, using the code that Storify generates for you.

Storify says this about what it is doing: "We are building the story layer above social networks, to amplify the voices that matter and create a new media format that is interactive, dynamic and social".

You can follow various publishers and broadcasters on Storify, including:

- The *Guardian*: **http://storify.com/guardian**
- *Washington Post*: **http://storify.com/washingtonpost/**
- CBC News: **http://storify.com/cbccommunity/**

on the website

Find a step-by-step guide to curating on Storify.

Curating a subject with Scoop.it

Scoop.it is good for creating a subject – you set up the area you want to curate and, if no one else has grabbed it, name it and set the sources. You go manually through content from the sources you have set and select the items you want to publish.

Scoop.it is best for sustained curation of a given topic, rather than for building a one-off story.

Here's their video introduction to curating with their platform:

I curate two topics on Scoop.it: Multimedia journalism and Brand Journalism. Here's a grab of my Multimedia Journalism curation:

You curate your topic by drawing on a wide range of social media, RSS feeds and web sites. You select the media you want Scoop.it to search, and the keywords it should search for in those media. Then Scoop.it feeds the items it finds, fitting your keywords, into your curation panel, and you either reject or accept them. The curation panel slides in from the right, like this:

Accepted items are added to the top of the published page. I have the Scoop.it app on my smartphone and tablet, so can curate very easily, wherever I am, whenever I have a few free minutes.

The key is to have the right sources set up. This takes a while to get right. I have a couple of hundred, here's a grab of just a few of them:

Scoop.it offers tips to assist you in your curation. Here are a couple of the best ones:

Keywords: Scoop.it uses them to help it suggest relevant sources to you. Keep your keywords specific and relevant to your subject matter.

Source selection: it is better to have a few highly relevant sources, rather than many marginal ones, which will throw up suggestions that are not particularly relevant.

You can also add your own sources, a Twitter list, a blog or an RSS feed, and get that content presented together with the keyword-identified content Scoop.it offers you for curation.

There is also a Scoop.it bookmarklet, which you drag to your tool bar and can click on whenever you are reading something you want to curate.

There's also a social side: others can offer you items to curate, which you can either accept or reject.

on the website

Find a series of video guides to every aspect of curating with Scoop.it

6B9

Exercises and projects

Exercise 1

Look out for a major story on which a number of news organisations choose to live blog. Monitor what they do, and compare their effectiveness. How often do they post? How good is their range of sources? Do they include valuable contributions from non-journalists and eyewitnesses? How do they ensure the context of the story is explained?

Exercise 2

Look at how one or more news organisations use live video. What apps do they use?

Exercise 3

Monitor the use of software including Bambuser, audioBoom, CoverItLive. Try to identify journalists who are using it well and analyse how they do that.

Exercise 4

Monitor the use of Storify and Scoop.it by journalists. Try to identify journalists who are using it well and analyse how they do that.

Projects

1   Select what you consider the most useful apps and pieces of software discussed in this chapter. Gather the means to broadcast and publish multimedia content to a live blog. You can use either a live blogging post area on your WordPress site, CoverItLive or any other app you have discovered.

2   Pick a subject on which to live blog. It could be an event in the area you cover or the beat you follow. A sports match would work well.

    If you can, work as part of a team. Assign an editor, reporters who will go into the field, and one or more curators or editors who will pull things together.

Research and plan your live blog thoroughly, and prepare as much material as you can in advance. Make your live blog multimedia - include video, audio and stills as well as text.

3 Curate a story using Storify.

4 Curate a topic using Scoop.it. Pick something that relates to your chosen journalistic beat or specialism. Make this a long-term project. Curate daily, or as often as the subject requires. Monitor how your following builds on the platform.

Notes

1 www.shinyshiny.tv/2011/03/bambuser_the_live_video_streaming_app.html
2 www.ojr.org/

chapter seven

Developing your abilities as a reporter and interviewer

In the book version of this chapter we will cover:

- The life cycle of a story and how to report on it at every point
- The difference between live news and scheduled editions or bulletins
- The value of in-depth reporting

Tackling challenging reporting assignments including:

- Reporting from press conferences
- Covering public meetings
- Reporting on public events
- Court reporting
- Difficult interviews and how to handle them.

At the end of the chapter are a range of assignments and projects to enable you to practise what you have learned.

In the online version of this chapter you will find:

- A wide range of examples to illustrate the tuition here on challenging reporting assignments
- A wide range of videos illustrating the material covered here
- A wealth of links to further information.

Have the companion website to this book open at www.multimedia-journalism.co.uk. That way you can easily click on the links to the stories discussed here.

Live news vs the edition, rolling news vs the scheduled bulletin

In this chapter we are looking in detail at how online and print work together, and how rolling news and news bulletins relate.

When deadlines were relatively few and far between, news had usually reached a fairly complete form before it was published or broadcast. News was formal and polished before the public read, listened to or watched it.

With online multimedia journalism that's all changed. Now there are as many opportunities to update a story as the story demands.

If we have a fast-moving story it can be changing and morphing as the minutes, hours, days and weeks pass.

This means that news stories are often in a state of constant evolution. Where once we could think of stories as having a particular angle or development for a particular day, now we find that they have many twists and turns during that day.

Because online is a news medium without deadlines or edition times, where most things can be published more or less instantly, most newspapers and magazines have an online-first policy for most content. This means there is no longer such a thing as the weekly newspaper journalist, the monthly or weekly magazine journalist, or even the daily newspaper journalist. And if you are in broadcasting, you no longer work solely towards a particular bulletin - the breakfast, lunchtime, 6pm, 9pm or 10pm news.

Today, almost all journalists must react immediately and craft their material first for online, after which it is adapted for print or a scheduled broadcast, sometimes by the reporter, sometimes by sub editors or online production staff, depending on the setup.

As multimedia journalists, we can publish before, during and after an event, using the medium - or combination of media - that are appropriate at each point in the lifecycle of any given story.

So, we can:

- tell them it's going to happen
- tell them it's happening, and
- tell them it's happened.

And, because reporting is a conversation, we can get our audience's feedback at every point along the way. If we listen to that feedback we often find that it shapes how our reporting develops. But more on that as we go.

Let's take those three points in the lifecycle of a story, and think about what we can do and when.

When we know it's going to happen

We can preview events. Tell the audience what is going to happen, and when, and what the likely outcome will be. Of course, some of this will be speculative. Our audience will have views on how things are likely to turn out.

You hear such previewing a good deal on some breakfast radio and TV shows. They see their early-morning role as what they like to call 'setting the agenda'. So, if the government is to make an important announcement during the day, they will focus on what the substance of the announcement is likely to be. They will have experts and both in-house and external commentators chewing over what they expect to happen.

You get stories that begin:

"Figures to be released later today are expected to show. . ."

Or

"A further slump in retail sales is expected to be revealed this morning when. . ."

Many media-savvy organisations are aware of this and co-operate with it. For example:

■ Government ministers will talk about why they are going to announce a new policy, even if they won't go into too many details on the substance of that new policy
■ Organisations that have a report published later that day will give a preview of its findings
■ A prominent person who is to make an important speech will release the text in advance.

Such previewing is an important function of multimedia journalism. It's all part of the conversation we are having with our audience. The sort of news coverage in which we only reported on something when it had happened is part of the old attitude to news; the 'here is the news' approach that is no longer appropriate.

As multimedia journalists we have great opportunities for previewing events. We can offer:

■ preview pieces in print and online
■ tips, steers and gossip in our beat blogs, and on social media

■ audio and video packages that set the scene by featuring those likely to be affected by, or with something to say about, the story that will break later.

In all of the above we can offer the facts as we know them, a range of comment and opinion, and invite our audience to comment on what is to happen, and take part in polls and other interaction.

We can appeal for those affected by the developing story to get in touch – many valuable case studies are sourced in this way. And we can plan our live coverage, as we did when we set out a strategy for live blogging in the previous chapter.

While it's happening

Once, only TV and radio journalists could go live to an event as it happened. Now any multi-media journalist can, using the tools we examined throughout Part A and brought together in Chapter 6 on live blogging. While a story is breaking, our role is clear: first and foremost we must deliver the actuality, and the facts, as quickly and directly as we can. But almost the instant it becomes clear that something has happened, then the how and why it has happened, and most importantly the 'what this means to you', must also be tackled. That involves opinion, comment and analysis.

We can cover events as they happen with:

■ a live blog to our website
■ social media updates
■ expert comment and analysis.

Once it's happened

Once an event is over, analysis, meaning and context are needed in our reporting.

questions

Think back to Chapter 1 and the quiz we did on which medium is best for a range of stories. Can you remember what we said was best for understanding complex facts and for remembering them? Don't read on until you have thought.

Text is best for complex, fact-packed analysis and for grasping the meaning of detailed information. Many publishers use this as the foundation of the distinction between the online and print versions of their publications. They use online for breaking news and the newspaper or magazine for analysis.

If you read a newspaper on a tablet app, for example, you will generally be able to choose between reading the edition (usually that morning's newspaper in electronic form), or live news. Some of that live news will probably come from staff on that title, but much of it will be from news agencies. It's that wire feed which used to be the private news-source for editors, but which is now made available to all.

This division between live news and edition news (or, on TV, rolling news versus a particular bulletin) makes sense because, if we have done our jobs properly, people often know what the news is when they pick up our print publication, read our app or watch our 9pm news bulletin. So if we give them it again we have to go far beyond the facts or they will stop reading or watching us. A former editor of the (London) *Independent* described his paper as a viewspaper rather than a newspaper. If that's true for a daily publication, it's even truer of a weekly magazine, let alone a monthly.

But online also has a key function here. It is a good place for grouping a range of stories about a particular subject. We can create a special area of the site where we offer an essential rundown of a topic – an election, a financial crisis or a major event such as the Olympics. If we organise it properly, readers can quickly find the detailed information they need. Such areas are often called special reports.

So, after the event we can publish:

- Analysis and comment in our print publication, or on our website
- The result of invitations to readers to comment, discuss or vote on the story
- Reflection, feedback and analysis of the outcome of the story on our beat blogs
- Discussions with experts via video or audio podcasts
- A special area online where extensive coverage of a long-running event is grouped together.

We can also point readers to a digest of our own and other people's news and comment through email bulletins.

Having so many opportunities to report can seem daunting. It can make us wonder when on earth we will get the time to do it all. One key to being able to achieve all of the above is to make our reporting a by-product of our research and of our news-gathering. Because, with multimedia journalism, the process through which we do our jobs – the things we read, the people we speak to, and the events we attend to ensure we are fully briefed, can be reported on along the way to the finished story. We aren't just gathering material to use later, when all is done and dusted. As is hopefully crystal clear by now, we are publishing at numerous points during the life cycle of a story.

Finally, a word about aggregators. Aggregators include search engines, which link to rather than create journalism. News is expensive to produce and the fact that it can be accessed without payment is a situation that has brought severe disruption to journalism – in particular to the print media. One response to that is paywalling – where publications such as the

FT, New York Times, Wall Street Journal and *The* (London) *Times* protect some or all of their content behind a paywall.

Many consumers of news take it from free sources. One key challenge for the modern journalist is to produce news that people are prepared to pay for. News that people will pay for needs to be perceived as valuable by the reader. Specialist, highly informed reporting falls into that category, and we look at how you can develop a specialism in Chapter 14. Some of the reasons people will pay for news and other information are:

- It helps them make, save, or avoid losing money
- It helps them do their jobs better
- It gives them an advantage over others
- It feeds a passion for a given topic.

Why the edition and the scheduled bulletin are still vital to our journalism

Bull QUOTE →

I want to stress that we should not allow our excitement at being able to report live, and update whenever necessary, to blind us to the continued importance of the edition and to scheduled news bulletins.

Long → QUOTE

Pat Long, head of news development at *The* (London) *Times* and *Sunday Times*, put the position succinctly here when he said: "In a world where news is freer than water on the web, and plays out in real time on social media platforms. . . prizing speed over depth is both a waste of readers' time and damaging to each newspaper's reputation as a whole."[1]

Long says that newspaper brands are defined by these characteristics:

- Quality of reporting
- Incisiveness of opinions expressed
- Expertise of journalists in providing context and analysis
- Wit of columnists
- Stridency of political views
- Value of campaigning.

The qualities on this list, Pat Long goes on, are often dispensed with when a publication races to break stories that are already becoming public in any case.

Long Paraphrased →

He believes that too much time is spent rewriting or reposting material that is on the wires. Competitors are all doing the same. No one wants to hold off publishing until they have fresh information of their own, or a unique angle on the story, so they end up publishing material that has very little value.

That's not to say we should never publish a story to which we have little to add. If it's big enough we must cover it. Long gives as an example the *Boston Globe*'s coverage of the 2013 marathon bombings. But, he goes on, we should not publish on a story just because we can. That is to confuse editorial strategy with platform capability.

We should follow our editorial strategy, pause before publishing and remember our strengths and core values. That, in an authoritative news organisation, means we should focus on strengthening readers' understanding of an event. We should use journalistic rigour and our expertise to publish in-depth, and not worry so much about trying to compete with Twitter.

It's arguable that the same should go for TV news bulletins, although - as we've seen - traditional broadcasters are often in a better position to create live content.

In short: go live when there is a good journalistic reason to - not just because you can.

on the website

Find a range of videos and other material that will enable you to look in greater depth at reporting online, in print, live and for mobile audiences.

7B2

Challenging reporting assignments

In Chapter 1 we looked at a number of typical basic reporting assignments and how to handle them. Here are some more challenging scenarios, related to multimedia and full story cycle reporting:

- Report at press conferences, product launches and police appeals
- Attend public meetings including those of local authorities
- Report on public events
- Report on court cases.

Report at press conferences

Beforehand – research

You must go to a press conference well briefed. Conferences are usually announced with a press release, and you may be sent documents, pictures and other material. You'll be told who

will be present, what access you will have to them, and arrangements for photography. Read through it all, and do a search in your archives for what you have written about the subject, and more generally to ensure you know what is going on.

Plan your questions.

Beforehand – reporting

If the press conference is to focus on an important issue - such as a major building develop-ment, or a company's plans for expansion - you can report on that right away. If you know the conference is to announce a decision that matters to readers, then tell them this in advance. You may be able to get a steer on what the announcement is likely to say.

It might be worth a poll on the website. Readers may want to express their concerns about what the outcome is likely to be. They may wish to express their opinions, or give their insights into what they feel is likely to happen.

If this has been a running story, you can link to key pieces about it on the website.

At the event

Is it highly newsworthy? Is it worth a live blog? Is it worth streaming live video from? Or can you cover it more effectively live via tweets and other social media updates?

Take stills, make video clips and record audio. Put the best of them live as soon as you can.

Can you get a quick one-to-one interview on video of the key person at the conference?

In all of this, never forget the vital importance of taking notes. Whether you do that on a keyboard or in a notebook, your written record is central to what you do.

Press conferences can range from glum events where you are one of only two or three report-ers present and where nothing newsworthy is being said, to huge scrums where it is very hard to make your voice heard. Of course, you can report anything that is said.

Just remember, the press conference is not news in itself, it's what is said there that your report should focus on.

The format is likely to involve an opening statement, and may include a video demonstration. Those holding the conference will be setting out their case in the most positive and persua-sive light that they can.

Then they will open up for questions. If it's a well-organised conference you put your hand up and wait to be called to ask your question. When asked, you stand up, say who you are and the news organisation you are from. You will probably get the chance for a supplementary question, but if you try to ask more than two, other reporters and the organiser are likely to get fed up with you.

Concentrate while previous answers have been given – don't waste your chance by being told: "I've already answered that."

You need a clear 'what's new' angle and some good verbatim quotes. If the issue covered is contentious you'll want to put the opposing view to the speaker – you need to pose the question that those opponents would express if they were there.

If you realise during the conference that there is something that is not being said which is hugely material to the story, you may be onto an exclusive angle. Reporters in this situation need to decide whether to ask the question and let everyone have the angle, or to keep quiet in the hope they can grab the speaker one-to-one immediately afterwards and keep their angle to themselves.

After the event – reporting

If the event is newsworthy you will want to follow up your live coverage with a full story online as soon as you can.

There may be additional reporting to be done. If the issue is contentious, you need the views of opponents. You will want to look at the implications of the announcement.

Perhaps a major piece is planned for print. If so, flag that up online. Once the breaking news for the web is sorted you can concentrate on additional reporting, updating online as required, and a considered piece for print.

The legal position

We are only covering law where it relates directly to the reporting situations we are exploring. You'll need to consult a media law textbook relevant to the legal system in the country where you do your reporting for the full chapter-and-verse on things. What I do say about law here refers specifically to the UK.

All sorts of contentious things might be said at a press conference. Things which, if said away from that conference, might be defamatory of a certain individual or group, and which could potentially land us in legal trouble. Defamation is the umbrella term for slander and libel.

Slander is publication in a transient form – speech; libel is in a permanent form.

Believe it or not, there is no one clear definition of defamation, but we can think of it as material which is calculated to injure the reputation of another by exposing him [or her] to hatred, contempt or ridicule.

It might also be a statement which is likely to diminish the subject in the eyes of right-thinking people.

Defamatory material is that which:

- is to a person's discredit
- tends to lower them in the estimation of others
- causes them to be shunned or avoided; or which
- causes them to be exposed to hatred, ridicule or contempt.

If someone says that a person is a conman, and we report it, then that is defamatory. Let's put to one side for a moment whether it is true. If they sue us, and we defend the statement, we'll have to prove it was true. However, if someone is called a conman in a press conference and we report it, we have a defence under the 1996 Defamation Act.

The act actually applies to public meetings, which we cover below, but also covers press conferences if they fit the legal definition of a public meeting. They fit that definition of a public meeting if the press conference is bona fide, lawfully held, for the furtherance or discussion of a matter of public concern.

If it is, then you are covered by what is known as qualified privilege. Which means that a fair and accurate report of such proceedings should be safe if published without malice and subject, on request, to a reasonable right of reply.

So you need to determine whether the matters you report on are of public concern. Not merely of interest to the public.

Matters concerning a person's job or profession, or the services they provide to the public, might be of public concern. So if at a press conference it is said that the town's mayor, or the proprietor of a company that our readers are interested in, is a conman, and that person sued us, we'd have the defence at hand of qualified privilege.

That person's private pastimes might not be of public concern, unless they are in a position of authority, particularly over children or vulnerable adults. So if the head teacher of a school was called a conman at a press conference or public meeting, we'd have the protection of qualified privilege in reporting that statement, whether or not it is true.

But what if you were emailed a press release with defamatory statements in it in advance of the meeting and decided to write it up from that?

The press release is not safe to use before the meeting. You would need to check if it was actually distributed at the meeting, so becoming part of proceedings, or given to all press before or afterwards.

Only what is said at the meeting is covered by qualified privilege. Things said outside it are not covered. So allegations hurled outside, after a heated meeting, are not covered.

Calling a press conference is a useful way for groups or individuals to air contentious issues, and helps you to report them more fully. But most press conferences are much more straightforward.

Press conference examples

Let's look at some press conferences, and see how stories are obtained from them. We'll deal here with general tuition in how to approach reporting at these events, and place contemporary examples on the website, where they can be refreshed when necessary.

Note: In order to keep these examples fresh and current, I am putting them on the online version of this module.

on the website

Find press conference case studies, including a product launch.

Police press conference

The police may call press conferences for various reasons, but there is one for a particular purpose that gives you special protection under law in addition to the qualified privilege mentioned earlier. That is a press conference when they are seeking publicity in order to catch a criminal. It is known as a police appeal. In such circumstances they are allowed to make all sorts of allegations that are clearly defamatory of the accused – and we are allowed to report them. They will also contain statements that are what is known as 'in contempt of court'.

I'll just explain briefly what contempt of court means before we move on. In British law we have an abiding principle – that the court's role is to determine an accused person's guilt or innocence. If we write anything that would tend to pre-judge a court's decision, we are usurping the role of the court and hence could be said to be in contempt of it.

Once a person is arrested, or charged, or if a warrant for their arrest has been issued, proceedings are said to be active. Those proceedings are likely to lead to a court case, and to a finding of guilt or innocence by that court. That means we can say very little about the case. We ought also, as responsible journalists, to be very careful when covering events that are likely, at a later date, to be the subject of a court case, but where proceedings are not yet active.

The police are allowed to make statements that are defamatory and in contempt of court when seeking to apprehend a suspect because the law determines that the greater public good is served in catching the accused person than in protecting their rights not to be defamed and to get a fair trial.

That's clearly the case if a serial killer is on the loose. It's much more important to prevent further murders than to protect the killer's rights.

But this special circumstance lasts only until the person is caught.

Public meetings

We looked at one type of public meeting in Chapter 1 – a council committee meeting. A much less formal public meeting might be called by a group of residents who are protesting about, say, traffic or crime.

There are all sorts of others.

One common problem can be that you have several, perhaps many, people making contributions. In a council meeting you can easily identify the people speaking. In a public meeting you may have no idea who they are and they may not give their name when they speak. In a crowded room they can be hard to get to.

One headache is getting quotes down from people saying interesting things, memorising their faces – and who said what – and then wading up to them or grabbing them afterwards to get the personal details you need.

You may want more from a particular speaker. Perhaps they have mentioned a personal situation that warrants more space in your story – or that lends itself to a video, stills or audio report.

A quick point of law

You have a statutory right to attend some meetings, some you can go to because they are open to the public or are concerning matters of public interest and you are a member of that public, as well as being a journalist, others you need an invitation to attend. See above under press conferences for a quick run-down on the law relating to reporting on public meetings.

Before the event – research

Learn the background to the story and why the meeting has been called. Read any documents you have been sent about it. If there is an agenda you'll be able to see the areas that will be covered. Check what has been written before, by you and others. Check any blogs or social media posts by participants.

Before the event – reporting

If the meeting warrants it, preview it in print and online. Online, link to any stories from you and others, and any relevant documents that will help readers understand what is coming.

At the event

A well-organised meeting will have an agenda and a chairman to ensure fairness. They will have rules about how they operate, called standing orders, and minutes, a record of the meeting, will be kept.

Speakers will be called, a debate will develop and a vote or votes will be taken to decide on the matter under discussion.

Less well-organised meetings can be much more haphazard. Perhaps the meeting has been called by angry residents. For example they may be worried about vandalism and call a meeting, demanding that a senior police officer come and address them. These are much tougher to cover effectively. As well as the practicalities mentioned above, you may not know what, if anything, has been decided.

After the event

If the meeting reached no clear conclusion; if it was just an opportunity for people to sound off, you may have to stay behind at the end and talk to the key people involved. How did the meeting go? Were they happy with what they heard? If there was a decision, did they agree with it and will they abide by it? What is the next step?

The fact of the meeting is not the main thrust of the story, it's what came out of it that gives you your news angle.

Even a well-organised meeting can leave some people dissatisfied. Is there conflict about what was decided? Very often you need to follow up after the meeting by interviewing key speakers and putting the points they raised to others who were not at the meeting - either officials who have an influence over whether what the meeting has asked for will be delivered, or opponents of the views expressed at the meeting.

questions

One legal point. Think back to what we said earlier about reporting at public meetings. Which act offers you protection in what you report from a public meeting? What protection does it provide you with? Do you have the same protection for things said outside that meeting?

Don't read on until you have your answers.

The Defamation Act 1996 offers us protection when we cover a public meeting. We have qualified privilege in what we report. Things said outside the meeting do not have such protection.

on the website

Find examples of reporting done at public meetings, including protest meetings.

Public events

It might be a carnival, a firework display, a concert or a street party. It could involve dozens, hundreds or thousands of people.

Before the event – research

You'll have got the picture here by now. If we are covering an event we owe it to ourselves to read up on it. Find out about its history, know who the organisers are and how to contact them, check what press facilities will be available. There may be a press area in which we can get coffee and food, and edit and file our reports.

Before the event – reporting

If it is a major annual event then the preparations for it, and details of the key highlights this year, will make for good advance stories.

At the event

Major events always have the potential to go wrong in some way. The thrill ride at the funfair on the common may malfunction. If 50 people are stuck at the top of the big dipper for half an hour and have to be rescued by firefighters, that's a big story, eclipsing the one you were expecting. So is a riot at a carnival, or at a football match.

After the event

How successful it was will be of interest to readers. If it's a big event, we can ask readers to send in their pictures and videos.

on the website

Find examples of how major public events were reported.

Court reporting

Local newspapers used to take covering court cases very seriously. They'd aim to cover a good proportion of cases in their local magistrates', youth and crown courts. Today, with small staffs, a lot don't bother unless it's a really juicy case. TV and radio tend to just cover the big stuff, and usually have specialist reporters – often the home affairs correspondent – who handles them.

On magazines, court reporting is hardly ever done. So why should you bother learning about it? Well, on some courses and for some accrediting bodies, court reporting is still considered an essential skill. Even if it's not essential on your course, you never know when you might have to do it. And trying to cover court when you don't know the rules is very dangerous.

Court reporting – in the UK at least – presents many pitfalls for the journalist who does not know the law relating to what can and cannot be said, when, and about whom. Indeed, this is the most dangerous place when you are training, because your mistakes can get you in serious trouble. A slip could cause a trial to be abandoned.

That said, because relatively few journalists now cover courts, I am putting detailed step-by-step tuition in court reporting on the website.

on the website

Find a full guide to court reporting, including:

- The law in England and Wales on court reporting
- The concept of contempt of court and how to avoid it
- How courts work
- The journalist's place in court
- Examples of how court cases have been reported
- Essential links to information about court reporting.

Even if that material is not for you, I do urge you to read up a little about court reporting.

7B3

Developing your skills as an interviewer

You will need to do some interviewing for most of the stories you write. Almost from the first word of this book, interviewing was involved, but now we are going to take our first systematic look at interviewing technique. A further detailed look will follow in Chapter 15 when we look at writing features.

Not all interviews are the same. The people you interview can be divided into three main categories:

- Well-known personalities
- Ordinary people, not usually in the news
- People speaking on behalf of organisations or firms.

Some interviews are arranged in advance, others just happen because an unexpected situation or opportunity arises to talk to someone relevant to a story you are writing.

Relatively few interviews are conducted face-to-face. Most are carried out either over the phone, or via email.

Whatever the method you use to get your interview, it is vital that you ask the right questions, in the right way, or you may not get the information you need.

Further tips on interviewing

As we discussed in Chapter 4, module 4A4, under the heading 'How to conduct your interview', the structure of an interview can be very different when you are writing a text report to when you are making a video.

It's a good idea to refer back to that module now to refresh your memory on the advice given there.

Here are a few thoughts on how to ask your questions, whatever the medium:

- Avoid questions that produce a yes/no answer. "Were you frightened?" is a bad question because it invites a yes/no answer. You could ask, "How frightened were you when x happened?" but they might just say "very" or "not at all". It's better to ask, "How did you feel when x happened?" Ask questions that will encourage the interviewee to talk. What happened? Why? This is particularly useful at the start of an interview
- Ask questions that will lead to clear answers. Such questions often begin with: who, what, where, when, why or how, and will help you get the information in a way that is easy to transfer into a story

- Listen. Don't interrupt with a new question until you are sure the speaker has finished their answer to the first one
- Think about what the answers mean. If you don't really understand, you will never be able to explain them for the reader, listener or viewer
- Clarify any vague answers such as "recently" or "about"
- Think about what the reader wants to know. While you are conducting the interview, try to think about what your intro might be. That will help you to think of more questions which will build your story up.

Other things to think about

- Check spellings of names and places
- Think about whether a photograph is needed, and if so take it
- Make sure your interviewee knows how to get in touch with you. They may think of something else that is important to the story after you have gone. Leave your business card or name, email and phone number in case interviewees would like to contact you
- Get their phone number, email and/or address in case you need to get hold of them again
- Thank them for their time.

How to conduct an email interview

If you can't interview face-to-face or on the phone, you may have to make do with an email interview. They can be tough. Here are some thoughts on how to get the best out of them.

Email is fine for getting a couple of quick quotes, but where you need a substantial interview it is very much second best to a face-to-face or phone chat.

Also, because it only takes a few seconds to ping off an email, you could easily approach an email interview too casually. You might find an interviewee who is happy to engage in a dialogue, answering one or two questions and then responding to your follow-ups, but most won't. So you need to ask a clear list of questions at the outset.

You should ask plenty of questions if you hope to get a decent piece out of this email interview, because you will need plenty of answers. You can't craft a 400 word piece out of the answers to two or three questions. Go for around 15, with a maximum of 20.

You could start your email with an apology for the length of the list, and explain that you are asking so much because you want to make sure you are able to write an in-depth piece, which completely covers a complex story or fully reflects the subject's role, achievements, successes or whatever. Your subject is likely to co-operate if they think that will win them a better write-up.

As with any verbal interview, open questions often work best, but you need to be careful how you structure them in an email.

Imagine you are conducting an email interview with the owner of a company. If you ask: "Was your product launch a success?" you may well get the one-word answer "Yes."

If you ask: "How successful was your product launch?" you may get the answer "Very."

That's not much use to you.

Ask a more detailed question: "How did you measure the effectiveness of your latest product launch and what did the results tell you?"

This should produce a considered, detailed response which has the sort of specific information you will need to build a piece.

With an email interview, try to come up with questions that need detailed answers supported by facts and figures.

One significant drawback with an email interview is that it is hard to get good, natural-sounding quotes. An interviewee who will give you a pithy comment in person turns out a bland platitude in an email.

You must try to get good reaction. You need quotes with words such as delighted, shocked, gutted, elated or amazed. For an interview to work you need some emotion and personality and, hopefully, some good quotes. Asking "How did you feel when. . ." is better than "Were you angry/upset when. . ." but you will probably find it hard to get good sharp quotes via email, however you phrase the question.

Finally, mention that if they would prefer a phone interview next time then that might take up less of their valuable time.

Difficult interviews

Sometimes interviewees are uncooperative. They either don't want to talk, or they want to control what you use from the interview they give, and how you use it.

Here are some key difficulties, and how to deal with them.

This must be off the record

There are some rules here. If an interviewee wants to go off the record, they need to make that request before they say anything more. You don't have to go off the record retrospectively.

If they want to go off the record it is worth asking why. Sometimes you can reassure them and keep everything on record. If they insist, let them say what they want to say, then, if it is good material, ask if some of it can be put on the record or, if not, whether it can be attributed to a source of some kind. A source close to the company/organisation or whatever is recognised by those who are media-savvy as identifying the person you have interviewed or someone very close to them.

Promise me you won't report this

Be very reluctant to make such a promise. After all, what your interviewee has said off the record might come later from another source. The most you should say is that if you do report the material they are worried about it will be because you have it from a second source, who may or may not be named.

Can I see your story before it is published?

This is generally a very bad idea. At the very least we get into the same territory we discussed under email interviewing. People who gave you great quotes get cold feet and want to withdraw them, water them down or rewrite them into something no human being would ever say.

Sometimes it is necessary to agree to some kind of disclosure of your story before it is published. If you have a contract with an interviewee they may have negotiated copy approval.

Otherwise, be extremely reluctant to allow your copy to be seen. Many publishers have a blanket ban on reporters doing this, which gives you an easy get out if the matter is raised. Know what the policy is and, before you go against it, make sure your editor approves.

A good halfway house – if you must – is to say you will let the interviewee check their quotes for accuracy, but not see the rest of the article. After all, quotes from others and the rest of the material you gather are not there for them to interfere with. If you have a full shorthand note or a tape of the interview, you can point out that you will only change things that you have got factually wrong.

There can still be struggles. Someone will say 'I may have said it but it's not what I meant. I meant this' – and then they give you a bland statement that has lost all its power or interest.

on the website

Read a demonstration of how a short press release about a boy trapped on a beach develops into a substantial interview.

7B4

Exercises and projects

Exercise 1

Follow a breaking story through a day or two. Monitor how it is covered by one or more outlets. Look at what they do before the event has happened, during it and in the aftermath. Analyse their coverage on social media, via live blogging, in print and/or on scheduled news bulletins.

Exercise 2

Identify a major product launch and follow how it is covered by one or more interested news outlets. Look at how the conference itself is covered, and what stories result from it.

Exercise 3

Look out for the next major story around the world that involves many people in a serious plight. It might be a natural disaster or man-made calamity. Follow the story as it develops over several days. Observe how social media, streaming video and other methods are used, by professional journalists, citizen observers and eyewitnesses caught up in events.

Exercise 4

Find a willing interviewee who is interesting for one or more reasons, and a number of journalistic colleagues. Take it in turns to interview the person. Leave it up to each individual what questions they ask. Tape or film yourselves and play the recordings back. How do you come across? How successful have you been in getting the full story and good quotes from your interviewees? Have others done better? Found better angles? Got better quotes? Write up a 500-word interview and compare your work with what others have produced.

Exercise 5

Practise email interviewing in a similar way to the approach outlined in Exercise 4. Work on developing lists of questions and phrasing your questions so that you get good answers. Write up a 500-word interview and compare it with the work of your colleagues.

Projects

1   Identify a major event in the area you cover and cover it intensively. The event might be an exhibition, a conference, trade fair, talent contest, carnival or other event with a lot of people to interview and plenty going on.

You should:

Set up a dedicated area on your website for the project, with an index page at level two of your site navigation and a number of pages at level 3.

- Preview the event
- Broadcast live video from it
- Create text reports
- Create picture galleries or slide shows
- Conduct interviews.

2   Identify a major press conference in the subject or area you cover. Where possible, preview the event. At the event, take as active a part as you can. Ask questions. Make sure you have all the material you need for a comprehensive text report, plus video or audio interviews and other footage.

3   Identify a public meeting and cover it though the story cycle. Preview it, cover it live and also after the event. Use the full range of media, and publishing platforms, at your disposal.

4   If court reporting is relevant to your projects, cover a range of magistrates' court cases, plus a major crown court case.

Note

1   www.journalism.co.uk/news-commentary/-why-newspapers-should-steer-away-from-the-mtv-model-/
s6/a556217/

chapter eight

Building proficiency with WordPress

In the book version of this chapter we will cover:

- Choosing a host and downloading WordPress.org to your computer
- Transferring your .com site to .org
- Choosing, downloading, unzipping and activating a theme in WordPress.org
- Recommended themes for creating magazine and news sites on WordPress
- Essential adjustments to make to your WordPress account
- Plug-ins you should add to your WordPress site to boost functionality
- Enhancing search engine optimisation on your content.

At the end of the chapter are a range of assignments and projects to enable you to practise what you have learned.

In the online version of this chapter you will find:

- Further, step-by-step tuition in developing your WordPress site
- Links to all the sources and examples cited in the book version
- Essential updates to using WordPress.org.

Have the companion website to this book open at www.multimedia-journalism.co.uk. That way you can easily click on the links to the stories discussed here.

Please note

From time to time platforms such as WordPress get a refresh. So while the description of how the site looks, and how to work with it, are current at the time of publishing, they may change over time. That's where the companion website to this print and ebook edition comes in. If things change, we'll update our tuition on the website.

Using WordPress.org

In Chapter 2 we discussed the differences between WordPress's two versions: .com and .org, and went on to create a site on WordPress.com. Now we are looking at upgrading, by transferring our site to WordPress.org.

We began working with WordPress.com because it is a very simple platform to use, but your ability to change the look and feel of the site you create is limited.

By transferring your site to WordPress.org you can customise that look and feel. You can install a wider variety of themes, add many WordPress plug-ins to extend functionality, and overcome the niggling restrictions that we have come across on occasion as we've worked with the software.

For a non-techie, looking at what you need to do to install and run .org can be daunting. But it needn't be. There are a number of hosting services that make it easy, some offering one-click installation of WordPress.org. But you do have to pay for their services.

WordPress.org offers a list of recommended hosts, and you'll find links to them on the MMJ website.

Alternatively, you can also choose your own hosting company. Tell them you want to use the WordPress operating system and they'll set you up an account on their server where you can administer your site. I use a local hosting company for many of the WordPress sites I run. I buy the URL, tell them which theme I want, and they set things up for me.

You can also pay for what WordPress calls a 'guided transfer', where they oversee the move with you. Click on **Tools>Export** in your dashboard and you get this under **Guided export**:

> One of our Happiness Engineers will transfer your site to a self-hosted WordPress.org installation with one of our partners. They will transfer over all your content, install and configure plug-ins to support features you have used on WordPress.com, switch your

domain(s) over, and provide support on your new WordPress.org install for a two-week period.

on the website

- Find a detailed guide to the pros and cons of .com and .org, and to transferring from .com to .org
- One WordPress-recommended host is Dreamhost, which you can trial for free for two weeks. You'll find a demonstration of using it.

8B2

Transferring your WordPress.com site to .org

on the website

Find a video that takes you through the process of transferring your .com site to .org.

I'm going to summarise the process here, but you may find the video easier to follow.

You need to have a hosting provider set up before you start.

- In your .com dashboard go to **Tools>Export**
- Download the export file that is now generated
- Go into your Dreamhost WordPress.org account and then to your dashboard
- Go to **Tools>Import>WordPress**
- Hit **Install now**
- Choose **Activate and run the installer**
- When prompted, choose the export file you have downloaded to your computer
- Now click **Upload and import**
- Click the box beside **Download and import file attachments**
- Click **Submit**
- Once the file has uploaded (it may take a while if you have a lot of video on your .com site) scroll to the bottom and click **Have fun**
- You'll see your site, as transferred
- Some elements may be missing. This is because WordPress.com has some built in plug-ins that, for example, play videos and lay out polls. You'll need to load those plug-ins in .org

- Go to Plug-ins on your dashboard, do a search for author and type in 'Automatic'
- In the list that appears scroll down to the Videopress plug-in and install it
- Do the same for other plug-in alternatives to installed widgets.

Recommended themes for journalism

Now might be the time to choose a new theme for your WordPress site.

Let's take a look at some that work well for journalism. You can demo them with your own content before deciding which one is for you. The following is a mix of free and premium (paid-for) themes.

on the website

Find links to many more themes that work for journalism.

One question to consider as you decide on a theme is how much you want your site to look like a print product or an online-native product.

Because we are very familiar with physical newspapers and magazines, aping their look and feel with a website is a useful visual shorthand – it gives the browser an idea of what the site will be like.

But there is a counter-argument that a news or magazine site created for online should have a look and feel that is relevant, first and foremost, to the online medium.

It really depends on what you want the presentation of your site to say about its content, and whether your target audience is digital natives or those who have transitioned from old to new media.

To help you decide, take a look at sites that have inspired you and helped you create the one you are working on. What approach do they take? What can you learn from them?

You also need to check whether the theme is responsive – that is, does it adapt depending on the device used to reach it: web, tablet or mobile? This is a very important consideration.

Find links to all the themes discussed below.

Newspaper-style themes

WordPress Newspaper

www.gabfirethemes.com/themes/WordPress-newspaper-theme/

WordPress Newspaper looks like a broadsheet newspaper, and gives a sense of authority and gravitas.

The Journal

http://demo.woothemes.com/thejournal/

The Journal is a more tabloid theme.

Magazine-style themes

The default theme we have been using so far is a magazine theme, but there are plenty of free alternatives that you might prefer. This guide to 60 free themes **http://premium.wpmudev.org/blog/60-free-WordPress-magazine-themes/** includes:

Surfarama

http://surfarama.com/

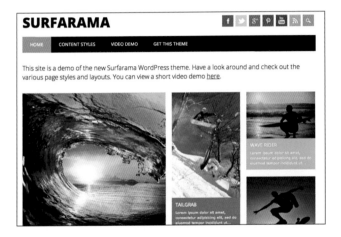

http://surfarama.com/video-demo/

Surfarama is a highly visual theme, ideal if you have a lot of high-quality images to show off.

Columnist

http://demo.wpmole.com/columnist/

Columnist is good for sites where the written word is important, but where you still want images to have a reasonable visual impact.

Designmagz

http://designmagz.com/

Designmagz is for a site where text is the most important thing.

Magazine Basic

http://demos.bavotasan.com/magazine-basic/

Magazine Basic is another theme that works well when the balance is towards words, and images are subsidiary.

Branford Magazine

www.wp-themes.der-prinz.com/branfordmagazine-free/

Branford Magazine might suit if you want your site to look like a print product.

Broadcast news-style themes

Focus

http://siteorigin.com/theme/focus/

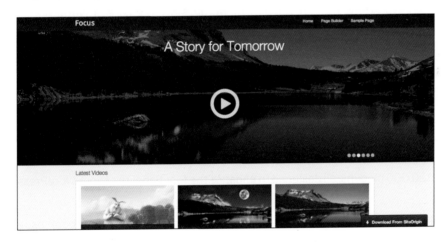

The 'Focus' theme could work for you if video is very much the focus of your work.

Vidiho

www.cssigniter.com/ignite/themes/vidiho/

This theme presents a selection of videos in a slider on the homepage, and lets browsers preview any video in an index page before deciding whether to click to view it full size.

8B4

Enhancing your WordPress.org site with plug-ins

First, what are WordPress plug-ins? Here's what the WordPress Codex[1] has to say:

> Plug-ins are tools to extend the functionality of WordPress. . .The core of WordPress is designed to be lean, to maximize flexibility and minimize *code bloat*. Plug-ins offer custom functions and features so that each user can tailor their site to their specific needs.

So, instead of piling lots of functions onto the generic site-building platform, WordPress gives you the basics and lets you add the other functionality you need by way of plug-ins.

What can plug-ins do?

There are around 20,000 plug-ins, all designed to enhance the functionality of your WordPress site in some way.

There are social plug-ins that display your latest tweets, or details of your Facebook page within your site. So far we've used widgets to perform the same function, because that was what WordPress.com offered us. But plug-ins offer us a greater variety of tools that will do similar things in ways you may find more aesthetically or functionally pleasing.

Where to find plug-ins

The official source for plug-ins is at **http://WordPress.org/plugins/**. It's worth taking a browse around to see what is available. You can think about what additional functionality you need on your site and then search for plug-ins that offer to fill the gap you've identified. A star system lets you know what others have thought of them.

How to install plug-ins

The easiest way is to navigate to **Plug-ins> Add new** on your dashboard's left-hand navigation.

If you know the name of the plug-in you want, enter it and the search will find it, or you can search using terms that describe what you want the plug-in to do.

Before committing yourself you can click **Details** to read more about the plug-in. Then it's just a case of clicking to install it and, after that, clicking to activate it.

Downloading plug-ins in zip format

You can also download plug-ins from other than the WordPress official library in zip format.

To install those, first download them to your computer – just as we did with themes – and then use the WordPress upload feature. When you click on **Add new plug-in**, there is an option to upload. Click on that and upload the plug-in folder.

Not all plug-ins work as well as you might hope, so it's worth testing them out and deactivating them if they just aren't working for you.

What plug-ins do you need?

That depends on two things – what you want your site to be able to do, and what functionality your chosen theme already has installed.

For example, on some themes, making sure that those who find you on a smartphone or tablet get a mobilised version of your site delivered to them is either automatic, or simply activated by clicking this facility from within your dashboard. With others, you have to find a plug-in to make the theme responsive. We'll avoid such themes – they are out of date.

Using plug-ins to overcome the problems we had with WordPress.com

You'll have noticed that, when our site was on WordPress.com, it was sometimes hard to get the functionality we wanted. Plug-ins can often overcome those problems. Let's take a look at a few examples:

Social media plug-ins

The official Twitter feed widget we installed in Chapter 3 is fine, but there are lots of other types of Twitter embeds available via plug-ins.

We added a like button for Facebook in Chapter 3, but there are lots of other ways we can integrate our WordPress website with Facebook.

on the website

You'll find other Twitter, Facebook and further social media plug-ins.

Embedding audioBoom clips within WordPress posts or pages

If you remember, that was a problem with WordPress.com. With .org it's not. Just mark the point within your text where you want your audio to appear with a row of xs, then go to the 'text' (html visible) version of your page or post. From audioBoom, pick up the embed code from the relevant podcast and paste it in here, removing the row of xs once you have. Click to preview the post and the player will appear, looking like this:

Adding an audioBoom player to your WordPress.org site

Here's another thing we couldn't do with WordPress.com. Go to **https://audioboom.com/ about/widgets** and select the player option. You can customise the player, setting a width and colour scheme, then copy and paste the code generated. Go to your .org site and create a page without a parent. That means the page will appear prominently on your homepage. Name it 'Podcasts', and then switch to the text (html) version of the page. Paste in the code from audioBoom, save and revert to the Visual (wysiwyg) version of the page. Now you have a player that shows the headlines of all your podcasts. Mine looks like this:

Adding a Bambuser video player to your WordPress.org site

In Chapter 5 we created a new live video page without a parent, which meant it would be listed prominently on your home page, but we could not embed the Bambuser player directly into it. Now we can.

Go to your Bambuser account and, under **Settings>Embed your player**, you can adjust the size of the player you create, and preview it, and then pick up the code you need. In WordPress, switch to the text (html) version of the page you are creating and paste in the code. Revert to wysiwyg and review how it looks. Once you are happy, publish.

Here's how my player looks on my WordPress site:

Live blogging

The WordPress liveblog plug-in (**http://WordPress.org/plugins/liveblog/**) turns any blog post into a live blog, to which you can post repeatedly, with text or stills (you have to drag

them in as there is no upload button). Each time you update your post, those following the blog get your new content, without either they - or you - having to hit refresh.

To find the plug-in, search for liveblog and look for the one authored by WordPress/Automattic.

There's a video explaining what it does here: **http://WordPress.org/plugins/liveblog/** and some screenshots here: **http://WordPress.org/plugins/liveblog/screenshots/**

Once I have it installed and enabled, when I open a new post I get this notification at the bottom:

If I click to enable live blogging the interface changes to this:

I add my content and click to publish.

I can drag in an image. If I drag in a YouTube video, only the URL appears in the post, but click on that URL and the video loads and plays.

Embedding a CoverItLive player into WordPress.org

That's another thing we couldn't do with .com but we can with .org.

Follow what we did in Chapter 6 but, when you set up your live blog, copy the code for embedding the CIL (CoverItLive) player and create a new, parent-less page on your WordPress site. Paste the code in there and you have your player.

If you follow the standard layout (you can customise the appearance if you like) it will look like this:

Simple page ordering

This plug-in lets you easily arrange the order in which your pages appear in navigation through a simple drag-and-drop process: **http://10up.com/plugins/simple-page-ordering-WordPress/**

Optimising your posts and pages for search engines

There are a number of plug-ins that help you make your content as findable as possible on search engines. They work by adding a series of dialogue boxes beneath each thing you write, into which you add your headline, key words and so on. They will also suggest keywords.

They are a useful way of becoming aware of the importance of selling everything you do as effectively as possible.

Take a look at some and try working with them to see how you get on.

Among them are:

All in One SEO pack: https://WordPress.org/plugins/all-in-one-seo-pack/

WordPress SEO: https://WordPress.org/plugins/WordPress-seo/

We'll look at SEO again in Chapter 16, but it's as well to become aware of the importance of it now. The analysis this type of plug-in gives you of your text is illuminating. They help you find the best-worded headline and intro, and to ensure your keywords – the main words you expect searchers for just the content you have written will use in their searches – are prominent within your text.

Here's a grab from WordPress SEO's analysis of a page on one of my websites. I used it to check I had sold the copy correctly.

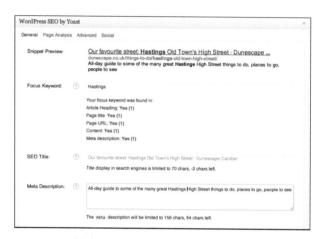

That's just the general page. The 'Page analysis' tab gives me more detail, and the 'Social' tab lets me write a description for Facebook and Google+. As I have this site set up to post new copy automatically to these and other social platforms, it makes sense to tailor the sell I give to each of them.

Other recommended plug-ins for journalists

on the website

You'll find more recommended plug-ins for journalism.

8B5

Exercises and projects

Exercise 1

Research media companies that use WordPress and see which themes they use.

Exercise 2

Research the look and feel that media companies go for in their websites. Compare and contrast one that goes for a print-look, and another that aims for a web-native style. What are the strengths and weaknesses of each in terms of how they present content?

Projects

1   Move your WordPress blog from .com to .org using one of the procedures outlined in this chapter.

2   Review the theme you are using and consider whether there might be a better theme to adopt. In deciding, take into account the type of website you are building. In particular, consider whether you would like your site to look and feel like a fairly traditional broadsheet or tabloid newspaper, like a magazine, a video-focused site or like a web-native creation. Also consider your target audience and what their expectations and experiences of media are.

3   Go through the widgets you are using and see whether any should be replaced with plug-ins. Ensure your site is effectively set up in terms of its

   ■   integration with social media
   ■   ability to embed audio and video within pages and posts
   ■   your ability to live blog within it.

Note

1   http://codex.WordPress.org/Plugins

chapter nine

Social and community journalism

In the book version of this chapter we will cover:

- Enhancing your presence on Twitter and Facebook
- Mining community content via Twitter and Facebook
- Advanced people and story search on Facebook and Twitter
- The role of the community reporter and editor
- Building a forums area on your WordPress site
- Managing forums
- Adding polls and forums to your WordPress site.

At the end of the chapter are a range of exercises and projects to enable you to practise what you have learned.

In the web version of this chapter you will find:

- Step-by-step guides to adding a forums area to your WordPress site
- More on journalists' role in community engagement, with case studies and examples
- Further examples and case studies in community engagement, and gaining community content
- More on managing forums
- A summary of the law of defamation and contempt as it applies to community content published by sites based in England and Wales.

Have the companion website to this book open at www.multimedia-journalism.co.uk. That way you can easily click on the links to the stories discussed here.

9B1

Developing our community journalism and use of social media

In this chapter we take the community and social media aspects of our journalism to the next level. We review, enhance and expand our use of social media. That's a logical next step, but there is much more we can do to truly engage with the community that consumes our journalism and which we need to be an active part of if we are to exploit the opportunities for news-gathering and -dissemination that social media offers us.

Engagement doesn't have to take place only on these other platforms. We can facilitate feedback and dialogue on our own branded sites. We can create forums where the community we seek to engage with can interact with each other and with us. And we can have journalists who take on roles such as community reporter, community editor or community manager.

Many news organisations now have such posts in place, and those that don't will probably acquire them in the near future.

But this is a new and developing area of journalistic endeavour, so we'll look at how a range of publishers and broadcasters are doing it, and decide how best to do it for ourselves.

9B2

Enhancing your presence on Twitter and Facebook, and mining community content on them

First let's make sure our social presences are working as well as they ought to be.

Twitter

In Chapter 3 we looked at adding a Twitter widget to your WordPress site. That's known as a Profile Widget, and is fine for a site where you are the only journalist.

But what if you are one of a number of journalists from a title who tweet?

And if your title has Twitter accounts for things such as breaking news, sport and other specialist areas of your content?

In these cases, how do you make it easy for your community to find the Twitter accounts they would like to follow from the range you offer?

The answer is to create a widget that brings all those accounts together.

For that you can use Twitter's **List Widget** option.

The *Guardian* has this one among others:

They also have a Find us on Twitter page here: **www.theguardian.com/users/2009/may/07/find-us-on-twitter** which lists all journalists who tweet, under the department they work in.

Here's how you create a list widget. First, you need to build a list on Twitter of all those you want to include. We covered creating Twitter lists in Chapter 3, module 3A2. You'll need to make a list of all those on your title who tweet.

Then, when the widget builder asks you to select which list you want to use, choose the list widget.

I've created a widget from a list of people who, I feel, journalists who are new to Twitter should follow. Here's the list pulled in to the widget maker alongside a preview of how the widget will look:

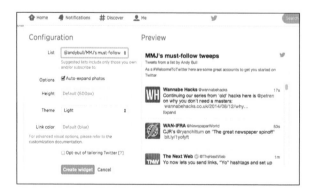

I can customise it if I like:

To set one up, go to the gear logo on your Twitter page, then to **Settings>Widgets>Create new>Lists**.

To embed it in your WordPress site, pick up the code generated and then drag a text/html box into the point on one of your sidebars where you want it to appear.

Other ways of letting several people tweet in the same account

As Twitter lets you tweet from more than one location, you can also have several people sharing one Twitter account – they just need the log-in details. But that could get messy.

One paid-for alternative option is called GroupTweet: **www.grouptweet.com/**

Managing your Twitter following and followers

As long as our Twitter following is growing, we tend to think all is healthy with our use of the platform. Certainly a declining following would be bad news. But it's good to know more about those who follow you. Who engages most closely with your content, for example – who favourites or retweets you the most.

Once you follow someone on Twitter it's likely you'll keep following them. That can mean you are following all sorts of inactive or no-longer relevant accounts. You need a clear-out now and then. There may also be people who ought to be following you but aren't – or were but have stopped for some reason.

Twitter itself will send you regular emails about your most popular posts, but there is more you can know and do. There are various applications that help you analyse your Twitter following and tidy up your account.

Just Unfollow

www.justunfollow.com/

Just Unfollow shows you various things including:

- Recent followers
- Recent unfollowers
- People who don't follow you back
- Followers who you don't follow back (called 'fans' here)
- Accounts you follow that have been inactive for one, three and six months.

One neat function is that you can follow all the followers of a particular Twitter account. Great when you want to look at the social circle around the subject of a story.

More about what it does here: www.justunfollow.com/help.html

on the website

Apps that help you manage your social media accounts tend to come and go, so we'll update this section on the website.

Improving the look of your Twitter page

Ideally your Twitter page should carry the same branding as your WordPress or other website. Under **Settings>Design** you can choose a background to your Twitter page from a gallery, or upload your own.

Twitter runs you through the process here

https://support.twitter.com/articles/15357-customizing-your-design

Note: because Twitter regularly tweaks the look and feel of the platform, we'll keep a step-by-step guide to improving the look of your page for the website.

on the website

Find the latest guidance in how to optimise the design and content of your Twitter profile.

Mining content on Twitter

There are a number of things we can do to ensure we are exploiting Twitter as a news resource as effectively as possible.

How to follow everyone who is following a particular hashtag

Blast Follow can be useful when a big story develops and you want to tap in instantly to everyone who is using the relevant hashtag. You can find it here: **http://brianmcarey.com/ blastfollow/**

Using Twitter search to the max

Find local sources

You can refine your search by using Twitter's advanced search page (https://twitter.com/ search-advanced) which lets you search by location. Type in your location and a key-word, and you can choose a radius of between 1 and 1,000 miles for tweets meeting those criteria.

As Poynter says: "If you find local people you want to interview, follow up with them on Twitter and ask them to send you a Direct Message with their contact information."[1]

Find specific conversations and forensically examine individuals' involvement in a story

You can also add filters for exact phrases, specific words, use of a certain hashtag and lan-guage. You can also look for tweets from one specific account to another, or mentioning a given account, set a date range, and look for positive or negative content, and tweets includ-ing a question.

With these filters you can forensically examine individuals' involvement in a story.

Turn investigations into collaborative storytelling efforts

Colorado reporter Wendy Norris used Twitter to seek help with an investigation in response to anecdotal reports that pharmacies across the state were locking up condoms and making them less easy to buy.

Instead of doing all the leg-work herself, she tweeted: "Heading to the grocery/drug store this week? Join fun, stealth crowdsourcing project. No disguise needed. DM me if you're in Colorado."

Poynter[1] reports that this tweet, plus a Facebook post and an email, brought Norris 17 volunteers, who went to 64 stores over a week to find out whether condoms were locked up.

In fact they showed the story was false. But you get the point.

Help your audience keep track of an ongoing story

Poynter recommends creating a separate Twitter account for a major, long-running story. For example:

> The Orlando Sentinel created a Casey Anthony Twitter account [related to a child murder case] that amassed nearly 42,000 followers. The Sentinel tweets links to its Casey Anthony coverage from that account, and reporters used the account to live tweet from the trial.

Facebook

Hopefully you'll know by now whether Twitter or Facebook bring you the higher level of social engagement. Most journalists respond to this by making one or other their main social media platform, and will tend to then link the platform that is less effective for them so tweets/status updates go automatically to Facebook/Twitter.

Improving the look of your Facebook page

Because Facebook regularly updates the look and feel of the site, we'll keep the step-by-step guide to what you can do on the MMJ website, where it can be instantly updated.

But here's some of what you can do:

- Use a cover photo similar to your branding on website, Twitter and elsewhere
- Likewise with your profile picture.

on the website

Find more on improving the look of your Facebook page.

Finding stories on Facebook

Maybe because so many journalists prefer Twitter, Facebook is working hard to persuade journalists and media organisations of its value to them. They will point out that they are responsible for many referrals from Facebook to media organisations' branded sites, and see themselves as an important part of the news ecosystem. They have set up FB Newswire

www.facebook.com/FBNewswire

to facilitate story development using the platform, but I find it unconvincing.

on the website

Find more on FB Newswire.

Advanced search on Facebook: Graph Search

Facebook has always been a good tool for finding people who are in the news, and identifying others they have connections to, and who might be sources of information about the person.

Facebook has developed that facility with Graph Search, which is designed to give you access to what the company calls a Rolodex of 1bn sources. It enables journalists to find people, content and photos around stories they are working on, but is said by Facebook to respect the privacy settings of the individuals and the content they have created.

on the website

At the time of writing, Graph Search was available only in Beta. We'll add a step-by-step guide to its use on the MMJ website.

A summary of what you can do on Graph Search:

Finding experts on Facebook

If you are doing a story on a company and want to interview someone at its New York office, you can search "People who work at ACME Inc in New York". You could also specify a particular job title.

Finding photos by location or topic

Graph Search allows you to find photos posted within very specific locations, using the location tags photographers put on them. That helps you find images of breaking news stories.

Discovering connections through Interests

You can search using a phrase that contains, for example, a particular job title with a certain interest or activity. Facebook suggests: "you can do searches like 'movies liked by people who are film directors' or 'books read by CEOs'".

You can find out more about Graph Search and how it works on Wikipedia:

http://en.wikipedia.org/wiki/Facebook_Graph_Search

9B3

Community engagement, and community or user-generated content

Social media sites such as Facebook are all about user engagement. They are designed to encourage users to like and share items of content. When they began, almost all of the content was also generated by those users. But pretty rapidly users began sharing things created by others outside the community - including from publishers and broadcasters who saw the sense in using Facebook and other social platforms as distribution channels for their content.

As I've said elsewhere, the hope was to reach a new audience who would enjoy and share our content and, through links, to draw some of that new audience back to our branded websites, where we could try to turn them into paying customers.

Conversely, those in the news - or who wanted to make news - now often turn first to social platforms. News-makers use social media: from warlords who put video of their latest atrocity on YouTube, to celebs who announce their marriage break-up on Facebook, and politicians who tweet their resignations.

One job of multimedia journalists is to monitor effectively the informal news wire that social media is, so that we can pull that news on to our own sites, and into our broadcasts and print publications. One phrase to describe the process is mining social media for user-generated content. We'll look at the science of that later.

Another job is to engage with our community - from what you might call the immediate family that we meet on our own websites, to the extended family that follows our accounts on social platforms, and on to the very distant relations in the far reaches of the online world who have barely even heard of us.

News organisations also set out to create areas on their own sites where that community can engage with our content – share it, comment on it, discuss it.

But we aren't Facebook. So how can social, community engagement work for journalism, and for journalists, publishers and broadcasters?

It's probably fair to say that that is still a work in progress. We're working on developing forms of community engagement that work for us as content creators. New job titles have been minted to reflect this area of social, community-focused journalism. So we have a range of titles including community reporters, community content reporters, plus editors and managers.

Here's a job description from the US's Gannett group:[2]

> **Community Content Editor**
>
> Main Function: Analyses audience needs and procures complementary community content for all platforms. . . stories, photos, videos, news briefs and blogs. Seeks partners, services and contributors to deepen products' reach and impact. Oversees. . . smooth editing and production of this content into both print and digital products.

We'll look at such roles later in this chapter. First, let's take a close look at what effective community or social engagement is, and how we can use it in our journalism.

Forms of social engagement

Social engagement, and the associated community content that can result from it, is the holy grail of many publications on the web. Publishers and broadcasters are desperate to get it for a couple of reasons. One is that, if you develop a community where your readers/users love to come and chat with each other, you have a site that is very sticky – it encourages people to come back.

Second, it is generally believed that content produced by users, rather than journalists, is free content. Gannett talks about complementary content but almost certainly means that it should also be complimentary. And all publishers like the idea of getting something for nothing. Adding interactive elements to online stories can generate additional news stories.

But it's not as easy to develop effective social or community engagement, and to obtain community or user-generated content, as many publishers once assumed. Many readers, listeners or viewers aren't particularly interested in engaging with us. When they do engage, a lot of what they share is of little interest. Am I being harsh? Next time a current affairs programme you are watching puts up a hashtag, follow it and see what is being said. The discussion is more likely to be about the clothes and hairstyles of the panellists than insightful contributions to the debate.

But sometimes really interesting contributions do come up, and a community reporter who is monitoring that Twitter stream can pick up great stories.

Let's look at community engagement, and community content in more detail, and at how it must be managed and developed if our conversation with our community is to be a rich and rewarding one from both sides.

First, what is it?

What community content is

Community content - once called user-generated content or UGC - can take various forms. At its simplest, the reader is unaware that they are providing it. Such content is a by-product of being on the site. So, a list of the most popular stories is generated without the people who read those stories doing anything.

Here's how the *Times Online* does it:

And here's the BBC's version:

These grabs were taken at the same time on the same day, and are interesting in that they show what people actually read, rather than what they might tell a researcher they read.

There were two mass catastrophe stories that day – one in Gaza, the other in Iraq, as well as the death of actor and comedian Robin Williams. Aspects of all three stories appear, alongside some you would not necessarily expect, and certainly would not put on your home or front page, or at the top of a news bulletin.

The tables also throw up an anomaly. The BBC list features a story from the time of Jimmy Savile's death. When he died, TV presenter and DJ Savile was generally an admired man. By the time this list appeared, he had long been revealed as a serial sex abuser.

The *Mail Online* berated the BBC for this, saying: "Fury at bungling BBC after tributes to Jimmy Savile are posted alongside website reports of Robin Williams' 'suicide'".[3]

The *Daily Mail* mined social media for people outraged at this, but quoted a BBC spokesperson saying: "Old stories reappear on the 'most read' part of the website when stories are re-shared. . ., sometimes long after the event, which means the old story moves up the 'most popular' list."

"When that happens," the BBC person went on, "they become more likely to be re-read and re-shared, with the result that the report remains in the list for longer."

The BBC does not delete archive stories, the spokesperson explained, which means that readers can still access news stories on the site whenever they were published.

Clearly no community editor is going to commission a homage to Jimmy Savile on the back of this, it's just a function of the way the web works.

Likewise, if you buy a book on Amazon you are told what other books were bought by those who purchased the one you just have.

Many e-commerce sites aim to offer you recommendations, based on your actions and purchases. News sites could do that, but they don't tend to.

You could ask readers to vote for the stories they like best, and that involves them taking action. They'd know they were contributing to the site. You could make that contribution easy. Let them hover their cursor over a row of stars and click on the number of stars they want to award to the story.

The next level of community-generated content requires readers to do a bit more. For example, you give them the opportunity to comment on a news story by adding their reactions below it. Or you invite them to vote on a topic – often one that is in the news.

Here's a voting opportunity from *PrintWeek* (**www.printweek.com/**)

Vote, and you get to see the results. That's great as far as it goes, but the voter could be drawn in to further discussion, by having a link from the poll results taking them to a forum with an appropriate discussion thread. A poll also offers a follow-up news story for the site and magazine.

Add polling to your WordPress website

Polling software called Poll Daddy (**www.polldaddy.com**) is integrated into WordPress.com. When you write a page or post you'll see an **Add poll** icon right by the **Add media** one. There is also a Polls submenu located underneath the Feedbacks menu on the left-hand side of your dashboard.

But with WordPress.org you need to install it.

on the website

Find a step-by-step guide to adding polls to your WordPress site.

Adding reader comments to a story

Commenting on a story is another step up in terms of the effort required. Often, comments on general news stories do not add to the story in any way. They are of value in terms of gauging readers' reactions to the story, but no more.

Comments can be really valuable, however, in specialist publications. The B2B title *Morning Advertiser*, which serves the pub trade, ran a story on how 31 pubs were closing each week.[4]

This was something its community of readers knew a great deal about, often at first hand. The story gathered 28 comments, a number of which took the story forward with significant insights.

Specialist publications have long been aware of the value of having a community of experts at hand, and the news-gathering and story development process benefits greatly from their input. Such communities are often eager to comment, but that's not generally the case with general news sites.

Likes, shares and reader comments on your WordPress site

The easiest level of feedback is to let readers Like a post or page on your site. The Like facility is built in, but you can choose whether to activate it or not.

It's there along with the share buttons and the comment box at the bottom of any of your pages or posts:

To turn Likes on or off on an individual post or page, you need to be on the Edit Post screen and to scroll down to the Likes and Shares module.

You can set the parameters for comments. Do that in the Discussions area on your dashboard. You decide whether someone needs to enter their name and email address in order to comment, and whether they need to be registered with your site. You can choose to moderate comments pre- or post-publication. If you select to pre-moderate, you set up alerts so you know there are comments waiting in the approval queue. There are also anti-spam and abuse filters available on this page. So there's a conundrum here. You want loads of community interaction, but you don't want spam and abusive comments. Pre-moderation may stifle discussion and takes up your time to handle. Post-moderation may lead to a level of abuse that puts many in your community off contributing. We'll look in detail at this issue later in the chapter.

Encouraging and managing community content

There is such a thing online as what you might call First Person At The Party Syndrome. Ever been the first to arrive at a party? You are tempted to back quietly out of the door and only come back when the place has filled up a bit.

Many comment threads and forums are like that. You find just a handful of people there – sometimes none. You find that hardly anyone contributes to the forums, and that their contributions aren't interesting.

Communities must be nurtured.

User inequality

The other problem is that most users don't participate very much. They are lurkers.

Jakob Nielsen[5] comes up with these figures:

- 90 per cent of your users never contribute
- 9 per cent contribute occasionally
- 1 per cent contribute frequently.

Why is that a problem?

Because a tiny minority, who may not have lives, dominate. If you want to get a good, accurate sense of a community's interest in a subject, it can be hard. The few make a lot of noise, the majority is pretty much silent.

So you get a biased understanding of the community. That matters, says Nielsen, because "many differences almost certainly exist between people who post a lot and those who post a little."

And you would never hear from the silent majority of lurkers – the mute majority who are your typical readers.

on the website

Read more from Nielsen on this point.

9B4

How to build a forum on your WordPress site

A forum is a substantial step up from a comment thread. Forums don't work on every site, and they may not work on yours. But you should still build one, and use it to get some hands-on experience of how to manage one. This is another vital skill for the multimedia journalist.

on the website

Find a full, step-by-step guide to building a forum area on your WordPress site with bbPress.

What forums topics should you start?

Once you have your forums area up and running, you could go ahead and add some topics to it and begin the work of getting discussion going. Your skill as a community host will be in setting up suitable categories that reflect your readers' interests.

Get on with that by all means. If you are working on your WordPress (or any other) site with a group of journalism students you could all pitch in and start to populate the area. But I'm going to move on now and look at some wider aspects of encouraging community content. We'll look at how to encourage contributions, and how to be a good community journalist.

Managing forums and the role of the community reporter, editor or manager

We've looked briefly at the difficulties of getting good community content, so what do we do to get great contributions from as wide a range of readers as we can?

We act like the editors that we are and recognise that we have to apply our editorial skills to encouraging, sifting and presenting community content.

Every multimedia journalist needs to engage with the community they report for, seek to inform and/or entertain. But there are also specific roles, where the focus of the job is to engage with the community.

We also recognise that a certain amount of inequality will always be with us.

Nielsen says: "Your only real choice here is in how you shape the inequality curve's angle."

We try to encourage contributions from more readers, so that we turn as many lurkers as we can into contributors.

Here's how we do that:

Make it easy to contribute

The less effort required, the more people will contribute.

So, clicking on a star rating is very easy.

Being more ambitious, you can pose a question that only takes one click to cast a vote. But, once a reader has voted, invite them to click through to a forum that is discussing the subject they have just voted on. You could also direct them to another news story, or perhaps a comment piece. With the software we have been discussing, you need the pro version of Poll Daddy to do that on its polls and surveys.

If you can encourage a reader to graduate from a simple step like casting a vote to reading further content, or going through to a poll, you are moving them up that triangle or pyramid of engagement that we have spoken of before. You are deepening the level of engagement they have with you.

Hit a controversial topic that your readers have strong feelings about, and you maximise the chances of getting them further involved.

Let's take an example.

Say a plan has been hatched to introduce traffic congestion charging in a city that you cover. You have a news story on the subject and, if the story has been a long-running one, perhaps an area of the website devoted to the topic that readers can easily find from your site's home page.

Ask readers to vote. Couch a simple, clear question that they can give a yes or no answer to.

Congestion charging - tell us what you think

Should motorists pay to come into the city at busy times?
Yes
No

The next step will depend on how good the software is that you are using for polls but, if it lets you, add a hypertext link from the result they see once they have cast their vote to a forum on the topic.

The problem on a busy forum is that the good comments get lost in a welter of so-so ones. If readers can't find them, they are less likely to get involved with the discussion that is going on, and to contribute to it themselves.

So you should find the good comments and highlight them. You can pick them out and add them to a Best Forum Posts area either on your site's home page or on what we might think of as your communities home page. Doing this rewards good participants. Pick the best news story comments, forum posts, blog posts, submitted stills and video and tell readers about them - in the forums area, at other places on the site where community content is asked for, in your email bulletin and in your print publication.

Nielsen says: "Promote quality contributors. If you display all contributions equally, then people who post only when they have something important to say will be drowned out by the torrent of material from the hyperactive 1 per cent."

Instead, he says, you should give extra prominence to good contributions, and to contributions from those who, as indicated by their reputation ranking, have proved their value.

You could copy a site such as eBay, and give them stars by their profile.

The role of the community reporter, editor and host

Successful community engagement takes time and effort, and has led to the creation of a new type of journalist called the community editor or reporter. But the need for community engagement does not end there. In many organisations, all journalists are expected to engage extensively with the community.

Let's take the local newspaper company Gannett as an example of how online journalism and community connections are central to job descriptions for many journalists. In 2014 Gannett developed what it called the Newsroom of the Future, with job descriptions that demonstrated a focus on measuring the online engagement a story generated – the metrics – and on journalists' role as "community connectors".

We've mentioned one role, community content editor, already. Another is an engagement editor, who "Plans and executes engagement opportunities to maximize community impact and story resonance in print, digital, community event and social media settings".

Reporters and photographers/videographers all, in addition to creating content, must act "as a public ambassador through community outreach."

on the website

Find more on Gannett's Newsroom of the Future job descriptions.

The Guardian's community engagement programme

The *Guardian* has journalists in roles including social and communities editor, and a community coordinator for news, as well as a moderation team working on its forums.

There is a community page:

www.theguardian.com/community

where readers are invited to comment on blogs and articles: "have your say on the big issues of the day, send us your pictures, share your travel tips and secrets, contribute to features stories and sections in print, and to get or give advice about careers".

On the *Guardian*'s Comment is Free (CiF) web area, a community of 400 commentators are invited to contribute each month.

A number of *Guardian* community journalists contributed to a conference on building communities.[6]

Laura Oliver, a community manager who is one of those 'embedded' within the news room and areas such as CiF said her role is to be the "voice of the reader", encouraging a "two-way conversation" and broadening the coverage. "Once a story is published, that's not the end of it as that's where the readers come in."

Oliver said the *Guardian* wants to go beyond asking readers to "send in pictures of snow", and gave the example of ensuring the team connected with those contributing from North Africa during the height of the uprisings and ensuring those commentators would come back to them.

She also highlighted the collaboration from readers and expert commentators during a daily blog on a major piece of government legislation, the Health and Social Care Bill, during its passage through Parliament.

Claire Armitstead, literary editor of the *Guardian*, talked about crowdsourcing and call-outs for reader responses and how they influence sections such as Books: "What this new journalism has opened up is new ways of responding to criticism within the arts," she said.

Dan Roberts, the *Guardian*'s national editor, explained how his team started by trying to capture witnesses to events, harnessing citizen journalists, and has evolved into opening up to publishing the daily newslist. The goal was to get assistance and feedback: "That way we know that we are chasing the things that readers care about."

So, another of the skills required of a modern multimedia journalist is the ability to run a community.

That means caring about the community, being a part of it, getting involved in what it does and using what you learn to inform your reporting.

When you set up a poll, monitor the comments. Select the best ones and promote them. Use the poll result as the basis for another news story. With the congestion charging example you can get a main story out of a poll that shows 80 per cent of readers oppose congestion charging.

The community reporter is looking for stories that get readers going. Stories that provoke a strong emotional response are often the ones to generate reader comment.

Find the Big Conversations

What we are looking for is what I'm calling the Big Conversations. These are the subjects that readers really care about and want to discuss. What these Big Conversations are will differ depending on your readership.

questions

What matters to the readers of the sites you have created? What Big Conversations ought there to be on your forums?

Really effective community content-rich sites take those big conversations - and the needs of their readers - very much into account when they plan the site, what it contains and how it can be used.

TESConnect

TESConnect is a good example. **www.tesconnect.com** is the online version of the *Times Education Supplement*. It is what I consider to be a trail blazer because, although it comes from a print publication that is news driven, it has found a strong identity online. Look at its home page and you'll see what I mean.

TESConnect is a great model for what can be done with community content.

Many websites are news driven. Indeed, one of the key distinctions publishers draw between their print and web publications is that fast, breaking news goes online, and more considered or featurey or analytical coverage goes in print.

TESConnect is different. The content of the print magazine is still there, and so is news, but the site is actually focused on the readers – their needs and contributions.

And it connects over 60m teachers and students globally through its community area. That's incredible. Many communities are much smaller.

In an interview with the Online Journalism Blog, the TES's Edward Griffith explained how the site came to be as it is.

on the website

You'll find a link to the full interview on the website.

He said:

> Some one noticed in the forums there were two big conversations going on. People were seeking support and ideas from each other. . .[and] sharing teaching tools and resources. . . So we developed a prototype resources sharing tool, and it went through the roof. It's grown 200% y-o-y ever since.

on the website

Find more on how TESConnect has built such a large professional community.

9B6

Managing forums

There are two main aspects to this part of the forum-managing job which, incidentally, might be part of the community editor or reporter's responsibilities, or might be a separate role.

One is about being a good host, the other is about being a sort of community police officer. Because not everyone is well behaved online. You need rules that encourage good neighbourliness, and to enforce them when users persistently overstep the mark and cause trouble.

How to be a good host

Be there. If you don't show up at your own party, why should anyone else?

on the website

Find out more on how to be a good host.

Moderating community content

Moderation is checking readers' contributions – from comments to blogs, submitted videos or other material – to ensure it is acceptable for publication. We need to do this for a number of reasons. For one we don't want certain contributors spoiling the atmosphere and putting others off from contributing. For another, we don't want them breaking the law. If they break the law, we are breaking it too, because we are the publisher. If they defame someone, we defame them too. If they commit contempt of court, so do we. We'll look at the law further after we've considered moderation.

Moderation can take three forms

1   **Pre-moderation** where material is moderated before it becomes available to users.

     The community editor has seen it and decided it is suitable for posting. This approach is necessary on sites where the users are vulnerable – children, for example, or other sections of the community particularly vulnerable to abuse – or where the subject matter is particularly sensitive.

2   **Post-moderation** where material is moderated after it is posted. The moderator effectively sweeps the site periodically, removing anything objectionable. This approach works for sites on which there is lively debate about current affairs.

3   **Reactive moderation** where it is left to site users to alert the moderator to offensive or inappropriate material. This approach is really only suitable for communities where few breaches of acceptable publishing practice is found.

Most comment and forums software includes a button marked "Report this post", or words to that effect, so that readers can alert the moderator to anything they find objectionable. This safeguard can be used in conjunction with any of the three approaches to moderation.

Not all sites are moderated, and you are deemed less liable for defamatory content if you don't moderate.

The law on community content

The law on what is acceptable in community content, and the responsibilities of the publisher to ensuring it is acceptable, is still being formulated and is confused. What we need to be aware of in the UK is essentially the law of defamation.

However, with community content as opposed to content created by a journalist, we have a bit more leeway. If a defamatory statement is published by a user we should move "expeditiously" to remove or disable access to it. We aren't required to monitor content, but if we *are* monitoring it we are expected to spot and remove anything objectionable. Some publishers decide not to moderate, but if you take that course you may well find potential community contributors put off by the nasty stuff they see on the site.

on the website

Find an outline of the UK law on community content.

When to intervene

Many situations that require moderators to intervene don't involve actual law-breaking, but rather upset the atmosphere in the forum.

You don't want to stifle debate, but there are occasions when things get out of hand, or when some posters set out to abuse, bully or gratuitously insult other users.

You can't allow racist, homophobic or otherwise threatening comments.

Your T's and C's - terms and conditions - should make plain what is acceptable and what is not. Think of them as house rules; an outline of what we consider acceptable behaviour. So read them and use them to moderate comment.

If users break the house rules

First warn them.

Remove their comment. If it's a situation that could become controversial, tell users what you have done and why.

Often, unacceptable comments arise from users not knowing the law. They name a defendant who is, for example, protected because of their age, or the victim of a sexual assault. Such breaches of the law must be removed asap, but you can also educate users, and even possibly avoid such breaches in the future, by publicly pointing out why you have had to remove a post.

on the website

On the website you'll find a link to the BBC's guidance on moderating community content.

9B7

Exercises and projects

Exercise 1

Look at a wide range of sites and assess:

1   The quality and amount of community content they contain.

2   The big conversations readers are having.

3   How welcoming the communities area is for users, particularly new users.

4   Is there a communities editor or host and how evident and effective are they?

Exercise 2

Take two sites and monitor them over a period of four to five weeks. For both:

1   Produce an audit of their community content.

2   Develop a strategy for improving the amount of community content on the site.

Projects

Develop community content on your website, including:

1   Invite comment on stories, monitor that comment and promote good comment.

2   Run regular polls.

3   Run forums and be active in them, beginning threads and contributing to them.

4   Look out for big conversations and reflect such interests and concerns in the content you produce.

Notes

1   http://www.poynter.org/how-tos/digital-strategies/146345/10-ways-journalists-can-use-twitter-before-during-and-after-reporting-a-story/
2   http://jimromenesko.com/2014/08/08/here-are-the-new-jobs-being-offered-to-gannett-journalists/
3   http://www.dailymail.co.uk/news/article-2722812/Fury-bungling-BBC-tributes-Jimmy-Savile-posted-alongside-website-reports-Robin-Williams-suicide.html
4   http://www.morningadvertiser.co.uk/General-News/CAMRA-CGA-new-pub-closure-figures
5   http://www.useit.com/alertbox/participation_inequality.html
6   http://blogs.journalism.co.uk/2012/03/25/how-the-guardians-community-of-commentators-contributes-to-the-story/

chapter ten

Email bulletins and creating your own RSS feed with Yahoo Pipes

In the book version of this chapter we will cover:

- How to write an email bulletin
- How to create and publish an email bulletin
- How to automate the content gathering and publishing process
- Using Yahoo Pipes to create an RSS feed for a bulletin.

At the end of the chapter are a range of exercises and projects to enable you to practise what you have learned.

In the online version of this chapter you will find:

- Links to all the examples discussed here
- Step-by-step tuition in creating your email bulletin
- Video demonstrations of all the applications discussed here.

Always have the companion website to this book open at www.multimedia-journalism. co.uk. That way you can easily click on the links to the stories discussed here.

10B1

Introduction to email bulletins

In this chapter we're looking at two more ways to distribute your content.

The first, regularly published email bulletins, are very useful for us and for readers. We like them because the reader doesn't have to remember to tap in our URL to get to our website. Instead, if they open the email bulletin they find heads and sells and can click from them straight into our site. Once there, they can move around, or go back to select another story they like the look of.

Readers like them because they are reminders to check on the news we provide and because of the ease of use. But they won't sign up to receive them unless they value our site.

Jakob Nielsen[1] summarises email bulletins' appeal like this: "Newsletters feel personal because they arrive in your inbox; you have an ongoing relationship with them. In contrast, websites are things you glance at when you need to get something done or find the answer to a specific question."

Nielsen says that newsletters can create much more of a bond between a user and a publisher than a website can.

You should sign up to email bulletins that are useful for your research just as you do to RSS feeds and social media accounts.

10B2

Writing an email bulletin

You'll be using a piece of software to write your email bulletin. We'll look in detail at using one, MailChimp, on the MMJ website. Any email client is a template. It will probably require you to write a certain number of elements at a certain length.

The first thing is the subject line. This is the text that appears as the subject of the email. You have about 60 characters and you should use them to present a taster of the material to come. You don't need to say who you are because that will be in the 'From' part of the line. Let's look at some examples.

The first is a financial bulletin from *The Times*:

> **KILL THE COMPETITION: Airlines unite. . . Dow chaos. . . Germany concedes**

This is from the publicans' magazine the *Morning Advertiser*:

> **Morning Advertiser: 'Refer beer tie to Competition Commission'**

Specific story teasers are much better than a generic line such as Breaking News, Latest Bulletin or News Update.

Generic lines don't tempt the reader with specifics and hence leave them less likely to click through to read the content.

Some subject lines are too long and only a fraction of the first news item is actually visible when you come to your emails. That's a lost opportunity to engage with the subscriber.

For example, this is from a B2B publication called *Construction News* (CN).

The full subject line said this:

> **CN plus Daily Newsletter: Bam Construct wins £35m Olympic academy job. . . Three battle for historic hotel refurb. . . Carillion signs £550m Abu Dhabi deal. . .**

In my inbox this cut off after "Bam Construct. . ." so I only got two words from one of the three news items they wanted to tell me about.

Writing "CN plus Daily Newsletter" in the subject field could be covered in the 'From' field. Remove those words and you have more space for actual content.

You can also use the name of the author of the bulletin in the From field. *The Times*'s Red Box, which we'll discuss in a moment, does this.

Writing the content of the bulletin

There are a couple of good ways to approach writing the bulletin, and the golden rule in both cases is to keep them simple. Bulletins should not take any more time to skim through than an email would. They should be written for easy scanning.

The head, sell and hypertext link approach

One good way of organising them is with the classic head and sell combination that we use for our online news story writing. It will be as effective with an email bulletin.

As with heads and sells on a home or main news page, readers must click on the link provided in the email sell, or the head, to read the story. Once they do, they are on our site. They have got there without having to type in our URL, which means that bulletins are a great way of keeping in touch with readers and encouraging them to return regularly to our site.

You can just take heads and sells from your top news stories and other items. Or you can select the best of the blogs, and the best comments from readers.

A site that has a strong community can list in its bulletin the top discussion threads on the forums, or the best reader comments and the best blog posts in addition to news.

The beat-blog approach

Some bulletins don't take this news-menu form. Instead, they take the form of a concise summary of developments in a given area. As with a beat-blog, you don't have to restrict yourself to your own material. Some titles' bulletins contain news and comment from their rivals.

questions

Why would we do this? Can you think of an upside and a downside to giving a rival's content publicity in our bulletin? Don't read on until you have considered.

The reason for doing so is that we know readers are busy and may well only subscribe to one bulletin that covers the sector we operate in, whether that is general news or a specialist area. We hope they will choose our bulletin, but we want to give them a good reason for choosing us over others: a reason above and beyond the quality of our own content. So we make our bulletin a comprehensive one. If it covers the opposition sufficiently thoroughly, then we hope that readers who could choose to subscribe to our rivals' bulletins will only subscribe to us. We save them time, we make their lives easier.

The downside is that we make them aware of rivals, who they can sample through us. If they prefer them, then we have lost them. The solution: be better than them.

To some this seems mad – you are inviting your readers to go elsewhere for their information. But we shouldn't be so defensive. The ethos of the web is openness. We let the reader go, indeed we help them to shop around, in the belief that they will come back to us if we are offering the best.

Few people read just one branded news or information site. They select what interests them from across the board, depending on their areas of interest. If they like politics they will want to read the main commentators from a range of titles.

Email bulletins are one easy way of reading what we consider to be the best reporting, comment and other material from a wide range of publications.

Some websites set out to do this – to aggregate by offering links to a wide range of content generated by others. *The* (London) *Times*, for example, runs a daily politics email bulletin called Red Box. It comes from a named political specialist on the title, and contains a summary of political news and comment from *The Times* itself plus from whatever other sources are required to give a reader the full picture of that day's political news and comment. You can sign up for it here: **www.thetimes.co.uk/redbox/signup/**

How often should we send bulletins?

Daily for a busy news site, weekly for a less busy one. If we are on a hobby site then weekly is probably best. Any less than weekly and the reader forgets to look out for them. Send them too often, and they find them a nuisance. Send them more often than you can cope with, and you find you have to repeat stories – and that turns readers off very quickly.

Subscribe and unsubscribe

Both should be easy. To get someone to subscribe, you can expect them to give you a little information. Their email address is clearly essential. We should not ask them for things they can't see the relevance of – their address and phone number, for example.

Unsubscribing should be really simple: ideally, by simply clicking on an unsubscribe button. If it is any harder, readers may decide not to unsubscribe formally, but simply to add you to their blocked senders list, and that's treating you like a spammer.

10B3

Creating your email bulletin

There are a number of bulletin – or newsletter – clients that you can use to create your emails. We are going to go step-by-step through the process of creating one with MailChimp (**www. mailchimp.com**). Because MailChimp regularly updates the services it offers, we will keep detailed tuition for the MMJ website.

on the website

Find:

- Step-by-step tuition in creating and publishing your email bulletin
- How to automatically generate a bulletin from your content
- Why email bulletins are another valuable way to distribute your journalism.

10B4

Creating an RSS feed with Yahoo Pipes

Say you do want to set up a bulletin from a number of sources. You could, as Red Box does, have one journalist read all those sources and write/curate the best content. Of, if you simply don't have the resources for that, you could automate the process, producing a curated feed.

We can use Yahoo Pipes (**https://pipes.yahoo.com/pipes/**) to create a new RSS feed that is actually a mash-up of a number of individual RSS feeds. And we can turn it into an email bulletin – or post it on our WordPress site as we did with our own content feed in Chapter 6, section B8.

on the website

See a screencast demonstration of how Yahoo Pipes works.

The screencast is probably the easiest way to get the hang of it, but here's what Yahoo Pipes is, and what it does, from Wikipedia: "Yahoo Pipes is a web application that provides a graphical user interface for building data mashups that aggregate web feeds, web pages, and other services, creating web-based apps from various sources, and publishing those apps."

"The application works by enabling users to 'pipe' information from different sources and then set up rules for how that content should be modified (for example, filtering)."

It's actually a lot simpler than it sounds, and thanks to that graphic interface, it's highly intuitive to use.

There is a simple logic to using Pipes that makes it a good first step in creating data mashups. We're only going to do one simple thing - create a mash-up of a number of RSS news feeds - but there is a great deal more that can be done.

on the website

Note: To avoid our step-by-step tuition in using Yahoo Pipes becoming dated, we'll cover the detailed tuition on the MMJ website.

10B5

Exercises and projects

Exercise 1

Subscribe to a number of email bulletins covering the same subject area. Compare how good a job they do.

Exercise 2

Find email bulletins that cover your beat or specialism. Add them to your regular story research routine.

Projects

1 Produce an email bulletin and publish it either daily or weekly, based on what is appropriate for your site.

You will need to follow the tuition on the MMJ website and:

- ■ Establish a subscriber list
- ■ Design and populate a bulletin
- ■ Send it to yourself and thoroughly test it
- ■ Publish it to your subscribers.

2 Create an RSS feed using Yahoo Pipes and turn this into an email bulletin

You should:

- ■ Identify a number of sources that together offer a useful curation of a specific area of news, information or entertainment
- ■ Get RSS feeds for each of them
- ■ Use Yahoo Pipes to mash them together and create one new RSS feed
- ■ Embed this in your website or blog
- ■ Create an email bulletin from your new RSS.

Note

1   Jakob Nielsen, www.nngroup.com/articles/author/jakob-nielsen/

chapter eleven

Stills, audio and audio-visual packages: Getting the best out of a digital SLR camera

In the book version of this chapter we will cover:

- Getting the most out of a DSLR camera
- Examining the types of audio slideshow journalists are making
- Gathering the material for your audio slideshow
- Editing an audio slideshow on your phone, tablet and computer
- How to use visually focused social media for your journalism
- How to use social audio platforms such as Spotify for journalism.

At the end of the chapter are a range of exercises and projects to enable you to practise what you have learned.

In the online version of this chapter you will find:

- Videos that take you step-by-step through mastering a DSLR digital camera
- Links to the videos and other material discussed here, plus additional resources
- Essential updates on all that is discussed in the book.

Have the companion website to this book open at www.multimedia-journalism.co.uk. That way you can easily click on the links to the stories discussed here.

Getting the most out of digital cameras

To create better still photographs, you need to become more knowledgeable and proficient in using your camera. You can stick with your camera phone if you like, but they still can't offer all a Digital Single Lens Reflex (DSLR) camera can.

Individual DSLR cameras differ in the functions they have and how you access them, but the following is a good general guide to the features such a camera is likely to have. You'll need to browse the manual to find out how to access these features with your particular camera.

You can just point and shoot, but most cameras give you two other options. One is a fully manual mode, which we'll discuss later. The other is a range of automatic options – selected by moving a dial or selecting from a menu.

Automatic options

They might be for taking portraits, landscapes, sports and moving subjects, close-ups and night photography.

Portrait setting will bring out the portrait subject in focus against a background that has been softened (photographer-speak for not in sharp focus). This gives a photograph a sense of depth.

Landscape

The camera will select the focus area containing the subject that is closest to the camera.

Sports

You get a fast shutter speed to ensure that an image is clear, focused. The camera will automatically focus continuously on the subject that is in the centre of the lens, which means it is easy to take a sequence of stills of an event.

Close-ups

Useful for small objects that you want to show in detail.

Night photography

The camera compensates for the low light levels and balances the main subject and background in portraits. Because light is lower, shutter speed is slower to enable the camera to gather the light it needs to illuminate the subject. If you don't hold the camera steady while the shutter is open, that can mean a blurry picture, so a tripod is useful.

Choosing a shooting mode

You can also choose a shooting mode. The camera will either take one photo when the shutter button is pressed down, or shoot continuously while the button is depressed. This is very useful when photographing sport or moving objects when you'd like to capture a sequence of shots of the action.

Self-timer or remote control

This enables you to get into the photo you take. It can be handy if you are out on a job and want to show yourself in the action without relying on someone else to take a decent picture for you. You can put the camera on a tripod, frame the shot you want, either set the shutter release delay (which typically gives you up to ten seconds) or take the remote control, and get into the picture.

Image quality and size

If you are shooting for print you will want a large, high quality image. If your work is to go straight to the web, you can shoot in reduced quality. Some cameras allow you to shoot in both formats concurrently, which means you have a high quality image for print and a low quality one for the web.

Manual mode

To get the most out of a DSLR camera you need to take it out of automatic mode, where the camera decides how the picture will be taken. Now you are in full control. Here's what it enables you to do:

Manual focus

This means you choose what you focus on, rather than the camera selecting the most prominent object. It can be useful when there is more than one object in view and you want to choose to focus on one rather than the other. Maybe you have a face close to the camera but you want to blur that and go sharp on a figure behind the first one.

Flash mode

In automatic mode the camera uses flash when it needs more light. If you want to override that – so you shoot in what can be referred to as either ambient, available, or natural light – you can turn the flash off.

Turning off the flash when light levels are low means the camera will need to extend the time the shutter is open. So, again, putting the camera on a tripod can be useful.

The two key controls

When you are in full manual mode you have control over the two key variables that determine how your photograph is taken. These are shutter speed and aperture, measured as F stops.

on the website

Find links to a wide range of video tutorials on all aspects of handling a camera in manual mode.

Shutter speed

Shutter speed can vary from the very fast, 1,000th of a second, to one, two or more seconds. This is the time the shutter is open and hence how long light is admitted and can reach the sensor on which your image is recorded. A standard photograph is taken at 250th of a second.

So, the less light that is available then the slower the shutter speed you need, the more light the faster the shutter speed.

Aperture

Aperture is the other variable. A lens has a diaphragm; a rotating section that, when turned, adjusts the amount of light coming into the lens and hence how much light hits the sensor. It will have a read-out beginning with F. The higher the number, the less light comes through – so F11 lets in less light than F5.6.

Depth of field

A manual aperture-setting controls not only the amount of light coming in, but also the depth of field. That is, how much of a scene – containing things in the foreground, the mid-ground and background – is in focus.

In manual mode you can adjust the aperture from F3.5 to F22.

All F stops allow a different amount of light in and give a different depth of field. It's like the eye of the camera, and adjusting the aperture determines how open the eye is and hence how much light is getting into it and reaching the sensor that records your image.

The wider the aperture, the more light is coming in and the shallower the depth of field.

So, when taking a photograph in manual mode you need to take account of how much light is available, and what depth of field you want in your photograph.

When light is low you will need to open the aperture up to allow more into the camera. But you also need to be aware of the shutter speed you are using, because if you are photographing action it could become blurred. When light is good you have plenty of options, when it is low your options are reduced.

Too much light leaves you with an overexposed photograph in which the colours are bleached. With too little light you get a dark, grainy image.

So if you are shooting action in low light you need a fast shutter speed, and to open up your aperture to get the light you need.

Shutter and aperture balance

Balancing shutter speed and aperture is the key to getting good photographs.

Here are the things you must balance to get a good photograph:

- The amount of light
- The depth of field you want
- The subject
- What the subject is doing.

Taken together they will give you the balance you need between aperture and shutter speed.

You need to look at the situation. If there is a lot of movement, you will need a fast shutter speed. If there is low light, you'll need to open up your aperture to compensate.

If you want a wide depth of field you need high F ratings – F20–F22. That setting means that things in the foreground, mid-ground and background are all in focus.

To have a subject in the mid-ground in focus but foreground and background out of focus use F2 – F4.

Medium settings – around F11 will allow you to see either foreground and mid-ground in focus, or mid-ground and background.

Aperture priority and shutter priority

It all sounds very complicated, but there is a half-way house that can help you master all this. You can choose either aperture priority or shutter priority. This enables you to give priority to one and have control over it, while the other is handled automatically by the camera.

You might use shutter priority when you are shooting action but want to slow the shutter speed and make the image a little blurry, to denote movement.

Aperture priority would enable you to set the depth of field, and shutter speed would be adjusted to work with that setting.

Camera lenses

Standard lens 50mm

Most cameras come with a lens that has a range, from say 18-55mm, or perhaps 18-77mm.

At 50mm the lens replicates the way the human eye works; it is close to the view we get without a camera.

Telephoto and wide angle lenses

Go above 50mm and you are zooming in on a subject, narrowing the view. Long lenses are called telephoto lenses. As you go progressively below 50mm you are widening the angle of the image you capture. At 18mm you have a pretty wide angle and can be close to a subject but still get it all in. There are so-called fish eye lenses that go down to 8mm, but distort the image in doing so.

You will be able to use 50mm most of the time.

Wide angle lenses are good for tight spaces such as when you need to show as much as you can of a small room, but are also good for panoramic shots of a landscape, or getting the whole of a building in, or perhaps a street or other scene where you want the subject - a person - but also plenty of the situation they are in - the background.

Audio slideshows

The audio slide show is one of the storytelling forms to have been born out of online, multimedia journalism. It is a great, hybrid way of telling stories. It combines some of the audio techniques we used in Chapter 4, when we created sound packages containing people's voices and actuality – atmospheric sounds that told the listener where they were or what they were doing. It also takes in the slide show storytelling technique, but brings to it the discipline of video storytelling, as discussed in Chapter 5, where the images must combine to tell a story: a story with a beginning, middle and end.

Types of audio slideshows

There are a number of different types of audio slide show.

on the website

Find a wide range of audio slideshow examples embedded, and discussed, on the MMJ website.

Here, we'll outline the types of package that are being created, but you really need to see and hear the examples, so head to the website first for this module.

The simplest audio slideshow just adds stills to illustrate what is being said. This is not particularly adventurous, but it can be a good deal more interesting than a video of a talking head.

The principle behind creating a good audio slideshow is to combine an interesting audio track with visuals that both complement the audio and make the package more interesting.

There are two general styles of audio slideshows developing. One is essentially a news report, combining a reporter acting as narrator with sound bites and natural sound.

Sometimes the reporter/narrator is absent, and the voices of the subjects take precedence. This second style of audio slideshow relies on the voices of the subjects to make a story more compelling, and draw the listener in more effectively.

Archive stills pictures can be combined with audio – including music and the spoken work – to create an atmospheric package.

Gathering material for an audio slide show

You need good audio and good pictures. Let's assume for now that you are not using archive material but gathering material afresh.

stills, audio and audio-visual
packages: getting the best out
of a digital SLR camera

Your audio will need to be of high quality, and gathered as described in Chapter 4. Indeed, it's probably worth thinking of the audio as driving the story, with the stills there to illustrate that audio. With the stills, think as you did in Chapter 5 where you wanted to tell a story with moving images, and needed an establishing shot, a series of shots of individuals and things/places in the story, many in medium close up, plus some detail shots.

Let's take an audio slideshow that appeared in a local paper called the *Croydon Advertiser* and analyse the story as it is told in stills and sound.

www.sitbonzo.com/scout/

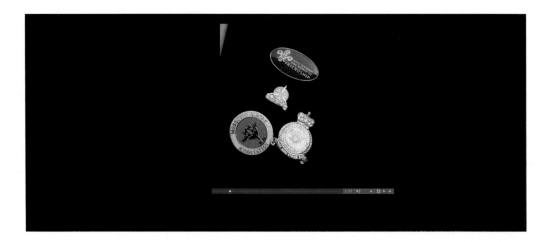

on the website

Watch the slideshow on the MMJ website.

This is the story of a scout gathering. The package starts with a caption, then a still of a sign made for the event. On the audio is a general hubbub of young voices.

Then comes an aerial shot of the event, followed by a still of a scout being helped by an adult. The audio is the same general chatter.

There follow stills of particular events, such as the scouts on parade, with audio of a troop leader taking them through the scout promise.

Then comes an interview with a veteran, now honorary scout member. A caption tells us who he is and we hear him talking about his time in the organisation. As he talks we get a series of stills that illustrate events at the gathering. When we see a picture of bacon frying we get an appropriate sound effect mixed in to the audio. Other interviews follow, with a wide range of stills of scouts, badges, books and other memorabilia.

The package is relaxed, it doesn't have a strong narrative thread to it, but it does capture the atmosphere, and you have a strong sense of the people featured telling their own story in their own way.

on the website

Find a second audio slideshow analysed in detail.

Getting started

Remember, you must tell a story. The images you use, plus the audio, must fit neatly together into a coherent story. So here's what you need:

Audio

An interview with your subjects that has them speaking as naturally as possible

You can choose whether to set the piece up with your own voice, or leave it to the subjects.

Actuality or wild track. If the subject lends itself to sound effects, get people talking while they work. If not, gather wild track to lay under the other audio.

Stills

An establishing shot of the place or event that the story is about.

Good shots of the subjects, preferably taken while they go about their business. Having them grinning straight at camera is not ideal.

Illustrative shots of the things they talk about.

Detail shots to bring as much interest and variety to the visual side of the report as possible.

Rather than just throwing together a bunch of interesting photos, select photos that will, when placed in a certain order, tell a cohesive story - creating a type of photo essay. When done right, this is one of the more effective ways of using online multimedia to tell stories.

It is at the editing stage that you sort out your running order and how stills and audio fit together, so let's move on to that.

stills, audio and audio-visual
packages: getting the best out
of a digital SLR camera

11B4

Editing an audio slideshow

Before we look at some of the software you might use, let's cover some general principles in putting the elements you have together.

You might start with a title or with an establishing shot. You will need to let that opening image sink in – give the viewer time to read the title or run their eye over the establishing still, absorbing the information it contains. You must give them enough time – not too little or they can't keep up with the story, nor too long, or they get bored.

This is called pacing, and applies to each image you present. A simple image might need only a second or two to be absorbed, but a more complex one – one with a good deal of detail – must be presented for longer.

However, you can gently move things forward by beginning the audio of, say, the first person to speak in your package, under the opening still. That way, the reader knows what is coming next. They'll expect to see the person speaking next or, perhaps, an image that relates clearly to what he or she is speaking about.

Whether you go to a picture of the person speaking at the start depends on how important they are to your story. With the manager of the second-hand wedding dress store we discussed on the web version of this chapter, or the 90-year-old man, that made sense. If the person speaking is not that central to the story – is describing events they were not directly part of, then their picture can wait. Indeed, it might not be needed at all.

Putting audio and stills together is probably the trickiest part. You will have some clear connections between the two – points at which what is being said can be directly illustrated with stills, but the link is not as close as it is with a video package.

Review all the stills, listen to all the audio and then begin to piece them together.

Getting the start of audio and the right opening still is a good first step. As with video, you can import your images and work out a rough order for them.

Next, work out the logic of the audio so that the story is told coherently. There will be points along the way when you should bring both together directly, as with the *Miami Herald* Pawn Shops piece where, when the names of the detectives are given, we get a coinciding shot of them. At other points you can vary the images to bring variety and counterpoint to the audio. The images become, in a way, asides or additions to the main thrust of the story.

You should also go for a variety of images – general shots, medium close-ups and detail shots should be interwoven to keep the visuals varied and interesting.

You can apply transitions between images as you did with video, but don't overdo them. A clean cut from image to image usually works perfectly well.

Your software will also allow you to zoom in or out of an image, or to pan across it. If you have gathered enough material you won't need to do this, but if material is limited – perhaps you are using archive material and have just a school photograph in which the subject of your package is a tiny face. If so, zooming in on that face, or out from it, can help prevent your visuals becoming dull.

You need to keep your audio track interesting too. It is just as important as with video to have high quality audio. Layering your subjects talking with wild track and appropriate music adds another depth of interest to the package.

Editing software

Windows Moviemaker and Apple iMovies can both be used to create an audio and stills package.

To edit on your phone or tablet, you should consider Vericorder software products 1st Video or Voddio.

on the website

Find links to presentations on creating an audio slide show in Windows Moviemaker and Apple iMovies, and on a range of other software.

 11B5

Visually-orientated social media

If images are important in the journalism you are doing, you can use visually-orientated social media as we have discussed using Twitter, Google+ and Facebook.

Here are two to try.

on the website

Find links to these products, and to further tuition in using them for journalism.

Instagram

Instagram is a sort of Twitter for images and short videos. Instagram lets users take photos and 3-15 second videos on their mobile phone, add filters and effects to them and share them instantly, both on the Instagram app and also to other social networks including Facebook and Twitter.

What sets it apart from most other photo-sharing platforms is the emphasis on high quality photography, and sophisticated photo enhancement and editing. To produce poor quality photographs is to invite the scorn of the Instagram community.

It's good for mobile social sharing, which some analysts say explains why Facebook, on which users share 250 million images daily, but which had not been strong on mobile photo sharing, paid $1bn for it in 2012.

You can use it to crowdsource images and short videos about a big event. CNN has used Instagram to source images from the public during major events such as presidential inaugurations.

It's also about location. As photos and videos can be geo-tagged, Instagram can work for you when location is in some way important to your journalism.

on the website

Find examples of how geo-tagged Instagram images have been used in reporting.

When you are on a story you can publish behind-the-scenes stills to Instagram, and give an insight into a story that is breaking, or which you are working on.

Live news events that involve many people can be tracked via Instagram. Events such as major storms that have people reaching for their camera phones are often played out on Instagram.

You can also give content previews on the platform. If you are interviewing someone, sharing a picture of the two of you on Instagram as you sit down to chat can bring responses including questions you ought to be asking. You'd tweet this picture too, obviously.

Pinterest

Pinterest is a photographic platform whose focus is on personal lifestyle. Users create boards, which are like scrapbooks, made up of pins – individual items. Pins and boards can be shared, and many users create boards from pins they've seen and liked on Pinterest, rather than sourcing original material. Along with stills, video and audio clips can also be uploaded. Unlike many social media platforms, Pinterest has a predominantly female community base.

Many magazine publishers have taken advantage of what's popular on the platform - food, furnishings, decoration and design, hobbies, crafts and other pastimes - by creating boards that showcase the feature stories they've published on these topics.

You can use Pinterest to have your consumer content shared and distributed among a much wider audience than would have found your title without it.

The *New York Times* has several dozen food, wedding and other boards

www.pinterest.com/nytimes/

The *Wall Street Journal* has several fashion boards, and has used Pinterest interactively around New York Fashion Week by asking readers, ahead of the event, to curate a board showing the fashions that influence their style. It then featured some of the boards and Pinterest users on WSJ.com.

The *Guardian* takes a particularly wide-ranging view of what can work on Pinterest. At the time of writing, it has boards on, among other things, a tribute to Andy Warhol, its own front pages, photography, cookery and data visualisations. Its On Our Radar board offers: "Intelligence alerts: incoming items of special interest", and its behind-the-scenes shows what is going on in the *Guardian*'s offices.

Audio social media

Finally, a further thought on audio-orientated social media. We talked about audioBoom in Chapter 4, but there are also music audio sites that we can use for our journalism.

Spotify

Spotify is the best known of the music streaming sites. Its facility to link to just about any music track means that, if you are reviewing new releases, or referring to particular pieces of music in an online article, you can add a link to it so readers can listen for themselves. Many online publishers now do that, making Spotify a great resource for creating multimedia journalism.

You can also create playlists, and share them. Some publishers, including *The* (London) *Times*, routinely get interview subjects to put together a Spotify playlist that they then share with readers.

on the website

Find a playlist from me on music with a journalism theme.

11B7

Exercises and projects

Exercise 1

Practise with a DSLR camera. Take pictures in a wide variety of situations in automatic and manual mode. Once you have a shot of a subject in automatic mode, move to manual and experiment with different settings to explore creating movement in an action photograph, with depth of field to add interest to a shot, and with the use of available light rather than flash.

Exercise 2

Look at a range of audio slideshows from a number of sources - including the sites of web-native titles, local and national newspapers, magazine and broadcasters' sites. Analyse the style of audio slideshows they produce. How good are they? Can they be improved? When you find a style that you like, apply it to the projects below.

Exercise 3

Research how a number of media outlets use visual social media including Instagram and Pinterest. Come up with a strategy for the websites that you are developing.

Exercise 4

Consider how you might use audio platforms such as Spotify in your journalism.

Projects

Do the following for each of the websites you are maintaining:

1 Create an audio slideshow that features a commentator - such as a sports reporter - discussing a game or event. Illustrate it with appropriate stills. Publish on your website.

2 Pick a news topic that lends itself to good stills, such as a weather story. Create an audio slide show in which you narrate the piece and conduct a number of interviews. Take appropriate stills to illustrate the interviews. Publish on your website.

3 Create a soft-news or features audio slideshow in which you record and photograph one or more individuals. Make theirs the only voices heard. Publish on your website.

4 Find an archive subject for which there are good stills, and find relevant people to interview. Create an audio slide show using just archive pictures and the voices of interviewees.

5 Establish an Instagram account and use it to both source and distribute news, information or entertainment.

6 Create a Spotify account for your website or beat blog and experiment with using music to develop your audience, interact with your community, and bring a multimedia element to your text music reviews or other content.

chapter twelve

Video

In the book version of this chapter we will cover:

- The future of video in news
- Getting the most out of video cameras
- How to film, edit and publish ultra-short videos using Vine and Instagram
- Shooting rough-and-ready video that puts the reporter and viewer at the heart of the action
- Improving your filming, story construction and editing in order to. . .
- Create broadcast-quality video.

At the end of the chapter are a range of exercises and projects to enable you to practise what you have learned.

In the online version of this chapter you will find:

- A wide range of videos to illustrate the techniques outlined in the following tuition
- Links to all the tuition and examples in the book version
- Essential updates on the tuition in the book.

Have the companion website to this book open at www.multimedia-journalism.co.uk. That way you can easily click on the links to the stories discussed here.

The future of video in news

By now you will have had a fair bit of practice in shooting and editing video. So what's the next step? That depends what style of video you are required to shoot. There is a strong divergence of opinion in the industry as to what form online video should take.

One school of thought is that online video should aspire to the high production values seen in traditional television news packages.

The other school believes that online video can be rough-and-ready and that good reports are not slickly produced, but instead show the reporter caught up in the thick of the action. This makes them much more immediate and compelling, the argument goes.

A third option is the development of ultra-short video reports of between 6 and 15 seconds. These can either be rough-and-ready or slickly filmed and edited.

This divergence is not a problem. We can cover all three approaches here, so that you are equipped to make videos in each style. For what it's worth, my view is that there will be situations for most multimedia journalists where they want to use one approach, other situations where the second is more appropriate, and further occasions where the third option suits the story, and the situation, best.

What the BBC has learned about doing video online – and what it teaches us

Steve Herrmann, editor of the BBC News website, said in a paper[1] that the familiar formats we currently know – the flagship bulletins, the rolling news channels – may change. He went on: "New technologies do not always replace old ones, but sometimes they do evolve and enhance them. I believe TV news is about to get much richer and more diverse as it becomes news in video, across many platforms."

That phrase "news in video, across many platforms" is a telling one. He doesn't think the flagship bulletins and rolling news channels are doomed – he believes they are more popular than ever – but he does say that TV news will have to adapt to changes in the ways people are watching news.

He goes on to outline changes and to pass on lessons learned about how people watch news on digital, on-demand platforms.

He says about 10 per cent of those watching video on the BBC News site are using mobile devices and interactive TV.

Short news clips

The BBC has discovered that short video clips which show the story, in contrast to traditional TV packages that tend to have a reporter telling the story, work well. Online, he says, there is often no need for the reporter as an intermediary, as a user will have already read the story.

These short news clips online work, if they show something visually compelling, not anchors or reporters outside buildings, but rather action, key soundbites, rare moments. But they must be kept short. Or very short.

They work best, he says, when they're embedded alongside or within related text stories.

We covered that in Chapter 5, so we will look in this chapter at video that can stand alone on a social network or website.

Traditional TV news packages

What about the traditional, well-crafted TV news package?

Herrmann believes that "one thing seems vital, editorially." It is that every TV news package has to be a piece of great storytelling. This is because there will be no bulletin to carry it, and so each will have to stand - or fall - on its own. This means that the navigation to it has to be simple to use, the labelling clear, and the report self-contained and strong. Any individual report, he goes on, could become a jumping-off point for related on-demand content - more video, text, or graphics on the same subject.

Traditional TV news skills

What about traditional TV news skills? Herrmann believes they will still matter in the future. He says the ability to recognise and gather great pictures, edit them skilfully, write concisely and clearly and tell compelling stories will be as important as ever. But, he adds, as TV news evolves into new forms, it will require skills such as developing clear labelling and signposting, simple navigation, concise headlines and summaries, balancing video and text, content that can stand alone, not as part of a linear sequence, and integration in the right places of short, sharp, unpackaged clips.

There is also the development of very short 6–15 second video clips in news reporting. We'll look at that later in this chapter.

Before we look at the different types of video and how to produce them, let's look at getting the most out of our camera.

Getting the most out of video cameras

A quick note: I'm saying video camera for ease here, but many DSLR cameras also shoot video, and many multimedia journalists use the one piece of hardware for both stills and moving images.

Having your video camera in automatic mode is a quick and easy solution for beginners. But, for more professional filming, you need to know how to use manual mode.

And, as with stills cameras, there is a half-way house on most camcorders, so you can set them to adjust to, and then act automatically, in a range of different conditions such as when filming sports, landscapes, in snow, at night, or where your subject is in a spotlight.

Then there are fully automatic settings.

Manual focus

Focusing manually on your subject means that, if someone or some thing passes in front of the camera, the focus will remain on your chosen subject. In automatic mode, the focus will momentarily change to this new, prominent object as it goes past.

Manual focus can also be useful if there are a lot of things going on in your shot. If you have control of the focus you can adjust it to take account of any movements your chosen subject takes. So if you are following a person in a crowd, you can keep them in focus as they move, and the camera cannot be distracted by anyone else who is in the frame.

To make things easy with a static subject, put the camera in auto mode and, once it has focused on your subject, turn to manual. Then the correct focus will remain, whatever happens.

Manual exposure

Manual exposure allows you to control the amount of light coming in to the camera. You can turn it up or down and, now that you are in control, if some extra light comes into the scene, the camera will not adjust to it. So a sudden flash of light, or if you follow a subject as they move from shadow across a brightly-lit window and back into shadow, will not affect the exposure.

You can also compensate for a scene in which your subject is being back-lit by a light source behind them, such as a brightly-lit window. In automatic mode the camera would take its light reading from the bright area it finds, and set its exposure to that. Which means your subject gets plunged into darkness. By manually adjusting exposure you can get the camera to brighten the whole scene, so that your subject is no longer in the shadows.

on the website

Find links to video tutorials on choosing and using a video camera.

Creating ultra-short 6–15 second videos

Let's look first at the development of very short video clips in news reporting. Leading the way here is the Vine app from Twitter, which allows 6 seconds of video to be shot and distributed as a tweet would be. Many other social platforms have followed with their own versions of ultra-short video, usually pegged at 15 seconds or less. Instagram, which we looked at in Chapter 11, has opted for 15 seconds max.

How the BBC and Guardian *are using ultra-short video*

The BBC has developed BBC Shorts, 15–30 second videos designed for social and mobile consumption. They range from simple animated graphics with voice over to short video clips of dramatic events accompanied by either captions or voice over.

The BBC is distributing such videos not just on its own branded platforms, but on social ones including Instagram. It has an Instagram account at **http://instagram.com/bbcnews**

The *Guardian* has GuardianCam, described by them as the "first truly global-from-the-start social account". Its videos often take the form of film plus voice over from an individual who illustrates a major story or issue. The *Guardian* uses the hashtag #guardiancam to broadcast on Instagram and Twitter.

Techniques of filming and publishing ultra-short video

It's worth experimenting with both Vine and Instagram – or any other platform that looks promising to you.

How to tell a six-second story on Vine

Vines (https://vine.co/) are ideal for short pieces of action, such as highlights during sports games – but beware of copyright issues.

Because you can stop and start filming as many times as you like within six seconds you can tell a story within a Vine, or explain something. You could show six slides featuring data, for example.

Editing Vines

You can save up to ten video posts as you're creating them, and delete and reorganise clips while constructing videos, which means that basic editing is possible within the app. Tapping the edit button at top right of your screen as your video plays back brings up edit mode, with the individual clips from your video arranged along the bottom of your screen, where you can drag and drop them into a different order.

There are apps available – such as Custom Video Uploader For Vine or Vinyet – that allow you to upload other video into Vine, meaning you can make highlight packages from other videos as tasters for big interviews or major news videos and promote them on Vine.

Publishing Vines on social media and in your WordPress website

You can add a comment or caption to your video, and post it to Vine, Twitter and Facebook. Sharing options include emailing the link. The link is the URL, and you can embed a Vine into a post on your WordPress website by pasting that link, in a line of its own, into your text, just as we have done earlier with other types of video.

You are allowed to embed Vines by you and others on your website or blog, but need to check the terms and conditions on using the logo here: **https://vine.co/logo**

How to tell a 15-second story on Instagram

Instagram videos can actually last from 3–15 seconds, but most people go for the upper limit. Facebook, which owns Instagram, offers advice for journalists on telling 15-second video stories which I summarise here:[2]

1   "Share breaking behind-the-scenes news clips". You can capture short video clips and share them from a reporting scene, giving a behind-the-scenes look into the event.

2   "Covering breaking news". You can find video from eyewitnesses and others caught up in a news event which will supplement the material you have, and very often enable you to get much closer to the story in your reporting.

3   "Crowdsourcing". You can prompt your community of viewers or readers to share videos from a news event by giving them a hashtag to include.

4   "Promote stories". You can use short video clips to preview stories you're working on.

on the website

Find examples of Instagram videos.

Editing Instagram videos

Using Instagram for video is almost exactly the same as using it for stills, but because processes in such a young application are likely to change over time, we'll keep step-by-step tuition for the MMJ website.

on the website

Find full tuition in editing on Instagram.

Publishing Instagram videos on social media and your WordPress website

Once you have published to your chosen social networks you can copy the video's URL, or choose to email it. If you email it to the private posting address we set up for WordPress live blogs you could have it added to that live blog automatically. Alternatively, pasting the video's URL into a WordPress page or post will embed it.

Aspiring to immediacy / capturing the moment

We know that video published on the web has some things in common with traditional TV packages. Some publishers aspire to the high production values of traditional terrestrial TV, but by no means all do. As video on the web develops, it is establishing a second style all of its own.

This style of video journalism is about capturing the moment, about the reporter being in the thick of things and of putting the viewer at the centre of the action.

It's fair to say no one really knows which form will become the norm – my hunch is both will become well-established.

Capturing the moment

When video journalism is about capturing the moment, it follows that the quality of the video is less important than what it captures. It might be about getting a picture that no one else has, or of hugely dramatic events seen from on the ground. No one complains if video, for example, of the survivors of a shipwreck or other disaster is grainy and jerky.

Today, it is often non-journalist eyewitnesses who do that, with the camera in their phones. Type 'capture the moment' into search on YouTube and you'll see a whole string of news stories in which the reports centre round a piece of footage shot by an eyewitness, even if it has been added to a professional package.

on the website

Find a video in which CNN anchor John Roberts expands on the importance of capturing the moment.

Roberts gives an example of how this technique need not always be applied in dramatic circumstances. In the US, fears of terrorist attacks on aircraft have led to the introduction of a no fly list. The list contains the names of people who are flagged up as a potential security risk to airlines. CNN reporter, Drew Griffin, is on it.

So how does he tell the story? By going to airports and putting himself at the heart of the story. He shows the queues of people similarly blacklisted and the hoops they have to jump through before they can get on to a plane. Roberts says this is: "The correspondent walking you through the story in a way that helps you understand it adds an element to video journalism that you can't get with any other form of journalism."

Putting the viewer at the centre of the action

Mark Davis is an interesting illustration of the solo video journalist. And the way he – and video journalists in general – shoot is considered by many to have an advantage over finely-crafted traditional TV packages.

In a profile in the *Melbourne Age*[3] the writer makes this point: "Some news broadcasters believe the public wants more of this style of journalism." Because of this belief, many media companies, especially those with current affairs programmes and online news outlets, see it as the future of journalism. As a result, they are training increasing numbers of reporters in how to become video journalists, with abilities as reporters, camera operators, film editors and producers.

The profile adds: "That the footage appears raw and the storylines unplanned can give television audiences a feeling of being at the centre of the action."

Michael Rosenblum is a former CNN and BBC TV journalist who got fed up with the instant, short, superficial packages he had to produce for the small screen. He decided he wanted to cover a story as a print journalist would – in depth – but using video. So he went to Gaza and lived for a month with a Palestinian family during the first intifada. He filmed every day and when he returned, got this very different, very personal style of video accepted by various networks.

on the website

Find a link to a video that takes the story on from there, and develops into an explanation of how video journalism has developed and his view of how essential it is for any news website. His opinion is that any news website simply has to have video, or it will lose out to its rivals.

Improving your filming, story construction and editing

It may sound obvious, but it's worth saying: people bring stories to life.

Often, the way we approach a story is not through a person, but through a diary event: a public meeting, an exhibition or some other community activity

Such stories don't often have obvious visual opportunities, so how do we bring them to life?

We do so by telling them through people.

Joe Fryer is a reporter at KING 5 NEWS (**www.king5.com/**) in Seattle. And like any reporter on a local TV station he is faced with a fair number of stories that are routine and hard to turn into interesting visual packages. Joe told a seminar at Poynter.org about how he approaches dull stories and strives to make them sparkle.[4]

He demonstrated with a video that shows how a story such as a public meeting about a planning matter could be turned into a more interesting tale. His original brief was to cover a transportation department informational meeting about what to do to block sound from a road-building project.

In showing how he tackled the project, Joe demonstrates the principles of TV news packages.

This particular kind of package, about a very local issue, is not something we see much of in the UK, because our TV news has not, traditionally, been that local. But with community TV stations popping up, and video proving a key draw on hyperlocal sites, we may see a lot more demand for it.

However, Joe's video took a news team a full shift to film and edit, but let's not worry too much about the resources issue for now, we'll look later in this chapter at a one-man-band video journalist who creates packages on his own, and get some tips on how to turn such packages around as fast as possible.

on the website

Find Joe's broadcast report, which is called "I want a wall".

Watch the video before you read on.

Here's what this story tells us we need to do to make a package:

Find a vibrant character, someone who will bring the story to life.

How do you find them? Go to the scene and ask around, very shortly people will tell you who you ought to be talking to.

Tell the story through this person

As Joe demonstrates, you can weave the essential information through the story, but you tell most of it through the eyes of the chosen central character.

And, as he also demonstrates, although the original brief was to cover a public meeting, you don't need to show very much of that meeting at all.

Most of Joe's film is shot at locations relevant to the story - by the bridge, at the man's house. Even at the meeting there is movement (arriving, walking and talking) and interaction between people.

Joe says he is looking for what he calls meaningful moments. Another phrase for them is good sound bites. Phrases from the central character such as: "I'll get down and beg".

Tight editing is key

The video moves fast. The audio is very tightly edited, with the reporter's voiceover (often including those snippets of essential information) slipped in between sound bites from the central character. Those sound bites are just a handful of words and a second or two long. This audio editing technique is, again, not something we see much of in the UK, but I think we can learn a lot from it.

One technical point. Once Joe had his central character, he put a radio mic on him and kept it there as he travelled to the meeting. Joe didn't know if the man would get up and speak, but a hunch that he would paid off. And, whenever he spoke to anyone, they had the audio they needed.

12B6

Aspiring to broadcast-quality

High-quality video reporting takes a lot of time and effort, as the example above showed. You need to take a systematic approach to an assignment. So let's go through an assignment step-by-step, so we can think about how to tackle it in some depth.

on the website

Find links to BBC video tutorials on all aspects of broadcast-quality video, and more examples of broadcast-quality video.

Planning before the shoot

Whenever possible, it makes sense to find out as much as you can about a story before you set out to shoot your video.

Having a clear idea of what the story is will enable you to make a list of the interviews you will need to conduct, the locations you will want to feature, and the main shots you will need.

To tell a story effectively through moving pictures you obviously have to have those pictures. Planning helps ensure you don't miss any essentials out.

So, here's a checklist:

- ■ What's the story?
- ■ What angle will you take?
- ■ What pictures will you need to tell it?
- ■ Who will you need to interview?
- ■ What locations will bring the story alive?

Here's an example.

You have a press release about increased truancy levels in local schools. This comes against the background of an average of two parents a week being jailed because their children were persistent truants.

Think about how you might approach this story, and go through the list above. Don't read on until you have thought about it.

- Here's our suggestion.
  We need to personalise the story, and focus on individuals who reflect its complexities.

- What's the story?
  Truancy levels are up. Parents elsewhere have been jailed. Why's this happening and is jailing parents the solution?

- What angle will you take?
  Find a parent whose child is a persistent truant. Interview the parent(s) and, with their permission, the child.

- What pictures will you need to tell it?
  School, parent(s), child and home. Children at school, truanting children.

- Who will you need to interview?
  Child, parent(s), school head, education authority official, perhaps another expert.

- What locations will bring the story alive?
  The school, the places the child and others hang out when they should be at school, the child's home.

You need to set up the interviews you need. Ideally get all interviewees in one of these locations to avoid talking-head-in-office footage. Find out from the child where they hang out when they should be at school. Can they introduce you to other truants?

If you are reporting in the UK for an organisation covered by either Ofcom (Office of Communications) or IPSO (the Independent Press Standards Organisation) you must follow their code on stories involving children. The details are on the website.

Setting things up

Write a summary for yourself of the story and how you want to tell it, with interviewees and locations.

building proficiency

Work out a shooting schedule that is achievable in the time available

What are the main interviews, locations and points you want to make? Some reporters like to rough out a story board so they can see what elements they need in the story, their order and to ensure the transitions between each is smooth and logical.

For example, with this story, the cue for the news reader, or the set up in print, can be an extension of the story summary we worked on above: truancy levels are up. Parents elsewhere have been jailed. Why is this happening and is jailing parents the solution?

First scene

Show the school, kids streaming in, with you in the midst of them doing a piece to camera, talking about the school, how many pupils it has and a line such as "Or at least, there should be 640 pupils in there today, but some are missing. And, on average xx of them will not be ill or have another good reason for their absence, they are playing truant."

Second scene

At "they are playing truant" cut to footage of truanting kids. Maybe a quick general shot of a bunch of them, perhaps hanging around in a kids' playground, then cutting to the truant you are going to interview. Over this picture you can give their name and, perhaps over footage of them messing around, give details of them.

Move to you interviewing them in the same location. Ask them why they truant. Don't they worry their parent(s) might be jailed?

Third scene

At home with the parent(s). Demonstrate their home life. Perhaps this is a single parent who has to go out to work and can't be sure that their child has gone to school. The interview with them can be cut with them and child at home – pictures that give a flavour of what life is like in that house. If the parent says the child spends all day playing computer games in their bedroom, show them doing that.

The key question of the parent(s) is: You could be jailed. Will that help you and your child?

Fourth scene

Talking to the head and/or education official about this situation and the situation generally. Avoid having them in an office if possible. Ideally get them together at the school, perhaps in the playground with children in the background.

Fifth scene

The expert who disapproves of jailings. Have them in the park with the truants on their bikes in the background.

Putting the plan into action

Your researches and initial interview with your interviewees should equip you well. You will be reasonably sure that what they will say, and know the locations and footage you need to tell the story visually.

When you are filming

Up to now we have kept our shooting very simple. The next stage is to add more variety to it, and to follow some of the rules used by broadcasters such as the BBC.

We talked earlier about three basic shots. Now we'll add three more, to add variety and interest to the videos we make.

These are the six shots you can use:

- Wide shot - the subject is small in the frame
- Long shot - the subject is shown head to toe in the frame but there is still a good deal of their surroundings in shot
- Medium shot - the subject is filmed from the waist up
- Medium close up - that's the one from chest upwards that we've used before
- Close up - head and shoulders
- Big close up - from forehead to chin, with the top of the head out of shot

You can also use one of three camera angles:

- High angle - a bird's eye view looking down on the subject
- Low angle - at foot level, often used to show a lot of anonymous feet when you can't identify those in the picture
- Eye level - the commonest shot, with the camera set pretty much at the subject's eye level.

Follow the five shot rule

You could just use one shot per scene. So, if someone is talking, you film their face in close up. Or, if they are doing something such as washing up, you film them in medium shot.

But we want more variety, and to shoot a range of shots that will cut together into an interesting logical sequence. There are five shots that we should film for each important scene that we want to capture, and using it is called following the five shot rule.

These are generally the shots to take, in this sequence, when we want to record someone performing a task:

- Close up of the hands
- Close up of the face
- Wide shot of them and what they are doing
- Over the shoulder shot, from behind them, of what they are doing
- Another shot from a different angle – you might film them from the side, or from a high or low angle.

If you shoot in this sequence the shots will edit together easily.

Remember, we are looking for pictures that tell the story. As we are telling the story visually just as much as verbally, we will only marry an image of a person speaking with what they are saying at certain points in our film. At other times, we cut away from their face as they speak to other shots, but what they say – the audio track – runs on beneath the various pictures.

One simplification if this filming approach is to shoot like this:

- The person
- The thing
- The person with the thing.

You can also shoot some material that can be used as cutaways – to a general scene of some kind – and cut-ins to some detail. These can be used to mask edits when you have two sections in which a person is talking to camera but you need to edit them together. If you have a cutaway or a cut-in you can insert a second or two of this, so that while the picture transition is masked, the audio of the person speaking runs seamlessly together.

on the website

Find links to video tutorials and other guidance on filming and editing.

12B7

Serving both broadcast and online: a TV news video package, and that footage unpacked for online

If you work for a broadcaster, the video you shoot will be needed in package form, but also unpackaged: as a series of online-friendly clips. That's what's required of many BBC journalists, who are shooting clips that can be fed into ultra-short videos for Instagram, material for more elaborate online reports, as well as creating highly-professional broadcast-style packages for the main news bulletins. As things only happen once, they need to shoot material that can serve all three publishing formats.

We'll look at a detailed example of how this can be done. But, because you need to watch a string of videos to follow the process, we'll switch over to the MMJ website for tuition on this.

on the website

Find a detailed examination of how a TV video package was adapted for use online.

12B8

How a solo video journalist can create great packages

The packages we've looked at so far on the online version of MMJ were created not by a solo video journalist but by a TV crew. But Jason Witmer (**http://witmervideo.blogspot.co.uk/**) demonstrates that you can create great packages on your own. Jason, a video journalist on the *Houston Chronicle*'s **www.chron.com** told a Poynter seminar on video storytelling[5] that he had been used to shooting videos in an hour and a half for quick upload to the web.

But then, videos like this one by Joe Larson showed him what was possible and made him want to develop as a video storyteller.

http://youtu.be/WZCEjTW-hMQ

on the website

You'll find the video on the website. Please watch it before reading on.

Larson has used all the elements of good storytelling in this tale of a very small town which has the only parking meter in 7,200 sq miles. He presents a range of characters, he gives a strong sense of place, and he introduces an element of suspense.

First he sketches a place where everyone knows everyone else, where nothing unexpected happens. Only once that is established does he introduce the unexpected element: the parking meter. It's by no means a big news story, it's a piece of whimsy, something which we rarely find on UK TV news shows, let alone on the web.

And the video points out one key difference between TV news packages and online video. On TV, with an anchor who can set up the video with clues as to what it contains, you can delay getting to the nub of the story until some way into the video.

On the web viewers expect a quick return: they want the video to get to the point right away. Or, at least, that's the conventional wisdom. But when you think of the sort of inconsequential, often amusing, whimsy that is popular on YouTube, we should probably be a little less ready to reject such material as wrong for the web.

There is also a great deal of technical skill in the video. There is effective use of natural sound - the meter being rolled along the pavement, grain pouring into the silo. Such sounds are used to bring the viewer into the story, and to punctuate the characters' sound bites and narration.

Those sound bites are very natural. You don't get the sense that the characters in the story are being formally interviewed. Instead, they are allowed to talk naturally, with the result that they give great, often humorous quotes, which bring great character to the story.

So Jason Witmer tried to learn from such video, and he came up with work of his own such as this:

on the website

The video is on the website. Please watch it before reading on.

This is a video with a lot of characters. They are all entertaining and often amusing, and Jason's narration is interwoven skilfully with their sound bites.

Such sound bites can't be got quickly. Jason says he usually films twice as many people as end up in his edited video. He says one essential is to know what the focus of the story is as you interview, so you avoid going off at tangents.

12B8

How to do video packages fast

Darren Durlach is an award-winning photojournalist and TV News Photographer of the Year currently at WBFF-TV in Baltimore

on the website

Find a video interview with Darren on how he makes shooting a story as fast and efficient as he can.

He also shared his tips on how to do stories fast at a Poynter NewsU seminar on video storytelling.[6]

Here's his advice for shooting a story fast:

Watch a video that demonstrates the tuition outlined below.

Plan ahead

Think about every way your video could open as you travel to the job, call the person you are to interview to talk it through, think of a beginning, middle and end.

Usually, by the time you are on your way to a story you know what it's about, and you can think of something to open with and something to close with.

As soon as you arrive. . .

Get the images and sounds that you might not be able to get later. So if it's a news story and there's a fire blazing, or a broken main spewing water into the street, get that immediately.

Get the moment

Get close to people. Darren calls this zooming with your feet. Rather than staying back and using the zoom on the camera, get close to them. He has a shotgun mic on his camera so he can pick up sound from them and, if necessary, he can whip it off and use it hand-held to conduct interviews.

Once the perishable stuff has been captured, he can go back and get clean shots, using the tripod, to cover the scenes he has already shot hand-held.

Shoot for the edit

Darren has a mantra he repeats to himself:

- Tight, medium, wide
- Get the moment
- Action, reaction.

By which he means getting the shots you will need to tell the story in a series of coherent sequences.

- **Tight, medium, wide** (medium are storytelling shots, wides are for perspective, tights are detail shots)
- **Get the moment** Capture things as they happen, keep your storytelling in the moment

- **Action, reaction** (for example, get the person being rescued from the building, then the reaction of the significant other who has been watching that).

Effective sequencing in the field

Sequencing is breaking an action down to its component parts:

- **Wide shot** to show the scene, and give an overview of the action (eg a postman walking to his van)
- **Medium shot** of the action: The postman reaching down to pick up a box.
- **Close up**: of the box

Darren does this because the viewer understands the story better if you are linking shots together effectively.

One further piece of advice: Don't edit two same-size shots in a row, ie don't use two medium size shots together.

on the website

Find lots more examples and tuition, including how to bring a touch of Hollywood to your videos.

12B9

Exercises and projects

Exercise 1

Experiment with a video recorder in manual mode. Shoot the same scene in a range of ways. Practise using manual settings.

Exercise 2

Practise shooting scenes using the full range of shots, and following the five shot rule described above. Create edited sequences from the shots you film.

Exercise 3

Take three or four sites on which video reports are included and look at how professional the packages are. If possible compare the same story covered on TV and in video on a website.

Exercise 4

Follow a number of news outlets on Vine and Instagram, and see how they use the platforms. What can you learn from them?

Exercise 5

Look for more rough-and-ready styles of video and compare their effectiveness with more polished packages. Do you notice a difference in the circumstances and/or subjects where this technique is used?

Projects

1   Use ultra-short video on Vine or Instagram to report on a wide range of stories. See how you can incorporate the techniques into live blogs.

2   Find occasions when it seems appropriate to make rough-and-ready videos in which you as reporter are in the heart of the action.

3   Make videos of as professional a quality as you can for your websites or blog. Use the techniques of preparation, filming and editing that are described and illustrated in this chapter.

4   On a story where you are planning a polished video package, try also to use Vine and Instagram while you are working.

Notes

1   The Future of TV News Belongs, In Part, To Multi-Platform Video, in *Brave News Worlds: Navigating the New Media Landscape*, published by the International Press Institute (IPI), 2013
2   www.facebook.com/journalists/posts/617595314919153
3   www.theage.com.au
4   www.newsu.org/about/instructors/joe-fryer
5   www.newsu.org/courses/video-storytelling-workshop-2010-package
6   www.newsu.org/about/instructors/darren-durlach

chapter thirteen

Data journalism

In the book version of this chapter we will cover:

- What data journalism is
- How to find data
- How to filter data
- How to create data visualisations.

At the end of the chapter are a range of exercises and projects to enable you to practise what you have learned.

In the online version of this chapter you will find:

- Practical step-by-step tuition in creating a range of data journalism projects
- Essential updates on tuition that take into account advances in data journalism techniques.

Have the companion website to this book open at www.multimedia-journalism.co.uk. That way you can easily click on the links to the stories discussed here.

What data journalism is

Defining data journalism

Data journalism involves taking large sets of figures and creating visualisations out of them - visualisations can be maps, graphs or tables.

What are these visualisations for?

They are to enable us to reveal stories that were buried in the data.

So, data journalism is about using computers to find stories in data. It's also about presenting visualisations that make a story instantly understandable. Visualisations are often interactive, which means that anyone else can delve into and then make their own connections, spot their own stories, and reach their own clearer understanding of the issues the data covers.

Why do we need to do it?

Journalists have always worked with data.

We've analysed council tax rates, changes brought about by budgets and other fiscal measures, plus all sorts of statistics thrown at us by government, business, unions, pressure groups and other organisations.

Our goal has always been to find the stories in the data - and it still is.

But how we work with data is being revolutionised because of the possibilities that using computers to make sense of huge data sets opens up.

Here's why data journalism has become an essential skill for any multimedia journalist:

- Much more data is now available. There has been a drive by governments and other organisations to open up thousands of databases
- Universally available, simple tools such as Excel and Google Spreadsheets make analysing data much easier
- Other simple tools make turning data into easily understood visualisations (or graphics to use an older term) much simpler.

Also, basing stories on open data increases transparency. The claims you make can easily be checked by others, and hence your stories can be trusted.

Do you need to be a skilled graphic artist?

No, because the tools we'll use make visualisations for you. But graphics skills can be enormously valuable to data journalism projects, as can the skills of a programmer.

No journalist should feel left out

Journalist and information architect Mirko Lorenz said:[1] "No journalist should feel excluded from this field. . .not all journalists working in tomorrow's newsrooms will be coders."

"There will be real coders, journalist/coders and journalists working with the output of such teams, being specialised in writing, photography and film-making."

Lorenz says that this is not so different from today's newsrooms. He believes it is not the case that only journalists with professional coding experience are needed for this.

As a multimedia journalist, you need to know how to do straightforward data gathering, analysis and visualisation.

on the website

- Watch a TED video talk on why visualisations work so well in storytelling
- Learn about the canon of data journalism: get a full historic perspective on how data mining has been the source of powerful stories for centuries, beginning with Florence Nightingale's data analysis on deaths in the Crimea.

13B2

Examples of data journalism, and what can be achieved

Mirko Lorenz, quoted in *Data-driven Journalism*,[2] gives this succinct outline of what data journalism can achieve: "Data is used increasingly to visualise very complex issues."

"The publication of the Afghanistan war logs by the *New York Times*, *Der Spiegel* and the *Guardian* have raised awareness that better use of data might lead to very big stories."

Similarly, he goes on, the way the *Guardian* handled the expenses scandal of British MPs in 2009 sparked interest in what data journalism can do.

"Think crowdsourcing," he says. Large stores of public data can be turned into open data that everyone can examine and share.

"Think uncovering scandals," he goes on, and using numbers to confirm the story.

Lorenz believes that data journalism can be used to help people make the right decisions when buying, insuring, participating or making life choices.

But journalists will have to learn new tricks, he goes on, in order to do that. They will have to work with tools that will help them to make data comprehensible.

on the website

Find a wide range of examples of data journalism.

Learn what types and sizes of data journalism teams various media organisations run.

The three steps of data journalism: gather, process, visualise

The easiest way to grasp how to do data journalism is to do this. . .

Think of what you do in more traditional practices of the journalism craft.

You gather information, you sift it, pick out the significant and interesting bits, and present it to the audience in as interesting a way as you can.

In short, you:

- **gather** raw information
- **process** or **filter** it, and
- **shape** or **visualise** it.

You do exactly the same when data is your source material, rather than a collection of quotes, documents and events.

Mirko Lorenz says:[3] "Data driven journalism can be viewed as a process of refinement, where raw data is transformed into something meaningful[. . .] complex facts are boiled down into a clear story that people can easily understand and remember."

But we mustn't get caught up in data for data's sake. What we extract from the data must be useful to the audience, it must make sense of a situation through turning a mountain of figures into a story they understand.

Mirko gives the example of a *New York Times* app called Rent or Buy?.[4] With it, a reader can fill in a few details and get a definitive answer - tailored to their specific circumstances - on whether they are better off buying or renting a home.

on the website

Take a look at Rent or Buy? on the MMJ website before you read on.

So how do we do data journalism? There are three stages in any data journalism project:

1 Find data

Paul Bradshaw[5] says of this stage: "'Finding data' can involve anything from having expert knowledge and contacts to being able to use computer assisted reporting skills or, for some, specific technical skills such as MySQL or Python to gather the data for you."

While you are learning you can get already-available data and use that as your raw material. Government data is one good source.

As we work on some projects, I'll identify data sources for you to work on, but as soon as you can, you should start finding your own.

Can you trust the data you have found?

Whenever you are thinking of using data, apply these checks:

- Who collected it?
- When was it collected?
- How was it collected?

If possible, find another source for the same sort of data and check whether data from the two sources is broadly aligned.

on the website

Find an extensive list of data sources that you can use.

2 Process or filter data

Before you can work with data to find stories, you need to learn how to access, structure and filter that information.

Filtering data, sometimes referred to as 'interrogating data', involves selecting what bits of the data you want to use for your analysis. This stage can sometimes be left out, particularly when you are learning, but it's an important skill to develop in order to be able to draw the significance, and the stories, out of raw data.

At its simplest, filtering can involve simply removing some lines of data or columns from a spreadsheet so that your chosen data-visualising tool can read the data properly.

Cynthia O'Murchu told Data-driven Journalism:[6] "the data published by governments (and others) is not at all user friendly. More often than not, journalists have to scrape data from PDFs, although the same information would be available from a database or Excel spreadsheet."

You also need to get your data into a state where the programmes we will use to turn it into a visualisation (a graphic, map or table) can work with it. Many of the tools used for data journalism can read Excel and other spreadsheets. So if you are gathering raw data, getting it into a spreadsheet – putting it into a readable form – is part of what I see as the filtering process.

As Stefan Fichtel said at Data-driven Journalism:[7] "a process is needed where the data is first understood and then visualised in a way that makes the connections visible at first sight."

And Frank van Ham[8] said: "There is a clear distinction between 'Data' and 'Story'. Data itself is a form of information." Van Ham says that, in order to extract information, the user has to go through a process. First, they usually have to clean up messy formats, and then structure and sort the data into a readable format before it can be visualised. He goes on: "Story is an interactive form of communication where information is brought into a context that people can understand, remember, discuss and tell others about."

3 Visualise data (as a graphic, map or table)

This is something that, traditionally, graphic artists (in print media) and programmers (in online media) did. But there are now a number of visualising tools that do it for you: they can take your spreadsheet and turn it into a range of different formats – the simplest being a bar chart or a pie graph.

The aim is to turn the data into something that can be immediately understood. A good, appropriate graphic can make the significance of the figures apparent; it can make the story revealed in the figures obvious.

It's important to remember that our goal in using data-driven journalism is to find stories and tell them well, just as we do in other forms of reporting.

If your visualisation doesn't tell (or show) an immediately compelling story then it's failed as journalism.

Frank van Ham said that the two main reasons for using visualisations were:

Explorative: understanding what is there (eg in research)

Communicative: display and discuss visualisations with the public, tell stories based on the data and the facts.

13B4

Your first data journalism project

Just to keep things practical, let's do a straightforward bit of data journalism right now, before going into more explanation and demonstration.

Note: Because data journalism is developing rapidly, we will keep all further projects for the online version of MMJ, but here is a simple starter to help you understand what doing data journalism involves. If this tuition becomes outdated, it will be amended on the online version of this module.

Find data

Go to Socrata (**www.socrata.com/**) which is an open data resource.

on the website

You will find the URLs mentioned here linked to on the website.

Also, watch a video about Socrata's mission.

You will find a data set which is about the comparative salaries in each US state, compared over a period of years at this URL. It's also linked to on the MMJ website:

https://opendata.socrata.com/Government/Average-Annual-Wage-By-State-Visualisation/u5h4-z7fb

Here's a grab of what some of that data looks like:

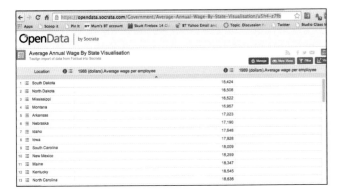

The next step is to export this raw data and convert it into a form where it can be read by the visualisation software we are going to use on it. We want to turn it into an Excel spreadsheet.

So click **Export** and then choose **Download as CSV**.

Do that and it will open in Excel. Name and save that Excel spreadsheet version of your data to your computer.

Here's a grab of that spreadsheet:

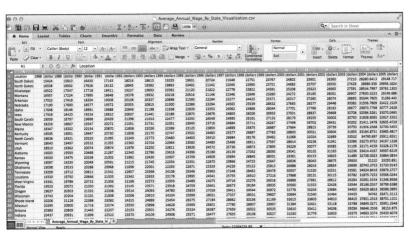

Process or filter data

In fact, this data doesn't need any cleaning up. But if, for example, there were rows or columns that I did not need, this is the point at which I could delete them, because the next stage is to copy the whole of this data set, and anything not deleted now will appear in the visualisation I am going to make.

Visualising the data

Next, open a website called Many Eyes (**www.ibm.com/manyeyes**) and create an account. Once you have been approved, go back in and click on the **Create a visualisation** option. Then select to upload a dataset.

Then go to Excel, copy your dataset by clicking at top left, holding and dragging diagonally right, so you have selected every cell of data.

Now paste that data into the empty box provided for it.

You'll get a preview, under the heading: **Check that we understood**. Fill in the details they ask for, and then click on **Create** at the bottom of the screen, and then on **Visualise** at the bottom of the next one.

The next screen gives a list of options for types of visualisation. Ignore the ones at the top under the **Analyze as text** heading and go down to the **Compare a set of values** options.

As this is a spreadsheet with columns of information, rather than plain text, the **'comparative values'** category of visualisations will work with it, but the **'analyse as text'** ones won't.

You can see how each visualisation looks, which work with this particular data set, and which don't work with it.

For this data set, here are the attributes and how they can be applied effectively to a good visualisation:

- It's got the **names of states**, which lend themselves to **a map-based visualisation**
- It also has **comparative wages**, which lends itself to a **bar chart** or some other form of comparative chart.

The bar chart has the states along the horizontal axis, and the relative wage on the vertical axis. The other variable was by year, from 1988 to 2007, and if you click on a year on the table to the left, the totals change to represent that year.

If I want to compare wages from different years for a particular state, to get an idea of how salaries there have moved, I can use **click and control** to select the years I'm interested in, and see them visualised on the bar graph.

Try these other types of visualisation:

Map

This visualisation puts the data on a US map, with the bubbles sized to demonstrate the difference in wages.

Bubble chart

On the bubble chart, you click on the drop down by bubble size, and that adjusts the bubbles depending on the year you have chosen.

Hover over a bubble and you get the year and the average wage per employee, with the total number of employees also displayed.

Publish your visualisation

If you like the visualisation you can click to publish it. You get a range of sharing options for social media, plus code for adding it as either a static image, or as a live visualisation.

When it appears on the website you only get one year presented in the embed, which is a static screen until you either click to interact, which means you can move around this year and see data displayed, or click on the top blue bar. Do that and the whole visualisation opens up for you, and you can move around within the data.

As Many Eyes doesn't make it clear how to get into the data in this way, you'll have to make sure you tell your readers how to do it.

So that's a visualisation. How good a story is it?

Well, it's certainly something that an audience can explore and use to find the particular data that interests them for themselves. It doesn't give you an immediate, visually arresting story though.

It may be that there is no great story here, but there may be, in the figures, a huge gap between best and worst-paid state. It may show a significant change from year to year, or over the time period analysed, but we can't easily tell that just by looking.

So it's not the best of visualisations; not the best of data journalism.

But it is certainly more readable than the raw data we began with, so this visualisation is still a definite improvement.

What about the bar chart?

With the bar chart it is immediately clearer what a difference there is in salaries by state, and if you click the top blue bar and go into the data, you can have a lot of fun comparing year to year.

How the *Guardian* does it

The *Guardian*'s work on the Afghan war logs is one of the most famous landmarks in the development of data journalism as a discipline.

on the website

Read Simon Rogers' full account of how the war logs were turned into data that could be visualised.

I wanted here just to extract from Simon's post[9] some key points about the wide range of skills and individuals that make up the *Guardian*'s data operation, and to relate their processes with the three steps towards data journalism that I identified above.

Simon is talking here about how they processed a huge Excel file from Wikileaks on the Afghan war.

Finding the data

Here's what they were faced with: over 92,201 rows of data, some with nothing in them, or the result of poor formatting.

To begin making sense of it they had to create a database. Simon says: "Harold Frayman, who with John Houston regularly wrestles data from PDFs and other formats for the Datablog – built a simple internal database."

This meant that reporters could search stories for key words or events. Suddenly, he says, the dataset became accessible and generating great stories became easier.

"The data was well structured. . . ie, events were categorised, sometimes more reliably than others."

Filtering (interrogating) the data

They had to filter the data so that they could look at key things such as the rise in the incidence of improvised explosive devices (IEDs).

They also filtered the data to help them tell one of the key stories of the war: the rise in IED attacks featuring home-made roadside bombs. The dataset was still massive, but it was now easier to manage.

Simon says that there were around 7,500 IED explosions or ambushes (an ambush being where an attack is combined with, for example, small arms fire or rocket grenades) between 2004 and 2009.

There were a further 8,000 IEDs which were found and cleared. The *Guardian* wanted to see how they changed over time – and how they compared.

The result was cleaned-up data which showed:

- IED attacks over time
- Where they happened by region
- Casualties data recorded in the database.

on the website

You can download the full overview spreadsheet of cleaned-up data.

Visualising the data

Next they needed to create visualisations that would make the stories in the data instantly 'readable'.

At this point, Simon says, Developer Daithí Ó Crualaoich came in. He helped the team map the latitudes and longitudes of every event, and also produced an editable map (one that is 'vectored', as designers call it).

Now, graphic designer Paul Scruton could make the map look attractive for the newspaper.

on the website

See the newspaper visualisation.

Visualising/presenting online

Conveying that information online is a different skill, says Simon. Here, Alastair Dant (with Igor Clark's help) created two interactives for the site:

- Interactive guide to all the IEDs
- Interactive 'front page' to their selection of 300 key events.

working from a spreadsheet with the geodata on (with design work from Paddy Allen and Mark McCormick).

on the website

Find links to the online visualisations.

13B6-9

More data journalism projects

To ensure the further projects covered in this tuition are still current, we'll keep them for the online version of MMJ.

on the website

Find a number of further step-by-step guides through data journalism projects. These include:

- Further use of data sifting and visualisation tools including Socrata and Many Eyes
- Using Tableau
- Using Google Fusion Tables
- Using Datawrapper.

13B10

Data journalism courses available online

Find a range of comprehensive, free courses in data journalism that you can complete online.

13B11

Exercises and projects

Exercise 1

Watch out for news stories or pieces of analysis that rely on data journalism. Identify where the data came from, and analyse how it has been visualised.

Exercise 2

Follow the additional tuition linked to on the website.

Projects

1 Research data sources relevant to the subject matter of your WordPress website or beat blog.

2 Take relevant data sets and extract stories from them. Use the data processing visualisation software and techniques covered either in the book version of this chapter, or the wider range of resources covered in the online version to turn them into visualisations.

In each case you must:

- find data relevant to your subject, area or specialism
- filter that data
- visualise the data
- embed visualisations in your website or beat blog.

Notes

1 http://datadrivenjournalism.net
2 http://datadrivenjournalism.net
3 http://datadrivenjournalism.net
4 www.nytimes.com/interactive/business/buy-rent-calculator.html
5 http://onlinejournalismblog.com/
6 http://datadrivenjournalism.net
7 http://datadrivenjournalism.net
8 http://datadrivenjournalism.net
9 www.theguardian.com/news/datablog/2010/jul/27/wikileaks-afghanistan-data-datajournalism

chapter fourteen

Building a personal brand, and developing a specialism

In the book version of this chapter we will cover:

- What personal branding is
- Why good branding must start with good journalism
- The goals of your branding, and how to measure your success
- The places to build your brand: websites, blogs, on social media and on cv/resume/port-folio sites
- Why you need a Google profile and to be recognised by Google as an author
- Branding on LinkedIn
- 12 journalism specialisms outlined
- Entrepreneurial journalism explained.

At the end of the chapter are a range of exercises and projects to enable you to practise what you have learned.

On the website we will cover:

- Further examples of journalists who have built powerful personal brands
- Further detailed tuition in using the platforms introduced here.

Also on the website

How to become a specialist reporter in 12 key fields including:

- Politics
- Showbiz and celebrity
- Music
- Film
- Fashion
- International reporting
- Health, science and environment
- Technology.

And

- A comprehensive guide to entrepreneurial journalism.

Have the companion website to this book open at www.multimedia-journalism.co.uk. That way you can easily click on the links to the stories discussed here.

What a personal brand is

Your brand is who you are, what you are known for, what you specialise in. If you don't like the idea of brand, substitute reputation. In this chapter we are looking at how to build your brand – or reputation – online. What you will find, if you have been doing everything we've been suggesting as you've worked through this book or ebook, is that you have already done a great deal of work on building your personal brand.

First, a bit of context

In old print media, the closest a reporter or writer could get to personal branding was their byline on a story. A broadcast journalist got their name superimposed at the start of their report, and their face briefly on camera.

Journalists who were employed to do something other than write or appear on-screen – sub-edit, run a department, edit the title, edit the programme – often got little opportunity to get their name out there.

On a magazine, if they were lucky, they got included in a flannel panel, where all staff names were listed. In TV, their name might whizz past in the closing credits.

Of course, some reporters and writers became big names. Some columnists, TV reporters and others had the power to bring large numbers of readers to a publication, or viewers to a news or current affairs programme. Their names might become as well known as the title or programme they worked for. They were stars.

But, for most journalists, that never happened. They remained more or less anonymous. A specialist reporter would gain the respect of those in the profession or area they covered, and be known to them, but that was about as much branding as the average journalist got.

Today, any journalist or student journalist can build their personal brand or reputation online – often independently of the title or programme they work on.

Some journalists are now as well known – or even better known – as the titles or programmes they work for. They often have a greater reputation – at least among the specialist audience that is most interested in what they do.

How has that happened?

Social media is one hugely valuable tool. So are beat blogs and personal websites.

Good personal branding starts with good journalism

A student journalist can use personal branding to get noticed and help win their first job. Good branding is like the job application that leaps out from the pile. But good branding only works if you are a good journalist.

A flashy website won't hide rubbish content.

If you can't write, can't headline, don't know how to use social media effectively, can't tell a story in text, stills, video and audio, that will be apparent. And your work in all those areas must be accurate, fair and credible. The work creates the brand, and the brand draws more people to your work.

Neglecting your branding can lead to your failure as a journalist – or, at least, a failure to get jobs and make money. Lots of good journalists are suffering today, as so many jobs disappear, because they remained pretty much anonymous; because they failed to establish their value with an audience.

If a member of a particular profession reads a certain publication because it helps them do their job, but they do not know who writes the content they value so much, then the title gets the credit, not the journalist. The title builds its brand, the journalist loses out.

A strong personal brand demonstrates your value – to an audience and to an employer. Fail to brand and you can become seriously undervalued.

One journalist who has branded himself spectacularly well

Here's an example of a journalist who became bigger than the brand that published him, and then took his personal brand away with him.

Half the people who came to the *New York Times*' website in the run-up to the US presidential election in 2012 were searching for a reporter called Nate Silver. Nate specialises in data-based political reporting and forecasting, and he wrote the FiveThirtyEight blog on the NYT's website.

New York Times executive editor Jill Abramson told a media conference: "He got huge, huge readership. They weren't coming for the rest of the *Times*; they came for him. You hope they will be tantalised by other things on the buffet table."

Alex Weprin, writing on the International Journalists Network (**http://ijnet.org/**) said: "In other words, Nate Silver has developed a personal brand that is bigger than the *New York Times* when it comes to the niche of political forecasting."

Indeed, his brand became so strong that he left the New York Times, taking FiveThirtyEight with him, to create a stand-alone website where he is editor in chief: **http://fivethirtyeight.com/contributors/nate-silver/**

Nate represents a fundamental shift in the way journalists now establish themselves as reliable, authoritative reporters and commentators.

The jobs market for journalists has changed radically

In a report called "Post Industrial Journalism: Adapting to the Present",[1] Clay Shirky, Emily Bell and Chris Anderson wrote of a new reality for journalism graduates in which the first step in their careers is not to be hired by, and to tie their reputation to, an established media institution, but to create their own reputation.

The report says: "Already, journalism schools are more like film schools than law schools, which is to say that the relative success or failure of a J-School grad is going to be far more variable than it used to be."

The report finds there are fewer entry-level jobs in metropolitan dailies and local TV than there used to be. These were once the jobs that served as unofficial proving grounds and apprenticeships.

Because of this, the report goes on, journalists will have to behave as film graduates always have, and go out into the world and create a name for themselves. This is a far less predictable environment, and the career paths are much less clear.

So, particularly for a young journalist starting out, good branding is vital.

A Pew Center Project for Excellence in Journalism report[2] found that, through search, email, blogs and social media, consumers were gravitating to the work of individual writers and voices, and away from institutional brands. The report said: "With journalism shifting toward an era of the personal, rather than the institutional, brand, students need to consider how they are going to stand out as the expert in a knowledge-based economy."

Strategies for building your brand

Let's go through a list of things you need to be doing to build your brand. I'm hoping that you'll discover you are already doing a lot of them – some very effectively, some to a lesser degree. We'll look at any actions you need to take to improve or build on what you are already doing. When you are accomplishing the majority of them, you are successfully branding yourself.

You must be findable

Entering your name in Google should bring you up on the first page of results. Those results should demonstrate a wide range of presences online – a content-rich website and a beat blog, Twitter, Facebook, LinkedIn (which we'll look at in a moment) and other presences, depending on what field you specialise in. Your email, phone and other contact details should be prominent on the pages returned in search results. Your CV/resume and portfolio should be easily accessible online.

You must be visible

People should see your name in comments and retweets. Your name should be quoted in coverage of, and discussion about, the area you cover.

You must engage with your community

You should regularly interact with the community around the topics you cover, via comments, retweets, likes and curation. Engagement brings followers, and enhanced opportunities to find out what matters to that community.

People interested in your field of journalism should know who you are.

You should achieve name-recognition and build your authority as a reliable, trusted source.

Your reputation should be verifiable

Anyone searching for you should be able to find examples of your work and your CV/resume or portfolio. Links to work on the sites you created it for are impressive. Use PDFs for work that is behind paywalls or is no longer available at those sites.

This means that a search for you should bring up at least one presence either on a site that bears your name as the domain, or on a CV or resume site (we'll look at some you can use shortly).

Those presences should present your best work, and a CV/resume that is accurate and transparent.

It should be clear what work experience you have. Make no overblown claims – if you say you were a freelance reporter on a title for several months when in fact you were a two-week intern you'll probably get found out.

Your online presences should represent you as a serious journalist

Which means any presences that present you in a less than professional light – a dodgy Facebook page, for example – should not be publicly available.

Your specialism should be evident

To build your brand, demonstrate your beat or specialism. You want people to follow you rather than your employer. The days of the general reporter are pretty much over. There is a view that the growing importance of personal branding reflects a move from generic labour – the jobbing hack – to the experienced, knowledgeable, expert specialist reporter.

If you are a named reporter it makes sense to build that name – it's important. Witness the rows there have been over who owns their Twitter account when a reporter leaves one news organisation for another. These Twitter followers are following a personal brand more than the media brand the reporter works for.

on the website

Find examples from the USA and UK of rows over Twitter accounts between employers and journalists.

You must be on top of the news in your specialism

Nothing succeeds in personal brand-building like breaking stories. When news is happening, getting out the first tweet, the first picture, the key quote or the first piece of cogent analysis will help build your reputation.

Be yourself

There will be opportunities to present your private self as well as your professional profile. People will expect you to show more than your straight professional face on social media, but you don't have to invent a persona. Just be yourself.

How much of yourself you share online is up to you. Not everyone is entirely comfortable making their lives transparent on social media. You choose where to draw the line between your public and private selves.

But make sure that, if you are sharing some of your off-duty thoughts and activities, these don't conflict with your profile as a professional journalist.

Pictures on Instagram of you walking your dog are fine, if you are happy to share them, so are Pinterest boards on your obsessions with scatter cushions or china owls.

Any activities that conflict with your role as a journalist, or that would embarrass your employer, are not fine. But there is flexibility here. If you cover heavy metal, say, you can get away with sharing something of your hedonistic lifestyle. If you cover accountancy, you probably can't.

Examples of student journalists whose personal branding has kick-started their careers

on the website

You can read more about these individuals on the MMJ website, and find some further examples.

Dave Lee[3] got a job as a technology reporter at the BBC while still at university through his website. It's no longer available in the form that won him that job, but it very effectively demonstrated what he could do with a range of stories over all media.

Josh Halliday[4] was hired as a media and technology reporter by the *Guardian* as a result of SR2, his hyperlocal blog covering Sunderland, which he founded while a student. You can read about SR2 here: **www.slideshare.net/joshhalliday/sr2-blog-the-concept-of-hyperlocal-2735342**

Not all get hired straight out of university.

Joseph Stashko built a hyperlocal blog in Preston, and was one of the founders of a live blogging platform called LiveBlog Pro before being hired by *The* (London) *Times* as digital news development editor.[5]

questions

Can you think of some journalists who are bigger brands than their employers?

Have a think before reading on.

Here are a couple of thoughts from me:

- Robert Peston
- Jeremy Clarkson
- Caitlin Moran.

14B3

Further personal brand-building opportunities

Here's what you should have done by now:

- You own the URL for your name or the name you are building your brand around
- Your naming/branding is consistent across all your online and social platforms
- You have built a website – either collectively or personally
- You have a personal beat blog, either as part of your website, or on a separate platform.

Here are three things we haven't covered yet:

- Establish a CV/resume/portfolio site
- Complete your Google+ profile and confirm your Google AuthorRank
- Create a LinkedIn profile and network on the site.

Establish a CV/resume/portfolio site

There are a number of such sites that cater for journalists. Do you need one alongside your website and beat blog? Yes, because with these sites you can summarise and promote who you are and what you can do, in a more focused way than you can on a website or blog.

Here are three platforms to consider:

Clippings Me

www.clippings.me

You can customise your pages, add a biography, and present all your work – in whatever media. It also takes PDFs, for work that you can no longer link directly to for whatever reason. You can track visits and see who is looking at and sharing your work.

Here's my profile:

Journo Portfolio

www.journoportfolio.com/

Journo Portfolio offers several templates to choose from, and you can add a CV and a contact form. You can create multiple pages and also blog directly on the platform if you like.

Journalisted

http://journalisted.com/

This is a UK directory of journalists and their work. Established journalists are included automatically, but if you have yet to establish yourself you can set up a profile and add your work here.

Complete your Google+ profile

We looked at doing journalism on Google+ in Chapter 3, but we didn't cover creating your Google+ profile.

Google+ is nowhere near as popular as Twitter or Facebook. There is, however, one important reason for seeing Google+ as central to your personal branding.

It has to do with the Google profile you set up when you create a Google+ account, with a Google algorithm called AuthorRank or Authorship (both terms seem to be used), and with the impact of these things on your ranking in search results.

Let's look at Google Profile first

When you create a Google profile - you can do it at **www.google.com/profiles** - you add in a great deal of information about yourself, including links to all your online presences and the content platforms that you use.

The profile you create links all your presences together, so it helps Google know who you are, and hence to deliver comprehensive search results about you when users type your name in search terms.

> Your profile is the way you present yourself on Google products and across the web. With your profile, you can manage the information that people see - such as your bio, contact details, and links to other sites about you or created by you.

Google describes it like this:

Use the advice in Chapter 3 to create a professional profile focused on you and your journalistic beat.

Google AuthorRank

Now let's add Google AuthorRank to the equation.

As Erin Griffith explains here:[6] "Google is verifying individual writers through its social network, Google+, with something called AuthorRank. If a website has connected its writer accounts with their Google+ accounts, search results show a writer's byline next to the result for their article."

As a result of this, Erin goes on, by-lined stories rank higher, and they get more "real estate" (display on the search result listing). Most importantly, she says, they return click-through rates that are 40 per cent greater than non-AuthorRanked results.

Google Authorship establishes you as the creator of a particular piece of content, and a contributor to a given platform. There is a section of the profile where you add a list of all the sites you contribute to.

You need to register as an author with Google. Then you need to tag each of your posts so Google can link them with you, and verify the content platforms you subscribe to with Google.

All of that creates what geeks call a circuit of verified trust, which sounds scarily like something from the movie *Meet the Parents*.

So how do you do all this?

Note: Because Google regularly updates the process of verifying Authorship we'll take this section to the online version of MMJ.

on the website

- Find a step-by-step guide to establishing your Google Authorship credentials
- Learn how to set up Google Authorship on your WordPress site.

Create a Google page

One further thing you can do on Google+ is to create pages, just as you can on Facebook. So you could create a page that is separate from your personal presence, and which might bear the name of your website or beat blog.

on the website

Find a step-by-step guide to creating a Google page.

Open a LinkedIn account

LinkedIn (**www.linkedin.com**) is a professional social network. People often use it to find work, or to join a community of people in their company, industry or profession. It's the most personal social network in that two people need to agree to connect before the link is made.

Which means those connections can be very valuable.

There's little danger of blurring your social and business lives on LinkedIn. It's clearly a work-related platform.

That's demonstrated by what it lets you put on your profile. Like Google+, it's extensive, and you can give a good account of yourself as a journalist – with your work experience, education and links to your other social presences.

Some key points on using LinkedIn:

- Make your profile as full as you can, with all your other platforms, portfolio and so on
- Update your profile regularly, and check who has been looking at it. Are any of them worth connecting with?
- Update your status to reflect what you are working on. Use the platform to request case studies, information
- Use it like an electronic contacts book – check out those you speak to at work and add them if valuable. Build up your connections – a large circle of connections shows you are networking hard. Connect with story sources, official bodies, any individuals who can help you do your journalism
- Write recommendations for those you find valuable as a connection, and (judiciously) request they do the same for you.

As a student or newly qualified journalist, you'll need to build in stages. As you come across a useful contact, the sort you'd put in your electronic contacts book, check whether they are on LinkedIn and, if they are, invite them to link up with you. The worst that can happen is that you are ignored.

LinkedIn lets you add connections by seeing who among your current contacts are already on the platform.

LinkedIn Groups

Another key element of LinkedIn is Groups. Groups are set up around companies, educational establishments, branches of professions and interest groups.

Joining groups links you in with experts in a particular field. Go to groups and search for ones that are relevant to your journalism. LinkedIn suggests groups you may like, and also has a full directory of existing groups.

If you can't find a group covering your area of interest, consider starting your own. If it proves popular, that's a great bit of personal brand-building.

on the website

Find a check-list on building your brand via Twitter and Facebook, just to make sure you are doing all you can.

14B4-16

Why you need a specialism, and how to choose one

For most newly qualified journalists, general reporting is their starting point – unless they choose the subbing and production route. If you want to remain a reporter long-term it's often a good idea to specialise: to choose an area of news that you cover intensively and on which you become a trusted expert and authority.

There are a couple of reasons for this. One is that specialist knowledge, and the provision of reliable, authoritative information, has a value above that of general news.

As we are seeing, it is almost impossible to get people to pay for general news online. In the UK, you have the massively well-resourced BBC pumping out a huge volume of general news, without needing to heed the commercial realities that other, private media outfits are governed by.

So, as a reporter, you need to be a purveyor of information that is valuable to the audience you are targeting – perhaps for their work, or for informing commercial decisions that they must make. Or, it may be information that gives them depth of coverage in an area of interest to them: a hobby or pastime perhaps.

The rise in social media has further devalued the work of the general reporter.

Because so much general news coverage is contributed by citizens in some way – whether through their eye-witness stills or video, or through celebrities tweeting what is happening to them – the general reporter sees their stock falling.

on the website

You'll find general advice on how to choose your specialism, plus detailed up-to-the-minute guidance in a number of popular specialisms, including:

- Technology
- Music Journalism
- Education
- Religion
- International Journalism
- Political Journalism
- Sport
- Celebrity and showbiz reporting
- Business and Financial Journalism
- Travel Writing
- Science, Health, Environment
- Fashion

Entrepreneurial journalism

Some self-employed journalists are going way beyond traditional freelancing.

Some are becoming entrepreneurs. They are developing start-up journalism businesses: creating their own apps or online and/or print publications. And a few journalism university courses are teaching entrepreneurialism

But, because this is such a new and fast-developing area, I'm going to address it in detail in the online version of MMJ.

on the website

Find a comprehensive guide to entrepreneurial journalism.

14B18

Exercises and projects

Exercise 1

Look for journalists who have created a strong personal brand. Try to work out how they have done it. Ask them what the secret is.

Exercise 2

Select one or two journalists from the area you intend to cover as a specialist. Pay close attention to the content they create in print, broadcast and online (as appropriate). Examine their use of social media, and identify the platforms they use, and how. Ask their advice on entering their specialism through whatever channel seems most appropriate.

Exercise 3

Identify a journalism start-up, interview the founders and create a full profile of the company. Apply the Cuny template (covered in detail in the online version of this chapter) to it and examine how the company has approached each point on the entrepreneurial check-list.

Projects

1 Do an audit on the strength of your personal brand. Check yourself against the criteria for success listed early in this chapter. Identify where you are doing well and where you might improve. Put a strategy in place to improve your branding.

2 Create a CV/resume/portfolio site for yourself.

3 Complete your Google+ profile and establish your Google Authorship.

4 Create your LinkedIn profile. Build up a circle of at least 50 connections. Become active in LinkedIn Groups. See if there is a group you could start for a subject that is not currently served. Work together with follow students if you can to create a vibrant group.

5 Develop an entrepreneurial journalism project, following the advice in the online version of this chapter. You may be able to take one of the publishing projects you have been working on, but if you can't, come up with a new idea.

Notes

1   http://towcenter.org/research/post-industrial-journalism/
2   www.journalism.org/
3   http://davelee.me/
4   www.theguardian.com/profile/josh-halliday
5   www.journalism.co.uk/news/joseph-stashko-joining-times-as-digital-news-development-editor/s2/a553404/
6   http://pando.com/2013/01/07/how-google-author-rank-could-change-content-marketing-and-journalism/

building a personal brand,
and developing a specialism

part C

Achieving professional standards

Aims of this section

In this section we aim to bring readers up to the level at which they could enter any branch of the media - from print to broadcasting or online - as newly-qualified journalists.

We will cover some familiar things in greater depth, and at an advanced level, but also introduce other areas of study that we have not tackled before.

In summary, we will work on bringing you up to professional standards in:

- Multi-platform publishing - creating smartphone apps, tablet computer editions and print versions of your content
- Advanced multimedia storytelling
- Long-form journalism
- Audio and video news bulletins and magazine programmes
- Features writing - general features, interviews, reviews, columns and comment pieces for print and online publication
- Creating in-depth special areas for websites
- Advanced online research methods
- Sub-editing news and features for print and online
- Search Engine Optimisation and Google Analytics.

chapter fifteen

Features and in-depth packages

In the book version of this chapter we will cover:

- Writing a wide range of text features for print and tablet computer
- Creating in-depth packages for online publication.

When looking at features we will work on:

- Interviewing for features
- Features structure
- Good opening sequences and endings
- General features
- Reviews
- Comment, leaders and other opinion pieces
- First-person columns.

In creating in-depth packages for online we will look at planning, structuring and populating an archive or specialist area on a website that contains a large amount of content.

The section will cover:

- Identifying a topic that has been covered regularly over a period of time, and that has a high level of public interest

- Selecting key items to add to an archive or special report on this subject
- Building the archive or special report, creating a welcome screen that sets out the subject matter and contains links, presented logically, to the individual story files.

At the end of the chapter are a range of assignments and projects to enable you to practise what you have learned.

In the online version of this chapter you will find:

- Links to all the examples discussed here
- A wide range of supporting material.

Have the companion website to this book open at www.multimedia-journalism.co.uk. That way you can easily click on the links to the stories discussed here.

15C1

Writing a wide range of features for print and tablet

In this section we will go deeper into features: an area of text journalism that has always been a mainstay of print magazines, and which transfers well to tablets, where the experience of flipping through a paper-product can be replicated electronically.

Such features are also read on websites, but they transfer there less well. It's really the tablet that best suits them, for reasons we'll go into in a moment.

Features defined

Way back in Chapter 1 we began by establishing a definition of news. We'll do the same now for features. Features differ from news stories in some ways, but they share many fundamentals with news.

Here is our definition of news:

News:

- Is new to our readers
- Is factual
- Is about people
- Is relevant to our readers, viewers and listeners - it affects them
- Is often dramatic and out of the ordinary
- Often involves conflict
- Can be something that someone doesn't want us to report
- Is perishable
- Is a good story well told.

News also needs a peg - a reason for running the story now.

The first thing to note is that a good feature has many - often all - of the elements of a good news story.

So all the above are important considerations when we write a feature. We should think of these news values as being at the core of a feature.

But there are some differences, and things we can do in a feature that we can't do in a news story.

For one thing, a feature is usually longer than a news story. While a news story might average between 200 and 400 words, features are rarely less than 600 words, and many are between 800 and 1,000 words. Some, particularly in magazines, can be much longer.

Features are longer for a reason.

With a feature we want to go into a subject in more depth, and to include more detail.

We often want to focus on one or more individuals in a feature, and to tell their story fully.

We can set the scene. If we interview someone, we can write about the place in which we talk to them, about what they are wearing, how they talk and other mannerisms.

Whereas a news story must be objective in its coverage of events, there is room for the author's interpretation in a feature.

So a feature is more subjective than a news story.

If a news story is there to give a reader the facts - quickly and without unnecessary details - a feature is often there to tell a story through an individual's experience.

If we are writing about a famine, the news story will concentrate on the number of people starving, the causes, the aid effort and other key factual elements required to tell the story.

If we write a *feature* about a famine we may well concentrate on the plight of a particular individual or family. We will describe their suffering, we will talk to them about what has happened to them. We hope the reader will relate to the individuals we talk to as fathers, mothers, children - as a family that has hit very hard times.

In doing so we will engage with our readers' emotions. If we have done our job well as feature writers, the reader will feel the plight of these people.

Often, it is not the news report about thousands of people starving to death that gets a reaction from the rest of the world; it is seeing the wide, frightened eyes of one malnourished child that goads readers or viewers into action.

Feature writers - or at least good ones - develop their own style. You could say they have their own voice. When we write a news story, we have no individual voice.

News has a rigid formula that requires an anonymous style. A feature allows the writer much more leeway.

Sometimes, the feature writer is the subject of his or her feature. But be very wary of putting yourself in a feature unless you have been asked for a first-person piece - a feature in which you are the main character, describing your experiences.

Features contain all the elements in our definition of news, with some important additions.

Features are similar to news stories in that they:

- Are new to our readers
- Are factual
- Are about people
- Are relevant to our readers, viewers and listeners – the feature affects them
- Are often dramatic and out of the ordinary
- Often involve conflict
- Are sometimes about something that someone doesn't want us to report
- Are perishable
- Are a good story well told.

Features differ from news stories in that they also:

- Contain colourful descriptions of people and places
- Often tell personal stories in detail
- Engage with the reader's emotions as well as their intellect.

Features are also:

- More subjective than news, and can include the writer's assessments of, and comments on, the situation they are writing about.

And, finally:

- Features writers can have their own style and develop their own voice.

The main types of feature

on the website

On the website you will find links to a range of good features, and to publications that regularly run high-quality features.

General features, often inspired by news stories

Features are often described as a 'look behind the news'. We take an issue that is mentioned in a news story and write about it in more detail and in more depth. Or we take a current news topic and write about one of the key people – or groups of people – that are caught up in it.

Such a feature gives the reader an insight into those who are caught up in events – what they are feeling, how they are suffering or coping.

Many news stories can be used as the peg for a feature.

Interviews

Some features – often involving a famous person or a powerful politician – are written as interviews. There is little else in them other than the answers to questions that have been put.

But interviewing is important to almost all features. Almost all features include quotes from people appropriate to the subject matter. There are people we want to talk to in order to bring a feature subject to life. We shall look at interviewing in more detail as we work through this section.

First-person features including columns

Here, the features writer can use 'I' a good deal, because the reader has come to read about them. It is very hard to write a really good first-person column. Many try, too many are published, few are worth reading.

Opinion pieces and comment

These are about the writer's views and opinions. The writer must draw on their expertise – either of an industry, if they are on a B2B publication, or of a subject (such as politics, or beauty products) if on a consumer title.

Reviews

Reviews are a features writer's assessment of a movie, a play or other kind of live or recorded performance, a book, a meal, a hotel or any number of other products or services.

Why features are better suited to print or a tablet computer than to the web or phones

It's because you really can't scan a feature. Or, if you do, you won't get much out of it. Features require reading closely, so that you engage with them. That said, there are some developments in features style and structure that help the scanner. Today there are fewer long feature reads in magazines and newspapers than in the past. Features are often broken up into boxes or other small elements. In some magazines, a feature is broken up further into bite-size chunks of a paragraph or so. Interviews become brisk Q and As.

We'll look at how to research and write the key types of feature.

Features inspired by news stories

Another way in which features differ from news is in how they come about. News often just happens. It lands at our feet and we write about it. News is often obvious. If a senior politician is arrested, a sports star dies in a car crash, a fire destroys a factory or a company goes bust, then the news interest is obvious.

We need to use our journalistic instincts to spot what news events might make a good feature.

For instance, if a sports star is in a coma after a car crash following an all-night booze and cocaine binge, maybe the accident is symptomatic of something. Perhaps it's an example of how hugely rich young stars lack the maturity to cope with their riches. Maybe there have been other incidents of drunken brawls, gambling addiction, drug addiction that can be tied together as examples around which a feature – a look behind the news – can be built. We can seek interviews with some of the affected stars, their managers and advisers. We can talk to sports agents, sports psychologists and other experts.

It helps if we have a headline in mind to give focus to the piece. We might go with: *Too much too young*.

Our feature will include quotes, colour, description and analysis. We'll want gripping content that engages the reader. If in our researches we find that the wife of the young footballer whose car crash put him into a coma is prepared to talk to us, and allow us to photograph her at his bedside, we may have either a very powerful opening sequence to the feature or, if the star was a big enough name, a powerful stand-alone interview.

Examples of features inspired by news stories

on the website

Find links to all the examples discussed here.

Features can be inspired by serious, high-profile news stories, or by less world-shaking ones.

Here's a serious one, from the BBC. The headline is: Is there a 'rising tide' of anti-Semitism in the West?

The standfirst explains how the feature will go behind the news:

> "Following the recent conflict between Israel and Palestinians in Gaza, there have been reports from a number of countries of attacks targeting Jews. But does the evidence support claims that anti-Semitism is on the rise?"

Now for a much less serious feature topic. In the (London) *Daily Telegraph*'s Life section is a feature headlined:

'How marriage to my toyboy husband (22 years my junior) ended in tears'

The standfirst beneath reveals the news peg: "A law firm has revealed that the number of younger husbands filing for divorce from older wives is up by a third in three years." It goes on to explain how the writer, Beverley Glick, married to a much younger man, will tell her story and explain why, for her, the report rings horribly true.

Interviewing for features

We looked at interviewing in some detail in Chapter 7. Now we'll develop what we did there by concentrating on particular types of feature. And we won't worry about interviewing for audio or video. This is interviewing purely for text.

A Life in the Day

This is a hugely popular feature that holds the inside back page of the (London) *Sunday Times Magazine*. It's a simple idea, and an incredibly effective one. The person is interviewed about their day, and in describing it they reveal a good deal about themselves and their life.

It's worth looking closely at how this feature works, because it is more complex than you might think. To carry out an interview that gives all the information needed for it involves a lot of time and care.

How the feature works

I suggest you go online and read a couple of Life in the Day features to get a feel for them. Later I'm going to look in detail at two:

1   **David Beckham**
    www.thesundaytimes.co.uk/sto/Magazine/a_life_in_the_day/article1368499.ece

2   **Jennifer Saunders**
    www.thesundaytimes.co.uk/sto/Magazine/a_life_in_the_day/article1366081.ece

on the website

Find those features reproduced on the website.

So read those, plus any others that look interesting.

Don't read on until you have done this research.

THE STRUCTURE

The person's day forms the structure of the story. The piece always begins with them getting up, and ends at the end of their day. This is fixed.

THE VARIABLES

There are two levels of variable:

- The superficial variables are the details of what they do – big breakfast or no breakfast, for example
- The more important variables come from the significance of each of these minor details for the individual.

To make it work

Everything you say about their day must be selected for its broader significance. Nothing is inconsequential, it is all pertinent to the portrait we are building up of them as a person.

The detail of their day shines a bright light on important aspects of their lives, such as their attitude to work, money, family, and who their key relationships are with.

The important variables

While the day is followed chronologically, the broader themes that are overlaid on the structure can be introduced in a variable order. This is dictated by what significance each point in the day actually has.

Breakfast, for example, might bring the reminder of a partner who died, and so the subject's sense of loss and loneliness might be the first broader theme explored.

But breakfast might introduce another broad theme – a dysfunctional attitude to food, for example.

questions

Look again at the two columns mentioned above, and note the superficial and important variables in each.

Below I've listed what I consider to be the important variables in the order they are introduced in the two columns. Make a list of your own, then take a look at mine.

1   David Beckham

Important variables

- Dealing with fame: Problems with paparazzi (triggered by taking children to school)
- Work: For charities, and commercial projects involving children (also triggered by taking children to school)
- Dealing with fame: Getting around without being recognised
- Attitude to food: Differences in diet between him and wife Victoria
- Dealing with fame: Friendships with the famous seem easier
- Dealing with fame: Visiting supermarkets and pubs, and normality won by gaining the trust and friendship of drinkers in a couple of locals

The overall picture we get is of a house husband. He deals with the kids both before and after school. His wife is not really present in the feature. Fame constricts his life and freedom considerably but he has developed strategies to keep life as normal as possible, including going to supermarkets and pubs.

2   Jennifer Saunders

Important variables

- Worry about overeating: No breakfast, light lunch, idealised rich, starchy dinner (triggered at meal times during the day)
- Worry about appearance: Make-up and clothes
- Health: Oblique mention of "with the chemo and everything"
- Family: Being a grandmother, children having left home, pining for family life
- Home and family: Devon "still feels like home, but after the kids left, it did seem rather empty".

The overall image we get is of a woman who hugely values family life, but who has had to come to terms with losing much of it, for whom food is a constant temptation. She has chosen to present herself when she is not working, and her desire for a very quiet life is paramount.

questions

We only get a very oblique reference to health problems. Is it an omission that we don't find out what the chemo was for and what the prognosis is?

Suggestion: Do some research into Jennifer Saunders and think of questions you would have asked to tease out more about her cancer. Do you think she will be reticent on this subject? Is it too painful for you to probe?

You'll find she wrote a book about her fight, described as "honest and uplifting" in the story linked to here:

> **www.dailymail.co.uk/news/article-2445091/Jennifer-Saunders-account-battling-breast-cancer-honest-uplifting.html**

In my view, it is a subject you can ask about.

How to interview a Life in the Day subject

To get all the detail you need out of your subject for one of these 700-word features will take quite some time. You'll need to ask them lots of things about their day, many of which won't find their way into the piece. Each question you ask about the detail of their lives is designed to probe for important things that you can then explore.

For instance, if they say they have a shower in the morning you can ask them what products they use. They might say they have no idea, that their partner buys that sort of stuff, or perhaps they might reveal a scrupulous beauty regime involving several expensive, exotic products. If they do then you can ask them if it is important to pamper themselves. Did they always have expensive products? What about as a child? Perhaps they say money was tight when they were growing up and they had to make do with a lump of green carbolic soap. Maybe they vowed that when they could afford it they would indulge in a luxurious bathing and beauty regime. This line of questioning might open up the key to their childhood and how it affected them.

If they say they walk to work you need to ask them about the route. Why do they walk? How far is it? What do they see? There might be nothing very interesting in the walk, but it could be the key to them. If the person says they count the number of buses they see and pray that the total isn't 13, or that they avoid stepping on the gaps between paving stones, it reveals something unusual about them.

With this, as in every other interview, you are trying to build up a fully rounded picture of your subject. After the interview you should be able to go over in your mind every aspect of them and their life, and have the answer to pretty much any question someone (maybe your editor) might ask you about them.

So, if they say they put on their suit, you need to know if they like wearing it, where did they get it, what did it cost? Do they have just one suit or many? Are they interested in clothes? What style of clothes do they prefer to wear? If the person clearly has no interest in clothes this is not an avenue we can go very far with, but if clothes are important to them then this is a significant aspect of their life, and we need to find out all we can about it.

So, how to get all this information?

Just as the day forms the framework of the feature, asking about it can form the framework of the interview. Take them through their day, building up in your mind an overall sketch of the shape their day takes. No doubt as they talk there will be some key points about the day that spark lots of subsidiary questions, or which get them talking without you prompting them much. You can let those asides run, get all you need out of them. The danger is that you forget the chronology. You forget at what exact point in the day they had got to and a jump occurs. If it does, you need to spot it and go back later to fill in the hole in your knowledge of their day.

After they have taken you through their day once in outline, you can go back and probe each part of it, checking for the significant variables that are revealed by the insignificant ones.

Working on a Life in the Day is a great way to learn the skills of features interviewing. The methods you use will stand you in good stead whenever you need to interview for a feature.

How to structure a general feature

Life in the Day is a good starting point because the structure is ready-made for you. But if we don't have a ready-made framework – and very often we don't – how do we structure a feature? And how do we decide what to say in the intro?

Features writing gives us much freedom. There are many ways to begin and structure a feature.

Whereas news writers have the inverted triangle as a guide, feature writers often lack a suitable scheme for beginning and structuring their pieces. We will look at some useful structures to use in place of the inverted triangle in a bit. But first – how do you begin?

With news you start with what's new, what has or will happen. With a feature you can start anywhere. Your intro isn't there to tell the reader what the latest is; it is there to hook them, to grab them and make them read on. But you must still have a focus. So the thing you choose to start with should be relevant to the theme you are going to develop through the feature.

So how do you decide, from all the information you have, what to put first?

You can ask yourself the following:

- What's the most interesting thing?
- If you have done an interview - what one thing do I remember?
- If reading through your notes, what is the key point?

Just as with news, you must hook the reader. Colour, detail, description, personality, all are good ways of providing a hook.

Let's use the earlier example of our *Too much too young* feature about sporting stars who go off the rails. The interview we have with the wife of the footballer in a coma after an accident is going to be very powerful. If she allows us to see her at her husband's bedside, that might give us a strong introductory sequence. Perhaps she puts the TV on whenever his former club is playing, hoping that the sounds and atmosphere, and hearing the names of his former team mates, might provide the stimulus to break the coma.

Describing this scene will give us a compelling start. We can take some time on this scene, and leave an outline of what the feature is about until later - maybe 200 or 300 words later. As we will very likely have a standfirst to introduce our broad themes this is not a problem.

So those are the two first elements in structuring a general feature.

1   Hook the reader. Give them colour, description, quotes or whatever it takes to engage their interest and perhaps their emotions. In a standard length feature - anything from 800 to 1,300 words - you can take 10 to 15 per cent of the total word count in doing this.

2   Give them the big picture. Say what the feature is about, how the example you have started with relates to the major theme you are exploring. That theme is summed up in the headline: *Too much too young*. So we can pose that as a question and support our asking it with a mention of other examples of excess.

This is the focus for the feature. It works rather like an intro on a news story, but it comes later than it would do in a news story. It says what the feature is about and should contain a mention of the main themes and areas we are going to cover. If we do that the reader knows where the feature is going and does not find any surprises later on.

Getting the intro right

There is a deal of subjectivity in deciding whether a features intro works. With a news story we have the simple yardstick: does it say what is new? Now we must apply the much broader test: does it hook the reader? Will they read it and then read on?

Because of this, it's likely that if ten writers had the same material from which to craft a feature, they'd come up with two, three or more different ways of intro-ing it.

Here are some examples of intros that I think work well. I'll explain why I like them. I've included links to the full feature where they are available online. You'll also find these links on the website.

> **1** Red petals scatter the stone steps of the Metropolitan cathedral in Timisoara, a city in western Romania. The petals have showered a bride and groom, and garlanded Dacia cars honk in jubilation. The noise is deafening.
>
> Fifteen years ago this month, these steps were spattered with the blood of fallen protesters, gunned down while crying "Down with Ceausescu! Down with Communism! We want liberty!" The people of Timisoara, like the rest of Romania, fed up with 45 years of Communism, the rants of President Nicolae Ceausescu, fear, corruption, queues for stale black bread, and grey cement homes, had risen against the totalitarian state. The noise must have been deafening.
>
> (Lee Karen Stow, *The Times*)

That's a great opening sequence because it packs in a good deal of information, both historic and current, about a city, but it does so by giving you two very vivid pictures that present very different images of the place now, and in the not-so-distant past.

> **2** I meet William Hague at King's Cross station at 8.15 in the morning. He is standing alone on the concourse, neat and shiny as a new pin, not just his head, the whole of him, a *Times* and an *FT* his only luggage, nothing else to spoil the cut of what he later says, when pressed, is a £2,000 Savile Row suit. He's been awake a long while, and had his porridge, as is his habit. We exchange pleasantries about Yorkshire: his hometown of Rotherham in the south, his constituency of Richmond in the north, my hometown of Hull in the east, which is where, as part of his publicity tour for his biography of William Pitt the Younger, we are bound today. Hague smiles a lot. For him, this is virtually a day off.
>
> (Robert Crampton, *The Times*)

This is a brilliant opener because it effortlessly packs a huge amount of information into its 135 words. But look at how much interviewing it will have taken to get all that stuff. Take the suit, for example. Like all the other details it is priceless because they build up such a detailed

portrait of the man. But ask him about his suit and I bet at first he just muttered something. Is it bespoke? Is it Savile Row? How much did it cost? Hague might not have wanted to say, so the interviewer might have had to say, ok, was it £5,000? No, no nothing like as much as that. "A thousand? A little more than that. . ." Ok I'm going to write £2,000 unless you tell me that's wrong.

Getting the information about his breakfast and other details will have been very similar to working on a Life in the Day. And the interviewer has subtly but firmly put himself in the intro.

> **3**   London, Paris, New York, Milan. . . and the Outer Hebrides. That's right: the Scottish islands are having what is known as a Fashion Moment.
>
> (Simon Chilvers, *The Guardian*)

That's a much shorter, simpler intro, but it uses the very effective device of a surprising contrast to hook the reader. It is intriguing, and almost challenges you not to read on.

> **4**   Later I am going to make you interested, for the first time in your life, in grout.
>
> (Bryan Appleyard, *The Sunday Times*)

I like this intro because I suspect most readers' instinctive reaction is: Oh no you're not. But he does. The feature is actually a lively but otherwise straightforward history of London's St Pancras station. At intervals through its 1,150 words the writer reminds us of the grout. After a couple of hundred words he is saying: "Both this grout and what it does are almost unbearably exciting. But you've got to work up to it, so first you must know about. . ." and off he goes into the history of the station. At one point he's stroking the grout. Later, approaching the end of the piece, he encourages us to stick with him: "Bear with me – we're nearly back to the grout."

I'll leave you to find out what the significance of the grout is by reading the piece, but it's a masterly example of how to introduce and sustain a thread that takes the reader right through your feature.

Here are two intros to features that I wrote. It's up to others to judge whether they are any good, but I'll explain why I wrote them as I did.

> **6**   A steady drip of Welsh rain falls from the high, round-arched apex of the concrete roof in Our Lady Star of the Sea. It lands with a metronomic tick on a green plastic kneeler, as if time were running out for this unique, modernist church.

I wanted an intro that communicated the atmosphere in an amazing church sitting on a cliff top in north Wales and slowly falling into ruin. While I was standing in it with the priest, the drip of water that I describe caught my attention, and seemed to me to offer a powerful yet simple and visually arresting indication of the state the place was in. In the intro I tried to include the place (Wales), that it's wet, that it's on the coast, some sense of the unusual design of the church, and the fact it is falling into ruin. And I wanted to do that in under 50 words.

> **7** Blackpool is "noted for fresh air and fun", Skegness is "So bracing", Brighton. . . well, in the words of Keith Waterhouse: "Brighton looks like a town that is helping the police with their enquiries."

The English seaside evokes nostalgia in those old enough to remember it before everyone took to jetting off to the sun in the summer. Each significant seaside town has its own character, and Brighton's is slightly disreputable. As I was going to go on to tell the story of George IV and the secret wife he kept in the town I wanted to establish its racy character right at the start, and show that there was some history behind the town's reputation.

When do you write the intro?

With news, its good practice to get the intro right first. Once you have, penning the rest of the story is fairly straightforward.

With a feature, it isn't always easy to get the intro right until a lot of the body of the feature is written. I often find that I have actually begun at the second par, and that the real intro suggests itself at some point in the writing process - sometimes not until the end.

Some useful structures to follow in a feature

on the website

Find a wide range of links to examples that demonstrate ways to structure a feature.

Let's continue with our footballer in a coma. We have the first two elements in our structure - the hook and then the focus of the piece - where do we go from there?

We have several aspects of the story we want to cover. After our focus at element two we begin to deal with those issues.

As our feature is going to be driven by interviews; with victims, experts and commentators, we can adopt a very simple but effective order in which we have:

Quote, transition, quote

This is a useful, and very simple, structure for when we have a substantial element of interview in our feature. You want to cover several areas, and you'll quote the person for several pars as you address each point. Between these segments you need a smooth transition, taking them from one area of discussion to the next. If you interview more than one person, you can use the transition to move on to the next person you'd like to quote.

on the website

See examples of features taking this structure.

So, with our footballer, our third element of the feature might be his wife on the shock of the injury and how life is so different now.

Among the other elements we have to place might be interviews with other sports stars or their families, quotes from a sports psychologist, quotes from a team manager, quotes from a sports agent.

The order we place them in depends on the quality of their quotes, and we use a transition between each.

If we have a feature that is not based nearly so heavily on interviews, but is structured around an examination of an issue, an industry, a problem, we can use a similar approach to structure. I call that . . .

The simple points-in-order approach

This is closest to the inverted triangle, and is regularly used in B2B titles where they often see features as extended news stories which, while topical, will go beyond the strict news peg to look at – say – a trend in a market.

In consumer publications the points-in-order structure can be used in features that are heavily factual and in which there are quotes, but no extended interviewing or colour.

To write these you should make a list of the main areas covered. There might be five or six of them. Then you can slot all the dozens of separate facts and quotes you have gathered into these categories.

The intro might be a very factual one, so you should pull the key points together and create your intro and second and third pars.

These opening pars should create the focus of the feature, covering all the main points you will expand upon later.

on the website

Find examples of features taking this structure.

The diamond

This structure works well when we have a strong news story, but have decided to introduce it with a personal tale.

The personal tale is an upright triangle, drawing the reader in to the story, engaging their emotions.

Then comes the peg - the news angle - of the feature. That is pretty much the same as the top line of the inverted triangle.

From there, the feature continues much as a news story would, amplifying each point and tying up loose ends.

This is another simple structure. You can turn a news story containing a short case study into a feature, very often, by taking the case study from the body of the text and promoting it to the top, so it replaces the hard-news intro. That hard-news intro drops down and forms the wide point where the upright triangle meets the inverted one. Like this:

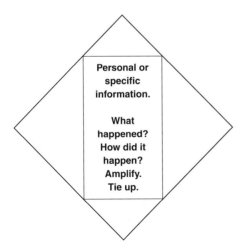

The hourglass

This is an inverted triangle balanced on an upright one – point to point. So the feature begins in a strongly newsy way – following the inverted pyramid with material in descending order of importance. Then in the middle, once the newsy half of the feature is told, it flips. From here we start slow, perhaps going back to the very beginning of the story and telling things chronologically.

For example, in a feature about a major crime, you could start with an actual crime, and recount the main events as you would in a news story, then switch to a chronological account of how the crime was allegedly planned and executed.

That's what John Follain has done in Is This the Face of a Killer?, which is linked to on the website.

The feature is about Amanda Knox, an American student who was in custody awaiting a murder trial when the feature was written. The victim, allegedly dispatched by her and boyfriend Raffaele Sollecito, was the British student Meredith Kercher.

The piece follows this structure.

A newsy intro establishing that Knox is a key suspect in the case, followed by an inverted triangle structure in which the case against Knox and other defendants is outlined. This tapers off to a summary of the autopsy report, at the narrow bottom of the first, inverted triangle.

Then we come to the opening of the second, upright triangle. It begins: "Knox was born and grew up in Seattle. . ." and takes a chronological sweep through her life, moving through the crime and Knox's imprisonment. At the end it comes right up to date, with the latest entry in her prison diary.

Using geography as a structure

Travel features about a journey are a clear example of this technique, but geography can also be the most logical way to organise a general feature.

For example, the *Sunday Times Magazine* ran a feature called The Irony Curtain which was about the stark contrast that remained on the ground after the wall between East and West Germany was torn down. It is as if an invisible wall still exists.

After the set up, and the introduction of the idea that a wall remains in people's heads, the focus reads:

> To find out why, there could hardly be a more poignant place to start looking than Wittenberge, and from there trace the stories of those along a section of where the border once followed the Elbe river – across which East and West German soldiers once regularly exchanged fire.

Using scenes as structure

This technique is often used in profiles, where the writer observes his or her subject in a range of situations.

Here's an example.

Headline: David Gandy's hot pants

Standfirst: The model has designed a range of underwear for Marks & Spencer. Deborah Ross talks briefs with 'the most handsome man on Earth' – and masters the art of self-control. Almost.

Deborah Ross is a really funny writer, who brings her wit to bear on difficult assignments such as this: an interview which has only been granted in order to promote a range of underwear. Many writers would fail to wriggle out of such a straitjacket. Ross manages it, and turns in a sparkling piece.

on the website

Find more examples of this type of structure.

Ending a feature

A feature needs a strong ending. That's another distinct difference between it and a news story, which tapers away at the end and can be cut at any point leading up to it.

Sometimes the circle technique – looping back to the beginning to reprise the scene you began with – works well. At other times you need some other strong final point: a good quote, a key fact, a shock statistic, a sobering thought.

Here's an example of the circle technique. Polly Vernon's feature about Paul McKenna, in the *Observer*, headlined Look into my Eyes, starts : "Paul McKenna wants to nail me into a coffin. 'Go on!' he says. 'It'll be great!' I'm cautious. 'Uh. . . not sure, actually. . .' I say."

Polly travels around with McKenna, and finds the man she expected to loathe grows on her. Eventually she trusts him enough to allow him to hypnotise her.

The piece ends: "After I've no idea how long, he wakes me up. I was, he says, properly gone. I believe him. And then Paul McKenna nails me into a coffin, and I don't mind a bit."

The broken up feature

Increasingly, features are not presented as one read but broken up into small sections. Typically there is a set up – 200 to 500 words in which the subject is established and explored, followed by boxes in which various aspects of the issue are focused on. The boxes might be interviews with contrasting people. This format lends itself well to surveys of products or services and is often used in consumer magazines.

on the website

Find examples of features that offer other great lessons in good writing and/or structure.

Some essentials and some pitfalls

Beware of dealing in generalities – many features fail on this point.

Use specifics, use detail. Specifics give us a picture in our heads, generalities do not. But use telling, relevant detail. Fiction writers are sometimes told that if they show the reader a revolver, they should make sure they use it. Do the same. As with A Life in the Day, dwell on the relevant detail.

Use quotes and attribution to give your feature authority

Another lesson from news – don't get lazy or turn the feature into an opinion piece unless that is exactly what is required.

Don't let chronology dictate your structure

Chronology can be the best way to structure a feature, but not if that slows it down. Dip in and out of it. Focus on some points in the story, move swiftly over others. And, even if chronology is the best way to structure the body of the feature, grab the best bit for your intro, wherever it comes chronologically.

Don't forget to tell the reader what you are doing – in analysis and fact-based features

Remember the advantages of the inverted triangle approach. It ensures that all key points are introduced – however briefly – high up in the story.

In an information-heavy feature, make sure you do the same. That gives readers a clear guide to where the piece is going.

Otherwise, particularly with a long, discursive feature, they regularly find new and important angles on the story that they weren't expecting.

Your standfirst can help a good deal here.

15C4

How to write a profile

A profile is defined as a portrait of a person which, rather than having an interview with an individual at its core, builds up a picture of them by talking to those who know him or her well. Often the subject is not spoken to at all, only their friends, enemies, colleagues, partners, victims – however many people it takes to build up the picture of them. Such profiles are often about a man or woman who is in the news.

In the following example, the headline and standfirst set up the theme for the profile, and establish the news peg. Here they are:

Headline: Scarlett Johansson: The sexpot superhero's great power is invisibility

Standfirst: The husky-voiced actress has made the catsuit her own and is back as a merciless warrior in her latest film *Lucy* but off-screen she can easily pass unnoticed – and that's just how she likes it.

on the website

Find a link to this profile, and others.

The bread-and-butter of such a profile is to run through the subject's life and career, including successes and failures, controversies and embarrassments.

So, along with the string of successful movies we get the episode when "she resigned as a global ambassador for Oxfam, choosing to keep promoting SodaStream, a company whose main factory was sited in the Israeli-occupied West Bank", and "One of Johansson's only brushes with the dark side of fame was when her phone was hacked and naked photographs of her appeared on the internet".

Her guts and bravery are also covered, including her risky decision to launch a second career as a singer. The profiler comments: "Most A-listers wouldn't have risked the ridicule of recording covers of Tom Waits."

But it's the theme of her success at keeping her life private that runs through the piece and makes it more than just a cuts job. So we learn: "So adept is Johansson at shielding her privacy that few knew until recently that she had forsaken New York for Paris and quietly become engaged to a Frenchman, Romain Dauriac. . . and is expecting his baby." Her anonymity is such, we are told that "In *Under the Skin*. . . she was able to drive a van around Glasgow picking up passers-by (so that her character, an extra-terrestrial, could kill them) without being recognised."

15C5

How to write a review

There are many ways to approach reviewing, but the following is a tried and tested method that works. Follow this format and you have a good chance of turning in something that your commissioning editor likes. It works whatever you are reviewing: book, film, band, exhibition, restaurant or play.

In general

Pick a theme. You can't say much in a short review, so what you include should be built on a coherent thread that takes the reader from start to finish.

on the website

Find links to the reviews discussed below.

For instance, in a review from the *Independent* of the singer Morrissey, the piece begins with the reviewer talking about how much he used to love him. He moves on to the disappoint-ments that Morrissey can drag his admirers through, then ends up: "I still love you but slightly less than I used to". Which has the added bonus of bringing things full circle and creating a neat ending.

1 First 100 words

Get straight into the story. Relate something specific that has resonance.

It might be the pivotal scene in a film, play or book, or the moment in a live performance that was most memorable or telling. You can put yourself into the review if you like – after all, a review is a personal opinion – and if what you are reviewing clearly has importance for you that will give extra energy to the piece.

In a *Sunday Times* review of Christina Lamb's *Small Wars Permitting*, about being a foreign and war correspondent, Patrick French writes in his intro: "It is 2000, and Christina Lamb is in Lagos, working against a deadline without any leads to locate the home of the family of Damilola Taylor, a 10-year-old Nigerian boy who has been stabbed to death in Peckham." Immediately we are in the thick of it, alongside a correspondent as they tackle a seemingly impossible task.

2 Next 100 words

Now give the context and the necessary background detail.

Having hooked the reader with an entertaining opening you can give the bigger picture. Why this performance, book or whatever is important/worth reading/demands to be seen. You can include here background information such as the film on which the director or star's reputation depends. You can say why the thing you are reviewing is significant enough to be written about. If it is brilliant, average or dreadful, you can say that here.

With Morrissey it's because there has been a huge revival in his popularity. With Christina Lamb, French writes: "Not all journalism deserves to be placed between the covers of a book. *Small Wars Permitting*. . . succeeds because it is so lively. Lamb does not enjoy theorising. Her interest is the human story behind global events."

If you are introducing a performer, author or other who is likely to be new to your reader, help them decide whether they are interested by making comparisons with performers/authors they will have heard of.

In another *Sunday Times* band review, of the relatively unknown Big Linda, Lisa Verrico gives this context:

> The ludicrously named Big Linda are a London-based hard-rock quartet who could have stepped straight from the 1970s. Their largest debt is to Led Zeppelin, whose scorching riffs, powerhouse drums and bluesy boogie they steal for most of tonight's up-tempo tracks.

3 250 words

This is the main body of the review. Make the key points you want to make. You'll probably have room for about three or four. Write about the performance, film or book in detail. Identify the best and worst bits. Treat the performance, book or whatever chronologically if that works.

The Morrissey review goes through the highlights and low points of the performance. The Lamb book review covers the main places, themes, stories and characters in the book.

4 Ending 50 words

Round things off either by finishing the chronology, looping back to the beginning or with another telling point. Don't let the review just trail away.

Morrissey we've mentioned. The Lamb review ends soberingly with a section about Zimbabwe, which she describes as "the most heartbreaking story I have ever covered." The final quote is Lamb remembering what an impressive place Zimbabwe was before Mugabe devastated it, with the best-educated population in Africa, neat buildings and lines of children with freshly washed uniforms. The reviewer ends: "Now all that has gone."

15C6

Columns and other first-person pieces

It's all about me, me, me. Many journalists aspire to column-writing. Far too many achieve it. Too many columnists run out of things to write about. A few are naturals. The persona they establish and the things they write about – which might be just the mundanities of everyday life – strike a chord with the reader.

To do so they have to embody a certain truth. Readers need to be able to identify with the columnist and their predicament.

Others are ostensibly writing reviews but a good three quarters of the piece is about them, and it is this bit they are read for.

Jeremy Clarkson and Giles Coren are both masters of the column that, whether ostensibly about cars or food, is really about them. Caitlin Moran puts herself into everything she writes, to the extent that, when – for example – she interviews the chef Jamie Oliver, she has him come to her house, to cook breakfast in her kitchen. Jamie's interaction with Caitlin, her children and friends means the piece is as much about them as it is him.

on the website

Find links to the examples discussed here.

Finding your voice

When writing personal pieces, finding your voice is hugely important. The column won't work without it. Competent general features writers, and star interviewers, also do it. Their voice in the feature gives it an appeal and a value all of its own. It becomes unique. That's how you become a star writer, as opposed to a jobbing hack.

Comment, opinion and editors' letters

You might think your days of writing such pieces are far away but, particularly if your first job is on a B2B publication with a staff of just one or two, you may well find yourself called upon to write comment.

The thing about an opinion column is that it has to have one. An opinion, that is. Sounds obvious, but often they don't. Poor opinion pieces say on the one hand this, on the other hand that, and I think we can all agree to disagree.

Leaders

Typically found in newspapers, they express the opinion of the publication (and often its proprietor) and go unsigned. Usually they relate to subjects covered at length in the newspaper – major current stories or important issues that are being covered in other sections. They are the place where the paper reviews what has been revealed in the news or other pages, analyses the import of it and gives a view. The paper often strives for balance in the news reporting of the issues covered, but then comes down on one side or other in the leader.

Comment pieces

Often called op-ed pieces in quality newspapers – traditionally because they appeared opposite the editorial page on which the leaders are placed. These are signed and present the view of the writer, which may not be the same as that of the publication. A balanced debate is not expected here. The writer is more like an advocate for a particular point of view, and there may be other writers advocating counter positions elsewhere on the page or in the rest of the paper.

Editors' letters

Usually found early on in consumer and B2B magazines, they often merely introduce the main pieces in the mag: "Have we got a great edition for you!" Sometimes they are more like leaders, expressing the view of the publication, and will tend to pick up on a contentious issue covered in the news or other sections of the mag. It's the latter definition that is relevant to our current discussion.

One thing common to all of them – they need a strong opinion, clearly enunciated.

To get that we need to consider these points:

- **What is our attitude to the issue?** Are we worried, angry, puzzled, outraged or wryly amused? What tone should we adopt?
- **What do we have to say that is new?** Not always possible to find something, but much better if we can.
- **Do we have a goal in mind?** Are we hoping to influence debate in material ways – to shift or support public opinion, to make legislators take notice, or industry figures adopt a particular practice or policy? Perhaps we want an official response.
- **Do we see a solution?** Very handy if we do, because we can develop a cogent argument, and conduct an analysis that leads up – hopefully logically – to the outcome, or the course of action, that we are advocating.
- **What are we adding to the debate?** Is this a view that has not so far been expressed? Do we have new material in this edition that takes things forward, and that facilitates a concurrent advance in the debate?

We must present a lively, compelling argument, and adopt a position that is a logical outcome of our analysis of events.

Creating in-depth packages for websites

This section will cover building an archive or special report on a key subject, and will include:

- Identifying a topic that has been covered regularly over a period of time, and that has a high level of public interest
- Selecting key items to add to an archive or special report on this subject
- Building the archive or special report, creating a welcome screen that sets out the subject matter and contains links, presented logically, to the individual story files
- Either importing these files into a designated area of the web site, or creating links to the relevant files but leaving them in their current locations
- Ensuring, where files are imported into the site, that text is evergreened: references such as 'yesterday' and 'tomorrow' are replaced with references to the relevant date – eg 'on 14 July 2007'.

Traditional publishers often feel themselves at a disadvantage when it comes to establishing a credible presence online. They often don't grasp the culture of online multimedia journalism as instinctively as younger, web-savvy outsiders do. They can both fear and look down on untrained practitioners.

They come from a world in which you had to be rich and powerful to own the means of production. Now, and this is a unifying theme of this book and online project, anyone can publish.

But what traditional publishers have that is absolute gold dust, and which they hold uniquely, is a breadth and depth of high-quality content. Take a company such as Haymarket, for instance, which owns an array of consumer and B2B magazines that are usually long-established, and often market leaders in their respective fields. One such title is *Autocar*. That became dominant, in print, by giving readers a pretty much unparalleled guide to cars. Its editors and writers were and are experts in the field. There are dozens of Haymarket magazines that are pre-eminent in their specialist area.

That unique depth of content is something that online start-ups can't begin to marshal. Which means that Haymarket and other publishers can punch with great weight online.

on the website

On the website you'll find a video interview with Mark Payton, digital editorial director at Haymarket Consumer Media, outlining the company's power online.

Here's a quote from it:

> Audiences now have a greater expectation of immediacy; they're accustomed to instantaneous coverage. But I'm convinced there's a need to make sense of the noise: the Associated Press research that was presented at the [World Editors'] Forum showed that 18 to 34-year-olds are crying out for context and depth.

Payton says that to compete in a "democratised" online environment, in which anyone can publish a basic site in minutes, the professional journalist's ability to research and place a story in context will become more important than ever.

So it's depth that gives traditional publishers the edge. Online, he says, a publisher can go for more vertical depth in a subject that they could ever afford to in print.

For example, if one of Haymarket's titles wants to create a car-buyer's guide, there is no limit to the depth they can go into: Covering every model, every age of car, every outlook on motoring. They can do it because they have an enormous wealth of authoritative content on all aspects of motoring.

That, he concludes, is very exciting for an editorial director such as him.

So this section is about depth. It's traditional print media's big answer to all the online start-ups: something they can do because they have the content.

Many newspapers and magazines have put their enormous archives online, and some are proving successful in charging for access to them.

But it's not just about archives, it's also about creating a rich content area that offers an in-depth analysis on a particular topic that is of interest, concern and value to readers.

We did a bit of that in Chapter 2 when we created a series of screens dedicated to a particular subject. We are going to do much more of it now.

Let's remember our family tree-style web structure here. In creating a special area we will be looking for a topic that is in the news regularly, and likely to remain so for some months or even years. Big subjects like this - the world economic situation is a good example - are complex and evolving, but there is a core of information that is always relevant to an understanding of them.

A newspaper or magazine that covers sport in great detail might create areas that contain a good deal of information. A national newspaper might have a Premiership site area that has a great depth of information about each team, its players and their form. There could be a good deal of historic information, including statistics.

A local newspaper/website might create an area that contained reports on all matches played in local amateur leagues - far more information than they could ever present in print.

If you edit a history magazine and website, you might create a site area about major historic events to satisfy readers' interest in drilling down to discover details they didn't know, or to check facts, or to conduct research. A Second World War area would cover the origins and causes of the conflict, the course of the battles, and the aftermath.

That's a useful example in that it happened a while ago. Most of what we put in such a section is fixed - it's not going to change or be made irrelevant by new events. However, many of the topics we select for special content areas will be evolving every day.

If for example, we create a specialist area on the rise of Islamist terrorism, the origins of the current situation are set. How it developed to date is to a large extent set, although we'll need to add to it.

What this means is we can create a tidy archive of material that will not need updating. Of course, much will be added to it over the days, week and months, but the core is static.

So we set up a site area, using our family tree approach, which has a landing page that sets out what is covered and provides links to the next level down.

Identifying a topic that has been covered regularly over a period of time, and that has a high level of public interest

So first we need to identify a topic. On a local website that might be schools and their Ofsted ratings and other material about them and their performance. On a B2B magazine it might be an issue that has an impact on the industry we cover. Perhaps a piece of government legislation has hit the industry hard and we are campaigning for its repeal. Say we are the *Morning Advertiser*, which serves publicans. The pub smoking ban of a few years ago was a major issue that hit the industry hard. They covered it in-depth, and readers wanted to refer to it over a long period, because it gave them guidance in steering their businesses over this major hurdle to continued profitability.

Selecting key items to add to an archive or special report on this subject

Once we have our topic we need all relevant staff to keep an eye out for stories that need to be added to it. Some media organisations rely on a mechanical approach to aggregating content for specialist areas. They simply pull in every story with a given tag. There are examples on the website which show why this approach is badly flawed.

Such an area is very useful, and impresses readers. Many of the major areas we build will tick along most of the time, with reasonable traffic, but as soon as we get a breaking story that takes the issue forward, we run it on our home or main news page and link from it to the archive we have built up. The reader is impressed because they find a wealth of background and valuable additional material available just when they are interested in it. They don't realise we had it all along and have just linked to it afresh.

I've concentrated on serious topics so far, but they needn't be. If we have a lot of showbiz on our site and the Oscars come around, we can post news stories and build new photogalleries and other elements. We can do that each year, and build a new segment in our Oscars area, but retain material from past years. Film fans can look back at the stars and movies that won in the past. Such an area lends itself well to video interviews, movie clips, slide shows of red carpet moments and striking frocks, and reader comment and other community content.

Building a welcome screen

The landing page or welcome screen for this area can be linked to from wherever we want – from our home page, from each new individual story that appears in our news pages, and also placed on our permanent nav bar.

Clicking on any of those links should take us to a welcome screen that gives the reader a clear guide to what they can find here. If this is level one of the area, level two should be the sub-divisions of the subject. At level three will come all the individual items - text reports, video and podcasts, slide shows and so on.

Evergreening content

Evergreening means ensuring, where files are imported into the site, that references such as 'yesterday' and 'tomorrow' are replaced with references to the relevant date - eg 'on 14 July 2010'.

Case studies

All this sounds pretty straightforward. But, surprisingly, few multimedia sites do it really well.

Let's look at how various news organisations approach them.

Note: to keep these examples fresh we'll continue this discussion online.

on the website

Find out how the BBC, CNN, *Guardian* and others create their in-depth, evergreened area of content.

15C8

Exercises and projects

Exercise 1

Find six features that have been inspired by news stories.

Exercise 2

Look at how features are written in a particular B2B magazine.

Exercise 3

Pick a news story from a B2B magazine and write a feature based on it. Use the points-in-order structure outlined above.

Exercise 4

Find features written in these formats: diamond, hourglass, using geography as structure, using scenes as structure. Explore whether the content could be rearranged to fit one of the other formats.

Exercise 5

Take a number of leader columns and identify how they draw on news stories or other items in that edition.

Exercise 6

Look at a range of archive or special content areas. Using the benchmarks we established above, determine how effective they are, how well organised, and useful to the reader. Consider their structure and content.

Projects

1   Write a feature inspired by a news story for your website.

2   Write a 700-word Life in the Day feature on someone of interest to the readers of your website.

3   Experiment with structure by writing features in each of these formats: diamond, hourglass, using geography as structure, using scenes as structure.

4   Write a leader column or editor's letter, following the guidance above, for your website.

5   Create an archive or special content area for your website. Select a topic using the criteria discussed above, and ensure that it is comprehensive, accessible, useful and well structured.

chapter sixteen

Advanced online research, search engine optimisation, analytics, sub-editing, and proof-reading

In the book version of this chapter we will cover:

- Getting the most out of Google
- Google's limitations
- Alternatives to Google
- Searching the deep or invisible web
- Sub-editing news
- Headlining news
- Subbing features
- Headlining features
- Proof-reading
- Sub-editing and Search Engine Optimisation
- What Google Analytics can tell you about your site's performance.

At the end of the chapter are a range of assignments and projects to enable you to practise what you have learned.

In the online version of this chapter you will find:

- The latest alternatives to Google search and developments in advanced search techniques
- Step-by-step tuition in using Google Analytics
- How to use the in-built analytic tools on social platforms including Twitter, Facebook and YouTube.

Have the companion website to this book open at www.multimedia-journalism.co.uk. That way you can easily click on the links to the stories discussed here.

 16C1

Advanced online research

As Google is the best general search engine, and the most popular, let's kick off where most journalists instinctively begin their searches.

Getting the most out of Google

First of all, there are a number of ways of improving our Google searches. Google is great, but a straight Google search can produce a wide array of types of results for your chosen search term. You'll get some news stories, government sites, fact sheets, and company websites.

When you are researching for a news story or feature you may well want detail and background that is buried way down the results Google returns and which would take a lot of trawling to find. So it pays to refine your Google search, and there are plenty of ways to do that.

Google provides a guide to the ways you can refine your search. It calls these refinements 'search operators', and has advice on using them here:

https://support.google.com/websearch/answer/136861

We'll go through some of their suggestions - with examples - and look at why, and when, they might be useful.

Narrowing your search

First step: Google offers various ways to narrow your search on the results page. You can restrict returns to just news, images, video, books and various other options. Clicking on the 'Search tools' option enables you to narrow things down by location and time. So if local search is important, or a search over the last few hours, days or weeks, you can specify that.

Search for a phrase ("")

Double quotes around a search term tells Google to look for that phrase, exactly as you have typed it. This is really useful when you have an unusual or defining phrase from a news story or report, for example.

Search within a specific website (site:)

If you want to find results from one particular website, you can refine your search term like this: Google allows you to specify that your search results must come from a given website. For example, the query **Iraq site:nytimes.com** will return pages about Iraq, but only from nytimes.com. The simpler queries **Iraq nytimes.com** or **Iraq New York Times** will usually be just as good, though they might return results from other sites that mention the *New York Times*.

Search within a specified class of site (site:ac)

If you want results only from, say, government or academic sites you can refine your search by following your search term with the site category: **crime site:gov** or: **crime site:ac**. If you want to search only on sites from a particular country you can use the country identifier from the URL, such as it for Italy and fr for France.

Search with an asterisk or wildcard (*)

You can use the asterisk *****, or wildcard, as part of a search term. When you do, Google treats the asterisk as a placeholder for any term. So, for example, if you are researching a politician's voting record, you can use this search term: **Cooper** [or any MP's name] **voted * on the * bill**, and get results that focus on Yvette Cooper's voting record.

Search with the OR option (OR)

Words such as 'or' would normally be ignored by Google – as would other very common words. But if you use the capitalised OR you can use it to refine your search. So, for example, **crime statistics 2014 OR 2015** will give you results for either of these years. The search term **crime statistics 2014 2015** would only bring results for pages that mentioned both of these years.

Search for erased content (cache)

Searching in Google's cache can be very useful when the material you want has been removed from a site. Perhaps something contentious, which would make a story libellous, has been removed from the latest version of the site. If you type this in the search dialogue: **cache:www.subjectsite.com** (replacing subject site with the URL of the site you are interested in) you'll see the version of the page that Google has in its cache. With luck the page before it was amended will be held here.

If you add to your search term the words you want to search for, by leaving a gap then adding them after the URL like so: **'www.subjectsite.com victim'** then those words will be highlighted within the cached document that is returned.

Search for definitions (define:)

You want to check the usage of a word or phrase? Put define: before your word or term and you'll get results that define it.

Search for stock prices (stocks:)

If you begin your search term with **stocks:** and then follow with the ticker symbols (the letters and numbers that are the official abbreviation of a traded stock) rather than the company name, your returns will focus on stocks.

Search for all words in a site's title (allintitle:)

Starting your query with this restricts your results to those with all of the query words in the title. For instance, **allintitle: garden ponds** will return only documents that have both garden and ponds in the title.

Search for all words in a URL (allinurl:)

Starting your query with this restricts the results to those with all of the query words in the URL.

The search qualifiers **filetype: inurl:** and **intitle:** are very useful for constructing search strings that reach deep within sites.

Search for trends

Searching for trends (**www.google.com/trends/**) gives you results presented on a timeline, and the graph that is delivered shows you how many times your search topic appeared in Google News stories. So you see peaks of interest. It also presents links to news stories, and indicates where on this graph they were written.

So, type in **HIV** and you get a graph of the peaks and troughs reflecting interest in the topic, and stories written at a number of points over that period.

Search by category

You may be searching for a word that has distinctly different meanings (is it Jaguar as in cat or Jaguar as in car, for example). After entering your search term, focus on the meaning you're looking for by clicking the **All Categories** button and then selecting a category from the drop-down.

Search scholarly papers

http://scholar.google.co.uk/

Search within books

http://books.google.com/

Set up a Google search on your own website

You can do that by following the steps outlined here:

www.google.com/cse/

Google's limitations

Google is justifiably the most popular search site, but the results it returns can be rather scatter-gun. It brings the most popular, sure, but the categories they come from can be very wide. If you are researching a news story or feature then you are likely to need background, and Google isn't the best for that. So let's look at some alternatives that will help you focus your search faster.

Alternatives to Google

Note: Because the available engines change over time, we'll keep specific recommendations for the online version of MMJ. Here we'll cover the general principles of what is do-able.

on the website

Find an up-to-the-minute guide to the available alternatives to Google.

Metasearch tools

Metasearch tools, or metasearch engines, search other search engines and aggregate their returns, categorising them to speed up the process of finding what you want. They are defined and explained here:

http://en.wikipedia.org/wiki/Metasearch_engine

However, as they are taking results from other search engines, they cannot be any better than those engines. Their only virtue is if they can sift the search results more effectively for you.

Find a wide range of up-to-the-minute recommendations of metasearch tools to Google that can help you find the information you need.

Vertical search

Broad search as practised by Google etc is horizontal in that it spans the whole web. Vertical search concentrates on an area of the web and drills deep. Drilling deep is often what journalists need to do. There are vertical search tools for subjects including:

- Business, economics and financial information
- Health
- Science

and many other areas.

Find up-to-the-minute recommendations of vertical search tools.

Searching the deep or invisible web

By no means all information on the web can be crawled by search engines, which means the result you are seeking might not be available through Google or another general search engine.

There is an invisible, or deep web: a vast repository of underlying content, such as documents in online databases. Deep web content is estimated to be 500 times as extensive as that of the surface web. To find these results you need to use an engine that can search these hidden databases. You'll find a guide to some here:

www.techgyd.com/search-engine-to-explore-hidden-web/7344/

Find a wide range of up-to-the-minute recommendations for tools that can help you search the deep or invisible web.

People search

One staple of the people search arena is 192 (**www.192.com**).

Research tools

There are a number of tools designed for librarians and academics that can help in journal-istic searches.

Searching the press

Identifying a newspaper or magazine that might have the information you need, and then searching through its online archives can be challenging. But there are engines that can help you do that.

Finding your own material

We've all mislaid files on our computer, or trawled for an email we are sure we received but can't find. Copernic searches your hard drive: files, emails and email attachments, Word, Excel and PowerPoint documents, PDFs and multimedia. Copernic Desktop Search: **http:// www.copernic.com**

16C2

Sub-editing

Traditionally, in print journalism, sub-editing was a distinct, separate skill, conducted not by editors or by news and features writers but by a dedicated team of subs. That's often no longer the case.

The web began this change. Most online writers sub and headline their own copy, and see this as an integral part of their job in telling the story. In broadcasting, by contrast, there was never the same idea of the sub. Broadcasters had producers who were the fixers and arbiters of what went, but often a reporter put their radio or TV package together, including writing a script, without passing it to a sub-editor for checking.

Subs have now disappeared in many areas. Which at the very least means that, even if you aren't employed as a sub-editor, any multimedia journalist needs to be able to sub their own material to a high standard. You may also be called upon to sub the work of others. Many publications now combine responsibilities, with staff doing some reporting and some subbing.

That said, subbing as a distinct skill will probably survive in certain areas of the media. Indeed, in recent years, national newspapers and others have taken on trainee journalists as subs, and there are subbing qualifications that prepare students specifically for copy editing. On tabloid newspapers, sub-editors often add huge value to the stories reporters write through the use of clever headlines. On glossy magazines, where production values are high, you need subs who can polish and refine the words and apply them to a complex layout.

So, with that confused, shifting picture in mind, let's look at how to be a good sub.

How to approach subbing

If you have written a news story and now have to sub it, it is important that you see yourself in a new role. You must try to forget you wrote the piece. You need to try to be objective about it. Will the reader understand? Have I left any questions unanswered?

If you are subbing other people's copy, achieving that detachment is much easier.

Let's look at what is done to a piece of copy at the sub-editing stage, and the roles of the sub-editor.

Quality control

This means ensuring that the story is accurate, well-written, adheres to house style and is legally watertight.

Here is a basic accuracy check list:

- Spelling
- Numbers and arithmetic
- Locations / geography
- Names and titles
- Dates / time references
- Law
- House style.

We are not covering law in any great detail in this book, but legal considerations are also vital when you sub.

The sub has two other roles:

Production role

This involves ensuring that the story and all other elements fit the space allocated to them on the web or paper page, and that deadlines are met.

Selling the story

This is achieved through the effective use of headlines, standfirsts, captions and other devices.

The sub's eye

Reading copy like a sub is not like reading it as a reader. The sub reads in a strange way, looking for inconsistencies, developing an instinctive feel for when copy is not right in some way.

Subs develop a sort of survival mechanism when they read. Once you have developed what I call The Sub's Eye, the essential checks you must make become automatic. You find yourself checking that a name in copy is consistently spelt throughout the piece, and in any captions.

If there are figures in a piece you instinctively check that, for instance, a list of percentages add up to 100, that if two dates are given and one is said to be 15 years later then the first, then that is the case. Figures that appear both in text and in a graphic are particularly troublesome. You must check carefully that they are consistent.

Sub-editing news

How to approach subbing a piece of news copy

Because the sub has a great deal to think about, they need to read copy more than once to make sure they have understood it and to make all the alterations that are required. Some subs will read a piece of copy five or six times before they have finished doing all they need to make it publishable. Each sub develops their own way of working, but they might follow a pattern something like this:

First read

The sub reads first for sense, without making many marks.

Put yourself in the place of the reader coming to the copy fresh, and ask yourself:

- What's the story about?
- What's new about it?

Beware of old news, or an old angle at the top of a story that has fresh information further down.

Second read

The purpose of the second read is to check the facts. If there is anything you are unsure about, you must look it up. Don't assume the reporter is correct. If you aren't sure of any aspect of the story – check it.

Third read

This is to check the structure of the story. Does it flow? Are the paragraphs in the right order?

Fourth read

This read is to tighten copy. Remove any unnecessary words or phrases, and cut the story - if subbing for print editions - into the space that has been given it on the layout.

Typographic amendments such as adjusting text to remove widows and orphans (short lines, often at the end of paragraphs, that fall at either the top or bottom of a column), and placing drop capitals, can be addressed at this stage.

Fifth read

This is a final check to make sure you haven't missed anything.

It is possible, once you are a confident sub, to combine reads one, two and three. But four and five can't really be merged with any of the others. So, to my mind, subbing takes at least three reads of the copy, and more if you can possibly find the time for them.

Exercises

In this chapter, the exercises appear right through the text, rather than at the end.

There is a lot for a sub to do. To help you make sure you have grasped each of the things a sub has to check with a piece of copy, we will divide them up, and give you a series of exercises that covers each point in turn.

on the website

On the website you will find model answers, with everything done to the raw copy that we feel it needs to make it publishable.

Checking for accuracy

First, let's look at correcting errors.

Exercise 1

Here are three short pieces of copy. Go through them, and check for errors. They are extracts from longer stories, so don't worry for now about unexplained references to organisation or whatever. Just check for factual errors in each case.

If you are not sure whether names or places mentioned in them are correct, you will need to look them up. Almost all the errors here can be corrected by searching authoritative sources on the internet, or with the use of a dictionary, a basic encyclopaedia or general reference book, but there may be one or two where you would need to check with the writer. If you find such a situation, make doing that your answer.

When you check on the web, make sure you do so with a reliable site. An individual or organisation's official site is always the best.

Check the following pieces of copy for errors in:

- spelling
- numbers and arithmetic
- locations / geography
- names and titles
- dates / time references.

1   A man who was washed out to see while trying to rescue his dog was saved by lifegards.

The man, who has not been named, was walking his dog on Bindi Beach, Sidney, Astralia, when the animal suddnly swam out to sea, chasign a seagull.

The man swam after his pet but, said rescuers, suffered an attack of cramp and went under the surface. Rescuers got alongside him and, grabign him round the waste, hauled him into their boat.

2   The Children's Aid charity said that 40 tonnes of aid had been flown to the airport on Tuesday, 33 tonnes was received on Monday, and 15 over the weekend - a total of 87 tonnes.

The agency said that health was improving. After the latest relief effort, only one in seven children was suffering from malnutrition, compared with one in 12 at this time last year.

3 George Warner Bush was re-elected president of the United States on November 2 2001. Both his supporters and opponents generally agree that his finest hour came when he showed powerful, decisive leadership after the attacks of September 9 2011.

Checking that the intro says what's new

Now let's look at making sure the story has the latest angle in the intro. As you will probably have recognised by now, if you write a story well you have done a lot of the sub's job for them. Subbing is doing to other people's copy what you ought to do to your own, as you write it.

Exercise 2

Take a look at the three short news stories below. Is the latest angle at the top? If it isn't, rewrite them so that it is.

1 Hundreds bought camping tickets yesterday for the annual countercultural Burning Man Festival, held in the deserts of northern Nevada.

But they were turned away from the site this morning because freak flash floods have caused the cancellation of the event, with the festival's Black Rock desert playa site turned into a quagmire overnight.

2 Cyclone Nargis hit Burma on May 3, killing tens of thousands of people in the main rice-producing areas.

Rice prices had already hit all-time highs after some weak harvests. Rice prices have now risen for a sixth consecutive day as global supplies continue to be stretched by cyclone damage to crops in Burma.

3   There have been many kidnappings of foreigners in Yemen in recent years. Two female Japanese tourists kidnapped by gunmen were just the latest.

They were seized as they visited Maarib, 176km (109 miles) east of the capital Sanaa.

Members of a tribe had seized the two to press for the release of a relative in government custody, a security official has said.

Other members of the tribe mediated the tourists' release, said the official. They had been held for less than a day.

Checking that the structure follows the inverted triangle

Exercise 3

Look at the three news stories below. Is the information in them in the right order? Put another way: does it fit the inverted triangle? If not, reorder it.

1   A former Kuwaiti detainee at the Guantanamo Bay detention centre was responsible for a suicide bombing in northern Iraq, according to Kuwaiti media reports.

According to the reports, Abdullah al-Ajmi and his two alleged accomplices, Nasir al-Dawsari and Badr al-Harbi, were able to leave Kuwait a month ago without alerting the attention of the authorities because they had wrongly been issued new passports.

They then travelled to Syria, where Ajmi is reported to have told his family of his intentions, before heading to Iraq.

The families of Ajmi and Harbi reportedly later received anonymous calls informing them that the men had died in Iraq.

The US transferred Ajmi to Kuwaiti custody from Guantanamo Bay in 2005.

He was later acquitted by a Kuwaiti court of terrorism charges.

Ajmi and two other Kuwaitis blew up two explosive-packed vehicles next to Iraqi security forces, media reports say.

A spokesman for the Kuwaiti government told the Associated Press that Abdullah al-Ajmi took part in an attack in Mosul on April 29 that killed several people.

2   James Naylor, from Islington, London, admitted that his Nissan Micra was not taxed, but said it didn't need to be because it was parked on his drive with only part of a rear wheel poking out on to the pavement.

Mr Naylor said he had planned to restore the car, but had not got round to it.

"I had decided to get rid of it, but then I came home from work the other day and it had been clamped," he said. "I don't know why they bothered – it doesn't go."

So he cut his car in half with a chain saw in protest.

The 30-year-old chef said the car was going to be scrapped anyway, but he wanted to make a point.

A spokesman for NCP Services, which has the contract to clamp untaxed vehicles from Mr Naylor's local council said half of the car was parked on the road and therefore should have been taxed.

3   Two-thirds of all HIV infections occur in Africa.

Yet researchers say that there is very little evidence to demonstrate the effectiveness of many of the prevention strategies used in the continent.

The multi-million dollar spending on promoting the use of condoms, HIV testing and vaccine research has had limited success in Africa, argue the researchers from Harvard University School of Public Health in the journal *Science*.

They say male circumcision and cutting the number of sexual partners should become the "cornerstone" of prevention.

They conclude that millions of dollars that is being spent to prevent the spread of HIV is being wasted on strategies that do very little good, according to American researchers who call for a "dramatic shift" in priorities.

Tightening copy

Now let's concentrate on tightening copy. Remove any unnecessary words or phrases in the exercises below. The number of words you should be able to save is marked at the end of each exercise. You should be able to cut the copy by this number of words just by tightening – there is no need to remove any information.

Exercise 4

1   Eminent researchers in the United States of America announce that they have found a significant new way to put to death a wide range of unwanted plants and of animals that have been known to hitch a ride in the ballast waters of cargo tankers.

It is postulated by the United Nations that a range of "invasive species" are often carried in the ballast water that is picked up by a ship in one part of the world and that is then finally pumped out in another part of the world and that this represents one of the four main threats that are faced by the world's marine ecosystems.

Tests, say the researchers, have shown that a continuous blast of microwaves in the tanks can and will remove all forms of marine life.

More than 80 per cent of the world's commodities are moved by ship and, as a by-product of this process, up to five billion tonnes of ballast water is transported internationally each year, this according to the UN.

The explanation of the process is this. When a ship's cargo is finally unloaded, the ship takes on ballast water in order to provide improved stability. When the same ship is ready to take on another load, often by this time on the other side of the world, this taken on ballast water is then discharged.

The findings from this study will appear in the journal Environmental Science and Technology.

Cut the above from 239 words to between 150-155.

2   It is estimated by authoritative sources that at least 8,500 persons have been fatally wounded by an extremely powerful earthquake that has shaken China's south-western province of Sichuan.

It is also suspected that many more people have been killed and injured elsewhere in the country during and in the aftermath of the quake, which experts estimate measured 7.8 on the Richter Scale, and which struck at 2.30pm in the afternoon.

It is also estimated that at least 60 bodies of earthquake victims have been recovered from the wreckage, debris and rubble of a children's school where it is believed that in the order of 900 students were buried alive.

China's President, Xi Jinping, has made a solemn pledge that there will be an all-out effort to rescue the victims of this earthquake.

The epicentre of the earthquake was said to be around about 92km distance from Chengdu, which is Sichuan's provincial capital.

Because of the fact that the earthquake has struck in the middle of the day, it is feared that many schoolchildren, who were at school at the time, may well be among the very many victims.

Cut from 187 words to between 110-115.

3   The introduction of face recognition technology that is said to be capable of preventing underage smokers from buying cigarettes from vending machines is set to deter the illegal purchase of tobacco products in Japan, and is being developed by a Japanese company.

The Fujitaka company is in the process of installing cameras in cigarette vending machines that are capable of counting the wrinkles and the skin sags of a would-be purchaser in order to check that smoker's age.

New Japanese government legislation to be introduced in July will mean that, from this date, the owners of vending machines could be faced with prosecution if they sell tobacco to anyone who is under the legal tobacco-product purchase limit of 20 years of age.

Should they fail this test, would-be smokers who fail the digital camera age test will have to show the machine an ID card in order to establish the fact that they are legally allowed to smoke.

The system works by comparing the facial characteristics of the prospective tobacco purchaser, including bone structure, sags and crow's feet around the eyes, against a database record that it holds of more than 100,000 people. It does so in order to estimate the age of a purchaser.

A spokesman for the Fujitaka company, Hajime Yamamoto, told the Reuters news agency that: "With face recognition, so long as you've got some change and you are an adult, you can buy cigarettes as before."

Cut from 239 words to 140–145 words.

Bringing it all together

The following exercises contain all or some of the faults we have been working on one by one above. Do whatever you need to and cut them to the length indicated.

Exercise 5

1   A hotel that is popular with celebrities, as stars such as Kate Mosse, Anne Hathaway and Brian Ferry are all said to have stayed there, while Gwynith Paltrowe cut the ribbon at its opening, was the scene of a dramatic event earlier today, police have stated.

Det Supt Jess Ruddell who is leading the investigation into the attack said hotel staff had been left "very shaken" by the raid and urged witnesses to contact police.

Two masked gunmen have stormed the hotel in central London and tied up a staff member before making off with cash and mobile phones, police said.

Dean Street Townhouse is a 39 bedroom four storey hotel and all-day dining room, located in the thick of buzzing Soho, in central London. The dining room is open for breakfast, lunch, afternoon tea, and dinner.

The four storey Georgian townhouse, once home to the Gargoyle Club, is rich in both its historic past and its Georgian architecture.

The men, said to be speaking in eastern European accents and wearing hoodies that were white in colour, burst in to the Dean Street Town House in Dean Street, Soho at about 03:00 BST.

According to its website, the hotel's bedrooms are individually designed and available in tiny, small, medium and bigger sizes. Each bedroom has either a king-size or super king-size bed, and is equipped with a Sony flat screen TV with Sky plus and DVD, free wireless internet, and a mini-bar packed with indulgent treats. Bathrooms are fitted with rainforest showers and stocked with goodies from the Cowshed spa.

The men who came in brandishing the gun threatened staff with a long-barrelled gun and tied one man up before making off. No shots were fired and no-one was injured at the four-story hotel.

One person was treated for shock.

"This is a very serious incident and we are working around the clock to identify those responsible," Det Supt Jess Ruddell said.

The 39 bedroom hotel is part of the Soho House Group chain, which owns a string of boutique hotels and private members clubs all over the world, including in New York, Hollywood and Berlin.

Cut to 190-200 words, it is currently 355.

2   It has no air conditioning, no electric windows and no power steering, but it only costs £1,500, but two deluxe models will be on offer.

One of the world's biggest motor companies, Renault-Nissan, has announced that it is entered a joint venture with the Indian motorbike manufacturer Bajaj to produce the vehicle, which will be aimed largely at the Indian market.

The car, so far known only as Codename ULC will cost roughly the same as another Indian cut-price vehicle – Tata Motors' Nano – which it claims is the world's cheapest car.

The Nano is a great advance for many people in India because it is now making it a realistic prospect for many people to afford to buy a car.who had previously not been able.

The Naon is a for-door five-seater car, and it went on sale from 2008, having a 33bhp, 624cc, engine that is mounted at the rear.

The naon has no air conditoning, no electrical windows and it also has know power steering, but two deluxe models also are on offer.

India's domestic sales of cars are predicted to be booming in coming years as a side effect benefit of the country's fast-growing economy and increased consumer spendign power.

sales of cars in India are predicted to more than four-fold increase to $145bn by the 2016. No details of the new car have been released, though production is expected to begin later this year.

Bajaj, the second-biggest maker of motorbikes in India, will manufacture 400,000 a year in a factory in Chakan, Maharashtra state, in the west of the country.

Cut to 110–120 words, it is currently 265 words.

3   Over six million of the children who are dying each and every year could have their lives saved if they were in receipt of basic health services, according to a new report by the children's charity Save the Children.

Save the Children carries out an annual survey of health care provision for the under fives in developing countries.

A spokesperson for Saving the Children said: "A child's chance of reaching its fifth birthday should not depend on the country or community where it is born.

"We need to do a better job of reaching the poorest children with basic health measures like vaccines, antibiotics and skilled care at childbirth."

In its latest report, just out and released to the press and broadcasters at a press conference today, it found the Philippines was performing best of all with almost 69 per cent of children in tht country being able to get health care.

In India and Ghana, on the other hand and in contrast, less than half of young chdilren under five years of age get the care they need.

Ethiopia ranks last – only 16 per cent of children under five get health care when they need it.

The report, called State of the World's Mothers, says that over 60 per cent of the 10 million children who die each year would live with basic health services provided by a health facility or community health worker.

Cut to 180-190 words, it is currently 236 words.

Headlining news

Now we come to the third of the sub's roles: selling. The headline a sub writes on a story is there to sell that story.

Bad headlines leave stories unsold and unread. Good headlines get the reader to begin reading the story. After that, the headline has done its job, and it is up to how good the story is, and how well it is written, whether the reader sticks with it.

So what makes a good headline? The key question to ask of a headline is: Would it make me read the story?

If it would, then it has served its purpose. But let's look at what makes a good headline in a bit more detail.

News headlines in print publications have a treble function:

- They attract the reader's attention
- They give the gist of the story
- They help order information on the page.

We are going to concentrate on the first two functions in this section. The third is more about the use of different type sizes to indicate the relative importance of stories on a page.

How to approach news headline writing

1   There will be some information that you must have in a headline.

Identify two or three key words that are essential to explaining the story to the reader.

This is your first building block for the headline.

If you only have a very tight space available, this element should stand alone as the minimum necessary to introduce the story.

Let's take an example.

Let's say you have a story about the Brighton Bomber - the IRA man who planted a bomb in the Grand Hotel Brighton in an attempt to kill Margaret Thatcher and her cabinet.

Imagine it's the 35th anniversary of that attack and the perpetrator is to return to Brighton for a meeting with some of the survivors and the relatives of victims. The organisers are calling it a reconciliation meeting, a healing of the wounds, but there is substantial opposition in the town to the visit. Those who oppose the meeting say that the bomber has never expressed remorse for the attack. You have very strong quotes from a survivor of the attack, condemning the bomber.

questions

If I said you only have three words to headline that story, what would they be? Don't read on until you have thought.

My suggestion is: **Brighton bomber returns**

In suggesting this I am assuming that my readers know the story of the Brighton bombing, and that by saying 'returns' it is obvious that he is returning to Brighton, not somewhere else.

So, **Brighton bomber returns** gives us our basic headline. It contains key words that tell the story as succinctly as possible. But very often we have headline space for more than three words. If we do, we can build on that nub headline.

2 Look at ways in which to add to the basic headline idea you have in ways that complete the thought.

Good headlines flow, they are a complete thought.

questions

How would you make the Brighton bomber headline a complete thought, using three or four extra words? Don't read on until you have decided what to do.

If we add to the end of the current headline an explanation of why the bomber is returning, that would fit the bill. We could say:

> **Brighton bomber returns**
> **for reconciliation meeting**

or

> **to face victims**

or

> **to 'heal the wounds'**

So now we have a headline that tells the story, but there is more we can do if we have the space.

3 Make the headline active. Try to introduce a dynamic element to it. This element might be emotion such as anger or rage. It might be about fears or dangers.

questions

Can you add two words to the start of your bomber headline to add this third element?

There is certainly anger at the bomber's visit, so we might write:

> **Fury as Brighton bomber returns to 'heal the wounds'**

4 There is a fourth thing we can sometimes do to a headline to make it more interesting. Look for opportunities to use your imagination, to pick on detail, a word or a turn of phrase that makes the story more interesting.

You can't always do this, just as you can't always do 3. If you are writing headlines for a B2B publication you are unlikely to get beyond points 1 and 2 very often.

But if there is an opportunity, you should use it. We don't really need to with our bomber headline, but let me tell you another story. This one is about Network Rail. The story is that several senior managers are to get substantial performance bonuses, totalling £1m, despite the fact that late-running of trains has not been reduced. So we can gather our key words, which will include bonuses, late trains and could include a phrase such as rail bosses. If we took these elements we could write:

> **£1m bonuses for rail bosses but trains still run late**

But let's say that, somewhere in the news story the bosses are described as fat controllers. That's the sort of phrase that can lift a headline:

> **£1m bonuses for 'fat controllers', but trains still run late**

Notice the use of single quote marks around certain words in headlines. We use them - never double quotes - to indicate that it is not us saying this.

So, in this instance, we have covered points 1, 2 and 4 in our headline. We haven't included 3, because the story didn't have any reaction from unions or passengers. If it did then we'd have an opportunity to tack something of this reaction on to the headline, perhaps at the start once again.

Here are some other things we should bear in mind when we headline a story

Headlines should say what has happened

Headlines should say what is happening or has happened. Headlines which say what has not happened are generally dull and a turn off.

> **No news on missing sailors**

is a turn off.

> **Fears grow for missing sailors**

is better.

Put the most important element first

> **US tells Israel**
> **'Stop the bombing'**

is not as good as

> **'Stop the bombing'**
> **US tells Israel**

> **Swedish knee surgery brings warning to hundreds**

is not as good as

> **Warning to hundreds over Swedish knee surgery**

Use short, concrete words

Headline words are short, direct and concrete because they have to get the reader's attention - and fit the available space.

Subs learn all sorts of short alternatives to longer, more abstract words:

- 'Bid' for 'attempt'
- 'Cut' for 'reduce'.

Harold Evans, in his brilliant book *Essential English for Journalists* (Pimlico) gives a list of hundreds of them.

- Instead of bankruptcy, for example, he suggests: collapse, crash, failure, fall
- Instead of assistance he suggests: aid, back-up, help, relief, rescue

Keep punctuation to a minimum

We use less punctuation in headlines than we do in text. If a headline needs punctuating, it's probably not a good headline. The odd comma or colon is ok, but keep them to a minimum.

British headline style – traditionally – is either all caps or upper and lower case with caps only for initial words and names. In America you tend to use initial capitals in all major words in a headline. UK publications are beginning to adopt the US model.

Quote marks in headlines are always single, and used to distance the publication from the words spoken or the opinion given.

Headline clichés

The media company you get a job with will have its own views on this, but as a general rule don't use words we don't use in normal speech, so avoid

- 'Caged' for 'jailed'
- 'Boost' for 'improve'
- 'Rapped' for 'criticised'.

Phrases from popular culture and common current usage are fine but they should not be over-used. The catch-phrases of comedians and others often find their way into headlines.

When I was a features sub on the *Daily Mail* they had us aim for a clever play on words in our headline writing. That meant that clichés were out because they were dull and predictable. A pun was ok as long as it was a clever one.

Here's an example of this technique in action.

A company has invented a new kind of office chair. It is highly sophisticated, and shaped rather like a cocoon, enclosing the sitter's torso, arms and head. It provides excellent lumbar support and, if the worker feels like a quick nap, it can be tilted back to the horizontal.

The headline on this story was: **The shut-eye pod**.

Don't use the same word in more than one headline

An important convention in headline writing is not to repeat key words in headline, standfirst, strapline and elsewhere on the same page or, for some publications, on a two-page spread. This can be a challenge on a specialist title. If you are writing for nurses, then the word nurse will suggest itself for pretty much every headline. If you write for publicans, then pub and landlord will have to be severely rationed in your headings.

A good shape for a headline

Headlines should be a pleasing shape. Some titles insist that all lines in a headline should be full out – meaning that there is no white space caused by short lines. Generally, you are allowed some short lines. But if a line is too short the resulting white space can attract the eye when it shouldn't. So, one-line headlines – lines are often called 'decks' in headlining – should be as full out as possible. With a headline of more than one line, the top line should be reasonably full out, and the second line shorter. The top line should never be shorter than any of the lines that follow it.

With a three-deck headline, the top line should be the longest, the middle line can be short but the final line should be almost as long as the top line.

Headlines are either centred, or set left, depending on your house style.

Here's how some different shapes look:

**This is a
very ugly shape**

**This is a much
better shape**

**With three lines
you need a
shape like this**

**This shape
for a headline
just looks rather odd**

Exercise 6

Write headlines for the three stories you subbed in exercise 5.

In each case, you have three decks of headline, and can use up to ten characters in each line. When gauging the length of a headline using characters, we count most letters as being one character wide. Narrow letters – i,j,l,t – count as half a character. Long letters – m,w – count as 1.5 characters. Most capitals are 1.5 characters, but M and W are two. A space between words counts as half a character.

You'll find some headlines from me on the website.

16C5

Subbing features

In many important ways, subbing a feature is the same as subbing a news story. All the basic checks on accuracy still apply. It is still important to tighten copy, and to structure it correctly. But there are differences.

The differences have to do with the variances in writing a feature as opposed to a news story. There are some essentials we must bear in mind.

First, features often don't have an intro that goes to the key point. Instead, they often have a scene-setting section at the start, with the key point coming a few paragraphs later.

Second, the ending of a feature is more important than the ending of a news story. We do not use the inverted triangle, often, with a feature, so the ending cannot be automatically removed without damaging the structure of the piece.

Because there is more leeway in how a feature is subbed, there is more room for error. Writing a new, newsy intro, cutting the ending and removing all sense of the writer's voice – just as you might in subbing a news story – will probably ruin a feature.

That's not to say you can't tighten copy, remove elements that slow it down and reorder things if they make the feature work better.

Because there is so much more leeway with features subbing, a sub needs a clear brief from the features editor, or to have developed a full understanding of how features are written on a particular publication.

16C6

Headlining features

Just as there are differences in the way we sub a feature as opposed to a news story, there are also different techniques we use when headlining a feature for a print publication.

With news we have to give the gist of the story. That involves getting at the essentials of the news the story covers, picking key words to get that across, and writing a headline that is as interesting as it can be.

With features in newspapers and magazines, we still want to interest the reader in the article, but we don't have to be as straightforward in the methods we use to get them interested.

While a news headline is clear, direct and specific, a features headline can be more oblique. It doesn't have to give the gist of the story. It just has to grab the reader's attention. It can be designed to intrigue; to puzzle the reader even.

Often, features headlines are twinned with a strapline - a second headline in smaller type, that tells the reader more. With this combination of selling devices, the headline can be used purely as a hook, while the strapline explains the headline and tells the reader more. The headline arouses the reader's curiosity, the strapline expands on the headline, and gives the reader more reasons to go ahead and look at the article.

Another common selling device on a feature is what is known as a standfirst.

A standfirst is longer than a strapline - often it can contain 20 words or so - and in a type size that is closer to that of the article itself. Standfirsts are often in 14pt or 12pt, while articles are set in 9pt or 10pt.

In a standfirst there is room to explain the headline, give the reader some highlights from the article, and include the by-line of the writer.

We don't always use this oblique approach with features. Sometimes they have very direct headlines. If you have an interview with a famous person talking for the first time about, for example, their drug addiction or their divorce or some other powerful subject, the headline could be very simple and direct: **My drug hell**, or, **Why my marriage failed**.

When you have a strong, newsy feature then a straightforward headline is often best.

Subbing and Search Engine Optimisation

Here's what search engine optimisation (SEO) is all about, and when it is relevant.

When readers find us through search engines, we have to work hard to make our content findable to them. Our content - for any given story - must be more easily findable than that of our rivals.

But if readers are looking at our print edition, reading us on a smartphone app they have downloaded, or in a tablet edition, then they have already found our content, and SEO does not apply. However, as it is highly likely that content is subbed only once, it often needs to be appropriate for every format in which it can be consumed.

Nevertheless, when we talk about SEO, we are dealing specifically with maximising the chances of your story being found by potential readers who are looking on Google or another search engine for stories on a particular topic.

To understand it, think of how you find things on Google. You type in search terms. The results you get are for files – news stories in the context of this discussion – that fit your search terms as closely as possible.

So, to get good at SEO, we have to know how the engines work.

We also have to think what a reader who is seeking a story we have published online would type into a search engine in order to find it. We also need to think about readers who might be interested in the subject, but haven't heard of the story we have, or of the events that we are writing about.

Search engines 'spider' your site to index its contents. They look for key words, words that give a clear indication of what the content of each item you publish is. The spider expects to find these keywords in several key, prominent places. The ones we as online subs and writers need to think about are:

- Headings – and particularly at the start of headings
- In your sell – the first paragraph of your body text
- In hypertext links
- In side headings.

Search engines expect to find the important words that define the scope of your story in these places.

Some people try to boost their rankings by stuffing keywords into these places. Not only is that repetitive and boring for the reader, it can also be counter-productive. Search engines expect to find a keyword density of about 1.5 – 2 per cent of total words. Any more and they begin to think you are trying to cheat.

Clearly, then, heads and other important areas of stories need to contain keywords that define the scope of a story. If they don't, then the search engines won't know what the story is about and won't be able to deliver it to the searchers you want to reach.

Because SEO is so important, content management systems (CMS) including WordPress have built in checks (or plug-ins) that help us check whether the piece of copy we are posting on our website is optimised for SEO. We'll look at how to improve SEO on our WordPress sites in a moment.

First, here's an example of a failure of SEO. The *Guardian* had an exclusive piece of video, posted on its website, that showed the violent arrest of a young woman outside a Sheffield nightclub in the early hours. The arrest, in which four police officers sought to restrain her and in which punches and kicks were thrown, was caught on CCTV.

The *Guardian* newspaper story, reproduced on the website, had this headline:

> ## Four men, five punches and a boot:
> ## A 19-year-old woman is arrested

There were two bulleted sub-headings:

- *Guardian* obtains footage of Sheffield police incident
- PC who dealt blows says he acted in self-defence.

The story didn't do well in Google and other rankings because it didn't contain the appropriate keywords.

It didn't have 'CCTV' for one thing.

A better headline, in SEO terms, would have been something like this:

> ## Police accused of brutality after officer beat woman during arrest at nightclub

Here's another example, this time from the *Wall Street Journal*. It had a story on the free access area of its otherwise subscription website about a coffee shop chain called Green Beans, which has outlets on US military bases overseas, opening its first café in the US for the general public.

The headline was:

> ## Green Beans Comes Marching Home

The problem with that headline, in web terms, is that it takes a human to interpret it. Search engine spiders simply aren't smart enough to know what the story is about from that headline.

As a consequence, the WSJ fell behind the Google rankings, beaten by, among others, a blogger who reproduced the story word for word but put better tags on it.

Also, if we are thinking about finding readers who are interested in coffee shops and coffee but don't know about this story, we are not going to reach them. In fact there is a more interesting way of telling the story. It is that Green Beans is planning to take on Starbucks. Few searchers will be looking specifically for Green Beans, but a lot will be searching for Starbucks for a variety of reasons, and for coffee and cafes.

So, a better headline would reads something like:

US military coffee chain takes on Starbucks with cafes stateside

In fact there is nothing particularly new about what we do when writing headlines with SEO in mind. But, just as with the way we write for the web, we are required to sharpen the skills we use for print.

And we have to recognise that clever, punning or oblique headlines that might be great in print don't work on the web.

The headline writing style I've described above is actually entirely appropriate for web headlines and for those in print or for tablet editions where the reader will not find the content through a search engine, but the features approach will not work when web search is involved in them finding a story. On the web, features headlines need to be like news ones, and contain appropriate key words.

The fact that most media websites get a large proportion of their traffic through search engines changes something really fundamental that print journalists have always held dear. With print, getting on the front page was a coup. It guaranteed you lots of readers. But if, say, 60 per cent or more of your users find you through search engines, your front - or home page in net terms - becomes an irrelevance to that portion of your readers.

Take a look at the highest ranking stories on any newspaper website and you'll usually find it very different to the ranking that was given to stories in the print edition. The front page lead is rarely the most-read story online. That means being on the front page, or on the home page, is much less important than we might think. What is important is that the right keywords are used in the right places to maximise the audience for a particular story.

The search terms readers use to find you are valuable in another way. They give you an insight into their interests and concerns. You learn about the angles they are interested in on particular news topics.

Improving SEO on a WordPress site

We looked at adding SEO plug-ins for WordPress in Chapter 8, module 8B5, and discussed how they can help you ensure you have correctly headlined and intro-ed your content and are using the best keywords. You might want to check back there before reading on.

There are some changes we can make to the settings of our WordPress sites that will enhance SEO, quite apart from what SEO plug-ins can do for us.

Note: As recommendations change over time, we'll deal with them on the website.

on the website

- Find step-by-step tuition in improving SEO on your WordPress site
- Find links to further aids to understanding and improving SEO including:
- Using Google Adwords to suggest keywords
- Google Insight to compare how often alternative keywords are appearing in relevant searches and
- An online SEO tutorial.

16C8

Proof-reading

Proof-reading is the final check that a sub-editor does before a page in a magazine or newspaper is printed. Web pages should also be proofed, but they often aren't because of time pressures.

Sound simple? Well it's actually very hard to proof-read effectively, and catch all the mistakes that might have crept into a piece of copy.

By the time we have finished subbing a story, we have become very familiar with it, and familiarity makes it harder to spot errors.

What happens is that we tend to see – and read – what we meant to write, rather than what is actually on the page.

That gets even harder if we are proofing copy we wrote ourselves.

So you must break the familiarity the copy now has for you. You need to use a range of techniques to ensure that you do not read what you thought was there or what you meant to put there, but what is actually there.

Not only that, but our eyes can deceive us when we are reading. To show what we mean, read the following sentence once and count up the number of fs in it:

Finished files are the result of years of scientific study combined with the experience of years.

How many do you make it? Three? Four? Five? Six?

Actually it is six, but most people see three the first time they read, then four or five, and eventually six. The problem is the fs in 'of'. Perhaps because we pronounce this word 'ov' it seems hard for us to spot that there are fs involved.

So we have to be very careful as we proof-read, and concentrate hard to try to stop our eyes deceiving us.

We should also be very clearly aware of the difference between proof-reading and subbing. Most, if not all, of the errors in a piece of copy should have been spotted at the sub-editing stage. When we proof, we must resist the temptation to improve copy in anything other than essential ways. We aren't subbing, we are only spotting errors that must be corrected, and doing so in a way that causes the minimum of work on the copy.

Proofing marks

Traditionally, proof-readers used a set of symbols to highlight errors in copy and indicate how they should be corrected. Computerisation has rendered them redundant in many situations, but not all. If you need to know proofing marks, you'll find links on the website.

It is very hard to proof-read effectively on a computer screen.

You need to have the document in a form in which you can see all of it at once. Seeing the material in a new form – printing it out – often brings errors to light that you had become blind to on screen.

You must try to distance yourself from a story you have written, edited or sub-edited yourself. Whenever possible, put the copy to one side after you have subbed it so that it is less familiar when you come to proof-read it.

One key thing about proofing – you can't rush it and expect to get it right. Accuracy is paramount, speed comes second.

Here are some tips:

Place a straight edge beneath the line you are reading

That makes sure you don't lose your place – and possibly miss an error.

Read out loud

By saying the words as well as reading them, we increase our chances of spotting errors.

Read backwards

This forces you to look at each word and helps you pick out spelling errors, repetitions and other errors at word level. When we read forward we can't help getting caught up in the sense of the sentence, and that can make us miss small errors – our brain ignores them for us! Reading backwards forces us to look at each word individually.

Share the task

If you can, get a colleague to follow the text while you read it out loud.

Rest your eyes

Take a break for 30 seconds every 10 to 15 minutes. Take breaks of 10 minutes each hour when you proof-read for long periods.

Here are common types of error that we must learn to spot

Spelling errors

You need a dictionary – either in paper or online form – with you at all times as you write, sub-edit and proof-read. A lot of people rely on Spell-Check, but it can let you down. You might have used a word that exists, but it is not the right spelling of that word for the context it appears in. Spell-Check can't spot that. For example:

> Analysts pour over statistics.
>
> It should be **pore** over statistics.

> The very young often enjoy read-allowed books
>
> It should be **read-aloud** books.

Transpositions in words or sentences

This means when the order of the letters or words has got switched around:

- gettnig instead of getting
- acocommodation instead of accommodation.

Repetitions of words

These are particularly hard to spot when the repeated word appears once at the end of a line and then at the start of the next line:

> He could see that the water
>
> water was coming in under
>
> the door.

Punctuation missing, or incorrectly used

For example:

> So what the terrestrial television companies offer in terms of advertising slot the 30 second television spot is becoming outmoded and replaced.

We need a pair of commas:

> So what the terrestrial television companies offer in terms of advertising slot, the 30 second television spot, is becoming outmoded and replaced.

Facts that contradict each other within an article

For example, a person's age may be given as 28 in the news story, but as 26 in the caption to their picture.

We need to check each mention of a fact such as a name or a place, a date or a figure, to make sure that they do not conflict. If they do, we have to find out which version is correct.

16C9

Using Google Analytics

Google Analytics tell you how many people come to your website, where they come from, what they do when they are with you and when they leave.

Analytics give you a detailed insight into what works on your site, what does not, and helps you improve your content.

We'll look at Google Analytics in the context of your WordPress website, but everything we say about the usefulness of the tool applies to any site you are running.

Note: Because Google regularly updates Analytics, we'll keep step-by-step tuition on using it for the online version of this module.

on the website

You'll find a comprehensive guide to installing and using Google Analytics.

16C10

Analytics tools on Twitter, Facebook, YouTube and other social media platforms

The in-built tools on social media platforms can also tell you a great deal about how you and your content are performing on them. Again, because the available tools and what they can do is updated so regularly, we'll keep discussion of them for the MMJ website.

16C11

Exercises and projects

Exercise 1

Try to develop your sub's eye as you read news in print and online. Look out for errors, inconsistencies, typos and other problems.

Exercise 2

Compare how a particular story is headlined over a range of media. Decide who has the best, and look out for smart headlining ideas that didn't occur to others.

Projects

1   If you are working in a team, set up a subbing system in which each person subs the copy of another member. Use the techniques outlined in this chapter to check and improve copy, and discuss your queries and the changes you made with the person who wrote it.

2   Practise writing headlines for your own and other people's copy. Have several people come up with a headline for a given piece of text and compare what they produce. Decide whose is best, and why.

3   Using the guidance above and the tools linked to on the website, assess how effective SEO is on your website and/or blog.

4   Apply the proofing techniques outlined here to material on your website before you publish it.

5   Install Google Analytics on your WordPress website, monitor how well it is doing, and use all the techniques outlined above to build your audience, deepen their engagement, and make your site more successful.

chapter seventeen

Multi-platform publishing and developing your skills as an editor

How to create smartphone apps, tablet computer editions and print versions of your content

In the book version of this chapter we will cover:

- Why multi-platform publishing is essential
- The creation of smartphone app editions
- The difference between web and native apps
- The principles of designing apps for smartphones
- Examples of successful apps
- Getting the right content on your app
- Simple software that lets you build smartphone apps.

Creating tablet computer magazines and print editions:

- The principles of designing and editing a magazine for tablet and print
- Getting the right content ideas
- How to commission text, stills, video, audio and more
- Templating

- Flat planning
- Why we need to build tablet versions of our websites
- The principles of designing tablet computer versions of your website
- Simple software that lets you build a print and tablet publication.

At the end of the chapter are a range of assignments and projects to enable you to practise what you have learned.

In the online version of this chapter you will find:

- Step-by-step tuition in the use of a range of publishing applications, including those featured in the book version
- Tuition in a range of alternative publishing platforms
- Additional resources and supporting material.

Have the companion website to this book open at www.multimedia-journalism.co.uk. That way you can easily click on the links to the stories discussed here.

17C1

Introduction to multi-platform publishing

In this chapter we are looking at professional publishing platforms for our content. Publishing often involves distributing our material concurrently in print, web, mobile phone and tablet computer versions.

If you work for a media organisation, or are on a journalism course where you have access to Adobe InDesign, or a comparable design and publishing system, then the work of creating mobile, tablet, web and print versions of your content is likely to be highly automated.

But it is also perfectly possible to work with simple-to-use, free or inexpensive software that will let you build and publish to mobiles, tablets and print.

Many WordPress themes will let you do the first two of these automatically, because they are responsive: they deliver a different version of your website, depending on what device visitors use to access you. But that doesn't adapt the content, just the way it is presented.

So, in this chapter, we'll look at how to create your own smartphone apps and tablet editions – plus create and publish your own print edition, all to professional standards.

We'll do this in the context of a professional newsroom, and we'll be drawing on the work you will have done as you've gone through your course, and this book, to develop a subject area for a news website, newspaper or magazine.

Note: The terms of use on the apps discussed here may change over time, and free options could be discontinued. Because of that, detailed, step-by-step tuition will appear on the website.

While we will be using a number of software platforms to build our apps, tablet editions and print magazines, all that we discuss is relevant to any other platform you might be using.

on the website

You'll also find tuition in the use of a number of alternative platforms to those described in the book/ebook version. Plus, as better platforms become available, we'll review them, and give step-by-step tuition in their use.

Now, let's look at why multi-platform publishing is necessary.

17C2

Why we need to build tablet versions of our sites, and create smartphone apps

Consumption of news, information and entertainment on portable devices rather than desktop computers is growing rapidly. Pew Internet Project Research[1] revealed that 43 per cent of Americans aged 16 or over have either a tablet computer or ebook reader. The same survey found that 57 per cent of men and 54 per cent of women have a smartphone.

As mobile internet access rises, desktop access falls.

In the UK, mobile internet traffic overtook desktop access in 2014.[2]

As we saw in the last chapter, for the site I demonstrated using Google Analytics, over 40 per cent of visitors were using tablet computers, and over 30 per cent were using smartphones.

If your website is built with responsive design, as many WordPress themes are, then when a visitor arrives at the site on either a tablet or smartphone, the version they are served will be rendered automatically to suit that device.

That's great, but is it enough?

questions

Think about the pluses and minuses of receiving traffic via the open web for a moment. What are they? Don't read on until you have decided.

The pluses of making our content available over the web are major. As we've covered at many points throughout this book, we can gain large audiences for our journalism by making it findable on the web, and by using social media platforms to distribute content and reach new audiences.

The minuses are that we risk devaluing our journalism. By making it freely available we let people dip in and out of it. And they do - rapidly. As we saw in the last chapter, the majority of visitors to our websites come for a minute or two and read just one or two stories.

That's OK, but if we think back to that pyramid of engagement we discussed in Chapter 3, it's only the start. We want to build our relationship with our audience. We want to reach those who will really value our content and convert them into regular visitors and - if we are in a commercial organisation - paying customers.

We hope there will come a point where a visitor who has come to know and like our content will want to commit to it. Tablet computer versions and smartphone apps offer us platforms on which we can serve the needs of a visitor who wants to read us regularly, and in depth. And that visitor is often prepared to pay for our journalism.

To some extent, these platforms are the modern-day equivalent of the newspaper that was shoved through your letterbox or dropped on your porch; the glossy mag picked up at the supermarket; or the TV news programme you sat down to watch at 6, 9 or 10 each evening. Those who use these mobile platforms stay with our content for much longer than a couple of minutes. Figures[3] show they read more news, for longer and from more sources. So these mobile publishing platforms can help us reproduce the relationship we had with those readers and viewers. They spend time with us, and they can be shown adverts and commercials along with our editorial content.

However, they have to make an effort to commit to us. They need to visit an App Store and download our smartphone or tablet edition. We can make it free, or free at first, to encourage them to do so. Many media companies set a version of metering, where you get the app and a certain amount of content for free, but have to pay for it after you've used up your allowance.

So what we give them on our tablet and smartphone versions has to be pretty good. It needs to work on those platforms, so it has to be designed to suit them.

Until recently, it's been pretty difficult for the non-coder to create a magazine for the iPad and other tablets, or a mobile phone app. What simple platforms there were for building phone and tablet apps often charged a hefty fee to host the content.

But there are now platforms on which a multimedia journalist, with the skills learned so far in this book, can do so. Their free offerings are limited, but those we will work with here all allow you to create a professional-standard app, and some let you publish for free, or free for a limited period. So they are great for learning how to create apps.

They are used by some mainstream publishers, though many prefer to have their own in-house platforms for publishing mobile apps and tablet editions. When you work for such a publisher, they'll train you in the use of their preferred platform – Adobe InDesign or something similar. What we can do here is teach you the principles of creating and populating smartphone and tablet apps. You can add a link to your app to your online portfolio, and use it to demonstrate to a potential employer that, if they hire you, they get someone with the skills required to work in this vital area of cross-platform journalism.

But what we'll also do – and this is crucially important – is develop your skills as an editor. Your app may look good, but without editing skills to match, it won't be worth reading.

The difference between web apps and native apps

We need to get the distinction between what are known as web apps and native apps clear at the outset.

Web apps can run on pretty much any platform because they are built on widely-used technologies such as html5. Web apps can run on mobile devices including iPhones, iPads, Android phones, Windows phones and Kindle Fire devices.

Native apps are built for a particular platform: iOS for Apple products, Android for many others, Windows for Windows phones and so on. Opinion is divided as to whether native apps have a future, but they are preferred currently by most of those who have the money and technical resources to build them because the user experience and functionality is better.

Native apps often look more professional, and are able to use elements from their native operating systems, such as the smooth screen transitions on iOS. They also come with many elements already loaded, so have to draw less information from the web when they are opened up and used, which makes them faster.

Native apps are easier to distribute – they are found in the appropriate App Store and can be downloaded with a click. Web apps have a URL, and you have to get that URL to your phone in order to load them.

If you get a job with a large media organisation, they will no doubt have native apps built for all the main operating systems. But many smaller publishers can't afford to do that, and so go for one web app. Others choose to do both.

We are going to look later in this chapter at creating web apps. But, first, let's look at the sort of smartphone apps publishers are creating, and see what we can learn from them.

Examples of good smartphone apps from news organisations

Some of the most popular news apps are Flipboard, Buzzfeed and Feedly. More traditional news organisations such as the BBC also have good news apps, as do the *Guardian* and others from a newspaper background.

They are popular for a number of reasons, among them:

- They are easy to read: content comes in short sharp chunks with engaging headlines and bright images
- They are customisable: users can decide what topics and interests to have in their feeds.

Buzzfeed

www.buzzfeed.com/

According to the *Guardian*[4] it is "a platform that combines artificial and human intelligence to detect, produce and increase viral content. It has taken social networks by storm, accounting for a disproportionate number of posts shared, liked and discussed online and offline." The *Guardian* praises it for quirky lists and interactive quizzes that, it says, have caught consumer attention worldwide and which are the "envy and nightmare" of marketers, publishers and "anyone obsessed with traffic and the battle of feeds".

It combines original and aggregated content, all of it presented in the brightest, most engaging way. And it makes social sharing very easy.

To emulate it, we need our app to be a mix of great, engaging content from us, and skilfully aggregated or curated content from others. We'll look at the technical solution to delivering that in a moment. In terms of creating engaging content of our own, we need to draw on everything you've learned throughout this book and on your course.

Flipboard

https://flipboard.com/

Flipboard aggregates more serious news content than Buzzfeed into a series of channels you can subscribe to. The content delivered to you can be endlessly customised until you have in effect set up your own personal news, information and curation service.

As its name suggests, you can flip through that content in a way that instinctively suits mobiles and tablets, but also replicates electronically the way we might flip through a magazine or newspaper. You can collect stories into 'magazines' to read later.

You can also connect Flipboard to Facebook, Twitter, Instagram and Tumblr to see what your friends are talking about.

Flipboard shows our app content does not have to be trivial - not that there is anything wrong with trivial. Our goal is to serve our audience, and we will need to learn what they want from us on their phone, their tablet, on our website and - if we get that far - in our print product.

Feedly

https://feedly.com/#welcome

With Feedly you add news sources of your choice, and are offered editors' choices and a starter kit of subject-streams. You can also search for sites you like and add them. That means your readers could add your feeds to their Feedly account and consume your content there. For instance, if you curate on Scoop.it, that stream can be delivered via Feedly.

BBC News

The BBC's smartphone app is a classic news site. You get a shortlist of top stories, delivered in a swipeable grid, and can also go live to the BBC's news channel. You can add or remove news categories and hence tailor it to your taste.

We can very easily set up our smartphone apps to stream our original news content from our website, our curated news streams and other material. We can also make our apps multimedia, and lock them into the main social networks.

Can we make smartphone apps like those we have been discussion?

Actually, we can go a long way towards creating an app that presents news, information and entertainment in a format that is ideally suited to consumption on smartphones, with navigation that suits the platform, and with built-in multimedia and social sharing. Let's look at how. . .

How to build a smartphone app

There are a number of applications that let you build your own mobile phone apps easily, without knowing coding or employing developers. Some have free options, others have fees set at just a few $/£ a month, and some cost a good deal more.

Note: Because mobile-building apps develop rapidly, we'll keep step-by-step tuition in creating a smartphone app with a range of them for the MMJ website.

The general principles of building an app without using any coding

All simple app builders work on the same principle – that content is pulled in from other sources, including your website or blog, RSS feeds and social media accounts. Some also allow you to add content direct to them.

They generally let you create several channels of content in the app, so you can upload, for example, the news feed from your WordPress site, your beat blog's RSS feed, plus your Twitter, YouTube, Facebook and other social media accounts.

In that way you can pull your main online presences together into one app.

You can also create feeds especially for your app, perhaps using techniques including Yahoo Pipes, discussed in Chapter 10, to create mashups of content that is particularly relevant to consumption on a smartphone.

With most such app platforms, the process of creating your app follows these steps, in more or less this order:

- Sign up and click to create an app
- Name your app
- Add your content, one feed at a time, via an RSS feed, URL or social media account name
- Customise your app, choosing from the range of templates and colour schemes offered
- Design an icon, which is the image that will appear on the app button your readers load onto their mobile devices
- Create a splash screen, which is the first screen that opens when the app is opened (only some platforms offer this with free accounts) and a background image
- Take the URL for your app and publicise it.

Users generally choose to load the app into their phones either by typing in the URL and then clicking to add the app to their home screen, by scanning a QR code (more about them later), or by sending the URL to their phones in a text message.

Note: While web apps can be viewed on tablets as well as phones, they are not designed specifically for the tablet format. We'll look at building specifically for tablet computers later in this chapter.

Gather your feed URLs before you start

It's a good idea to gather the feed URLs for the content streams you want to add to your app before you start. That way you can quickly paste them in to whatever platform you are experimenting with. You could build on three or four platforms and decide which works best for the kind of app you want to create.

Choosing the content that will work best on your smartphone app

You want short, sharp reads. Any bite-size streams such as gossip or showbiz updates will be popular. So a breaking news feed should work well. Video and stills suit the platform, so your YouTube channel and Instagram are suitable. Social engagement and sharing should be integral to the app, so you want your social presences there as well.

In addition to your own content, you could create a mashup from the best sources of, say, showbiz news, or commentary on a particular sports league.

Creating a magazine with both tablet computer and print editions

In Chapter 15 we looked at creating a wide range of features, and other content well-suited to both print and tablet computers. Now let's look at building platforms on which to publish such material. We'll look at the big picture, covering:

- Commissioning content
- Design, templates and flat planning
- Why we need to build tablet versions of our sites
- The principles of designing tablet computer versions of your website
- Software that lets you build a print and tablet publication.

Many publishers of print magazines also create tablet computer versions of them. On the tablet they can replicate the look and feel of the magazine, and include the same content, but can also enhance it with multimedia.

But let's not get too hung up on the mechanics of publishing at this stage.

Instead, we'll take an overview of the whole process of creating a magazine for print and/or tablet.

If you've been working on a magazine as one of your projects, now's the time you can realise your dream.

I'm going to assume that, at this stage, you have a title for your magazine, a target audience, mission statement and all the rest of it. If you haven't and you want to create a really professional magazine, I suggest you flip back and take another look at what we said in Chapter 1, culminating in the project section.

on the website

Find much more about the editing process, from generating ideas, choosing writers, briefing writers, working on submitted copy and the rest of the editorial process.

Here we'll look at pulling your first edition together.

So that involves:

- Assigning roles: choosing an editor, news editor, features editor, production editor and so on
- Commissioning articles for the magazine
- Planning the magazine – creating a flat plan
- Editing copy and images
- Laying out pages
- Sub-editing
- Proof-reading and, finally, publishing.

We also need to consider finding a magazine-publishing platform, if you don't already have one.

Choosing a publishing platform for your magazine

on the website

Find step-by-step tuition in using the current best-available free or inexpensive publishing platform.

The editorial process – from idea to published article

Ideas

In journalism, ideas are absolute gold dust. Those who can come up with great ideas, and turn them into compelling news stories, features or whatever, are highly prized.

But where do ideas come from? And what makes an idea right for the audience you seek to serve, and the media organisation you work for?

Where do ideas come from?

From all sorts of sources. We discussed this at length in Chapter 1, but here's a reprise of what we said there:

Ideas come from, among other sources:

- the news and events in general
- issues that are in the air
- your audience, through interaction with them
- contacts, meetings
- press releases
- editorial brainstorming (the more informal, the more creative)
- contributors and freelances
- specialists.

Ideas often seem great when they first occur to us, but are they really that good? An idea is not tested until you've spoken it out loud. How does it sound, how do others react to it?

Keep an ideas file, or forward-planning diary, full of things that might not be right now, but could be good at the right point in the future.

What makes ideas right?

Ideas are right if they produce content that appeals to your audience. We set about defining our audience in Chapter 1. By now, we ought to be confident that we know who our readers/viewers/listeners are and what they want from us.

Balance

You may have six brilliant ideas, but can't use some of them because they are too similar to each other. You need the right balance of ideas in a publication: a mix of the light and the serious, interviews and profiles, first-person pieces, analysis and comment. You'll need to balance coverage of the different interest areas you handle – whether that's defined by geography, branches of showbiz or whatever.

How should the idea best be handled?

Should it be an interview with a particular person? A first-person piece by someone intimately involved in a story? A piece by a writer, pulling in various interviews and other material?

Most stories can be handled in numerous ways. You have to pick the best angle – taking into account what options you have, and how to make the piece a good fit with other things in the edition.

Commissioning

Ideas will be run past an editor in a planning meeting. Those that are approved must be commissioned. Maybe you'll be briefed on what is required, or perhaps you'll be the one doing the briefing.

How do you commission successfully?

You need the right project for the right journalist. It's called good casting, and you learn it by getting to know writers and their work and seeing what they can – and can't – deliver.

Some ideas are best for a hard-news reporter, others for a colour writer, some for incisive interviewers. Knowledge or experience of a subject can be important. Sometimes you want a non-journalist to do a piece. Perhaps you need the authentic voice of someone intimately involved in a story, or the knowledgeable analysis of an expert in a given field.

Finding writers

You'll get to know who on the staff, or in your range of regular freelances, is good for a given piece. But sometimes you need to find a new person – an expert, a victim, someone with personal experience of a story. Maybe a prominent individual who has personal experience of the particular issue you are interested in.

We often take features, comment pieces or analysis from:

- Specialists
- Academics
- Pressure groups
- Politicians.

Briefing contributors

The commissioning editor needs to have a clear idea of what they want, and to give solid guidelines to the contributor. If they have a headline in mind, great, it's the perfect thing to work towards. The contributor needs to take careful note of what is wanted, and to work hard to deliver exactly that – and not some other, very interesting news story or feature that the commissioner didn't ask for.

It sounds simple, but it's not. Too many commissioning editors don't know what they want, or aren't clear about it. Too many contributors ignore the brief they are given.

It's a good idea for editor and contributor to talk through an idea, and for the commissioner to follow up with an email outline of the brief. If, as they work on the piece, the contributor finds they can't deliver exactly that, they need to tell the editor, so an alternative way forward can be agreed upon.

Negotiating fees for freelance contributions, and the question of copyright

A commissioning editor needs to be clear on:

- The rates you have
- The budget you have
- The flexibility you have.

Rates paid to different contributors can vary enormously on the same publication.

A contributor needs to be clear on:

- How long it will take to complete a given commission
- The nominal day rate they need to achieve.

For staffers, all they create while under the terms and conditions of their contract of employment with their employer belongs to that employer. Some employers will share syndication income generated by a staffer's work.

For freelancers, rights need to be negotiated.

All literary and artistic work is copyright, which means that it cannot be reproduced without the permission of the copyright owner.

The owner of the copyright in freelance material is the freelance contributor. Editors usually require a 'licence' to print this material. In the UK, where no other agreement is reached, writers sell a licence called first British serial rights. This is the right to publish, once only, in a magazine or newspaper circulating in the UK. Extra rights, for example the right to syndicate the article to publications outside the UK, have to be negotiated separately. Publishers often want greater rights than this, usually to cover online and other electronic publication, and inclusion in databases.

Some ask freelances to assign copyright. Others ask for an unlimited licence giving them all rights in every country and medium. Conde Nast is most vigorous in insisting on all rights, even from star photographers.

To acquire extended copyright you have to have the contributor's agreement in writing. So you should send them two copies of an agreement, both signed by you, one of which they will sign and return. It is good practice to include in this contract the brief, deadline and fee.

on the website

Find out more about copyright law.

Deadlines

No professional journalist will break a deadline. Ever. But deadlines need to be realistic, for both the contributor and the editor. The contributor needs to be sure the material can be delivered within that deadline, and the editor needs to set a deadline that gives them enough time to assess the contribution and see it through the production process.

Sometimes a contributor asks what the REAL deadline is. They don't get it.

If an editor knows a contributor is reliable, they can shave off time from the leeway you need for lesser-known quantities such as first-time freelances.

You need if possible to build in time to rework disasters, or have other contingencies in place.

Assessing contributions

When commissioned material comes in, editors must decide on its merits. Usually, the department heads will get things the way they feel they should be, before submitting them to the editor for his or her final approval.

On occasion, content needs to be reworked. When do you do it yourself? When do you re-brief the contributor and have them re-shoot? That often depends on what is easiest. If you as editor know what needs doing to make the contribution publishable, and it's quicker to do it yourself, that's probably the best way to go. Other times you need the contributor to do more work – more interviewing, gather more material, in which case you are in their hands.

When all the content is in: the process of creating a magazine

The editor, often in conjunction with the production editor and designer, decides what goes where in the magazine. There will be fixed points – regular columns and features, that are always in place, but as this is your first edition you'll have to decide what, for example, goes in the first few pages – often short nuggets of news or information – where columnists appear, what the main feature is, and where it goes in relation – say – to the big interview piece. And what feature rounds things off on the final editorial page?

Your layout software often helps you do that. In working with it, you'll need to follow this process:

- Choose your overall magazine template – that gives you a style for your magazine
- Flat plan your mag – assign the items you have in the right order
- Laying out pages – choosing the right templates
- Assigning text and images and having them subbed
- Writing headlines
- Proof-reading
- Publishing.

How many pages?

Twenty-four is the minimum, but if you can double the pagination, great. That gives you enough space to experience what it's like creating a magazine for real.

Creating your magazine

If you don't have access to InDesign or a comparable layout platform, you'll need an alternative.

17C7

Creating a newspaper or magazine for tablet only

So that was building a magazine that works on tablets and in print. Now let's look at creating an edition of a newspaper or magazine that is for tablet only.

As we mentioned early on in this chapter, the tablet computer offers us the chance to create an edition of our publication that is distinctive; that is true to our principles, brand values and content criteria, but which works particularly effectively on the tablet platform. When any media organisation designs a tablet app, it has to think about the extent to which it needs to reinvent itself on the platform, and also how to transfer its core values – the things that make it valuable to its audience – onto this format. Let's look at how a range of organisations have approached that challenge.

Examples of newspaper tablet editions

The *Guardian*'s iPad edition is the result of much work and deliberation. When someone familiar with the *Guardian* brand – either off or online – comes across it, they instantly recognise it as the *Guardian*, but find a publication that has been adapted to suit the tablet form in terms of navigation, design, integration of multimedia, and the balance between content from a fixed-in-time edition, and a live stream of breaking news.

The FT

The FT's app is arranged into two distinct editions – 'Morning' and 'Live' – so readers can choose news as it was at a fixed point, or as it is now. Both versions, which you can switch between with the tap of a button, share the look and feel of the print product, down to the pink background colour.

Readers can 'clip' articles to read later, and they go into My FT Hub, which also contains a list of what they have read most recently, as well as recommendations based on what they have already been reading.

The FT scrapped its native iOS app and created a web app instead because, it was reported, of[5] "concerns about the lack of data Apple made available around user activity from the App Store. Not to mention the 30% cut Apple takes from any in-app revenues generated."

on the website

Read the FT's explanation of how it works, and watch a demonstration video: **http://apps.ft.com/ftwebapp/**

The London Times

The *Times*'s tablet edition is also divided into Edition – as published that morning – and Live News, which is a simple feed of new stories and updates to existing ones, most of them from *Times* staff. These stories often form the basis for the reports that will publish in the next day's edition.

So it's a way of having the *Times*-quality reporting that readers value, but as soon as it breaks.

There are videos embedded into most major news story, a limited number produced by the *Times*, the majority lifted from Sky News, another company in the Murdoch stable. On a selection of its features, *The Times* produces video that complements the print versions of the

article, which are identical in print and tablet editions. So they may have a video of part of an interview with a major figure, or a video version of an art exhibition or a car road-test from the author of the text piece. Video is also gathered on an index page:

A newspaper staple such as the Times Letters Page is redrawn as Readers' Forum, in this format:

And there are interactive versions of some stories, for example ones where data can be used to produce information specific to a given reader. When, for example, the A-level results were published, the *Times* tablet edition story asked: "How many kids did your child beat?"

Enter their subjects and grades and you get the result:

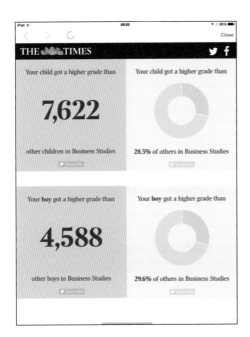

So, again, *The Times* goes for a mix of tradition and innovation.

The NYTimes

The NYT offers metered access, with (at the time of writing) ten free articles per month. It too shares very much the look and feel of its dead-tree ancestor, but there is a video section, and an area for saved stories.

Of the major newspaper titles we've looked at so far, this app is probably the least adapted to the tablet format (at the time of writing). You can't swipe through articles, for example, as you can with most tablet apps. Instead navigation is through a section index that you tap to see, and then via a long (sometimes very long) vertical scroll through the articles in that section.

To get live news you tap to subscribe to a series of alerts.

17C8

Building your own tablet computer edition

Let's recap for a moment on the characteristics of tablet editions, as discussed in the last couple of sections of this chapter (in book or online versions combined), so we can get a handle on what we need to do to create a worthwhile, bespoke tablet edition of our publication.

Tablet apps usually incorporate:

- The look and feel of a print publication
- Combined with navigation appropriate to a tablet
- The vast majority of content is processed semi-automatically from print or web editions into the app
- The choice between a static edition and a live one
- The ability to embed multimedia including video
- Interactive storytelling
- Social connections and sharing.

Note: Tablet apps are developing fast, so we'll go online to work with the best currently available one.

on the website

Find step-by-step tuition in creating a tablet edition.

17C9

Exercises and projects

Exercise 1

Study a couple of publishers' smartphone apps in depth. Assess their usability. How do they look, are they easy to navigate?

Exercise 2

Compare a range of tablet apps. Assess how they best tackle issues including design, navigation, the balance between a static edition and live news.

Projects

1   Build a smartphone app, using either one of the platforms discussed on the website, or another that you discover. Add a range of feeds to it.

2   Create a magazine as a group project, using the recommended platform on the MMJ website if you do not have access to InDesign or comparable platforms.

3   Make a tablet edition of your print publication or website, using the application recommended on the MMJ website, or another appropriate platform.

Notes

1   www.pewinternet.org/2013/10/18/tablet-and-e-reader-ownership-update/
2   www.intelligentpositioning.com/blog/2014/01/mobile-and-tablet-traffic-set-to-overtake-desktop-by-mid-2014/
3   www.journalism.org/2012/10/01/future-mobile-news/
4   www.theguardian.com/media-network/media-network-blog/2014/feb/11/18-reasons-readers-love-buzzfeed-publishers
5   http://thenextweb.com/apps/2013/04/03/the-ft-launches-an-all-new-ipad-web-app-featuring-per-sonlized-myft-hub-a-morning-edition-and-more/

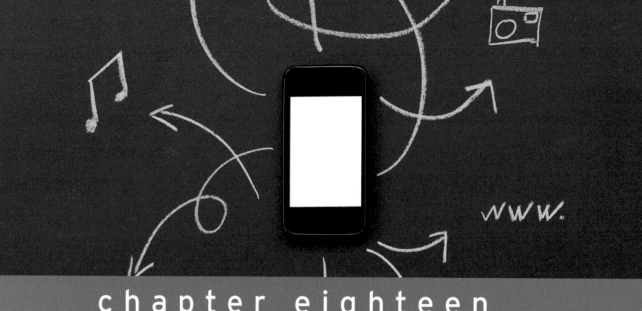

chapter eighteen

Advanced multimedia storytelling

In the book version of this chapter we will cover:

Advanced multimedia storytelling:

- Examples of advanced multimedia storytelling
- How multimedia story packages are made
- Software used to make multimedia stories.

Mastering further multimedia storytelling tools including:

- Infographics
- Timelines
- Maps.

Augmented reality – adding active content to static print media.

- Examples of augmented reality applied to print products
- How to create your own augmented reality version of stories on your website or in a print publication
- Using QR codes to link to multimedia content.

At the end of the chapter are a range of exercises and projects to enable you to practise what you have learned.

In the online version of this chapter you will find:

- Full step-by-step tuition in each of the applications covered here
- Links to alternative software packages
- Essential updates to the tuition contained here.

Have the companion website to this book open at www.multimedia-journalism.co.uk. That way you can easily click on the links to the stories discussed here.

18C1

Introduction to advanced multimedia storytelling

We spoke early on in this book about determining the best medium in which to tell a story - or an aspect of a story. We've considered how, as multimedia journalists, we are able to select from our range of storytelling skills to create text, stills, video, audio, and various types of visualisation.

We have worked, as we have built websites, smartphone and tablet apps, to combine those elements into a series of coherent, multimedia storytelling packages.

Now we'll take the next step, and look at ways in which these many diverse elements can be combined as seamlessly as possible into a format that I'm calling advanced multimedia storytelling.

Let's look back at a *New York Times* initiative called Snow Fall. Snow Fall was a forerunner among efforts to create a really cohesive, seamless format for multimedia storytelling, and we'll analyse it and other examples of the genre.

We'll also add to our skills by looking at the creation of some further elements to enable us to tell stories via infographics, timelines and maps.

Then we'll consider one particular interesting aspect of augmented reality: how multimedia such as video can be accessed by pointing a smartphone or tablet camera at images in a print publication.

Examples of advanced multimedia storytelling

Snow Fall

www.nytimes.com/projects/2012/snow-fall/#/?part=to-the-peak

Snow Fall was heralded as the future of storytelling, and won a Pulitzer for its creators. This and the other examples here are experiments in making long-form journalism work online. In-depth material has always been a strength of printed media, and these examples are partly attempts to translate that strength into an immersive experience well-suited to online media.

Take a look at Snow Fall before reading on.

on the website

Find a link to Snow Fall.

Snow Fall is told through a text story into which multimedia is embedded: video clips at key points; background on participants in the story served via hyperlinks; a graphic timeline that plays through the story; images and a map.

As you scroll down, videos of interviews are embedded alongside the text, and you can play them either by clicking on the video player itself or on a link within text.

questions

What do you think of it? Consider your answer before reading on.

I think it's technically impressive, but don't feel the story is particularly strong, or well told. The grab above shows the extent of the sell, which is minimal and doesn't do enough to persuade me to read on.

The piece is written in a very gentle, featurey way. We know there's been an avalanche but we are told nothing at the start about what the consequences of that avalanche might have been. And as I read on I don't find the story interesting enough to keep me scrolling and clicking through this amount of material.

But it's how the story was created that is of interest to us, more than what it says, and Poynter.org spoke to NY Times graphics director Steve Duenes about that.[1]

> Duenes told them the goal was to "find ways to allow readers to read into, and then through multimedia, and then out of multimedia. So it didn't feel like you were taking a detour, but the multimedia was part of the one narrative flow."

Normally, multimedia is segregated from text, but with Snow Fall it is almost seamlessly integrated. The intention, Duenes said, was to get as close as possible to a coherent and seamless article that contained all the multimedia elements that made it strong.

Snow Fall required collaboration between writer John Branch, the sports editors and graphics editors, Duenes said. It was essential to get all those elements to fit into the narrative flow, he said. That took a lot of coordination between departments. They couldn't just dump the finished text article on the graphics desk.

As John Branch wrote, the other journalists involved in creating the package were looking at his drafts, thinking about where multimedia elements could be embedded. So the project took shape on parallel tracks, with text and other elements being developed simultaneously.

Effects such as the opening full-width header with background video and audio of windswept snow are impressive, and this effect probably does more to pull the reader into the story than the text sell I've been complaining about.

Further down, there is what's known as a flyover animation, which is designed to transport the reader to the mountains and ski areas where the story takes place. That took a lot of work. Graphics Editor Jeremy White had to gather LIDAR elevation data (**http://lidar.cr.usgs. gov/**) and satellite imagery for the terrain, then use it to create a virtual model and generate the animation.

The Jockey

on the website

Find a link to The Jockey. Take a look before reading on.

questions

Is this better, worse or just different to Snow Fall? Don't read on until you have your answer.

With this story, as you scroll the video fills the screen and plays automatically, so there is even less need to click around than there is on Snow Fall. Again, the story doesn't grab me enough, but I do think this is a development of some of the techniques used in Snow Fall.

on the website

Find out how The Jockey was made.

Snowden NSA files

on the website

- Find a link to the Snowden story
- Read about Snowden and what he did.

Take a look at the story linked to on the website. Again, decide what you think of it as a piece of storytelling.

Edward Snowden is an American computer professional who leaked classified information from the US National Security Agency.

The piece takes significant areas of leaked documents one by one and, in each case, explains what has been revealed and the significance of this through text, embedded video clips of talking-head experts, and a range of graphics or visualisations.

In the first section, video fills the screen and plays automatically, there is no text to scroll through. In section 2, as you scroll through text you reach embedded video clips of talking heads that play automatically, offering commentary or illumination on the text you are reading.

Copies of leaked documents are embedded in the text, and can be scrolled through. Simple visualisations, or graphics, are used to make information more easily absorbed.

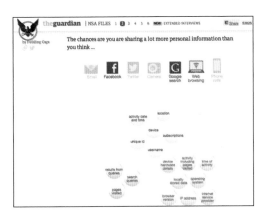

In this one, if you click on one of the buttons at the top, you get the information that is gathered on your activity on that platform in the bubbles below.

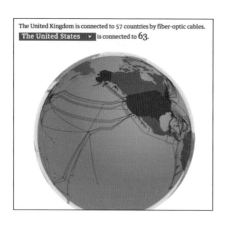

The United Kingdom is connected to 57 countries by fiber-optic cables. The United States ▼ is connected to 63.

In this, the fact that much of the world's communications pass through fibre optic cables controlled by the USA and UK is demonstrated through mapping on a spinning globe.

It goes on to look at 'Are your details secure?' and other aspects of the story. It's worth running through to see the range of graphics/visualisations used.

I find this a particularly effective package. It's like concurrently watching and reading a documentary. And the embedded documents let the reader drill as deep as they like into the subject matter at any point they choose.

How to make your own multimedia story package

Software that enables the non-techie journalist to create their own multimedia packages with all the elements seen in the examples above tend to come and go. When Cody Brown published a version of Snow Fall he said he had made in an hour on a start-up software package called Scroll Kit, he was ordered to take it down by the NYT.

So we'll keep recommendations for software you can use on the MMJ website, where the information can be kept updated.

on the website

- ■ Find further examples, including the latest developments in multimedia storytelling
- ■ See how the BBC approaches multimedia storytelling
- ■ Find the latest information on software that will enable you to make multimedia stories like those described here.

18C2

How to make infographics

Information graphics, or infographics, can be defined as visual representations of data or other information. A good infographic can present complex information quickly and clearly.

Infographics need the right structure, headline and content. Let's take a look at how they can be sold and structured. Examples taken from Piktochart.[2]

A good headline

As with any story, the headline is there to sell it. It's no different with an infographic. Go for four to eight words.

> Why do freeways come to a stop?

For example: **Why do freeways come to a stop?**

or

A throwaway culture

An informative, compelling strap line. . .

After the headline you will probably need a strapline to help you give enough information to convince a browser to stick with your infographic. For example:

A throwaway culture

How much do we really recycle?

A standfirst (sometimes)

When you need more words to introduce your graphic, a standfirst works well.

For example, an infographic headlined Healthcare Costs by State has this standfirst alongside the heading which talks about how there is a heated debate over the issue of public health care but that, despite lobbyists spending over $1m a day, senators are evenly divided falling evenly on the issue.

Body

This is where you present your information graphically. There are several ways of doing that. A common one is to open with a graphical summary of your information - some big picture stats that have high impact.

That can be followed by some supplementary information that sketches in the detail, such as taking a number of subsidiary stats or facts and presenting them on the next level down.

Conclusion

Finally, you want a strong sign off. That can be done statistically, or with text.

Here's an example of that typical structure:

The infographic opens with an introduction - a big picture - and then elaborates points that support the premise. It ends with a strong piece of information: what every useable email address is worth in terms of active giving. But there are other ways to structure your infographic.

Alternative structures

One piece of information

Some graphics only have one piece of information, for instance comparative statistics presented on a map, such as the healthcare costs by state infographic we mentioned earlier.

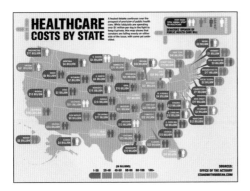

Comparison structure

This is where you want to compare two things. That goal dictates this sort of graphical arrangement. Here's an example, comparing two models of iPhone:

Process flow

You use what is known as a process flow design when you want to illustrate a sequence of events, or cause and effect. Such as this on the shape of the modern newsroom and how people work in it.

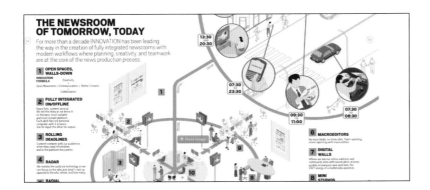

Here's a detail:

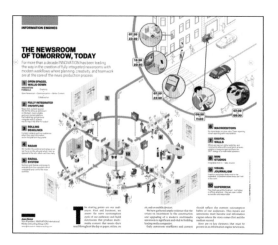

on the website

See the graphic enlarged.

Or this on 'Why do freeways come to a stop?', the headline of which we looked at earlier.

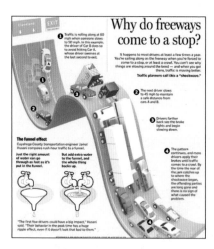

Building an infographic with Piktochart

Note: because Piktochart and other software is updated regularly, we'll keep the step-by-step tuition in how to use it and other platforms for the MMJ website.

How to make interactive timelines

Dipity

www.dipity.com

Dipity is fast and simple to use. You just click to create your timeline, name it and add in some details, then get building.

Here's an example:

A timeline such as that can be built in an hour or two.

You build up your story by adding items to your timeline. Each time you click to add an event you get an interface into which you can paste in a headline, image, text, a link back to the post you are sourcing the information from, and video.

You can adjust how much of your timeline is visible – a few days, a week, a month or more.

Embedding is easy, just customise the dimensions of your player if you need to, and the appearance if you like, then take the code.

on the website

Watch video tutorials in using Dipity, follow a step-by-step guide, and see further examples of timelines created with it.

18C4

How to tell stories via maps

Maps can be elements in a story, or they can be the medium by which the whole story is told. We can make a map the underlying, linking structure for a story where that is appropriate. A map can be the way the reader navigates a story. We can create a map for an individual story, or add numerous stories on a particular theme to one map. We can embed multimedia at points on the map, so the reader can understand the context in which something happened.

We can also add an RSS feed of geotagged data to a map, which will mean that information related to points on that map will appear and be clickable to the reader. So, for example, adding a FixMyStreet RSS feed for a given area to a map of that area will create a live map of local incidents.

As we saw in Chapter 13 on data journalism, spreadsheets can also be mashed up with maps.

In this section we'll look at software that lets us create sophisticated mashups where the map is the background on which the story is told, but where a good deal of rich media can be added to the map.

Examples of simple maps used in news storytelling

on the website

- See easily achievable examples of what has been done, just to inspire you to think about what you could be doing
- Find links to the maps discussed below, and to others.

Here's a simple example from the *Guardian* of the Boston Marathon bombings, where images of the explosions are embedded at the locations on the map where they occurred:

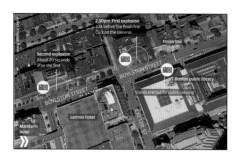

This from the *Brighton Argus*

www.theargus.co.uk/news/special/sussex_torch/map/

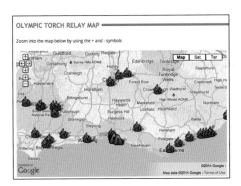

dates from the run-up to the 2012 Olympics and lets readers check to see where the Olympic torch was coming close to them during its journey around the country and which celebrities would be with it – much better than a long text list of locations and names. It's built on Google Maps, and involved simply adding a spreadsheet with the locations and other information to a map.

More complex maps

Here's another map on the same topic, for the 2016 Olympics, that uses a more sophisticated piece of kit, StoryMap JS from KnightLab.com.

Mapping gunfire near schools

http://datatools.urban.org/features/everydayviolence/

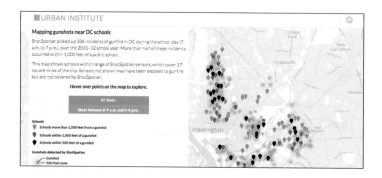

This map mashup combines information on gunfire and school locations in Washington DC.

How's it gathered? Data from a network of sensors that triangulate sounds of gunfire and map the results is added to a map, to which school location data is also added. Images of locations are also embedded. Take a look via the link above, which is also on the MMJ website, and see how many shots are heard during school hours, compared to total shots fired.

> It takes this text to give you the story: "ShotSpotter picked up 336 incidents of gunfire in DC during the school day (7 a.m. to 7 p.m.), over the 2011–12 school year. More than half of these incidents occurred within 1,000 feet of a public school."

The dogs of LA

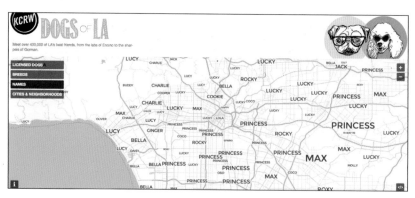

Breeds and names are mapped across the city. Why? Maybe because you can.

questions

In storytelling terms, is there anything wrong with these last couple of maps? Don't read on until you have decided.

Here's my view. They don't give me the story, they give me the information within which many stories may be lurking. While all of us can enjoy scrolling around in such maps, what we lack are the headlines hidden within them. For example, how often are DC schoolchildren's lives placed in danger because of gunfire close to their schools? Often? Sometimes? Never? We need to know before we can decide whether this is a story that ought to interest us.

And the Dogs of LA map is fun, but I want a story from it, I need text, images, video, portraits of dogs and their owners.

We need the specific points of interest drawn out by a smart journalist, and a story or feature built around them. The maps don't bring the stories to life, it would take a journalist to do that.

So, a lesson - we mustn't let the smart technology that is at our disposal blind us to the fact that we need to find a good story to present via it.

Applications that let you tell stories via maps

Google Maps is the best-known and the most widely used, but it's fallen behind the field: the range of rich media it allows you to add is limited, and there are plenty of rivals that let us do more. But let's not dismiss it.

on the website

Find links to a full guide to using Google Maps for storytelling.

There are several alternatives to Google Maps, including:

- StoryMap JS from Knightlab **http://storymap.knightlab.com/**
- Storymaps **http://storymaps.arcgis.com/en/**
- Henagoo **http://heganoo.com/**
- ThingLink **www.thinglink.com/signup?buttonSource=4dots**

They vary in exactly what they'll let you do, but all work on the principle that they let you embed rich media into a map or sometimes an image. That includes:

- Video – often including YouTube, Vimeo, Vine and Bambuser among others
- Audio – such as Spotify, SoundCloud and audioBoom
- Images – including Flickr, Instagram and Photobucket
- Social media – Facebook, Twitter, LinkedIn
- E-commerce – Amazon, Etsy, eBay
- Utilities – Wikipedia, Slideshare, Google Docs.

We'll look at one of them here: Storymap JS.

Storymap JS from Knightlab

http://storymap.knightlab.com/

This is a more sophisticated piece of software, which enables you to create very slick and professional multimedia stories that render very well on tablet computers.

Your story is told in a series of slides, combining text, mapping and embedded rich media, so you can add headlines and explanations to what the map shows in order to tell a story. You build your slides one by one.

on the website

Find guides to using StoryMap JS, examples of maps created with it, and my step-by-step guide to how I created a StoryMap on it.

Find tuition in alternatives to StoryMap JS.

18C5

Adding augmented reality to your print publications

Print has a problem. Print is static.

With digital news platforms you can combine video and audio, interaction of all kinds, and links to all sorts of other content. With print, what you see on the page is all you get.

Or it was.

Augmented reality changes that. It removes print's disadvantage by making it possible to create links within printed images that open up from them into an entire digital world. It turns a static medium into a dynamic one.

OK, we know how easy it is to embed multimedia content into a website or blog. With augmented reality you can, effectively, embed it into print.

Pointing your smartphone or tablet camera at a still image that has been turned into a trigger image for a piece of augmented reality makes that media play.

You make this possible through the use of an augmented reality app or, less sci-fi-sounding, via a digital browser.

There are a number of outfits that make this possible. The one we are going to work with is called Aurasma (**www.aurasma.com/what-is-it/**) and it has been used by leading publications including *The Times* (of London) and *GQ Magazine* (**www.aurasma.com/partners/#/gq**).

The *Times* and *Sunday Times* have run a number of special, augmented reality editions of their magazines, using Aurasma to link still images, in adverts and editorial, to videos on the same topic. So the magazine cover pictured right, for example, featured a figure which, when viewed through Aurasma, sprang into life via a short video loop.

Aurasma say: "Aurasma is available as a free app for iPhones, iPads and high-powered Android devices or as a kernel for developers. Aurasma uses advanced image and pattern recognition to blend the real-world with rich interactive content such as videos and animations called 'Auras'".

How to create augmented reality with Aurasma

There are three essential building blocks to creating augmented reality content with Aurasma:

- Trigger images
- Overlays, and
- Channels.

Trigger images

are the still pictures a user has to scan with their phone to unlock the augmented reality content associated with them.

Overlays

are the content you link to the trigger image – usually a video.

Channels

are the places you put your content for publication, so users can find it.

on the website

Find a step-by-step guide to using augmented reality in your storytelling.

questions

Once you have completed the tuition on the website, consider this question: Do you think this form of augmented reality will become widely used? Don't read on until you have decided.

My view: maybe, maybe not. It may prove to be too much trouble for most people, given that tablet versions of print publications are proving popular. How many people will be prepared to go to the trouble of downloading an app and then having to point their mobile device at this static print object when they could just get the print product's app on their phone/tablet in the first place?

Nevertheless, I don't believe we can afford to dismiss augmented reality at this stage. So we'll see online how to use an application such as Aurasma to create multimedia journalism.

Using QR codes to link to multimedia content

QR codes offer another, very simple, way to link to multimedia content.

QR – for Quick Response – codes are often seen on adverts – particularly on static ads such as street hoardings and posters, but have not proved particularly popular for editorial purposes.

A QR code is – potentially – a very convenient way to get people who are on mobile devices to take a look at your content. They don't have to find your app's URL, nor send it to their phone, just hold their phone before a QR code to be taken to your content. That could be a web page, an app, a video clip, a business card, your contact phone number which is then dialled. In fact, it could be pretty much anything.

Maybe they'll take off, maybe they won't. Because of the uncertainty we'll only deal with them briefly here.

on the website

Find a guide to creating QR codes for your journalism.

Here's Wikipedia's definition of Quick Response codes:

> A QR Code is a specific matrix barcode (or two-dimensional code), readable by dedicated QR barcode readers and camera phones. The code consists of black modules arranged in a square pattern on a white background. The information encoded can be text, URL or other data.

To create them you need a QR-writing application such as Kaywa: **http://qrcode.kaywa.com/**. The app will turn your URL into a QR code, just as a URL shortening service such as bit.ly truncates your URL.

To read them, you do three things:

1   Install a QR code-reading app on your phone – and there are loads to choose from in the app stores.

2   Open the app, which opens your camera.

3   Point the lens at a QR code and the information linked to it opens.

Exercises and projects

Exercise 1

Study the latest multimedia storytelling packages, compare them to Snow Fall and assess how far this type of storytelling has developed.

Exercise 2

Research infographics, and reach your own assessment of how to create a successful one.

Exercise 3

Study the use of timelines, and produce a report on how best they can be used in storytelling.

Exercise 4

Write a report on the use of mapping in storytelling.

Projects

Using either the software packages covered on the website, or others that you prefer, create:

1   An infographic.

2   A timeline.

3   A storymap.

4   A virtual reality addition to one of your text stories.

5   A QR code that links from a static location such as a page in print or online, to a piece of multimedia content.

Notes

1   www.poynter.org/latest-news/top-stories/198970/how-the-new-york-times-snow-fall-project-unifies-text-multimedia/
2   http://piktochart.com/

chapter nineteen

Long-form video journalism, audio and video news bulletins and magazine programmes

In the book version of this chapter we will cover:

- Long-form video journalism
- How to compile, edit, script and present a video news bulletin
- How to compile, edit, script and present a longer, magazine-style programme
- Ensuring your performance at the microphone and on camera is professional and authoritative
- The professional approach to voice coaching
- Using an autocue.

At the end of the chapter are a range of exercises and projects to enable you to practise what you have learned.

In the online version of this chapter you will find:

- Links to all the examples discussed here
- Video and other further tuition in key areas
- Additional resources
- Essential updates to tuition in the book.

Have the companion website to this book open at www.multimedia-journalism.co.uk. That way you can easily click on the links to the stories discussed here.

Long-form video journalism

We'll use *Vice* magazine as a case study for effective long-form video journalism. *Vice* has its online magazine at: **www.vice.com/Vice** and its wide range of YouTube channels clustered at: **www.youtube.com/user/vice**

on the website

Find the links to these and all other resources discussed here.

Vice is a former fanzine, which became a magazine for the under-30s filled with "sex, drugs and rock and roll", and is now primarily a creator of highly original long-form video journalism.

It began life in the 1990s as a free fanzine called *Voice*, distributed in Montreal, Canada. Today it produces documentary series for HBO; has launched a cookery channel, in partnership with Fremantle media, that aims to disrupt the cosy world of TV cookery shows; and long-form video documentaries in which it covers compelling stories in a lively, irreverent style.

In 2014 *Vice* gained exclusive access to the Islamist militants proclaiming an Islamic state in parts of Syria and Iraq, scooping all the major established networks. It's a great model of how to build a modern news, information and entertainment brand using multimedia journalism and harnessing the power of online and social networks.

on the website

Watch *Vice*'s Isis videos.

On YouTube and elsewhere, *Vice* has a network of channels covering fashion, music, travel, culture and art, and has an international presence and profile. It's worth around $2.5bn.

Vice's Dan'l Hewitt says that[1] while the magazine is still hugely important, it now accounts for only around 5 per cent of total revenue.

The move into online video began when channels including YouTube and Vimeo flourished, and the price of video-producing hardware and software fell.

Vice's long-form video documentaries have attracted a lot of attention. A film looking at the historic rivalry between Scotland's Rangers and Celtic football teams – produced by Vice's UK team – involved a reporter and cameraman/producer being embedded with fans for weeks. A Vice US film series covered a journey into the Amazon to hunt down rare hallucinogens.

Hewitt says[1] that when they go out and film their documentaries, they do it very differently to traditional media businesses. "We won't go into places with big film crews, so our founder Shane [Smith] has been to North Korea, for example, and we tend to go in slightly guerilla in fashion."

Documentaries can take months. Hewitt says that this allows them to produce content quite cheaply because the resources are low, but it also gives them an "intimacy with the people" who they are spending time with, which he believes means that trust is also built up.

Take a look at either Vice's magazine site or YouTube channel and you'll find great, highly professional but unstuffy long-form video. Just up while I was researching this was a 20-minute documentary about a bunch of jewel thieves called the Pink Panthers.

Another was a portrait of London street-biker culture.

Alex Miller, executive editor of Vice UK, told a news:rewired conference[2] that Vice filmmakers travel the world and produce long-form videos for the web on anything from current affairs to the environment. They say they like to trick people into caring about the planet.

Alex was part of a team that filmed riots in Greece. The team did not have press cards and did not stay at the hotel many journalists from other news outlets booked into. Miller said: "We were right in the thick of it. . .We are an alternative voice. . .By the very nature of us being Vice, us being different, we got very different stuff – which was probably closer to truth."

on the website

How does Vice make long-form video journalism pay? Find out on the MMJ website.

Video bulletins

Vice also has a news channel (**https://news.vice.com/**) with comprehensive coverage of the main world stories, and a short daily bulletin on the main news of the day, presented as a package of video clips with voice-over from a news reader, and called a news capsule.

While the bulletin itself can only summarise a big story, an on-screen invitation to 'click here to read more' during a particular story clip takes you to a detailed text report. Within those text reports there are often links to long-form video documentaries on the subject. So *Vice* is using short-form video on social media to draw users in, then offering context and depth via text, followed by a major exploration of the subject via long-form video.

Here's an example.

on the website

Find links to the examples below.

The news bulletin is here, grabbed at the point when a story on Yemen is featured.

www.youtube.com/watch?v=RH3BQPrxje8

The text report is here:

https://news.vice.com/article/what-do-the-protesting-houthis-really-want-in-yemen

The long-form video documentary is here:

There are also links to in-depth text-based material within that documentary, including this:

https://news.vice.com/article/a-justice-department-memo-provides-the-cias-legal-justification-to-kill-a-us-citizen said to be a CIA memo providing the legal justification for killing a US citizen.

How to add links into your YouTube videos

YouTube has a facility it calls annotations, which allows you to add text and embedded links into your videos on the channel. They say:

> "With annotations you can layer text, links, and hotspots over your video. They help you enrich the video experience by adding information, interactivity and engagement."

At the time of writing these annotations don't appear in all contexts – go to the MMJ website for any update on this.

on the website

Find more on how to add annotations to your videos, or use this link: **https://support. google.com/youtube/answer/92710?hl=en**

News bulletins from brands

Many brands and other organisations for whom journalism is not their main business are now creating their own video news bulletins as part of a brand journalism offering. Manchester United, for example, creates a daily bulletin of short club-news items.

on the website

You'll find an example on the MMJ website.

Gathering material for video bulletins

You'll need time to gather material for your audio or video bulletin. If it's an early morning one, you will want to have created a good deal the day before, perhaps taking the afternoon or evening to record and edit interviews destined for next day's bulletin, then beginning again two or three hours before you publish so you can add the latest news, and ensure that anything you did yesterday is still relevant.

A lunch-time bulletin might again involve a split shift, with the previous afternoon or evening used for gathering a certain amount of material, the morning devoted to breaking stories and writing the script.

With a bulletin going out in the evening, much if not all is usually done on the day.

Not all bulletins contain a majority of original content. On a local news website they may well do, but if you are producing a bulletin of national or international news – such as the one for *Vice* – you will be selecting from material made available to you from sources including other multimedia journalists in your organisation, agencies and freelances.

On a B2B site, you may well be gathering the best stories destined for the website that day, taking the first couple of paragraphs and adapting them for your bulletin.

If you are doing hourly bulletins, it's a question of getting your agenda set for the day you are covering, and then adapting and freshening things up on each subsequent bulletin.

Some bulletins are very simple, and we've looked at a number of them as we have worked through Chapter 5. What we are doing here is focusing on bulletins that involve a high level of skill as a reporter, editor and presenter.

on the website

Find links to the bulletins discussed here.

Lloyd's List, a print-legacy B2B title for the shipping industry, runs a weekly short news bulletin called On The Radar which, they say, "provides concise insight into the week's biggest stories and issues facing shipping as well as a preview of what's to come in the week ahead. Your weekly guide to what matters most in the industry."

Liz McCarthy, publisher at *Lloyd's List Intelligence*, has several years' experience creating the bulletins. While she was responsible for the script and presenting, a second journalist covered the production side – filming, editing and publishing the bulletin.

Liz began by looking at the 10 or 20 most read stories on the website – so popularity is at the basis of the selection process. She cut them down for broadcast, taking three top stories and then a series of others relevant to key areas of *Lloyd's List*'s coverage – the dry bulk industry and the tanker industry – finishing up with a number of briefs to end the bulletin.

She read the script aloud as she added items, rewriting them where necessary to make sure they worked when spoken, and tried to keep everything in the present tense.

Liz says the toughest thing to master was her breathing: "It's very hard while reading aloud to breathe at the right time to make the sentence come across as it should do."

After the recording, the production journalist takes over, working on Final Cut Express and adding their spinning globe background (created in software called After Effects), captions, stills to illustrate the main stories and, when they have them, video inserts. They have had dramatic mobile phone footage of a shipping disaster in the past. Stills used to illustrate items of breaking news come from the web editor. They also insert snippets of interviews when they have them.

Selecting material for a bulletin

Item selection and order are crucial. Your editing skills will often be heavily tested in boiling down a mass of information, much of it clamouring to be broadcast, into a three-minute bulletin. The word count on that is probably about 500 words – not much more than a page lead in a newspaper or a couple of online news stories.

Whether your bulletin is for a locally based website allied to a newspaper, a B2B publication or a national or international audience interested in general news, there are some general principles.

- You will have to be highly selective
- The bulletin needs to give a fair, rounded picture of what matters to your audience
- The bulletin must have variety: a mix of heavy and light stories.

Deciding on a running order

As ever, put the audience at the centre of all that you do. In selecting material we go for a range of items that are important to them, plus – depending on the general tone of our coverage and our audience – some information that is less vital but nevertheless interesting, entertaining or out of the ordinary.

As you get more experienced your instincts will take over and you will know what is your lead, what to follow it with and just the right light item to end with. There's no real short cut to getting there other than practice, and while we practise we will try to be as objective as we can about our item selections and running orders – always acknowledging that journalism is an instinctive art as much as a practical craft.

Here are some questions to ask to help us sift and order items. They are keys to good editing and apply just as much to editing decisions in a print publication or a text-based website as they do to audio and video bulletins.

- How significant or important is the story?
- How many of our readers does it affect, and to what degree?

    - All of them a lot?
    - All of them a bit?
    - Some of them a lot?

- Will it change their lives, or affect how they behave?

If a story affects all of them a lot that gives us a good idea that this is a top story. All of them a bit and some of them a lot are harder to judge against each other. Here are some more considerations:

- What material impact will the story have?
- Will it cost them money, or make them money?
- Will it advantage or disadvantage them in some significant way?

On a B2B title, questions of financial or commercial advantage or disadvantage are vital, for a general audience also important.

Here's another key question:

- What will the audience's reaction be?

Will they be angry, shocked, delighted, mildly amused? We are including items of human interest here, where the strict significance of a story may be low but it is nevertheless of great interest. Such items can become major talking points. For example, one woman dying of breast cancer is a much bigger story if that woman is a very well-known TV personality, and interest in her plight crosses all audience boundaries.

- Will they expect to hear about it?

Sometimes we are behind on a story, or shut out completely from someone else's exclusive. But if the audience is aware of it from other sources, and it affects or interest them, we need to get in on the act.

- How fresh is it?

News just in is valuable for a bulletin - especially if we are doing bulletins hourly and struggling to make them different during the day and to point-up developments in the stories we are covering.

Fresh stories often jump into a bulletin high up, just because they are fresh, and this freshness may not be balanced entirely by their significance. Sometimes we reflect afterwards and wonder why an item was the lead in a bulletin for an hour or two. The answer can be that it was fresh. Later it may drop down the rankings.

Audio and video

The fact that, for video, we have good pictures and, for audio, good actuality, can affect an item's inclusion and placing in a bulletin. For an audio bulletin, shouts of anger at a demonstration, with the reporter describing the police charging the demonstrators, batons drawn, bring the story to life, as do pictures from the thick of the mêlée in a video bulletin.

We have to consider whether we are over-promoting a weak story just because we have good sounds or pictures. If we are excited by great footage that's understandable, but we must not lose sight of the audience and their level of interest in the story.

Stories that go together

When it gets to the order of items, and we have two or more that focus on different aspects of a story, then it makes sense to keep them together, otherwise the bulletin can seem disjointed or repetitive.

And finally

Finding a light item for the end of a bulletin helps round things off. In a general bulletin, sport is often used to end on a lighter note. Then there are the lighter, human stories - the skateboarding ducks that ITN's News at Ten used to specialise in, when it was still a national institution.

On a B2B bulletin, a lighter story about an industry event or other, softer news item can be used to round things off.

Scripting the bulletin

on the website

Find links to a BBC guide to scripting a bulletin.

In traditional broadcasting organisations there are very strict guidelines on how a script should be put together. Scripts have a great deal of information in them. If the bulletin is for TV, then the words spoken at each point by the presenter will be in one column on each page of the script with, in the other, a note of whether or not the presenter is in vision, or if stills or graphics are filling the screen. Cues to video inserts will be given, together with the first and last words spoken - the in words and the out words - by the reporter on the tape. On radio, the same applies to recorded audio items.

Exact, second-by-second timings will be given for each element in the bulletin.

With online multimedia bulletins, practices vary. In some organisations, broadcast procedures have been adopted. In others, things are less formal. If you are producing a bulletin yourself, things are simpler. If you are part of a team, and others are responsible for cueing in clips of video or audio, they need to know exactly when to run them.

You may not be expected to work to traditional broadcast standards, but as production values in online video bulletins rise, it's increasingly likely that you will be, so let's look at what those standards are.

Here's an example of how a script for a broadcast news bulletin is presented. Exact formats vary, but most look quite a lot like this:

Simon (the name of the presenter) I/V (short for in vision)	A cull of elephants is to be allowed in South Africa, for the first time in 15 years.
Still: bull elephant	In a statement, the South African government said a cull was needed to control elephant numbers.
Still: herd of elephants	The elephant population is thought to have grown from 8,000 to 18,000 since culls were banned in 1995.
Simon I/V	The statement acknowledged that the issue would rouse "strong emotions", and the news will anger many animal rights campaigners.
Still: tourists riding on elephants	The capture of wild elephants, and their use in elephant safaris will also be banned.
Simon I/V	In the statement, Minister of Environmental Affairs and Tourism Marthinus van Schalkwyk said culling would be an option of last resort that was acceptable only under strict conditions.

Here's how a pre-recorded report is marked in the script:

Simon I/V	The people of Looe in Cornwall spent the day reinforcing flood defences following yesterday's severe flooding.
Still: flooded town centre	Shops in the town and over 150 homes were swamped.

Simon I/V	There are fears that exceptionally high tides will bring further problems tonight. Emily Sutton has this.
In words: "To begin with, the water. . ." Supers [captions that on TV are inserted live when a person is interviewed as part of a video] Jane Townshend, mayor 22" ["=seconds] Robbie Albery, lifeboat coxswain 45" Out words: ". . .could face even more serious flooding." Time: 1'22"	

If you have to write a script which you will deliver live to fit visuals – video or stills – that have already been edited into a sequence, then each still or sequence in the video will be marked, so you can time your reading to coincide with the appropriate image. Here's an example where a series of stills have been edited into a slide show.

The timings here show the period from the start of the report when each item should be read.

Simon I/V Cue 3" Simon OOV [out of vision] GVs remains of car in crater	Two car bombs in the Iraqi capital Baghdad have killed at least 19 people, Iraqi police say.
Cue 5" GVs shopping centre	The most deadly attack was a parked car bomb in a shopping area on the east bank of the Tigris.
Cue 12" GVs bodies	It killed at least 15 people and wounded 45.
Cue 15" GVs damage to police station	A suicide car bomber also attacked a police headquarters in east Baghdad, killing four people, including two officers.
Cue 21" GVs damaged houses	There was widespread damage to houses hit by the blast.

The skill here is in balancing our words to our pictures. Stills can be held, but the viewer will get bored if they have had time to absorb the information in the still long before it is replaced by the next shot in a sequence.

Likewise, if we have a five second video clip we can only accompany it with five seconds worth of words - or about 15.

If necessary, we must find a second illustration that addresses the same point so that our words can run over two clips and still be relevant to what the audience is being shown.

19C4

Presenting the bulletin

In US television the news anchor is highly prized. To a lesser but still important extent in British TV, the person who reads the news is a key figure, and their personality and the impression the audience gains of them is vital. That's less so in radio where there's no talking head to scrutinise, tie to dislike or hair style to critique.

Also, with short bulletins the presenter - on video as with audio - is businesslike and needs just to be easy to watch and/or listen to; to be believable. Awkward presenters whose eyes are glazed as they focus on the autocue don't do a bulletin any favours.

As a multimedia journalist you are expected first and foremost to be an effective news gatherer, but if you have an aptitude for presentation as well it will certainly help your progress.

Your look

You don't have to be good looking, but it helps. What you should do is avoid, as far as you can, having anything in your appearance or dress that distracts the viewer.

A good microphone voice

We talked briefly in Chapter 5, unit 5A12 about the basics of a good voice. Let's deal with this in more detail now.

A good microphone voice is one with richness, depth and resonance. That goes for women as well as men, and means that voices that are high pitched and lacking in power do not work nearly as well.

You need to take an acting lesson, or voice training, to read really well.

If you've ever noticed an actor read, followed by a non-professional, you'll hear the difference. The actor uses their voice almost like a musical instrument - sorry to be pretentious - they don't gabble, they instil the script with full and rich meaning. They learn to emphasise, to fit pace to words and generally make the most of the text.

How fast to read

In broadcasting, there is a wide variety of reading speeds, depending on whether you are doing a bulletin for a fast-paced pop station or a serious news channel. The word-per-minute count can be anything from 140 to 220.

A good average for radio is 180 wpm, or three words a second. TV can be a little slower.

Knowing how many words you need per second is the vital building block when you are writing a script and timing material.

You might introduce a video report with a 20-second, 60-word cue. A 30-second clip of audio or video is going to be about 90 words.

If you are struggling to deliver your script clearly at the speed required, practise by slowing things right down. Read the script at a pace that you feel comfortable with, that allows you to form the words correctly. Tape yourself and listen to it back. Work on the points you recognise are unclear. Get others to critique your performance. As you get more confident, speed things up until you get to the right pace.

Here are some common problems and how to tackle them

Speech impediments can be a problem although minor ones can be overcome - look at Jonathan Ross.

They are a problem for the presenter when they affect clarity, such as if you pronounce your THs as Vs. In her advice on how to speak clearly, US voice coach Ann S Utterback[3] warns about the erosion of consonants in words. She says: "This erosion can turn the word 'centre' into 'sinner' or 'ask' into 'ass'."

You must articulate words correctly. That means, she says, using our articulators - lips, teeth, tongue and jaw - to enunciate the individual sounds, the phonemes in a word, and form each word correctly.

She says correct enunciation is vital because "intelligibility, credibility, and precision of pronunciation are all linked".

Often the endings of words are blurred or left off. That affects understanding. She recommends: "Try taking some copy home and marking all the ending plosive sounds (/t/ /d/, /p/ /b/, /k/ /g/) with a highlighter." Ann says that these sounds should produce "an explosion of air" when they are produced correctly. She recommends that you practise by over-pronouncing those endings. When you do that, she says, your brain will register the new, precise articulation more readily.

Ann makes it clear that she is not suggesting marking ending consonants on your actual on-air script. That might cause you to sound overly precise, she says. Rather, the goal is to sound conversational while articulating most of the ending consonant plosive sounds.

on the website

Find links to a range of additional tutorials and resources covering voice.

Warm up your voice

Utterback recommends you stretch your facial muscles by opening your mouth wide and moving your jaw from left to right. Hum or sing. Go through the vocal range from high to low and back again.

Breathing

Good breathing improves your voice. It should be deep – from right down in the lungs – not short and shallow. Sitting cramped or hunched makes it harder to breathe properly. Sit upright, with your back straight. Using your full lung capacity gives you plenty of air in reserve as you read. You have the capacity to pause, to emphasise and not run out of breath mid-sentence or mid-clause.

Take a couple of deep breaths before you start, and another deep one between stories. The time it takes to do so is a sufficient pause between items. You can take a quick breath at a full stop, and a shallow one at a comma. Such breathing works with the rhythm of your bulletin. After all, a comma is designed to indicate a short pause and a full stop a bigger one. They organise our words on the page, and we can use correct breathing and pausing to organise our words as we read a bulletin.

You might take a tip from good public speakers, and replace or overlay conventional punctuation with slashes.

Pauses and emphasis

It works like this:

Here's a complex passage from President John F Kennedy's inaugural speech:

> Now the trumpet summons us again - not as a call to bear arms, though arms we need; not as a call to battle, though embattled we are; but a call to bear the burden of a long twilight struggle, year in and year out, 'rejoicing in hope, patient in tribulation'.

The speech is easier to read if you put a slash (/) between words where a pause is needed. It can be used alongside or in place of commas, semi-colons, colons and full stops, but it can also be used for points where a pause for emphasis would help the delivery of the item.

And you can use one / for the shortest pause, // for a slightly longer one and /// for the longest. Think of them as units of pause, and adapt them to the speed you are required to read at.

Do that and the speech looks like this: "Now the trumpet summons us again//not as a call to bear arms/though arms we need// not as a call to battle/though embattled we are//but a call to bear the burden of a long twilight struggle/year in and year out/ 'rejoicing in hope, patient in tribulation'/."

Let's face it, conventional punctuation is designed for silent reading, and may not work nearly as well for spoken reading. The slash system works better for that.

It's also a good idea to read your script through to identify points of emphasis. You want your delivery to be conversational, but with a few enhancements. Stresses on important words will help.

Go through your script and decide on the words you need to emphasise to keep what you read interesting, and easy to understand. You need to find the essential words in your script - the ones that, when emphasised, give the gist of the story and make meaning crystal clear. Mark these words either with an underscore or put them in capitals.

These words that need to be stressed are often known as the operative words. You should:

- Raise or lower the volume of your voice when speaking the operative words
- Alter your pitch on these words, going either up or down the scale a notch
- Alter your rhythm, pausing either before or after the operative word.

Change speed as you read. Keep your speed up as you move through less important information, but slow down when you get to the key bit that needs emphasis.

Pitch

Pitch is the ups and downs your voice takes as you read through a sentence – again to aid meaning. If you've ever listened to the football results being read out you may have noticed that the announcer tends to read the winning team's name on an upward pitch, peaking at the goals scored. The losing team is read on a downward pitch, with the score being at the lowest point. Try it out:

> Chelsea, 3, Manchester United, 1

Or:

> Chelsea, 1, Manchester United, 3

If you haven't noticed this, look out for it next time. You'll find you can often predict who has won by the pitch the reader uses.

Sentences usually begin on a rising pitch, ascending to the middle of the sentence, and then take a downward pitch to the end. So you go up a hill, pause on the flat top, then roll down the other side. In some cultures a rising pitch is common at the end of the sentence – which can make each one sound like a question.

Projection

Telling a story with your voice is about more than just reading it out. The best scripts don't sound as if they are scripts at all – rather, that the speaker is ad-libbing. Projection is not about shouting, but it is about pitching your voice with strength. Think of your job as lifting the story off the page, and projecting it through the radio, the TV screen or that tiny online video interface. You must overcome the constraints of the funnel you have to speak though, and get right to your listener's ear. Deep breathing and speaking from the diaphragm will help, as will the other elements we have analysed above.

Microphone technique for audio

Get too close to your microphone and you get a nasty popping noise as you speak. If you are wearing headphones you'll hear it, and can either move a little away from the mic or turn it slightly to one side. A good mic distance is about 15cms.

Getting close to the mic can help if you have a weak voice.

Paper rustling will also be picked up by your mic. Picking up your script and flipping through its pages will be picked up. But how do you avoid it? You could keep the script flat on the table, but if you do your head is facing down and your voice can become muffled – and you will undo the good work we put in just now on projecting and keeping your voice strong. To avoid it, lift each sheet from your script as you come to read from it, and hold it between fingers and thumb at the bottom of the sheet, folding it slightly to keep it upright. As you near the end of the sheet transfer it to your left hand – or to your right if you are left handed, and pick up the next one. Don't put the first sheet down until you are reading from the second. And so on.

Using an autocue

With video you will want to dispense with a script completely. If your university or employer has a fully equipped studio then an autocue will be available which projects your script onto an area close to the camera and scrolls through it as you read.

If you don't have one, or if you want to practise reading bulletins, there are a number of free software applications that turn your computer screen into an autocue.

on the website

On the website you'll find links to a couple of free autocue applications.

19C5

Creating a magazine-style video programme

In a magazine video programme you are likely to have a number of items. There may be some pre-recorded elements, and there will often be an interview or discussion element.

To front up a programme like this needs confidence and skill. It's a big step up from handling a three-minute bulletin. It also requires resources. You need a plausible-looking studio set. And you need a team of people with a range of skills: director, producer, a couple of camera operators, plus sound, light and editing.

I spoke to Philip Smith, head of content solutions at Haymarket Brand Republic Group who developed a broadcast-quality video magazine programme for his organisation.

BrandRepublic describes itself as "the home of the advertising, media and marketing communities online. BrandRepublic.tv brings the issues at the heart of those sectors alive with a series of monthly video bulletins."

Philip describes the programme he created as: "The show which reviews the things everybody in advertising, marketing and media are talking about."

BrandRepublic.tv uses professional studio facilities. Its programmes, which average 20 minutes, have a strong visual element. The one Philip had just created when we spoke was titled: "How Hovis returned to TV triumphant".

on the website

Watch it on the MMJ website.

Hovis had done so with an impressive £15m commercial. It lasts 122 seconds, one for each year the brand has been on the market. It tells the simple story of a boy popping to the corner shop for a loaf of bread, but while he starts out 122 years ago, time ticks forward as the ad runs, through seven different historic periods. So he goes through the First and Second World Wars, the swinging sixties, ugly eighties and, in the final seconds, arrives in the present. The idea was to show that while things have changed a great deal, Hovis as a brand is timeless.

Philip took me through the process of creating such a programme. First comes the idea, and that needs to be something highly visual: a story that can be told well with the use of video. He stresses that the correct approach to creating such a programme is not to start with a story and decide how to tell it, but to start with the requirements of the medium. He needs stories for which good visuals are available, and a plus is that they won't be told by anyone else. So, with Hovis, they had the ad, and they had footage shot on location while the ad was being filmed. This was something that viewers would not see elsewhere.

Such exclusivity is key, and was built into the planning process for BrandRepublic.tv:

We said to a lot of advertising agencies 'what have you got that we don't normally see?' What you may not know is that, with a lot of ad agencies, they will be shooting behind the scenes when they are filming on location for a big production like Hovis, so there is some great footage of the extras and how this street was set up for the ad, and this incredible time-travelling event and how they brought all that together.

"In the days of just print you wouldn't necessarily see that video. It would only be available in the agency or on the director's show reel, so only certain key people in the industry would see it.

Once we knew that was available: there's an award-winning ad, there's some footage you can't see elsewhere, you can get the people involved on, and there's our show. But the big thing is we are telling a story that can't really be told in a different medium.

Philip stresses that if compelling visual material is not available, there is no point trying to tell a story – however good it might be and relevant to the audience – using the medium of video.

Knowing that he has the constituents he needs, Philip writes his script. He uses a format similar to that outlined above, with words and video inserts both presented, but says: "Don't be too rigid with the script is my advice and my experience."

With this programme the segments he used were, in order: the ad, a studio discussion, footage shot on location while the ad was being shot, and more discussion.

Philip then wrote his introduction to the programme, his links between the elements and his final comments. While he sticks to his linking parts of his script closely, he will be flexible with the interview, ready to ask supplementary questions picking up on things the interviewee has said, and also to cut questions if they are no longer necessary or if a long answer to a previous one has meant time is pressing.

Then he'll show his script to the director, who will tell him if it is too wordy, and who can plan how he is going to film things. They tend to use two cameras, one on Philip, one on the guests, and mix general shots with MCUs of the person speaking.

There is an autocue, but Philip does not rely on it. He does, however, have a clipboard with his script on it, and the director talking in his ear to keep him on track.

The show is shot as live and, says Philip: "It's very rare that we will go back and re-record anything. We'll only do that if I need to sharpen something up, improve the pace."

The video inserts are not screened during the recording, which gives a chance to tell the guests if they are going to be come to next.

Once filming is complete, an editor will do an initial edit, which Philip will look over and amend if need be.

I asked Philip if he aimed for broadcast standard on BrandRepublic.tv and he said:

> We were very conscious that this had to be shot in a professional setting, in a studio-type environment, because the calibre of the guests and the conversations we wanted to have with them.

> We've tended in the trade press to think about our stories in terms of how they look on the page. When you start thinking about video you have to really start thinking about how you tell a story visually. It's not just about a video anymore, it's also about is there footage, is there real video we can put in there. And, of course, something like Hovis lends itself to that because it had a very exciting ad that broke a few boundaries, that a lot of people in the industry were talking about. So we were able to show the creative, show behind the scenes of the making of the ad – that's something that we just couldn't do in print before.

The studio discussion is there

> to bring those ideas to life. And often, thinking about the stars in an industry, it's actually intensely powerful to bring that person to life with video, because you see when he really does mean something, you can hear him actually explain it, and he does talk to you in a very different way than when you see the words reproduced in black and white.

Philip says that producing such packages is demanding.

> If you feel that your video needs to be of a studio-based variety, you will need people who know what a good studio is, people who can operate at least two cameras, people who can edit well, and you will need all of those so-called TV production skills.

> That said, my broadcast training was a long long time ago, and while I made sure that I was up to speed with my presenting skills, you also need people around you who say 'that works', or 'that doesn't work'. So yes, it's a big team, and you do need to take the best from it.

> You don't always need the big production but, for this project, we felt we did.

So, here's what you need:

- A studio and set
- A team with the skills of director, producer (Philip says that, with his films, producer and director are pretty much the same thing), camera, light and sound, and editing
- A script that your director can discuss with you, amend and work from
- Compelling video to screen
- Authoritative studio guests.

And finally. . .

If you are frustrated at the loss of quality your video suffers when uploaded to YouTube or via your blog or website, there are free high-definition video upload services available. One such is Vimeo:

http://vimeo.com

Exercises and projects

Exercise 1

Look at a number of *Vice* long-form videos. Analyse what it is that makes them effective. Or, if you don't like them, decide what it is that puts you off.

Exercise 2

Look at a wide range of online video bulletins. Assess what they get right, and what can be improved. Look at:

- news selection
- studio setting
- the presenter's appearance
- the quality of the presenter's reading
- the editing of the bulletin.

Exercise 3

Look at a range of online magazine programmes and carry out a similar exercise as the one above on bulletins.

Projects

1   If you have the resources, make a long-form video documentary about a topic that will interest the audience for your website.

2   Either working individually or as part of a team, set up a weekly news bulletin for your website. Establish its purpose and develop an editorial policy for it. Gather material, either from that generated for the projects you are working on, or by re-working other content. Experiment with the *Vice* model of linking from within the video to other content.

3   Develop your skills as a presenter. Follow the guidance in this chapter and have colleagues critique your performance.

4   Create a format for a magazine-style programme. Determine the staffing it requires and the roles individuals should fill. It should include a studio discussion, and one or more filmed inserts. Plan, record, present, edit and publish a programme.

Notes

1   www.journalism.co.uk/news/how-vice-became-a-video-success-story/s2/a550133/
2   www.journalism.co.uk/news/how-vice-tricks-people-into-caring-about-the-planet-/s2/a551478/
3   http://newslab.org/articles/speakclearly.htm

chapter twenty

The future

In the book version of this chapter we will cover:

- The latest developments in devices, including wearables, and in automated storytelling
- The development of Web 1.0, Web 2.0 and a vision for Web 3.0
- Developing journalism for new and future technologies.

At the end of the chapter are a range of exercises for you to practise what you have learned.

In the online version of this chapter you will find:

- Updates on new developments in software and hardware
- Case studies of emerging journalistic enterprises
- Tuition in new techniques.

Have the companion website to this book open at www.multimedia-journalism.co.uk. That way you can easily click on the links to the stories discussed here.

20C1

Pointers to the future

The danger about talking of the future here, in the book edition of MMJ, is that it will no longer be the future when you get to read about it.

For that reason, I'll just map out here the way things are developing, and build on this with regular updates, and appropriate new tuition, on the website.

One trend that will inevitably gather pace in the future is the adoption of wearables - web-enabled devices such as watches and glasses.

New devices bring new apps and require new ways of presenting content.

Watches need very brief bursts of text, appropriate to their very small screens, a bit like the pagers of old.

Eyewear products such as Google Glass (www.google.co.uk/glass/start/) need visual and voice recognition software, and are particularly appropriate for interacting with the world you see through forms of augmented reality.

So one way the future will develop is in finding ways to present our content on these devices. As journalists we need to think about that, and in module 20C3 we'll look at the ideas media companies are coming up with.

It also seems likely that automation will take over the creation of much routine content. Software that can write sports, market reports and straightforward breaking news is already with us.

But there is a bigger picture, and it's to do with a vision of how the web will develop, and the place that content - including journalism - will have in it.

20C2

The bigger picture: Web 3.0

First, what is it with all this 3.0 business? And where did 1.0 and 2.0 get to? The numbers are a way of charting the development of the web.

Web 1.0 was about commerce

Commerce was the driver in the early days of the web. This was the time when online institutions including Amazon and eBay were created.

Web 2.0 was about community

Community sites including Myspace and Facebook and hundreds more often niche players drove development.

Web 3.0 will be about joined-up thinking

Actually, at the time of writing, no one can be entirely sure of what Web 3.0 will be like, but the simplest way of looking at developments that will shape it is to say that they bring things together.

Because the web is so useful, we tend to enjoy its benefits without looking too closely at what could be done to make it better. Let's face it, it's pretty disjointed at present: the fact that you have to go to one place for content, another for community and another for commerce. OK, many organisations are aware of this and are trying to knit the three together, and in doing that they are ushering in Web 3.0, the web of connectedness.

Let me quote from an incisive article at PCMag.com, which is linked to from the website and which offers four pictures of the way Web 3.0 will develop. They are:

The Semantic Web

This is a Web in which machines can read sites as easily as we can. They can compare and connect, pulling information from several and bringing it together in ways that make our lives easier. The simple example PCMag gives is this: "You ask your machine to check your schedule against the schedules of all the dentists and doctors within a 10-mile radius – and it obeys."

There are many more ways this interconnectivity can help us - particularly as journalists and in reaching our audience - and we'll look at this in a lot more detail in a bit.

The 3D Web

A Web you can enter, by slipping on a suitable wearable such as a headset, or glasses. So from your armchair you can go shopping, travel geographically or through time. You could create a world where you can interact with others and do - virtually - pretty much everything you do in the real world.

The Media-Centric Web

A Web where you can search not just with words but with all other media. A photograph of a favourite painting entered into a search engine brings you hundreds of similar paintings you may also like. Searches could be done with sound, video, anything.

The Pervasive Web

A Web that's everywhere. So not just your computer is online, every device you use is too. So your fridge orders the food you are running out of from the online supermarket, and checks your diary to ensure it is delivered at a time when you will be at home. Your garden irrigation system checks the forecast to see whether it needs to water. Your windows do the same to decide when to open.

Let's look in more detail at the elements that Web 3.0 brings together. For this I'm quoting from Sramana Mitra, an entrepreneur, strategy consultant and author of the technology business (**www.sramanamitra.com/**).

She sees 3.0 as bringing together and developing everything from Webs 1.0 and 2.0 - content, commerce and community, or what she calls the 3Cs, and adding to it a fourth C - Context.

She says it also brings personalisation, plus vertical search. So, if you like equations it looks like this: **Web 3.0 = (4C+P+VS)**

Vertical search has been under development by some during Web 2.0, and we looked at it in Chapter 16. Vertical search, unlike Google which searches across the web, drills down into a niche area.

Personalisation has been limited because of the lack of an appropriate context (the fourth C) within which to develop it.

Mitra says:

"In Web 3.0, I predict, we are going to start seeing roll-ups." She envisages what she calls 'a trunk' that emerges from the **Context**. That context might be film (Netflix, for example), music (such as iTunes), cooking / food, working women, or single parents. The roll-up, she believes, will assemble the Web 3.0 formula that addresses the whole set of needs of a consumer in that Context.

She gives an example of how it would work, which I summarise here:

Context: The personal profile of an individual, which might include their body size, colouring, personal style and fashion preferences which only certain designers resonate with.

Commerce: This individual wants a personalised version of their favourite fashion store – say SAKS Fifth Avenue – which carries clothes by those designers, in her size.

Content: This individual also wants a personalised version of their favourite fashion magazine – *Vogue*, for example. This personalised *Vogue* will contain articles about her personal style, favourite designers, and other emerging ones who are like them.

Community: She want to exchange notes with others of her size-shape-style-psycho-graphic and discover what else looks good. She also wants the recommendation system to tell her what they're buying.

Personalisation and vertical search: There are also some basic principles of what looks good based on skin tone, body shape, hair colour, eye colour, and this individual wants the search engine to be able to filter and match based on an algorithm that builds in this knowledge base.

Such a context could be built for any individual. For each and every one of them, Web 3.0 could become their online personal shopper, or trusted recommendations engine. And that online personal shopper will include content.

Sramana came up with this formula as long ago as 2007. So, surely, with the frenetic rate of development we are used to hearing about in matters of technology and connectedness, this ought to be history by now? In fact, it's not. In 2014 she wrote: "The web has not evolved according to this vision quite as rapidly as I had imagined. We have hardly seen the fragmented web mature into a more deeply personalized user experience."

20C3

The C-for-content in Web 3.0, and the opportunities for journalism

Clearly content is still very valuable in this vision of Web 3.0. High quality, reliable, well-informed and trustworthy content will be of great value to an individual, as part of a coherent and rewarding online experience. What is vital is that we get our material into that C-for-content element of the overall package. If it's not us but a rival, we have been left on the outside of a viable and lucrative collaborative venture.

In her example, Sranama included *Vogue*. In fact *Vogue* developed an app that brought the various elements together as she describes. It was called Vogue Stylist and it fused *Vogue* fashion content with commerce and the other elements of Web 3.0 in this way:

- **Context:** The user adds their own personal style and characteristics into the app, including pictures of their outfits
- **Commerce:** Purchasing opportunities are tailored to a user's taste in fashion, size, favourite designers and stores
- **Content:** *Vogue* content personalised to the individual user
- **Community:** The user can share what she does on the app, and her thoughts about fashion, with friends on social media
- **Personalisation and vertical search**: Search is built on a knowledge base about the user and her taste.

The app, launched in 2010, is no longer available, but other fashion players have entered this field.

on the website

Find links to apps that combine the elements of Web 3.0 enterprise.

Wearables: content for glasses and watches

We've seen how new hardware drives the creation of new applications. The iPhone heralded the age of the app, and now all media outfits have learned to adapt their content to this format.

New wearable formats are driving the creation of forms of content appropriate to them. And we are seeing elements in the vision of Web 3.0, such as image search and personalisation, becoming reality.

John Hashimoto, senior director of product development at CNN[1] says:

> As the device makers become more creative or innovative, they push us and other providers of content to be more innovative and creative about how our core competencies can be leveraged in that way as well.

CNN developed news apps for Google Glass eyewear and Samsung Gear watches, but has not, at the time of writing, created distinctive content for Glass. Instead it puts out the same headlines and videos as appear on its smartphone apps.

On Google Glass, CNN's community content platform iReport takes advantage of Glass's photo and video capabilities, and allows users to submit content which is then assessed by editors for publication. Audio also has a role on Glass. A platform called Urmano offers audio versions of text-based content they would have read for themselves in another context.

The FT developed the fastFT app for Samsung Gear, where text is delivered one word at a time, at a speed set by the reader. It was developed with the technology company Spritz and designed for on-the-go reading, where you can't read in the conventional way.

Visual search and augmented reality are further technologies with particular relevance to eyewear. A startup called Image Searcher[2] created a version of its CamFind image recognition app that works Glass. The wearer can have CamFind's visual search facility identify an object he or she is looking at in seconds, and access content linked to that trigger image.

on the website

Listen to a podcast on wearables in news.

Automated writing

Kristian Hammond, of robot writing firm Narrative Science, thinks 90 per cent of the news could be written by computers by 2030.

Hammond says it's possible because many forms of news writing are formulaic. Most obviously, stock reports and sports reports are based on statistics and numbers. A stock rises or a footballer scores, and software that has been programmed with a wealth of data on that stock and or that player can not only report the facts, but add interpretation based on the data it holds. The stock may have risen against expectation, the player may have scored for the first time this season.

The *Guardian* reported:[3] "In engineering their software, Narrative worked with trained journalists to help the software determine an angle. For example, in the case of sports, the algorithm answers key questions like, 'Who won the game and by how much? Was it a comeback or a blowout? Any heroics or notable stats?'"

The Narrative program chooses an article template, then strings together sentences, and spices them up with catchphrases. A typical piece of automated copy might begin: "It was a flawless day at the dish for the Giants." It reads pretty much as a piece of human-generated sports copy might.

As the journalist input, and the writing ability of software, develop, so more complex and nuanced stories will be generated automatically.

Robot writing opens up the possibility of writing a different story for every reader – which would be the ultimate in personalisation where news is concerned.

The *Guardian* reported[3] that Hammond was convinced automated writing will show what it can do when it is merged with another technological advance: the individual tracking of billions of consumers, through their purchases, internet browsing habits and mobile communications.

on the website

- Find a detailed explanation of how robot writing software works
- Find links to the latest developments in journalism, and current predictions for the future.

20C4

Exercises

Exercise 1

Consider the opportunities and threats that Web 3.0 holds.

Exercise 2

Investigate how media organisations are adapting their content for wearables.

Exercise 3

Research the current state of play with robot writing technologies.

Notes

1   www.journalism.co.uk/news/how-wearables-are-already-delivering-the-news/s2/a562539/)
2   http://venturebeat.com/2014/09/24/camfind-app-brings-accurate-visual-search-to-google-glass-
    exclusive/
3   www.theguardian.com/technology/2014/sep/12/artificial-intelligence-data-journalism-media

the future

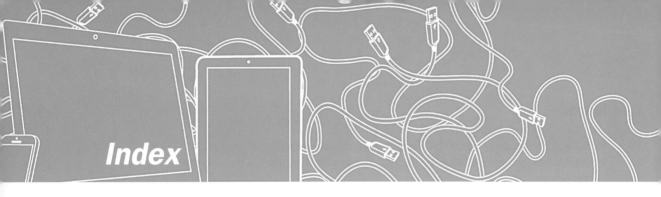

Index